MIGUEL MARMOL

by
Roque Dalton

translated by
Kathleen Ross and Richard Schaaf

preface by
Margaret Randall

introduction by
Manlio Argueta

CURBSTONE PRESS

© 1982 Editorial Universitaria Centroamerica
translation © 1987 Kathleen Ross and Richard Schaaf
ALL RIGHTS RESERVED

printed in the United States by R. R. Donnelly & Sons

cover linocut by Dea Trier Mørch

We thank the family of Roque Dalton for the
photograph of Dalton and Mármol used on
the back cover

LC: 87-70059
ISBN: 0-915306-68-9

The translators wish to thank the
New York State Council on the Arts
for their generous support.

This publication was supported in part by
The National Endowment for the Arts
and the Connecticut Commission on the Arts,
a State agency whose funds are recommended
by the Governor and appropriated by the
State Legislature.

distributed by
The Talman Company, Inc.
150 Fifth Avenue
New York, NY 10011

CURBSTONE PRESS
321 Jackson Street, Willimantic, CT 06226

MIGUEL MARMOL

PREFACE

Some Thoughts for the English Edition of MIGUEL MARMOL

There are books without which an understanding of a particular time or place would not be complete. Jack London's prose opens a window on the great northwest. Without Willa Cather's *Death Comes for the Archbishop* we would not know the southwest as we do. We owe our knowledge of the iron range to Rebecca Harding Davis, our image of the south to William Faulkner and Zora Neale Hurston. In Central America there are books that are records. *Mamita Yunay* is such a book. And *Miguel Mármol.*

Most people in the United States have no idea that the first "soviets" in Latin America were in El Salvador. Indeed, most Salvadorans, if they depended on the history texts taught them in school, would not count within their collective memory an uprising so powerful, a rebellion of impoverished farmers and workers so complete that it took the slaughter of 30,000 human beings to wipe it from official time.

Miguel Mármol is a book that sets the record straight – for Salvadorans, for North Americans, and for anyone else interested in this century's history in a country that daily claims our interest through a conflict no amount of covert or overt aid will quell.

Roque Dalton – revolutionary poet, political analyst – is the only one who could have written this book. His was a passion for his country's history so insatiable and a knowledge of its culture so deep, that there was practically no area of research, during

ix

his active writing life, untouched by his genius. His poetry pushed its way through literary innovation of all types; and when a single voice was insufficient to say what he needed to say in verse, he invented other voices for varied explorations. His essays of the sixties and early seventies probed the problems of political content most vital to his nation's time of change. He wrote novels, even one "posthumously," that kept his generation on the cutting edge. And *Miguel Mármol* – biography, narrative, oral history – became not only a brilliant story of a working man who shaped his country's destiny, but as well a popular and useful history of the revolutionary movement in El Salvador, in Guatemala, and in all of Central America.

Dalton himself had already paid heavy dues when he met Mármol. Imprisoned on several occasions, exiled more than once, he was living in Prague where he edited the Latin American edition of the INTERNATIONAL MAGAZINE, where "unknown thugs" attacked and beat him up one night in the streets of that European city. Mármol was in Prague on his way back from a workers' conference in the Soviet Union. The two men met, and Dalton who was hospitalized and recovering from his beating persuaded Mármol to delay his return to El Salvador long enough to tell his story. It is Mármol as protagonist, historian, and storyteller as well as Dalton as listener, writer, and political analyst that make for the unique and compelling strength of the book you hold in your hands.

This is a story of a struggle told by a man who lived it, to another man who also lived – and later died – for it. The reader will meet the leaders of the 1932 rebellion, learn about their dreams and their failures, their successes and the legacy they willed to those fighting today for a nation where justice may be constructed. Mármol is a Party cadre, but never a blind or dogmatic one. Again and again he moves in and out of political favor, as he – and generations of good men and women – grapple to find the best, the most honest way to justice.

You will find dozens of memorable scenes in this book, but none more memorable than the one in which Mármol survives his own execution. For that scene alone, taken from the rigors of real life, this book should long ago have been a film.

Curbstone Press has taken on a commitment that larger and more solvent publishers might have undertaken several years back. For the translators, this has been a labor of love – and an excellent one. I could go on and on speaking about this masterpiece you are about to read. But why? You have the book itself!

– Margaret Randall
Albuquerque, Fall 1986

PROLOGUE

In 1833, Anastasio Aquino, indigenous leader of the central zone of El Salvador, rebelled against the governmental power headed by the Creole families, the sole beneficiaries of independence from Spanish rule. The sowers, the indigo plant cutters, and the makers of the natural dyes produced from the plant, rose up to challenge the political power of the landholders. They attempted to touch the sky with their soiled hands. Aquino pronounced for the first time laws for the distribution of land and the just application of the penal laws (the only laws applied to the poor). The army rebels, who had first discovered the use of the guerrilla ambush with the cry "one hundred below and one hundred above," were defeated: Anastasio Aquino's head was nailed onto a stake in the center of the park in San Vicente, and there it remained for several days as a lesson and an example for whomever might dare to question the authority of the newborn oligarchy.

One hundred years later, in 1932, the body of José Feliciano Ama, another indigenous leader, hung from a tree in the park in the city of Izalco, this time in the western zone of the country. The insurrection of 1932 has recently ended. The massacre is repeated, and silence and terror imposed. The events of the insurrection must be forgotten. No one dares to deal with it, to analyse it, the facts are hidden, including the newspapers in the archives of that period. But the story is kept alive by word of mouth, from ear to ear. And Roque Dalton collected it from that peasant-artisan with an incredible memory and sense of humor: Miguel Mármol.

In the history of El Salvador, the power of the landholders was always ready to unleash its fury and rage against those who

xiii

rebelled, that is, against those who lived a life of misery and, at the same time, produced the nation's wealth; against the peasant masses who had acquired the "sui generis" qualification for the labors of the field. Since 1600, dye factories had existed in the countryside. The Indians, using techniques belonging to their ancient culture, now worked under the whip of the colonialists for the benefit of the Creoles and the emerging European industrialization, in the textile branch of industry.

The history was obscured, but it spread by word of mouth, from ear to ear.

Synthetic dyes were discovered, and the Creoles replaced the indigo haciendas with coffee plantations.

Since the end of the 1600s, there were dye factories in the countryside. The Indians manufactured, with the techniques from their own culture, the colors and pastels designed for the new European textile industry. The colonialists became great exporters and therefore needed to expropriate large tracts of land and to fully exploit indigenous labor. The cultivation of coffee beginning in the second half of the 19th century didn't alter conditions for the great masses of workers in the Salvadoran countryside. The laborer had ceased to be a semi-slave, but the injustices continued to be reflected in miserable wages, horrible punishments and forced labor. The National Guard became an army of occupation throughout the countryside.

In the second decade of this century, the government of the coffee growing families had witnessed the approach of social unrest under the banner of the obstinate workers' organizations. The peasants arrived in the city and became artisans, "the best artisans in the world," says Roque Dalton in a poem. The field workers kept on living in their thatched huts, and the artisans in the city inhabited the shacks of the surrounding barrios.

Different factions of coffee growers were contending for power in the elections of January, 1931, and there was no better way to win those elections than to win over those organized masses, calling for reforms that the workers' organizations had been demanding for a long time. After all, the problem of the elections was a question of numbers. And these masses constituted 80% of the population. The candidates of the oligarchy, the only ones who can participate in the elections, talk about agrarian reform, credits for the small farmers, doing away with the shameful, punitive laws against those who refused to work for a certain boss.

Those elections open up a tiny window for the dreams of that army of workers, who were containing their insurrectionist impulses with the calm inspired by the hope of winning a few of their demands for just treatment, through one of the landholding candidates.

No one could hold back that storm without satisfying those needs. A kind of conditional past was reached between the workers' organizations and the candidates representing the coffee growers. The one who offered the best hope, naturally, won in the elections. But once in power, the proposals conflicted with the interests of the oligarchic families. No other road was left open to the organized masses than to repeat their historical deeds; those transmitted by word of mouth, from ear to ear. The only form of communication known to those almost illiterate peasant sectors, without the least access to education, health and to the benefits of a life with dignity. Human dignity hasn't existed for this 80% of Salvadorans. Western civilization or Christian culture had always meant a terror that became more sophisticated with the technical advances in firearms, torture and extermination apparatuses; in greater advances by the army and National Guard towards achieving an effective state of submission.

"What is exceptional about El Salvador, among the nations of Latin America (says Thomas Anderson: *Matanza: El Salvador 1932, Communist Revolt*), is that nothing differentiates it so much as its past history; it is a chronically unhappy country, not only in its history but in its past."

But there is something more exceptional: that at a high cost in lives, it has struggled to change the society of horror, which has been equally exceptional. And it continues to search for the social peace that has been unknown in its history. "Even an outsider like myself could write a letter in April, 1948, commenting on the problematic future that awaited a society where 95% of the wage earners received a wage of less than one dollar a day" (states Murrat W. Williams, ex-ambassador of the United States to El Salvador, referring to the latter country in the prologue to Charlie Clements' testimony of experiences in the region of the Guazapa Volcano).

That history has been long, before the Monroe Doctrine and the so-called East-West conflict. And the Salvadoran army has continued the same, not bound to the least nationalist or patriotic sentiment; its tradition of a mentality of servitude to the sovereign rulers is too strong to change it with paternalistic or interventionist claims. After what Henry Kissinger (in his Report of the Central American Commission) called "the impressive elections of 1982," Charlie Clements reveals another reality in that same place: "Unable to trap us, the soldiers unleashed their rage against the people. They killed all the livestock they found. They even killed the dogs . . . The clinic was totally destroyed, as was the school . . . A photo of Monseñor Romero was covered with obscenities" (says Clements in his well-known testimony, describing first a bombing raid and then an invasion of the populated zones in Guazapa).

Thirty-two years after what Murrat W. Williams describes, in reference to 1948, the figures continue to be pathetic: "66% of the national income was received by the richest 20% of the population, while the poorest 20% only received 2% of the same income," says the Report of the Kissinger Commission.

The history is the same as ever. But it will not be in the cold analytical laboratories where the social and political problem of El Salvador will be solved; nor with the economic and military assistance that attempts to maintain the situation, or at best "to improve it," overlooking a reality represented by thousands of lives sacrificed by the oppressed.

Whatever has been the effort of Salvadorans to liberate themselves from oppression, the enemy has always been

xvi

internal, and when it has seen itself in danger it has asked for the assistance of its natural foreign allies, mainly the government of the United States. This was evident in 1932 when North American warships arrived off the Salvadoran coast, prepared to disembark troops if the military government failed to put down the rebellion. It is the only proof of foreign intervention we have dating from that period.

If we compare those events of '32 with present times, we see that now elements of a consciousness accumulated through that cultural reality are at work. The history, the "chronically unhappy" past about which Anderson speaks in his book *Matanza*, has gone through changes, the major one being the rise in the collective consciousness, the regrouping of social forces that always ended up defeated in that chronology "plagued by poverty and repression," as the Report of the Kissinger Commission repeats with almost the very same words. A report that at the same time gives equal weight to external factors as being the cause of the situation, but only those external influences by enemies of the United States "that exacerbate the difficulties of the region and exploit the anguish." If we could take up this argument with the peasants of Aguacayo, Izalco, Guazapa, perhaps they wouldn't see evil intentions in the ambiguous conclusions of this report, but they would think their leg was being pulled, given the mental gaps that exist between the computerized analysis and the reality, a reality that has been repeated for more than one hundred fifty years, where the massacre of '32 is small compared to the "dragon flies" that cut through the skies in this decade of the '80s; and the fields are in flames from the incendiary bombs in this country barely the size of New Jersey. What we experience through Dr. Charlie Clements' book is, though limited, filled with a great sensibility. El Salvador today. And is *Miguel Mármol* El Salvador yesterday?

At eighty-one years of age, Miguel Mármol continues to live in political exile. He has survived not only '32, but '45, '52, '60, '80. He is the living document of a history that is changing through the efforts of Salvadorans. "The most bloodthirsty army in the world," as affirmed by Robert White, United States ex-ambassador to El Salvador in the early 1980s, will not be changed through the good graces of foreign intervention without attacking the underlying causes that give rise to a hundred-year-old conflict, of which Miguel Mármol is living testimony.

Miguel Mármol by Roque Dalton is the expression of an exceptional culture. On the one hand, the forces that want to hold back time in the darkness and backwardness of an oppressive system. On the other, the consciousness attained by Salvadorans seeking a peaceful and just society that cannot jeopardize anyone's security.

Nevertheless, the warplanes continue to cut through the skies over El Salvador. And the threats of direct intervention continue in force. The ones who haven't changed are we Salvadorans, except for our consciousness, being forged under the roar of the bombing raids. Miguel Mármol hasn't changed, nor has the history he narrates with an imagination and memory that allows us to confidently wait for our denied dreams. To recover the human dignity that was stripped from us. *Miguel Mármol* is El Salvador yesterday and El Salvador today. But El Salvador in the future will be different. That is what we are saying.

Manlio Argueta
Central America, 15 August 1986

INTRODUCTION

1.

I'll always consider having had the opportunity to collect the life testimony of comrade Miguel Mármol as one of the greatest satisfactions of my life. As a writer and militant revolutionary, as a Latin American and Salvadoran, I consider this opportunity a true privilege, since the gathering of that testimony involved the gathering of some fifty years of Salvadoran history (particularly with regard to the organized worker's movement and the Communist Party) and a segment of the history of the internationalist communist movement and the Latin American Revolution. I don't say this out of modesty nor as a simple gesture: it is enough to understand, for example, what it means for a writer and a Salvadoran militant to receive detailed information (and to be authorized to transmit it publicly) from an eyewitness, a survivor, of the great anti-communist massacre of 1932 in El Salvador (which is the most important social-political event of our country thus far in this century, the event which has most determined the character of the national, political development in the republican era).

But it wouldn't be worthwhile to make an analysis of comrade Mármol's testimony simply to show my deep satisfaction or to point out the importance that I personally give to the collected material. My task in these present lines is, on the contrary, fundamentally determined by:

1) the fact that the revolutionary history of El Salvador, the history of the Communist Party of El Salvador, the details of the events of 1932 in our country (when, after an unsuccessful insurrection led basically by the Communist Party, more than

thirty thousand Salvadoran workers were massacred by the military-oligarchical and pro-imperialist government of General Maximiliano Hernández Martínez – the true instrument behind the definitive incorporation into North American imperialism of the national-social-economic structures of El Salvador – massacred, I repeat, in a matter of a few days) and, above all, the relation of those processes to Salvadoran, Central American and Latin American realities of today, are extremely complex phenomena, as yet unknown in their details by the world revolutionary movement; and by:

2) the fact that, independent of the extraordinary political, historical, human (anthropological, you could say) quality of Mármol's testimony, it is basically a *personal* testimony, which is the same as saying, far from any pejorative connotation, *biased.*

These two facts: the complexity of the Salvadoran process and the fact that it is unknown outside of El Salvador, on the one hand, and the basic though relatively biased quality of Mármol's testimony, on the other, have made me decide that an introduction principally intended for the non-Salvadoran reader is useful (let's not forget that these pages have been collected and edited between Prague and Havana and that, because of the present state of the Salvadoran political regime, it is very possible they'll be read first by an international public – which doesn't negate that my concerns and those of Mármol have *what is Salvadoran* in mind as a final objective, and not only in this book –), a very brief and general introduction that would be meant to:

1) locate the testimonial subject in an historical, cultural and political context that will make it unequivocal and, to that extent, as useful as possible to the revolutionary movement of today, providing complementary information which doesn't appear in his testimony for reasons of a diverse nature; and to:

2) place on record the form and method of work (the interview technique, literary handling of the text, political difficulties that arose between the time of the initial interview and transcription, and the time it was considered ready for publication, and that have conditioned the editing of the final material, etc.) which

20

were employed to gather the testimony, and to place on record the literary, political, historiographical, etc. intentions that have governed my work as an interviewer, editor (and eventual analyst) of the text, etc.

I don't propose here, however, at least not as a principal question, the examination of the disagreements, doubts, partial denials, etc. that some statements by Mármol regarding the concrete problems of contemporary revolutionary history, as much national as international, might have aroused or, in fact, did arouse in me. I can say in general terms that I don't necessarily share *all* Mármol's viewpoints on Salvadoran history nor do I agree with every judgement Mármol makes about numerous figures (dead or alive) of Salvadoran history or of the world revolutionary movement. I even think at some points Mármol commits possible errors due to memory difficulties or to a lack of concrete information (as would be the case about the communist militancy of the greatest bourgeois leader of the masses that El Salvador has produced since 1932, namely, Doctor Arturo Romero, or about the participation in communist party work by elements known from way back for their fascistoid thinking, such as Doctors Antonio Rodríguez Porth and Fernando Basilo Castellanos – facts at the least very doubtful). The reason these things appear in the text is that Mármol held to his original statements even after I had expressed my doubts (and the contrary opinions of other Salvadoran comrades) and, therefore, I felt they couldn't be excluded without calling into question the authenticity of the testimony. Neither do I totally share Mármol's view of the international communist movement. I think that's perfectly natural. When I was born, Miguel Mármol had already been a militant communist for five years and he'd been shot once, had travelled to the Soviet Union and had been in prison in Cuba. Mármol was educated in communism when Stalin was or seemed to be the cornerstone of a system, when the possibility of being "the new man" consisted in becoming "the Stalinist man." I joined the Party in 1957, after having seen the first symptoms of "de-Stalinization" in the U.S.S.R., and, personally, I had behind me a very complex class

21

origin, a bourgeois education and a social position of an intellectual nature. I didn't become more or less fully familiar with the problem of Stalinism and the "cult of personality" critique until 1965-67 in Prague, and I learned of it as an almost theoretical problem, one of information. At all events, I came to understand it as an intellectual. A Party intellectual, to be sure, but in the last analysis, an intellectual. Which of course isn't the confession of a crime, not in the least, but a statement of fact. Because of this generation gap between Mármol (basically a party organizer) and myself, there was next to no chance of us seeing eye to eye on everything. All this, independent of (and now I'm speaking on a level of temperaments) my natural tendency to complicate things, which bristles seriously at Mármol's tendency, to simplify them. But there is yet another matter that must at least be pointed out, and which seems to me to be more important than this incidental focus on differences that could be constituted by the improper historical "Stalinist or non-Stalinist" perspective, or by temperaments. I am referring (not to offend modesty but to exercise a minimum of responsibility) to the distinct positions Mármol and I maintain concerning the problems of the Latin American revolution at the stage ushered in with the Cuban triumph. Mármol supports, for the most part, the positions of the Latin American communist movement expressed concretely in the line of the Communist Party of El Salvador. My positions in this respect (about the paths of revolution, the driving forces, forms of struggle and methods, relative importance of international experiences, class realignment of the Party, changeability or unchangeability of the Party, regionalization of the armed struggle within the country, global imperialist strategy, new instances of international solidarity, etc.) have been publicly and principally expressed in my book on the theses of Régis Debray (*Revolución en la Revolución y la crítica de Derecha,* Casa de las Américas, Havana, 1970) and in diverse political and cultural articles published in Cuban and Latin American journals. I have no disagreement with the Italian review of my book on Debray when it points me out as a writer and militant "belonging to the critical current that emerged on the triumph of the Cuban Revolution and on the influence exerted by Che Guevara." Notwithstanding, or rather, due to these reasons it seems to me that an *insistence* on the mutual conceptual differences of opinion between Mármol and myself can be avoided. More than to argue with Mármol, I feel my duty as a Central American revolutionary is to *assume* him: just as we assume, in order to see the face of the future, our terrible national history. Which doesn't hamper, I repeat, the effort to extract experiences, conclusions, hypotheses of work, from the historical realities that spring up, that issue from the testimony of Mármol, an effort I'll try to fulfill in the specific material of the text. Neither will I particularly point out my agreements with Mármol's points of emphasis, as I believe they'll become obvious to the reader in the course of the text and in the orientation of my conclusions. Nor will I speak to the many and broad areas about which I had no opinion after Mármol, with undeniable authority, made us conscious of them. Therefore, the limits of this introduction are those set out above.

2.

Miguel Mármol is a legendary figure among Salvadoran communists, a well-known communist among Marxists and revolutionaries in Guatemala and a revolutionary almost unknown by today's Latin American revolutionaries.

Activist in the organized workers' movement in El Salvador from the '20s; founding member of the Young Communist League and of the Communist Party of El Salvador (Section of the Communist International); first official delegate of the Salvadoran organized workers' movement to a worldwide communist trade union congress (Congress of the World Red Trade Union Federation–PROFINTERN–held in Moscow in 1930); arrested in Machado's Cuba that same year, under suspicion of being an international agitator and spy; participant in the preparations for the aborted armed insurrection of 1932 in El Salvador; captured, executed, and miraculously a survivor in this latter event; important element in the slow, difficult reorganization of the Party and of the clandestine workers' movement after the massacre; recaptured by the tyrant Martínez in 1934 and held incommunicado and shackled for many long months, until his parole in 1936; reorganizer of the open workers' movement under the Martínez dictatorship, principally with the shoemaker's guild; entrenched in the internal struggles of the fragmented and weakened Communist Party of El Salvador, between those years and the beginning of the decade of the '40s; indirect participant in the events that surrounded the overthrow of the Martínez dictatorship in April of 1944 (initiating the fall, one by one, of Central American dictatorships after the Second World War); mass political leader under the brief, provisional government of Andrés I. Menéndez; activist and clandestine propagandist under the terror of Colonel Osmín Aguirre y Salinas (21 October 1944–28 February 1945); exiled in Guatemala and active militant with the Guatemalan workers' movement after the fall of the Government of Jorge Ubico, as well as inspiration for the first Guatemalan Marxist circles at that stage; founder and leading cadre of the Guatemalan Workers' Party (communist); militant and leader in the new era that, for the Communist Party of El Salvador, began with the rapid development of the Salvadoran popular movement of the '50s; member of the Political Bureau of the Central Committee of that party in said era; peasant leader in the '60s, captured, held incommunicado and tortured for many long months by the El Salvador National Guard; member of the Central Committee of the SCP at the time he gave me his oral testimony (1966), etc., comrade Mármol is the prototypical incarnation of the Latin American communist worker and peasant leader of what is usually called "the classical period," "the heroic era," of the Parties that, as sections of the Communist International, sprang up and developed in nearly every country on the Continent.

And that isn't everything I could say about the personality of Miguel Mármol, even without intending to exhaust its every important aspect. These are the facts of his life that must be located within the historical, political, cultural, ideological, etc., context.

Though touched from a young age by the worldwide influence of the Great October Revolution in Russia, today Miguel Mármol is ideologically a product of the most general concepts disseminated throughout the international communist movement since 1930. Surely readers are aware of the acting currents of this stage, both within and on the "periphery" of the communist movement. But at the same time it is necessary to say that comrade Mármol decided on a communist line – that is, on the line pushed by the Third International – from within an incipient organized movement of workers as was the Salvadoran workers' movement during the '20s and at the beginning of the '30s. That is to say, a very heterogenous labor movement with a large preponderance of artisans, peasants, etc., and profoundly, even simultaneously, influenced by the anarcho-syndicalist, reformist, "minimum-vitalist," etc. positions. In accordance with the deformed structure of the working class in a country such as El Salvador – whose history is a long progression from one dependency to another – the proper class location of Mármol is ambiguous and, in any case, to conceptualize it we would need a composite definition. Mármol himself repeatedly raises this problem, in terms whose consistency and appropriateness are left up to the judgement of the reader, when he refuses to be seen as an "artisan" or as "a revolutionary with an artisan mentality." To all this has to be added that in the course of his revolutionary development, Miguel Mármol had but sporadic opportunities to engage in more or less profound, prolonged Marxist studies. This is particularly evident in his military life up to 1946, which is, by the way, the most turbulent, the most productive and interesting period of his life, from every standpoint. Up until then, during all that period, Miguel Mármol extracts his experiences and thoughts almost exclusively from direct contact with the reality upon which he *acts*; he is almost exclusively a practicing revolutionary. Which doesn't mean, of course, that he didn't have access to the very general rudiments and especially the

25

agitational-operative aspects of theoretical Marxism, obtained in the "schools of Marxism" which were founded by foreign cadre who were sent into the country by the Communist International, as well as from articles in pamphlets and from informational, agitational and propaganda materials – all of which Mármol places on record in his testimony. But it is clear that the level of education received by one means or another didn't diminish in any appreciable way his, I repeat, almost exclusively practical revolutionary nature. Even, let's say it once and for all, a relatively *empirical* nature. Nor does such an assertion detract anything major from the fact that his practical experiences (trade union and political organizing work with the workers in the countryside and cities of El Salvador; first clandestine experiences; attendance at the World Red Trade Union Congress in Moscow; preparations for the popular armed insurrection to seize power and realize the bourgeois-democratic revolution, etc.) are so clearly *charged* with political ideas and the impact of political ideas, and convey in themselves certain levels of elaboration, including theoretical ones (the level of elaboration isn't important). It is in Guatemala and from Guatemala on, as corresponds to the level of political consciousness attained, at that time, by the most advanced study groups in the Central American region, where Mármol has the greatest – and more and more organized – opportunities to study Marxism (even to the extent of having taken a very important course in political-trade union leadership and peasant organizing in the Peoples' Republic of China at the end of the '50s). I've said all this not to oppose in Mármol's personality the initially practical with the later eventually theoretical-practical, but because it is necessary to understand that Miguel Mármol gave me his life testimony (in which, as we've said, the most important events happened around 1932) as recently as 1966, which implies the elaboration of a viewpoint on those earlier problems by means of a process that has been developing ever since. Miguel Mármol tells us all about the events of the '20s, 1932 or of 1944 through the political thought he possesses in 1966. And though the testimony may demonstrate great objectivity

26

and a constant preoccupation with letting the facts speak for themselves, and though Mármol isn't in the habit of hiding his positions and even his political sympathies and antipathies, this situation deserves special consideration and evaluation, regardless of how obvious it appears, in order to reduce as much as possible the eventual margin of political error or disorientation in the conclusions.

But without doubt Miguel Mármol is, ideologically, *also* a product of what Lenin called "national culture in general," that is, of the cultural resultants of Salvadoran history – past and in progress – which formed around our source insofar as his socio-geographical *habitat* conditioned them. In this sense, it should be pointed out that Mármol spent his childhood and early youth in the suburban area around the Salvadoran capital, specifically in the region of Lake Ilopango, where there has been – at least since the turn of the century – a mixing of what the jargon and charts of North American anthropologists would call *cosmopolitan cultural components* (mainly European in origin): the *local upper-class*, the *new middle strata*, the *unstable, mobile rural workers* (peons, cutters), the *stable rural workers* (small peasants, fishermen), *urban workers* (mainly artisans), etc.,[1] and including the *corrupted and surviving components of indigenous culture* (ladinized Nahoas). And, from our point of view, the cultural elements of every exploited social strata and class in the country, within the context *of a national culture:* that imposed by the dominant landowning and exporting oligarchy, and by its fundamental instruments (the state apparatus, the church, army, security forces, ideologues, etc.), and by the outside influence of various imperialisms which, by then, were vying for control of the Central American region (North American imperialism among them, and more and more preponderant), continuing and reinforcing our societies' dependency. The elements of democratic culture produced by the exploited strata and classes within the "national culture in general" conformed and conform to what we call the *revolutionary tradition of the Salvadoran people* which, at the time of the formation of Miguel Mármol's personality, manifested itself in

27

different ways. Such as the at once communitarian and revolutionary-agrarian tradition of the peons and day laborers (agricultural proletarians in the process of development), concentrated in the heroic deeds of the Nonualco peoples led in the first half of the XIX century by Anastasio Aquino (the historical figure who most impressed the little schoolboy Mármol in Ilopango, as he states in the first chapter of the testimony), the Nonualco peoples who rose up, arms in hand, against the "government of the whites" to obtain land and socio-economic rights, and who, as did that tradition, received one of their worst blows with the abolition of public and communal land decreed under the government of Zaldívar (1876-85), the basic means of concentrating Salvadoran agrarian property into the hands of the Creole oligarchy, also in a process of development;[2] the liberal and anti-conservative political tradition of the most advanced fathers of Central American independence, of Francisco Morazán (the great Central American unionist born in Honduras), etc., that had had its great figure and martyr in Captain General Gerardo Barrios (author during his governmental reign [1859-63] of sweeping liberal reforms, introducer of the intensification of coffee production, etc.), and that even managed to initiate paternalistic and very relatively anti-oligarchical forms of government – at least in opposition to the most obscurantist sectors of the oligarchy – as was the case with the government of Ezeta (1890-94) and even perhaps with that of Manuel Enrique Araujo (1911-13), about which Mármol now tells us in his testimony; the quasi-lyrical tradition of the "ideal of Central American union," of the *great fatherland*, etc., etc. A whole, long tradition (disregarded as a general rule in the diverse "histories of Central American ideas"), very positively reinforced by the development of the revolutionary struggles of the peoples of the world, whose principal feature starts to become, as the century moves on, anti-imperialism, visible to El Salvador principally through the echoes of the Mexican Revolution, the Great October Revolution and, through much more than echoes, in the heroic struggle of General Augusto César Sandino against the North American Marines in the jungles of neighboring Nicaragua. It isn't strange, then, that the first Salvadoran peasant trade unions carried the names of murdered Mexican agrarianists, or that Mármol read – along with the inevitable Salgari of early youth – a newspaper that arrived quietly from Panama and was called *The Bolshevik Submarine*, and that he informs us there even was, in El Salvador in 1918 and '19, a "Bolshevik style," a "Boshevik fashion," that is: Bolshevik shoes, Bolshevik bread, Bolshevik sweets; and neither is it strange that the most important individual figure of the Communist Party of El Salvador during the period from '30 to '32 was Augustín Farabundo Martí, who had earned in combat the rank of Colonel in the Defending Army of Nicaraguan Sovereignty led by General Sandino, and became Sandino's Private Secretary. Many other Salvadorans, I ought to say in passing, fought against the Yankees at General Sandino's side.

I don't mean to say we can simply dismiss all attempts to classify Miguel Márgol by saying he was the unequivocal incarnation of the perfect fusion, the total (dialectical) amalgam of Marxism with the national, cultural resultants of El Salvador, particularly with the "domestic elements" existing within the "national culture" (everything receiving the echoes or feeling the direct impact of the international situation at that time). It has to be kept in mind we aren't referring to Marxism in general, but to that system of ideological rudiments of Marxist origin that arrived in El Salvador between 1917 and 1932, and one has to understand (after becoming aware of) the chaotic, embryonic, backward – underdeveloped – nature of Salvadoran culture, even in its role as an object of study in the process by which our country's militants acquire revolutionary consciousness. And one has to also keep in mind the always relative quality (even at present) of the later political development of Mármol, which makes him ask at the end of the interview: "Why am I a Marxist? In what sense am I a Marxist?" One could even question whether that fusion, that necessarily dialectical encounter between Marxism and the national culture ever occurred (and lasted) in El Salvador in general, historical terms. This

29

questioning would immediately bring us to the nature of the instrument that necessarily had to have been the agent of such a fusion (the Marxist-Leninist party of the Salvadoran workers), to the consequence of its political line in the face of the national dilemma in this historical period – the basis for its real revolutionary perspective – but I think it would mean, as far as El Salvador is concerned, beginning at the end. One could arrive at the theoretical-historical solutions to these problems (this book with its limits being, of course, just one of the ways) through the discussion of the lessons of experience that the testimony of Miguel Mármol may eventually start in our country (in light of present realities and needs), and not before.

Of course one could also study or simply raise, in some detail, the inner-world of the so-called "individual ideologies" deep within Mármol: those elements of his family upbringing to which he himself gives such importance, strongly determined by the personalities of his grandmother, his mother, etc.; his being an *illegitimate* child and therefore a boy doubly discriminated against in the small town of Ilopango; the superstitious atmosphere, firmly rooted in the people, that goes back to indigenous mythology, and has created in Mármol himself an undeniable "psychology of the extraordinary and supernatural" that, though it doesn't usually present a problem from the standpoint of his political and philosophical positions, does do so at some particularly intense moments during the course of the testimony. A psychology that, moreover, provides a very unusual climate for different examples of his rich array of anecdotes. But to study this I would need to have more than a layman's knowledge of ethnology and psychology. And then there would be too much about a very complex area that I prefer to maintain in the narration simply as shading, at a level that won't disturb the essentially political intentions of comrade Mármol's deposition and of my elaborative work.

The essential complexity of the thought and personality of Mármol, whose social and ideological conditioning I've touched upon very briefly, is reflected in his different levels of expression. In the language of Mármol is mixed the everyday-colloquial, almost folkloric expression, the gamut of *popular speech*, with a style of language charged with the catchwords and clichés of traditional Marxist-Leninists of Latin America, and even with a new kind of political-literary language of undeniable formal quality. At different times during the interview I myself had to make an effort to accept that there was nothing incongruent in that the very man who told me about his childhood with the style of a bucolic-constumbrista poet, was also capable of structuring, with an extreme, indispensible verbal harshness, an analysis of the military errors of Salvadoran communists in '32, or the examination and characterization of this or that Salvadoran government on the basis of the state of the relations of production and productive forces at a given moment. I have refused to carry the irremediable "technical treatment," to which I had to subject the text, to an extreme that would achieve a stylistic uniformity that simply doesn't exist in the person giving the testimony. Nevertheless I've wanted to place this fact on record, which, in any case, would be noticed by any circumspect reader because it has to do with the problems proper to the linguistic structure of the testimonial book, a new genre for us, whose very problematic begins to reveal itself to us in practice. At the same time as this genre offers revolutionary writers and researchers a mechanism and a set of techniques highly appropriate for the profound understanding of the reality of our countries and our era, it is necessary we work out its fundamental characteristics along the way. That is why I'll permit myself in this introduction to emphasize several of the merely formal, elaborative aspects of the points of view, methods and even mere "recourses" that comrade Mármol and I had to deal with in our joint labor.

3.
    When, how and why was this book written? When did the idea occur to me to structure it in its present form? I clearly remember that at noontime on the 13th of May, 1966, I was sitting comfortably at a table in the Novinaru Club (the Press

31

Club) in Prague, in front of a large window through which you could see a part of the dark, massive building that is the National Museum, crowning St. Wenceslas Square. The atmosphere started to get saturated with distinct odors: slivovitz, goulash, American cigarettes and Cuban cigars. Bohemian crystal was everywhere in the shape of ashtrays, sconces, lamps, table ornaments, glasses, goblets, platters. I was nursing a drink made with a lot of vodka and a little vermouth, and I was wearing for the first time a tweed jacket that I should have saved for the following day, on my birthday. From somewhere came the melody of Waldemar Matushka's latest hit song. I had arrived at the Club in my capacity as representative of the Communist Party of El Salvador for the *International Review* ("Problems of Peace and Socialism"), accompanying, or rather, guiding comrade Miguel Mármol who had arrived in Prague from Moscow (where he had participated as a guest in the XXIII Congress of the SUCP) in order to attend the sessions of the XIII Congress of the Czech CP on behalf of our Party. A Czech journalist had arranged an interview with him to get his impressions of the Congress and here was comrade Mármol, with a big mug of beer in his hands, conveying party views to the local press. The last time I'd heard of Mármol (I thought then, smiling inside) had been under very different circumstances and in a very different atmosphere. At the end of 1964 I was arrested in San Salvador, handed over to the Guatemalan security forces and, finally, thrown by agents of the latter into the Suchiate River. After crossing, I was able to reach Tapachula, now in Mexican territory. After having asked the Mexican immigration authorities for asylum, I was subjected to a very detailed interrogation. There I was with no socks (they'd been left in the Guatemalan police barracks), my shoes and ankles caked in mud, the right leg of my pants torn clear up to my knee from the jungle thicket I had to go through between the Suchiate and the nearest road, without a centavo in my pocket, without papers and without a bite to eat for almost two days. One of the last questions of that interrogation was if I knew or had information about Miguel Mármol, a Salvadoran citizen. I had heard news that Mármol had been arrested in El Salvador some months earlier, tortured savagely by the Salvadoran National Guard despite his age and, finally, sent to Mexico, under pressure from the workers' movement that demanded his freedom, by the same means and in the same way as I. The Mexican police insisted on getting information about that Salvadoran "little old man," who had also gone to the immigration offices in Tapachula to ask for political asylum some weeks before, and who, afterwards, disappeared as if the earth had swallowed him up, despite the surveillance that was set up all around him. I denied knowing Mármol or even having ever heard of him, since I had started out by denying my militancy and all contact with Salvadoran communists, in accordance with instructions I had been given for such an eventuality. The police insisted on getting me to talk about Mármol, telling me they were worried that the "savage Guatemalan police" might have had second thoughts and re-arrested Mármol in Tapachula itself, in order to abduct and murder him in Guatemalan territory. Fortunately, what in reality had happened was what I supposed, but what I was very careful not to say: Miguel Mármol had returned clandestinely, "through channels," all the way to El Salvador in order to return to his responsibilities on the peasant front of the Party. So, that Mexican policeman wasn't the first one to tell me about Mármol. From even before I joined the Party (in 1957), news of "the survivor of the massacre of '32" had reached my ears, though very distorted and incomplete. Later on, through my party work, I had the opportunity to get to meet him personally, though our relationship was never close, nor even near to it: he was working with the peasants and I with the university students and intellectuals. And except in a couple of clandestine meetings, in a friendly session among comrades, I don't remember having seen him again. Then came my prolonged exile, my clandestine, severely restricted returns to El Salvador, which absolutely limited my personal relationships, even with respect to most of the party members in the capital. That's why sharing with that man the comfort of such an exclusive Prague restaurant (at my side, right there on the big couch were piled the latest issues of *Les Temps Modernes, Rinascita,* the *Revista de Casa de las Américas* –recently arrived from Havana and still unpacked, a manuscript of the Spanish translation of the poems of Vladimar Holan, bulletins of the European communist parties and a copy of "The Apocrypha," by Chapek) seemed to me all at once a paradox, an echo from my past, and a kind of premonition with a hidden political meaning. I had felt something like this a year before, talking with a young Frenchman named Régis Debray.

When Mármol finished conveying the usual things in that very typical interview, and was sure the journalist was completely satisfied and definitely ready to bring it to an end, he took a big swig from his beer and starting talking about how happy he felt to be in a socialist country, spending such a pleasant time among friends and comrades, making an explicit allusion to that "greatest part of his life" when he went around "with his life on the line," that is to say, in imminent danger of losing it. Then the conversation became anecdotal, full of zest, but the Czech journalist became bored (or he had other commitments) and left before Mármol could finish relating the adventures of his execution. I felt like I was transported back to my country, the heaven-and-hell where my revolutionary ideals were born (an historical, intellectual, sentimental even – why not? – time and space whose ability to affect me had been sleeping in deep hibernation for the past year). At one moment when Mármol stopped talking to take a sip of the tea that had just arrived steaming at the table, I hinted, almost timidly, that maybe it would be good to organize some facts of his life for the purpose of writing an article for some Cuban or Latin American newspaper or journal. Since Mármol didn't show any opposition to the idea, I told him we could meet the following day so he could fill in the details of the "sequence of events" surrounding his execution, which I thought would alone be enough for a narrative article, a story or something along that line. I was even thinking of a poem, but I didn't tell him. So in fact we got together on the morning of my 31st birthday, the 14th of May, 1966, in a hotel room at the Czechoslovakian Party hotel, and

34

began working out the format for an article. Mármol talked and I wrote down what seemed interesting, like a reporter for the press who'll later make a story or article from his "notes." From his narration of the execution, many questions started coming up with respect to persons, situations, antecedents and outcomes. Why did they arrest him in the street, defenseless, unarmed, on the eve of a popular armed insurrection in whose planning and final approval he had participated at the level of the Central Committee? Who was that "Russian" who died on the execution wall at Mármol's side: a man with the International, a hero of revolutionary internationalism, or an innocent victim, a simple seller of wooden figures of saints in the Salvadoran countryside? Were all those executed with Mármol communists? Wasn't it possible to organize actions against the small firing squads to rescue the prisoners? Was any kind of legal process employed in the executions of '32? How did Mármol integrate himself back into the struggle after his "escape from the dead?" Mármol himself was hinting at connections with other incidents that came to mind, depending on how more or less interesting they seemed to him. The possibility of simply talking about two or three ideas characterizing Mármol quickly multiplied a thousand times for me, branching out as my anguish grew, in about an hour of probing conversation. I began to realize that to write about Mármol I'd have to go into — and not superficially — the history of the Salvadoran workers' movement and the CP of our country, and that to go into that I'd have to try to "dismantle" the image of the government of the Laborite Araujo, to reconsider the government of Martínez (about which we militants of my generation have a view that begins in 1944, precisely with its overthrow), to delve into the international situation during a period of world crisis, into several decades of history. And that couldn't be done in a couple of articles. It was then that I began thinking about a book. During my petty bourgeois birthday lunch, I proposed to Mármol working longer, for a few weeks, on what I imagined as a long interview about his life and his era. Mármol agreed and I petitioned the Czech CP to invite him to stay for the necessary

35

time in Prague, a petition that was immediately accepted. Thus, conditions were satisfactory for our work.

The interview proper lasted almost three weeks, with daily work sessions that varied between six and eight hours in length. On some exceptional occasions the session managed to take up to ten hours. Also, there were "spontaneous sessions" resulting from conversations in restaurants or during walks. The interview was taken by me directly, writing it down by hand into a big notebook. I didn't use tape recorders or any other technical means at any time. With respect to the limitations that manual writing supposes, I want to say there are hardly any in my case, because I am very familiar with it. I could go all the way back to my high school and university student days, when I had to take very quick notes in class, almost in calligraphy, simultaneously synthesizing and going into details. Similarly, it should be said I've had a lot of experience as a reporter and journalist for the written, radio and television press, and that during the years I worked as a counsel for the defense in the criminal branch, my daily job was to interview defendants, authorities, corroborators and technical witnesses, synthesizing their statements, collating them and using them in arguments against the prosecutor's case, etc. Also I have to be credited with the "parliamentary" practice within the student political movement, in which the work of preparing oral statements and arguments from hurried notes was indispensible, as well as with my job on the editorial staff of the *International Review* where I had to do the same thing almost on a daily basis. In such a way that, even taking into account that the amount of interview material with Mármol was really extraordinary, I think I can say that taking the testimony down by hand was the method best suited to my abilities and, therefore, the one that best guaranteed rigor and authenticity. In my case, the use of a tape recorder would have resulted in an abridged version, not only because of my lack of practice and skill with using one, but because of the fact that we had relatively little time for the interview and because, once Mármol had returned to El Salvador, I wouldn't be able to count on his collaboration later. There was no guarantee that at some future time conditions would be right for us to meet again to make technical changes and discuss the problems that might arise from a close scrutiny of the text, etc. Writing it down by hand had, in light of these uncertainties, the advantage that, before leaving Prague, Mármol could look at and revise the collected material – expanding it, reducing it, modifying it, correcting it directly on paper and in my presence. Also you have to understand that all the work of this book, in all of its stages, had to be carried out directly by me. I haven't had technical equipment, nor secretaries nor typewriters. Therefore it was necessary to have a basic or absolutely outlined text from the beginning. Time would confirm that the direct method of writing the testimony down by hand was correct. Especially because since 1966 I have hardly received any complementary material, recommendations, etc. from Mármol, either by mail or in person. Essentially, we've fallen out of touch with each other: Mármol's position within the political situation of our country has imposed it on us. This fact alone gives the book a provisional character in some aspects, since despite its length the book covers only a part of Mármol's life, and even this part contains some facets that are barely sketched out. Perhaps in the future conditions will allow Mármol and I, or, more likely, Mármol and other comrades to fill in the gaps, the innuendos, the absences and hasty points of emphasis that may appear in the present text. This, independent of the fact that the book covers, from a chronological standpoint, the period between Mármol's birth and his Guatemalan experience, which lasted until the fall of Arbenz in 1954. After then, Mármol refrained from going on with the testimony, considering – very rightly in my view – that the facts and people to which he would necessarily have to refer could provide confidential and useful information for the class enemy, for the organisms of anti-communist repression of the dominant Creole classes and of imperialism. This is another vein of Mármol's life that might possibly in the future be used openly without danger to revolutionaries.

Finally, I think it would be fitting to make it clear that my intentions in collecting the material about Mármol are eminently political, even though the collected material lends itself at different times to historical, ethnological, etc. approaches. It exempts me from having a specialized knowledge of anthropological matter, for example, which has been present in the work of Oscar Lewis, Jan Myrdal, or, among us, Miguel Barnet. My level of knowledge in this area is one of an average Latin American political cadre who almost finished his Law degree, who studied a year of anthropology in Mexico, who is relatively familiar with the history of his country and has studied the most noteworthy works of "documentary literature" produced in the last years, and who is, moreover, a journalist and professional writer. The rigor that must be pursued then in the pages of this introduction, in the epilogue, and in the form in which Mármol's testimony is carried to the reader, isn't so much technical-scientific as it is political, as much on the expository as the interpretive levels, and on the basis that the author attempts to guide his work within the principles of Marxism-Leninism. I am not a cold, impartial witness to a testimony that has to be located in a world of watertight compartments, labeled pigeonholes. I am a militant revolutionary immersed in the history that Mármol has begun to relate to us and I absolutely share the vital passion of the narrator for bringing that history in its present phase to the wellspring of the popular masses. It is useful to clarify this since, to all appearances, the "events of '32" have begun to attract the attention of scholars and specialists, of Latin Americanists, in North American universities. Decades of forgetfulness have passed over these events, as dramatic as they are important, but in the last two years at least two works – in mimeograph editions – of some length and importance by North American authors have appeared about the anticommunist massacre. They are: *Matanza: El Salvador's 1932 Communist Revolt* by Thomas Anderson (Connecticut, U.S.A.), and *The Communist Revolt of El Salvador 1932* by Andrew Jones Ogilvie (Harvard University, Cambridge, Massachusetts, U.S.A.).

I think these and other publications make the transmission of historical reality urgent: and no one can inform us better

38

about a massacre than the survivors. With this understood, some of the concrete objectives I work towards in preparing Mármol's testimony for publication would be, among others, the following:

—To help elucidate a number of unknown political facts within the process of revolutionary struggle by the Salvadoran people and the Communist Party of El Salvador, so that they may enrich the experience of every Latin American and Salvadoran revolutionary confronting the facts and problems of the present.

—To counterpose the eyewitness testimony of a revolutionary on the history of the principal struggles of the Salvadoran people, between 1905 and the middle of the century, with the reactionary versions that have already become *traditional, official history* with respect to that very period, and with the seemingly impartial, "technical," etc. versions of phenomena such as the massacre of 1932, the eventful days in April and May of 1944, the nature of the governments of Martínez, Aguirre y Salinas, Arévalo (in Guatemala), etc. that have begun to appear in El Salvador and in other countries.

—To aid the search for political precedents in our national history that may eventually support and reinforce truly revolutionary positions in their struggle against pseudo-revolutionary, anti-Marxist and counter-revolutionary positions within the peoples' movement of our country and our continent.

—To confirm, with the wealth of facts of an unmistakable Creole nature that inhabit the testimony of Miguel Mármol, the profoundly *national* character of the Salvadoran revolutionary struggle inspired in Marxism-Leninism.

—It is evident that such objectives implicate another: that of denouncement. The direct and unconcealable denouncement of imperialism and the Salvadoran dominant classes, of the capitalist system as an international means of domination and exploitation of man in this historical stage — the sources of our people's backwardness and misery. I believe that in very few published materials of El Salvador and Central America the magnitude of the historical crimes caused by the capitalist system in our country is as manifest as in this "incriminating testimony." And not only through these terrible *frescoes*, in which Mármol tremulously narrates the huge collective massacres, but also in that everyday form of dying, which is the life of the workers in the countryside and cities of Central America, and which is embodied in the *day-to-day existence* of Mármol to secure bread for his children and for himself, to secure basic rights, the minimal conditions of human existence.

–Therefore, in the face of Miguel Mármol's testimony, I rejected the first trap suggested by my writing vocation: that of writing a novel based on him, or of novelizing the testimony. I quickly realized that the direct words of the witness for the prosecution were irreplaceable. Especially since what most interests us is not to portray reality, but to transform it.

Havana, 1971.

---

[1] RICHARD N. ADAMS. "Cultural Components of Central America," in *American Anthropologist* (Vol. 58, 1956, No. 4, pp. 881-907). Spanish translation by R. Bogrand.

[2] It isn't a question of being nostalgic for obsolete, archaic forms of production. But it is true that, in El Salvador, the liquidation of the communitarian forms of land possession was done in favor of concentration of land into the hands of the "semifeudal" landowners, which was the material basis for the maintenance of the country's underdevelopment, and was carried out at the same time El Salvador was gradually falling under the yoke of the imperialist railroad. It is interesting in this respect to compare the views of Mariátegui ("Seven Essays") on the indigenous "community" and the *latifundio* in Peru with the theses of A. Gunder Frank on "the development of under-development." Mariátegui points out how, in Peru, "communal property does not represent a primitive economy which has been gradually

replaced by a progressive economy based on individual property," but rather that "the communities have been stripped of their land to the benefit of the feudal and semifeudal *latifundio*, by its very nature incapable of technical progress." And for what concerns us here, Mariátegui further points out that "by dissolving the community, the regime of feudal *latifundismo* not only has attacked an economic institution, but also a social institution that defends the indigenous *tradition*, preserves the function of the peasant family, and represents that popular judicial sense of things to which Proudhon and Sorel assign such high value."

1

Origins. Childhood. Adolescence.

You're asking me if everything I've done and experienced was already written in my destiny? Only an academic would ask that kind of question, and it makes me think of that song about "what might have been and never was." On the other hand, why get uppity about it. Old as I am, experienced as I am, these kinds of things still bother me and make me complain. A lot of people who know me say that, without a doubt, I showed up in this world to cause trouble, but then they have to add right away that I'm in the same crowd as Jesus Christ, who they say once told the Christians so nobody would think he'd been tricked when it came time to be stoned: "I didn't come bringing peace, but war." In any case, supposing that has been my destiny, trouble and me have been together for a long time, that's for sure. Whether I made trouble or it found me, is another story. Just to begin to show you how things were in my own life, listen to this: As soon as it was obvious that my mother, Santos, was pregnant with me, my grandmother kicked her out of the house. Since the guy who got her pregnant was nowhere to be found, her swelling belly was an unpardonable dishonor. I could never figure out why we poor people make such a big fuss over these things, but the truth of the matter is we can't keep calm when faced with a daughter who's been knocked-up. And it's not just because we're afraid of another mouth to feed, there are other, less straightforward reasons. All this even though in El Salvador the number of children born to legal or church marriages are still just a drop in the bucket. So with my mother in such an unhappy state, chased out of the house, I came into this world in Ilopango, Department of San Salvador, Republic of El Salvador, on the 4th of July in 1905, Saint Berta's Day and, God help me, Independence Day in the United States of America. When I was 8 days old, with my belly button still sticking out, mother took me over to grandmother's to see if my little face and my crying

45

would soften her up. But the problem was that I was pretty ugly, and they say the tears of the ugly inspire anger, not pity, and since my mother insisted on keeping my father's name a secret in spite of all my grandmother's ranting and raving, what happened was – like they say, it takes two to tango – grandmother sent us to hell all over again. My mother fainted with me in her arms, and for the first time in my life I was saved just when I was about to be crushed. My mother's oldest brother, Uncle Hilario, picked her up off the floor and carried her into the hall where he treated her with alcohol and mugwort until she came to. But meanwhile nobody paid the slightest bit of attention to me, whining and crying muddy tears on the dirt floor.

Grandmother's big story was that she'd married my grandfather with all the legal stuff and a big party and everything – something that, like I said before, even today in El Salvador isn't your everyday thing to do – and besides which my grandfather had been a Creole of Spanish blood, a magnificent figure. "I married a poor man, but a handsome man," she used to say. "We are ugly Indians, and I wanted to better our race with my gorgeous Perfecto." And she used to add, ironically, "It would have been good for me to have gone out with the big-nosed chiefs from Santiago Texacuangos." And it seems that my grandmother, Tomasa Hernández, the Widow Mármol, had been all her life sure of herself, active, having great authority and decisiveness because of her hard, mean life, yet at the same time willful, proud and stubborn. Even though a fanatical Catholic, she had liberal leanings when it came to General don Gerardo Barrios, whose picture, along with that of his wife, doña Adelaida, she kept in a pretty, hand-painted viewing box. But the greatest pride of her life had been and still was her husband. She never shut up about his handsome face, about his beautiful body, his modesty and goodness. My grandfather was killed outside of Santa Tecla while he was working as a laborer on a coffee plantation. That was at the end of the last century. And, in fact, it seems that he, besides being a gentleman, had been a very special person because all you

46

heard about him were wonderful stories. I remember this one: One time, when the season for harvesting the corn had arrived, a huge wave of insects swarmed through Ilopango and threatened to destroy all the fields. The farmers desperately ran off to save their crops from that ravenous plague with all the means at hand, that is, tin can noise-makers, rattles, torches for making leaf fires, etc. Only my grandfather stayed at home, in town, calmly smoking his Honduran cigar and rocking in his hammock. When everyone returned with the news that the plague had destroyed the crops, he went off to inspect the fields. They were untouched. Then he announced that he would divide up his corn among the poorest families in town, those to whom the plague meant certain starvation. It was for this sort of thing that they used to say Perfecto Mármol stood out from all the rest in Ilopango. Marrying this kind of man, and especially in Ilopango, a town of *ladinos*[1] where there were only ugly names and everyone was an Echeverría or a Payés, was something that went to my grandmother's head. She was an Indian woman descended from the families of Tonacatepeque and Texacuangos. And so when my mother took me over to her house, the real reason why she got so angry was seeing all her plans for bettering the race go completely down the drain with her new grandson, an ugly little Indian and a jackass like all the rest.

So my mother went through some bitter and hard times. As she told me later, when I was able to understand, we survived because of the kindness of a gentleman named don Simón, who every day gave us a handful of corn to make tortillas with. When I got big enough to eat without dying of indigestion, they taught me to eat mashed-up tortillas to go along with my mother's milk. I think that's why we poor people have such tough hides. Because if you can eat tortillas when you're still at the breast you can eat stones, if necessary, for the rest of your life. Life, though, was a whole lot harder for my mother than it was for me, since I wasn't her only worry. She had two little girls, who had a different father, and who were almost school age when I was born. So with this situation at home, mother had to

47

leave me very early. I stayed at home with my two sisters, Pilar and Cordelia, who took care of me and fed me even though they were so little, and my mother started to work carrying big bales of tobacco on her back, transporting them from Ilopango to San Salvador. She made two trips a day, the equivalent of 40 kilometers, half of it under a heavy load. Sometimes she made three trips because the pay was barely enough for food. As for shoes or clothing, forget it. We all went barefoot and in rags, according to what my mother has told me. My crib was a nest made out of the dresses and bits of dresses my mother and sister had thrown away. Fortunately, mother got a job as a cook in San Salvador, and after that she worked as a domestic servant. She got to be a very good cook and wound up in the private home of Dr. Manuel Enrique Araujo, a prominent doctor in San Salvador, just before he was elected President of the Republic. Dr. Araujo was very good to her, and while she was working in his house we ate three squares a day in ours. Leftovers, probably, but they took care of our hunger. But after that there were long periods of unemployment when we had to find food by whatever way possible: stealing fruit from the farms nearby, fishing, picking things we could use out of garbage cans, like boxes and rags to sell to the cardboard factories or to the washerwomen. Naturally, I didn't do this sort of work, but my sisters did; mother had to take them out of school in order to provide us with a minimum of food every day.

As time went by, grandmother Tomasa's resentment of me grew less, and little by little she began coming around to the shack where we were living – a shell made of straw, set over two forked poles, with mud walls held up by strips of palm and cane rods – to try and help us out. She was the classic "grandmother" of that region, with her happy and irritable moods, but generally speaking she was just pure bitter fruit. One of her first meetings with my mother after throwing us out of her house was made on the pretext of getting my sisters and me to go to the catechism classes she gave in her house at six in the evening to all the children in Ilopango. In those days, she was always talking about the Last Judgement, about the angels that were going to come

48

down from Heaven with their trumpets announcing the end of the world, the moment when all the dead will be raised to be judged by God, with all those who'll go to Glory lining up on the right, and on the left those who'll go to Hell, etc. I remember all this because for several years I assiduously attended my grandmother's catechism classes. I also remember how she insisted all men were equal before God and that no human being should humble himself or bow down before another. She always blessed me when we met, when I arrived or when I said goodbye, but deep down she never forgave me for being such an ugly little kid. But I was always kind to her: when she was sick I brought her fish soup with cabbage and lemon that my mother made, and flowers that I had picked by the side of the road. At that time, I vaguely remember, Ilopango was a beautiful little town with lots of flowers in bloom. The streets were lined with orange trees and myrtle that perfumed the air in the morning and at dusk. When my grandmother saw me coming with the soup or flowers, she'd give in for a little while, kiss me lovingly, and say I was her little man who wouldn't let her die of hunger or sadness. But she never brought me fruit in the basket she carried on her head, only for my sisters. And she hit me for any reason whatever, for touching her pictures of the saints or for messing up her basket. And although she always became so angry with me that she would hit me, she'd then break into tears and talk about her past, about the hardships that forced her to emigrate to the eastern region of the Republic, following her father, on foot, sleeping on mountain paths where one night she almost got eaten by a jaguar.

My sisters were in school now and all our money went for them. That Pilar, she wasn't a good student and all she thought about was playing, but since she was funny and was always making us laugh, we loved and adored her. Cordelia, on the other hand, was good at her studies and intelligent, and she had artistic talent. My mother was often asked to let her participate in the school pageants or in the town pastorals. Since you had to pay for your own costume for those occasions, mother would call us all together and ask us if we

49

would agree to go without new clothes for the holiday so our money could go for Cordelia's new costume. We always said yes because we were proud to have a sister who was a star, who everyone applauded, and we resigned ourselves to showing up among all the kids in their new little outfits wearing our rags from the year before, all mended and patched, but clean and well-pressed even so.

My mother, Santos Mármol, was the most important thing in the world to me. She had a normal build, clear skin, wavy brown hair, a friendly glance and a light step. She was cordial, resigned and tolerant, but when her patience was used up you had better go lose yourself. You could say she was like most poor mothers in El Salvador: Catholic, ignorant, strict and very capable of bringing up her children to follow her own example in the face of the worst possible circumstances. From early on, she tried to instill in me good attitudes, love and respect for others, and a sense of justice. I don't think my later development can be explained without understanding my mother's struggle to raise me to be a good man. When I did something wrong, she punished me and explained at length why what I did was wrong. Sometimes she would let me get away with one, two, even three wild pranks, and then when I was least expecting it she'd come and say I'd done this and that so many times, and now she was going to punish me. But she made me think about my mistakes, I didn't resent it and I tried to correct myself. She began to nurture my religious sentiments and, in spite of my young age, I was soon devoted to the Virgin Mary and to St. Francis of Assisi. When I had problems, or got into trouble or into fights, I'd go to church and pray the way my grandmother had taught me in catechism. I prayed for my mother and my sisters, for the few friends I had in our poor neighborhood, and for the little animals that sometimes called our house their home even though they only showed up when they were hungry. But I tried to pray when the priest wasn't around because I didn't like him, he smelled like vinegar and all he ever wanted to do was pick you up and kiss you with those spiny, dagger-lips of his. My Catholic faith was also tempered by

50

our worst problems, and the solutions they often necessitated. There were days when it was already ten in the morning and we still hadn't eaten anything. Mother would light the fire so it would look like we'd be eating soon, to calm us down. Then she'd kneel in front of the altar to the Virgin she had next to the oven and she would hold me so I'd pray with her. Before we had finished praying, the woman next door would call out to her, "Hey, Santos, I've got some dough left over, wouldn't you like it to make some tortillas with?" And that's how we ate. Mother said it was a miracle of the Holy Virgin, who never abandoned us, and she stressed the importance of faith and prayer as something you should never forget in life. Now that I'm older, I know there was another reason for what happened. Everything was due to the fact that my mother was always helping her neighbors, who were as poor as she. She was a helping hand, But this was why our neighbors always thought of us and tried to help us out whenever they had a chance. In the scarcity and neediness of poor people also lies their generosity of heart.

The holidays in Ilopango were wonderful and, from a very early age on, I've had glowing memories of them. At various times of the year there were religious ceremonies for St. Joseph, St. Christopher and for the Holy Virgin, and at the same time there were all kinds of popular festivals following in the old traditions, among which I especially remember the revelries of the farmers, workers and fishermen. It was common to organize community outings to nearby Lake Ilopango, when all the families in town would go together to eat and drink on the sandy beaches under the big fig trees and fir trees. There was guitar and mandolin playing and the young women would recite poetry. There were never any fights. These were times of peace, tranquility and beauty. At Christmas the ceremonies which were the most fun were the pastorals in which all of us, young and old, participated. I never missed going as a shepherd, singing that song, "Shepherds, shepherds/let us go to Bethlehem/to see Mary/and the Child." Later on, with the construction of the International Airport and the Air Force installation, that whole way of life would be destroyed. The airport and the Air Force barracks killed Ilopango and brought corruption and hatred. It was only a few years ago that Ilopango, because of the intensive industrialization, came back to life. Now the people of Ilopango are industrial workers.

But don't be fooled by the pastorals and the town holidays. There was tremendous poverty throughout the country, and all you have to do is reread what I said about my family's life to get the general picture. And it wasn't just hunger that ate away the heart and guts of the Salvadoran people. Around 1910 General Fernando Figueroa was President of the Republic, and if he was known by the nickname "Bitter Orange," it wasn't just a joke. That old thief held the country in a perennial state of siege and under tremendous repression in response to the national protest movement against the general economic and financial situation, which had grown more chaotic after the war with Nicaragua started in 1907. Of course, at that time I wasn't aware of anything, and I spent my time catching lizards in the bramble bushes around our poor house, scarcely worried except when there wasn't anything to eat and hunger began to gnaw. Although, I do remember, I felt sorry for the farmhands who came to town vainly looking for work, and for the sick people who came from San Salvador. But mostly, I was moved by the cart-drivers who, through the severe winter storms and under the scorching sun of summer, passed by tormenting their overburdened oxen, prodding them with goads that made them bleed, half-naked themselves and sometimes totally drunk. I used to think it would have been great to have a lot of money so I could have a great awning of shade trees built for them, covering the whole length of the road from Ilopango to San Salvador so they would be protected from the sun and rain and their lives wouldn't be so hard. I remember one time, as though in a fairy tale, when down the same road the cart-drivers went yelling and swearing at their oxen, a beautiful white carriage flew by right in front of my eyes, pulled by two white as cotton horses that had to be Chilean, big and lively as they were. An elegant and very fair coachman was driving, giving light touches of the whip to the animals, and inside was a lady whose face was

52

hidden behind her black mantilla, but it seemed to me that she had to be incredibly beautiful, like the Virgin on the great altar. It was dusk, and I still remember the whole scene like someone looking at a Japanese postcard or watching a movie in color. Back then I was a real dreamer, but that carriage was no dream, as I would later discover. When winter came and the Salvadoran sunsets turned brilliant with the humidity, and also sad and melancholy, I'd watch the low clouds pushing themselves by, almost at arm's reach, lying around in an old straw hammock, and I'd say to my mother that we all should be able to fly like the parrots that travelled in flocks or like the mysterious birds of prey. My dream was to fly to Mexico, which I thought was the end of the earth. "My poor little son," mother would say jokingly, "he's so weak, he's gone absolutely crazy on me."

I wanted to know who my father was, and I tried to get my mother to tell me. But she considered that a secret between him and her, that not even me, the fruit of that secret, should know. When some well-dressed and good looking man would go by, I'd run to call her to come see, and I'd say: "Ma, couldn't that man maybe be my father?" She would laugh and I'd show my disappointment since I would have liked that man for my father. Finally, moved by persistence, she told me that my father was Captain Carranza, who lived in San Salvador. I immediately started telling everyone so they'd all know I had a father, too. A name was a big deal for me, and I was as happy as if I had just gotten a new toy or something. But it wasn't true. He was just a name my mother had made up to get me to quit bothering her. My father was then Mayor of Ilopango, Eugenio Chicas or "Eugenio the Chicken," as they called him. A well-off farmer, he was the son of the famous Francisco Chicas – "Chico" Chicas – who was thought to be invincible with his sword made from the calabash, and who roamed the roads at night looking to do battle with the Devil or with other evil spirits. Chico Chicas had died from a heart attack, late at night, on a road near town, caught in the grasp of a ghost that had everybody terrorized. My father didn't inherit my grandfather's combativeness; rather, he was hardworking, quiet and easy-going. However, he was totally irresponsible when it came to his illegitimate children. And there were plenty of us. My poor mother felt obliged to hide his paternity because he was married and she was good friends with his wife, doña Crescencia. I found out that Eugenio Chicas was my father the same year they killed President Araujo, that's 1913 if I remember correctly, when I was about eight years old. My father, who didn't look like nor act like my father, but who was simply the Mayor of Ilopango, named me marshal of my barrio in the Festival of Our Patron Saint, an honor usually reserved for older boys or for grown men. I did my part in the main procession with an extraordinary seriousness of purpose, and my father was really impressed. That night he threw down a few belts of rum and confessed to his friends that I was his son. The news spread throughout Ilopango until it reached the ears of doña Crescencia and her daughters, my half-sisters, who were much older than me. They screamed bloody murder and my half-sisters went looking for me to beat me up. They found me coming back from doing an errand for my mother, and they threw rocks at me, splitting my skull wide open. I came home all bloody and when I told her what happened, she fixed me up as best she could and furious took me with her to the local Justice of the Peace to file a criminal complaint. My father caught up with us on the way, feeling all contrite; he'd found out about the incident, too. He apologized for what his daughters had done and said he had already punished them, pleading with us not to file the complaint in court. Mother, who was still furious, said to him: "I hope to God that one day this boy knocks-up one of those damned daughters of yours!" And that's why it's better not to curse anybody, not ever, because that curse of my mother's almost came true. Though in a different way. Since my father was such a womanizer and had so many children, at one point I was going out with a girl who turned out to be my sister. And if my mother hadn't told me, I would have married her. Well, anyhow, mother and father had it out with each other and we never did go to court. Years later, those two sisters of mine who had thrown the rocks and split my skull open were good to me and helped me out a lot. But, in the end, when I was a known communist, they went back to denying that I was their brother. Blood ties aren't absolute and, on the contrary, they have – like they say – their ups and downs.

I have happy memories of school. That's because even though I'm older now I still like defiant kids better than obedient ones – I was a good boy and spoiled my teachers. Since they trusted me because I was so well-behaved, they made me monitor the other kids during recess. But I hated having to write up my classmates every time they broke the school rules, and that's what I had to do. Neither did I like it when the other kids tried to bribe me with candy and soda so I wouldn't report them. I felt hurt, and right away I'd write down what they'd done, so they would learn. My favorite subjects were geography and history. My teachers taught me to respect and admire the heroic feats of our native ancestors during their struggle with the Spanish conquerors, and the Fathers of our Independence, like José Matías Delgado and Manuel José Arce, were my heroes. But the historical figure who impressed me the most was the 19th century Indian *caudillo*[2], Anastasio Aquino. My teacher said he had committed many atrocities and that his followers were a gang of bloodthirsty Indian thugs, but I really liked the idea that a humble peon on an indigo plantation could make the government of the rich tremble. I liked geography because behind every name I imagined fabulous cities, mountains that reached up to the sky, and magical rivers. I used to whiz through reciting the most important cities of every country in Latin America, but the ones I liked the best were the cities in Bolivia that sounded so musical: La Paz, Sucre, Potosí, Oruro, Cochabamba, Santa Cruz, Tarija and Trinidad. At least they were music to me. Music, or a litany. I hardly ever fought with my classmates. There were only a couple of times that I tangled with some of them, and I recall coming out on top. My mother had given me a lot of advice on the subject: "If they pick a fight with you, remember that God gave you legs to run with; but if they catch you, remember that God gave you teeth and fists to

55

defend yourself with." The toys we played with the most in those days were wooden tops, homemade kites, marbles that we called "baby turds," wheels, and slingshots using buttons as ammo. But none of them really excited me. My school-age playground was the Ilopango lagoon. That's where I felt the happiest, because I was a terrific swimmer and had great lung capacity, so much so that I was the champion of the whole region in underwater breath-holding. In the water we played games like "dive for the ring," "tag," and "cops and robbers." On the other hand, on land I was always so quiet and calm about everything. Mother scolded me for that, and said I should be more of a "man," that when she was young the boyfriends she liked were happy and joked around a lot. She also said that she herself had been a tomboy and had loved to play rough. She used to cross rivers hanging from branches, and she remembered how she once broke her shin when a branch she was on broke and she fell against a rock. She had tried to reach a beautiful, ripe fruit on the tree before the boys she was playing with did. But people liked me precisely because I was quiet and well-mannered, besides being courteous and thoughtful. I helped everybody in the neighborhood with their housework or I ran errands for them. And for helping out they gave me gifts of fruit, fish and other things. When I brought them home, mother used to say: "Maybe they give you so many things because they think you're always begging with a hungry-looking face." Another activity I really enjoyed was the military war games. They built the local barracks of the National Guard next to our house, and I used to like going over there to watch them cleaning their rifles and to talk with them about battles and what military life was like. I quickly learned by heart the names of every part of a Mauser, as well as facts about world military history. Because of The Great War, cigarettes were sold with pictures on the packs depicting all the big battles. And since I collected them, I was always offering to buy cigarettes for the guardsmen. It was because of those picture cards that I wound up being pro-German. The Commander of the barracks was in the habit of having me read the newspaper every morning, filled as it was with news of the war, and all the guardsmen would sit around and listen while I read. I would emphasize the news of German victories and try to play down their defeats. The guardsmen, who had caught on to the fact that I was pro-German, would argue with me and I'd wind up getting mad, crying and going home swearing I would never read to them again, not for anything. But the next day I'd go back, like a dummy, as if nothing had happened. I insisted that Germany was right in her fight with the Allies simply because I defended her right to freedom of the seas, which the Allies wanted to deny her. I had read that somewhere, and I used it as the basis of my argument. My lagoon playmates and I never talked about these things, only about school. I only talked about the war with the guardsmen or with grownups. And in town they said I was "quick" and that I had a great future. "That Miguelito will go far," they'd say, "we have to pray to St. Christopher for him."

As my sisters and I grew and our needs became greater, the work at home got to be too much for my poor mother. Permanent jobs, though, were harder and harder to find. So hunger became a daily visitor in our house. We went around with our stomachs bloated, our eyes stuck into our skulls, and we were even seeing things. I don't know if it was the hunger, combined with the superstitious atmosphere of Ilopango in those days, that made me believe for a long time in spirits and goblins, absolutely convinced as I was that I'd seen them on several occasions. That mental process is funny to me now, but something like it must have happened. Early on, we three children had to quit school in order to go to work so we could survive. I was eleven and had barely begun to study in the fourth grade. I started working as an apprentice for a group of fishermen who had me doing everything and they paid me in kind – two or three fish after working all night long. But I was happy because they treated me well and they liked to talk a lot, especially about the gross, vulgar things distinguished men would say and do. Even so I really missed school and it made me angry to think I would be ignorant for the rest of my life. I consoled myself by believing I was becoming a man in a job as hard as fishing. My mother was living with a man at that time. He was an ugly, terribly cruel Indian named Julián González, who was known in town as "Loose Shoe." I felt both furious and ashamed that such a bastard was my mother's husband, but so as not to upset her I was obedient and respectful to "Loose Shoe." Since he was also a fisherman, he decided that I should work for him, and so I quit working for the other fishermen. He fished only with bait, because he had nothing else. The others fished with whatever they had, even with dynamite and *barbasco*, a poisonous root prohibited by the authorities. Bait fishing was done at night in an operation that required extreme patience and silence more than anything else. My stepfather was particularly strict about this. When I made the slightest noise, he'd say that I had frightened the fish away, and he used it as an excuse to beat me, without giving a damn about what a scandal it was to punish a kid in the middle of the lake, late at night, in a little old fishing boat. Sometimes he even hit me with the oars and threw me overboard so I'd have to swim back to shore. There were plenty of nights when "Loose Shoe" started work completely drunk, and then he would really let me have it. By itself the work was hard under any circumstances. For example, the bad winter storms that often capsized our canoe. We had to hold on to it and head it back to shore so it wouldn't sink to the bottom of the lake or just drift around, allowing the other fishermen to pull it in and keep it for themselves. It was hard maneuvering it in the pitch black darkness in the middle of the thunder and lightning. And then the violent waves would throw us up against the rocks, where we could have lost our lives, or at least we'd be tossed up onto the shore covered with brambles that cut us all over. I spent two winters doing that hard work. It toughened me up and got rid of a lot of my fears from before. All of a sudden I had quit being a kid for good. But by then my stepfather wasn't just beating on me. He spent all of the few cents we got from fishing on liquor, and when he came home drunk he'd beat my mother up and even my sisters. I

58

hated him down to my very soul. But now I don't know, maybe I don't hate him anymore. When I'd try to defend my mother, he would threaten me with his machete and he'd lock me up in a filthy shed we had added to the house for storing firewood, where the hen laid her eggs. All of that turned my heart to ashes. I asked for advice but nobody gave me a good answer. Everybody just said to be patient, that this was the Vale of Tears and that everyone, if they thought about it, was more fucked over than everybody else. But my situation was so desperate that one day I decided to kill myself by jumping off a high cliff onto the rocks of a little bay in the lake. I climbed up to the top and when I got there, I knelt and prayed to Saint Christopher of Jesus for guidance in my decision; either to support me and give me the courage to do it, or else to give me a better idea that would put me on top of the situation. Just at that moment a great idea came to me. And I didn't kill myself. I went home and told my mother: "Ma, I can't stand it that Julián keeps beating you and I'm going to kill him today." You could see my mother start trembling, but she tried to look calm. "And how are you going to kill him?" She asked. "When he comes home drunk and goes to bed in his hammock, I'll wait till he's sound asleep, then I'm going to sew him up tight in the hammock with fishing line so he can't fight back, and then I'll kill him with my sharp knife." My poor mother started to cry and she said, "I can see you've thought this over, and if you've made up your mind I know you'll do it." Then she told me to forget that crazy idea, that she promised to leave Julián González forever, that she didn't love him either and never had loved him, and that she'd only gotten involved with him so all of us wouldn't die of hunger. Then we went together to pray and vow our promises to St. Christopher. I winked at St. Christopher as if to tell him that only he knew how that stuff about killing Juilán had only been a bluff to scare mother, and that I was grateful everything had turned out all right. Mother thought I was promising not to kill "Loose Shoe." At any rate we both kept our promises, my mother's real one, and my fake one. But all these things didn't get our minds off our hunger. The situation throughout the whole country was miserable, awful, aggravated by the recent quake of 1917 that destroyed San Salvador and killed many people. Another disaster was that by then the damned Meléndez-Quiñónez dynasty had enthroned itself in power.

To understand this period it's worthwhile just to briefly go over some past history, maybe even go back to the government of Generals Carlos and Antonio Ezeta, which began in 1890. Contrary to what's been said in El Salvador during these last years, the Ezeta government was one of the most progressive in our history as a Republic. I personally remember that it was a farm laborer from the village of Los Amates who cleared that issue up for me, because even I had come to believe the stuff they were saying all around me, that the Ezetas had been thieves and enemies of the people. That comrade from Los Amates was named Jesús Cárcamo, but we called him "Archive" because he had so many historical facts stored up in his head. "Archive" was blind, but when he talked about the past, you could see history unfolding before your very eyes. He was barely twelve when the Ezetas were in power, but he remembered in detail every one of their progressive measures. General Carlos Ezeta, acting as President of the Republic, ordered the landowners to modernize their estates, he forced them to build adequate housing and to introduce various improvements in the living conditions, and he passed a law forcing them to use all their land to grow coffee. And any owner who opposed him was an owner without land, or who at least was threatened with having his land expropriated from him. And Ezeta had the balls to do it. The "work-loads" in the fields were reduced and the same wage was fixed for each one. Up to then, one work-load brought 18 centavos, and how it was measured was arbitrary. Under the Ezetas one work load was farmed in an area measuring ten brazadas by ten cuartas, and it was worth one colon. That means that the work-load was less than it is today, since now the area measures 13 by 13. At that time the field hands could easily do two work-loads and earn two colones a day, for whatever a colon was worth in those days. "Archive" worked as a water-boy and earned one colon a day. The bosses

60

also had to provide three nutritious meals a day and enough coffee for the worker and his family, so all that hot air by today's Salvadoran politicians about an alimentary quota isn't anything new. Money spilled over everywhere in the countryside, and the men loaded down their belts with bills and change. There was lots of gambling, and in just about any good spot groups of men would take off their wide leather belts and start to bet. Peasants started using rough woven material for their clothing, like what was then called the "Colombian blanket" that has been worn ever since in the Salvadoran countryside, and that for a while became the uniform for the rural population. Peasants also began buying hats, machetes, candles and many handicrafted items. There was a sudden flowering of craftsmen in the cities. From the 75 cents a day they had been earning, they were now earning four or even five colones a day. The looms in Candelaria and San Jacinto were humming, employing a great number of workers. A good import market started to flourish as well. Of course, at the same time that what today is called the standard of living for workers was rising, so was inflation, that later badly damaged the country. But our class and all the poor people of El Salvador were happy under the Ezetas. The main obstacle was feudalism. The fight between the liberals and the conservatives was cooling off in El Salvador, but it was still affecting us through Guatemala. Because of the general economic and political chaos throughout Central America, the feudal lords had never consolidated their power at any time before in El Salvador's history. Force was always used, but governments only survived when they defended the strongest of the feudal interests. Foreign imperialism didn't as yet seem to be a decisive factor. It would begin to be a few years later. It has to be said, of course, that foreign imperialism in its modern form, that is, in this century, intervened for the first time in Central American affairs in response to a Salvadoran request: it imposed a peace settlement when we were at war with Guatemala in 1906, during the Escalón regime, and also when we fought with Nicaragua the following year. The Salvadoran soldiers always acted like big bullies, but when the moment of

61

truth came all they could do was yell for help, so big daddy would come and save us. The government of General Carlos Ezeta, a primitive liberal-democrat, ran directly against feudalism. It's true it was a hard-line government, but at bottom it had as much foresight about the peoples' needs as the government of Gerardo Barrios did. The Church, the feudal bosses and the conservative Guatemalan government began to conspire together. There were secretly backed military uprisings, like the one led by the famous General Rivas or by the Child Murderer of Cojutepeque, Horacio Villavicencio, but they were all immediately put down with the popular support of the people. Finally, there was an insurrection in Santa Ana, backed by the Guatemalan government, that was successful. It was the famous "rebellion of the 44," a reactionary mob that defended feudal interests and that bourgeois historians couldn't record by its true name, because those 44 were 44 rich good-for-nothings and 44 traitors and 44 sons of bitches. The Ezetist forces marched from San Salvador and set siege to Santa Ana in order to impose the government's progressive laws, but the siege was broken by the rebels and their mercenaries, with the decisive help of the conservative Guatemalan government, which was the blackest in Central America, a gang of Papist, ultra-rightist murderers. The clergy had fired up the people of Santa Ana, who were courageous and long-suffering but ignorant and superstitiously Catholic, assuring them that the Ezetas were heretics and that General Antonio Ezeta, Chief of the Armed Forces, had sworn he would have breakfast in the rebel city over the ruined statue of Our Lady Saint Anne. In spite of everything, the luck of the battle favored General Antonio, but the President, his brother Carlos, fled to Panama and everything got screwed up. General Antonio went into exile in Mexico, where he became a big reader of the Marquis of Volney: *The Ruins of Palmira* was his bedside reading until the day he died. One of those 44 rich boys, Rafael Antonio Gutiérrez, became the provisional President, and the city of Santa Ana was named The Heroic City. An absolutely oligarchic title, though, and today when the poor people of Santa Ana brag about it they're only putting a noose around their own necks. Men make history, said General Martínez. What balls: the ruling class makes history. The economic situation became miserable for the people, including Santa Ana, because in spite of everything the Ezeta government was more for the people, while that of the 44 was fundamentally an enemy of the people. As expected, the government put all the problems on the backs of the workers. The wage went back to 18 centavos a work-load in the fields and 75 centavos a day for city craftsmen. Misery returned, even worse than before. The craftsmen, who had fast become accustomed to a better living, sank over their heads into debt. The poor peasants lost their small plots of land. There weren't enough cops in the country to capture, bring down from the mountains, and throw into prison all the insolvent debtors. Gambling stopped being a game and became a dramatic, desperate way to get money. A crime wave broke loose in the countryside around places where darts and cards were being played, and where beer and rotgut rum were sold. Famous criminals and robbers came on the scene, like the often-mentioned "Whiteface" who stabbed countless people to death, and assaults became an everyday occurence. That's when the custom began in El Salvador not to count your money in the street, and not to wear jewelry in deserted places. That's when places like the crossroads of Calavera, or the sidewalks of Soyapango and Ilopango, la Garita, etc., became known as dangerous, as places where gangs of "thugs" and "scum" attacked passersby and murdered them in order to steal their gold teeth, if they had any. That chaotic situation lasted twenty years, getting worse all the time. And it's so easy to say that, twenty years, but not to say one bad word would be incredibly difficult. But that's been the sad story of oligarchic domination in El Salvador. Popular discontent was always at an explosive level and the initial enthusiasm for the so-called principles of the 44 was quickly forgotten. There were various changes in government, but the basic situation remained the same. It was the time of the governments of the drunk Regalado, of Escalón and other similar criminals. The bad deal the 44 gave the people is like today's so-called "Revolution of the 48" led by Osorio, the gringos and company. The same demagogic monkey with another tail, and the people on the bottom, fucked over. In 1911, as I said before, Dr. Manuel Enrique Araujo became President of the Republic. He was a doctor of great prestige and respected for his generous, charitable nature. His candidacy was proposed and backed by the feudal reaction, whose idea it was to use him as a buffer for popular discontent, and the truth is that the people turned out to vote for him in droves. The mandarins' plan had a rude awakening, though, when Araujo began to install a progressive, free government. He pressed for public works, spoke out against a policy of loans that would mortgage the country, and he even went so far as to take some independent stands on foreign policy, as in the case of North American intervention in Nicaragua. His measures that benefited the people, such as the abolition of debtor prisons and the establishment of workman's compensation for farm laborers were blows to the feudal bosses. Araujo noted that all these measures complied with international law, but international laws have always meant beans to the rich in every country used to screwing the people. Neither did the reactionaries go for the institution of compulsory military service for all citizens without discrimination, and not only – as was customary – for the poor people in the country. It was for supporting this measure that Dr. Miguel Tomás Molina, then Interior Minister, began to gain in prestige. Araujo took steps to protect citizens against crime and organized a corps of rural police. That was how the National Guard was born, modeled on the Spanish Civil Guard, which in those days was still an honorable group. The engineer and general, don José María Peralta Lagos, one of the great Salvadoran writers of all time, author of *The Death of The Turtle Dove* which has sold out many editions in the Soviet Union, was Minister of Defense and he brought in military instructors from Spain. The National Guard began to function. In the beginning it played a magnificent role in cleaning up society, it was on the front lines in the nationwide fight against delinquency and it created a network of barracks through much loss of blood and sacrifice. On the roads, delinquents attacked pairs of guardsmen and on occasion even entire barracks were wiped out by mobs. The majority of guardsmen were craftsmen from the cities, in good physical condition, and those battles toughened them up and strengthened their group spirit. It was during the time of the Meléndez-Quiñónez dynasty that the government bestowed on the National Guard the character it still has today, that of a terrorist, criminal body that represses political activity. Also, during that period, a rivalry started between the Army and the Guard to establish which of the two was the better from the technical and organizational standpoint. But returning to the subject of the Araujo Government, it should be said that it had to end in the same way as that of the Ezetas, since its crime was the same: to dare to challenge the feudal interests. Of course, the death of President Araujo himself was much more dramatic, because as everyone knows he was hacked to death by paid assassins while he was resting defenseless in a park in the center of San Salvador, as was his habit. The assassins had been trained on the estate of the instigators, practicing with their machetes on coconut after coconut until they were sure of killing him with the first blow, with the first two-handed stroke. The instigators? Well, now they're called the fourteen families, the coffee barons, the landholding oligarchy. Their last names are just disguises. I remember the day Araujo died: when I got home, I found my mother crying disconsolately. When I asked her why she was crying, she said they'd killed her old boss, Dr. Manuel Enrique Araujo. "They don't know what a man El Salvador has lost," she added, "God keep him, because he saved my aunt Juana when he operated on her stomach and didn't charge a single centavo." In those days mother signed up to work in the Army PX because they said we were going to war with Guatemala, but it was all a demagogic smoke screen to cover up the murder of Araujo and the identity of his true assassins. The ones who had carried out the murder, a pair of illiterate Indians who'd been promised the heaven and earth,

65

were shot down before they could open their mouths. One of them was called Little Mulatto.

When my mother left Julián González, she started working on her own selling fish, since there was no breadwinner at home. Starting at dawn she'd go down to the shore to buy fish and shrimp, carry it back in a big basket on her head, and go door to door selling her merchandise. Sometimes she went all the way to San Salvador and often she came home with her basket still chock full, without having earned a single centavo. Our situation was so bad that the guardsmen in the nearby barracks decided to give me a job to help us out. They had me sweeping up the place and fetching water in an earthenware jar for the latrine, and they paid me a colon and fifty centavos every ten days. So my pay was fifteen centavos a day. But since I was a good worker, they quickly gave me other things to do, and in the end, when the bosses knew who I was, I became a sort of assistant to the officers, which made me feel like a real big-shot because the title "assistant" was a military rank and they addressed you and gave you orders by your title. Before, they'd just say, "Miguelito, get that," "Miguelito, clean this up," etc. The Commander of the outfit was a Lieutenant named Funes, and he was the first who took me on as his official assistant. This is how I got the job: Lieutenant Funes had an assistant named Ismael, who was sixteen and stronger and taller than me. This guy Ismael for some reason held a grudge against me and he was always looking for an excuse to hit me and humiliate me. One day, for no good reason, just for the fun of it, he gave me a good whack in the face with the rubber bands of a slingshot. Instead of crying, I jumped on him absolutely crazy mad. We fought for like fifteen minutes and even though he was bigger and stronger, he couldn't beat me. Finally the guardsmen, who had formed a circle around us enjoying the fight, broke us up and started making fun of Ismael. Since I'd made his nose bleed, they pointed at him and laughed, "Somebody threw a strawberry at Ismael." Lieutenant Funes congratulated me and

66

had them give Ismael 25 licks for being a coward and a bully. Then the Lieutenant himself brought me home to my mother so she could take care of my wounds, especially a big lump on my forehead that looked like the horn of a little bull, and besides that he gave her five colones so she could buy me a new shirt, since Ismael had ripped to shreds the one I'd been wearing. When we returned to the barracks, Ismael had taken off enraged from having the pants beat off him, and I automatically became by rights Lieutenant Funes' assistant. It wouldn't be the only time I'd have to use my fists to get somewhere in life. Lieutenant Funes was very good to me, he gave me food and money to bring home, and I made sure to carry out my duties down to the letter. His clothes always had to be ready, his shoes shined and his weapons where they belonged. I didn't feel bad being a "pet-servant," as we say in El Salvador, because going hungry was worse. But now, I don't know, because it pisses me off that I was a flunkey for a guardsmen, though he personally was a nice guy. He began talking about me with the other officers and some of them made me offers to come be their assistants in other large towns and even in the Central Barracks in San Salvador. Captain Bonilla and Colonel Duque even got angry with the Lieutenant because he didn't want to let me go. Besides doing my job, every day I exercised with the Guard, and in no time I was strong and agile. So much so that one time when a sergeant gave me an order in an insulting kind of way, I refused to carry it out. He then tried to hit me with a strip of bark from a banana tree, but I managed to get it out of his hand and started hitting him with it until he had to run away. That's how I began to be known as a scrappy fighter and the guardsmen respected me, not as a kid, but as a man. Lieutenant Funes was proud of his assistant, and when he spoke with me he used to say he was going to help me and protect me so I'd continue in a military career, where a great future awaited me. And I wasn't opposed to it. I dreamt of being up on a horse wearing a general's epaulets, inspecting my troops and with a whole bunch of assistants running behind me with a glass of water every time I licked my lips. In those days, the opposition activity

67

against the infamous Meléndez dictatorship intensified. The conspiracy wasn't only made up of civilians, it had also penetrated certain sectors of the Army. One day it became known that Colonel Tomás Calderon Jr., Chief of Arms in San Miguel, and Juan Amaya (who they called "Juan the Chicken"), Chief of Arms in Cojutepeque, were going to meet with their troops in Villa de San Martín, our closest barracks, and begin military maneuvers to attack the Capitol. Lieutenant Funes received orders from San Salvador to pull together under his command all the forces of the National Guard in the surrounding villages and to march on San Martín. Since there was in any case a shortage of personnel, they even signed me up, a boy of 13. They gave me a rifle and fifty bullets and I became one more soldier. Life can be really nuts: the first time I picked up a rifle it was to defend a criminal oligarchic dictatorship hated by the people! Of course I didn't give a damn about the government. I still wasn't politically aware enough of the problems to take a position against them, and if I was willing to fight it was in reality because of the esteem I had for my immediate boss. I don't remember being scared, rather I prepared myself for battle with enthusiasm and I was even happy about it. Nevertheless, the invasion by the opposition forces in San Martín didn't happen and after a few tense hours just outside that city, we went back to Ilopango. But from then on, all the barracks were under stricter control from Guard Headquarters in San Salvador. Inspectors started to visit frequently and the garrison personnel had to always be on alert. This new activity even affected me, since based on my experience in the prior mobilization I thought that if a similar circumstance came up again I'd have to fight, so it was better to be prepared. Up to that point, like I said, I liked everything having to do with the military, but I really didn't know anything specific about the duties of a soldier. So I decided to overcome my ignorance. First, I learned by heart the code of the National Guard. I remember that the longest article was number 22 and all the guardsmen messed up on it, but I sailed through it. I was like a tape recorder playing back every detail so accurately that the Inspectors always held me up as an example for the others. The poor guardsmen studied the code in such a way that they could only recall the articles in their exact order. I was the only one who could say them out of order, in order or backwards. That was when I learned about theory and practice, about marching in formation, battle commands, how to carry a rifle, and how to load it and unload it. In a few weeks I even became an expert shot. And I was one of the best in the rifle exercises, the obstacle course, fencing with a fixed bayonet, and in disarming the enemy. And the political situation at that time offered plenty of opportunities to put those violent skills into practice. On another occasion, they put us all in the Headquarters of the National Guard in San Salvador, located then in a building that later became the Central Penitentiary and that had to be demolished because of the state it was left in after the earthquake of 1965, so that the same ass-lickers as always could build a park dedicated to "John F. Kennedy." We had gotten word that Colonel Juan Amaya, alias "The Chicken," had rebelled again and was coming with masses of troops from San Miguel to march against San Salvador. Our quarters were to prepare to resist the possible assault and to use the National Guard as the main force in the counter-attack. So for a few days I lived in an atmosphere that I would later recognize in adventure movies, like *Gunga Din*. We assistants were responsible for transporting ammunition from the munitions dump to the walls, the gates, and to other sites. It was all very exciting for me and I still remember the state I was in during all that time. For a thirteen-year-old, the imminence of war was like a chance to play a forbidden, grown-up game, and that's why I felt so proud. I didn't understand back then the meaninglessness of struggles between factions of the military that bloodied each other for the exclusive benefit of the ambitions of a handful of colonels and generals. I only saw the superficial aspects of war. Fortunately, staying for a couple of days in the general headquarters also provided me with some positive experiences that were an important influence on my way of thinking and on my future life. What happened was that in spite of the preparations to repel the supposed attack by Colonel Amaya (an attack that like many

69

others expected in those days never happened), the daily police activity of the National Guard was not suspended and it was all there for me to witness in a way I had never imagined: every day contingents of prisoners were put in jail for various crimes and offenses – thieves, drunks, peasants who had been in brawls and had hurt someone, suspected contrabandists, moon-shiners, gamblers and card sharks, young guys who wouldn't get married, people denounced for a thousand and one reasons. It was there that I witnessed a practice of the Salvadoran police and judicial process that I'd never had the opportunity to see directly in Ilopango: torture. Since the job of transporting ammunition had me poking into every corner of the building, I discovered that in some dark, dank interior rooms the guardsmen whipped prisoners savagely so that they would confess to the crimes of which they were accused. I saw some hanging from the ceiling by their thumbs with their hands tied behind their backs, and they were being beaten with a bullwhip, the whip that hurts the most. They also hit them with rifle butts until they bled. One time I saw them torturing three of my neighbors, honest boys from Ilopango who they accused of stealing cattle. They hung them up with their arms behind their backs and a guardsman hung himself from them to increase the pain with the weight of his body. I can still hear their screams. All those savage, criminal acts made me violently indignant, even more so when I knew the victims were innocent people. I couldn't stand it any more. I went outside into the courtyard and exploded, cursing them up and down, while I cried my eyes out. I knew it was all horribly unjust, and that I couldn't do anything to stop it. A Colonel Flores heard me swearing and came over to me, but instead of reprimanding me or punishing me, he put his arms around me and said he was glad to see I was sensitive and good. Then he told me not to be so upset by what I'd seen, that life was like that, that sometimes honest, decent people paid for the sins of evil people, and that it was all a matter of orders from above and following normal procedures. The colonel's words didn't convince me and I felt that from that moment on something in me had changed. For one thing, I could never

70

look a guardsman in the face again without asking myself how many poor, innocent prisoners he must have tortured, and for another, the real danger that one day they'd order me to do that kind of barbarity ate at me. I started asking myself if it was right to continue supporting myself in the Guard. And also, when we got back to Ilopongo, upsetting things kept happening. On several occasions the officers suggested that I should spy on the guardsmen themselves, and on other assistants. They wanted me to inform on what the guardsmen talked about among themselves or with other people, what they did when they went out on a pass, who they associated with, etc. That went radically against the way I'd been brought up, and I not only refused their suggestions on a variety of pretexts but I also felt a growing disgust with the whole military corps. And I think that all these attitudes of mine are a reflection of the way my mother brought me up from earliest childhood. In the basic questions of life, she kept teaching me lessons that would last forever. For example, once when I saw a strange man kissing the hand of my half-aunt Chepita, I ran off to tell my mother about it. She scolded me and then warned me:"If I find out that you told anyone about it, I'll burn you alive." From then on, I knew the meaning of the saying "eyes and ears open, mouth shut." And I could say the same thing about the basic feeling of respect for people that I hold to this day, above all for people's differences. I remember once when my mother had a really awful fight with one of our neighbors. The next day when we were passing by her house, that same lady just happened to come out, but I didn't say hello to her because my mother didn't. So then my mother yelled at me and said the argument wasn't with me, and she made me go back to say "good morning." Our neighbor greeted me, but she and my mother stayed on the outs for a long time. But I'm really getting off the track. Finally something happened that was the last straw, my patience broke and I left the cowardly ranks of the National Guard. Just in time, as we'll see. It was like this: In Ilopango there was a certain Major López, who was really a mean petty officer and second in command of the barracks. He hit the guardsmen even when

71

they were in uniform – an act expressly forbidden by the military code – and when he was drunk, which was often. Life in that barracks was sheer hell between his insults, his absurd, capricious orders and his cruel imagination. One day after he got drunk in San Salvador, on the road from La Garita to Soyapango he lost his sword, and when he got back to the barracks he was burning mad. As luck had it I was the first assistant he ran into and at the top of his lungs he ordered me to go look for it, warning me that if I came back without his sword he was going to tie me up in the middle of the courtyard and personally whip me to death. I put on my uniform, checked my rifle and made some pine torches to light my way. I combed the entire road from Ilopango to Soyapango and La Garita, but the fucking sword was nowhere. Either it was buried under the thick dust, or someone found it and took it. It was already dawn when I returned to Ilopango but I decided not to go into the barracks to tell the Major. Soon a guardsman passed by and asked me what I was doing just sitting there. I told him the story and he said that in spite of everything I should go see the Major because otherwise it would be worse. "I already decided I'm not going in, and I'm not going in!" I answered. "And how do you think you'll get away with that?" he asked me. "As a last resort," I told him, "with this rifle I've got in my hands, and the fact that I know how to use it." The guardsman bit his lips and told me in a firm voice, "You've taught me something, kid. It's true that these officers are really sons-of-bitches." By a twist of fate, at that moment Major López's servant was passing by, arriving at the crack of dawn to make his breakfast, and she didn't waste any time running in to tell him we were saying bad things about him. Major López, who'd been boozing it up all night long, rushed out mad as hell, and after insulting the guardsman he made him hold his rifle with one hand with his arm stretched out in front of him. When López came over to punish me, the guardsman said to him in a voice that you could tell was barely controlled, "Lift my punishment, Major, because if you don't you'll be sorry. The first thing I'm going to do is report that you lost your sword because you were drunk." Meanwhile I had moved back next to

72

a bush and, while the guardsman was talking, I put a cartridge in my carbine. The Major saw that the guardsman meant what he said, and he backed down. He lifted the punishment and went inside the barracks son-of-a-bitching to no end. That same morning I asked Major López for my discharge, and he immediately gave it to me. Although he slapped so many charges on me that I was left without any pay in my pockets, all in all, I was incredibly lucky, because that very night, the first time in many months that I hadn't slept in the barracks in Ilopango, the earthquake of 1918 – also known as "the one that dried up Ilopango" – struck. All the guardsmen and officers were buried under the collapsed buildings. The only one who was saved was my old protector, Lieutenant Funes, who'd been away when I resigned. And he survived, too, even though when he saw all his comrades dead, he shot himself in the head. He survived the earthquake and his own bullet, that dumb ox. Like they say, life loves a winner.

---

[1] *ladino*: citizen of Spanish and Indian blood, half-breed (translators' note).

[2] *caudillo*: a personalist political leader; a military strongman (translators' note).

2

Trade apprenticeship. Entrance into guild activity. First revolutionary influences. Foreign imperialism in national politics. The first strikes. First political experiences and the first persecutions. First love.

When I left the National Guard, my mother said she'd do anything, make any sacrifice, so I could get started learning a good trade. She always wanted to make sure I never ended up working in the fields, doing farm labor, because the way the bosses and foremen mistreated you was horrible, especially if you didn't have even a tiny piece of land, as was our case. Mother didn't know anything about politics, yet she'd say that working in the fields was like being a slave back when the Jews killed Our Lord. And you have to think that those years I'm talking about weren't even the worst times El Salvador has suffered! We tried to get me admitted into the Teacher's Training School, but there was no way we could afford all the expenses. If you aspired to be a teacher, you had to pay for your tuition, for all your clothes – everyday clothes as well as your good clothes – all your personal belongings, books, food and medicine, shoes, etc. Then, I almost became a telegraph operator, but our efforts in that direction also failed. Finally, I decided to become a shoemaker, a trade that enjoyed a lot of prestige as well as being pretty lucrative. I began my apprenticeship in Ilopango, in the small local shops, but I quickly realized that I wasn't going to get very far there and that I needed to go to San Salvador so I could get started in a large shop where they did a wholesale business and where the latest developments of the trade were in practice. After a few frustrating days of looking for work, I found an opening as an apprentice in the capital's shoe factory, "La Americana," owned by Felipe Angulo, which was located then in front of what is now the Central Post Office, and what used to be the National Treasury. Over a hundred operators were working there, and it was the largest shop in the country. At first my work consisted of sweeping up the premises and hosing down the street and sidewalk to keep the dust and dirt from blowing around so

77

much. I had to start at five in the morning, so when the first worker arrived he'd find the whole place already swept clean. My poor mother was still carrying basketfuls of fish between Ilopango and San Salvador, and she gave me fifty centavos a day for breakfast, lunch and supper. When master Angulo saw what a good job I was doing, he quickly moved me on to other jobs more related to the actual handiwork of shoemaking: making paste, transporting sole leather and other raw materials. And when he realized that I came to work from Ilopango, which meant I had to get up before three in the morning in order to get to work on time, he officially made me an apprentice and gave me a salary of three squares a day at Meléndez's little market, which was nearby. I was really able to learn the trade then. In no time I was an expert in taking shoe sizes and ordering styles for special customers. Along with my progress on the job, I was gaining the trust of master Angulo to such an extent that he also put me in charge of the billing and, soon after that, to spare me the long daily trek back and forth from Ilopango, he let me stay in his house. Although he was illiterate, he wanted very much to be informed in every detail about national and world events, and he used to always go around getting into discussions of every type and on every topic, essentially of a political nature. I used to talk with him about the war in Europe and what came of it, about scientific developments, the planets, poisonous animals, social theories, and I always found him to be a man with formed and solid opinions. In his time, he'd been a shoemaker in El Zapote, the National Guard barracks in San Salvador. When I started sleeping at his house, he'd ask me to read him the newspapers and different magazines and books, such as the publications that arrived all the time from foreign countries. In those days, the dictatorship of Meléndez was particularly oppressive and fed an underground rumor of growing popular discontent, but the repressive apparatus was still very primitive and didn't pay particular attention to, for example, agitational propaganda coming in from outside the country. The national daily press, on the other hand, was filled with propaganda against a revolution that had happened in a far off country, which I had hardly heard of, except that it participated in The Great World War: Russia. Its revolution was called the Bolshevik Revolution because that was the name of the communist party that led it. When I read about the atrocities that Salvadoran journalists and international news agencies attributed to Soviet power, master Angulo explained to me that they were just lies that the worldwide interests of the rich were raising against the fact that the poor and humble workers in Russia had seized political power. He said this was how it had to be, that the workers had to be in charge because it was they who produced the clothing and the food and the houses and everything, and that what happened in Russia was someday going to happen here, in our country. All of this inspired me with an ardent sympathy for that word which still wasn't real for me, and which you had to pronounce very carefully under your breath: Revolution. And with a magazine which at that time was from Panama and which was called *The Bolshevik Submarine*, communist propagada found in me an enthusiastic, sympathetic and interested reader. Along with those very politicized readings, which shed light on many of the basic principles of liberation, we read short adventure novels, like *The Malasian Tiger* and others by Emilio Salgari and Jules Verne. Verne's works had us discussing a lot whether all the things he talked about – trips to the moon or to the center of the earth – might possibly become reality someday. And without really having a clear and complete understanding of it all, I started to realize from all these readings that the most beautiful capacity of man is the capacity to struggle, to struggle against injustice and misery, against the obstacles that keep us bound under miserable conditions, to struggle for the freedom and happiness of everyone. Master Angulo was a big help to me since, as I've said, he wasn't simply just an attentive listener, a digester of international readings that caused him both pleasure and discomfort. But more: periodically – and more and more often – he organized secret meetings in his house with people from different social sectors. At these meetings they would lock themselves in a room and talk so low you couldn't hear a word of

79

what they were saying. Again, I say, all this inspired me, fired me up. My only regret was that I couldn't attend those meetings because Master Angulo thought I was too young. It wasn't from a lack of trust since he trusted me almost totally, so much so that I was the only person permitted to read *The Bolshevik Submarine* to him; not even his own stepson who was a university student and who occasionally viewed the Bolshevik Revolution in Russia as a positive thing. The conspiratorial atmosphere which you could almost touch in master Angulo's house wasn't, at that time, an isolated case. In the shop, for example, there was constant agitation, people were speaking out against the Meléndez-Quiñónez dynasty, talking about the achievements of the Bolshevik Revolution and about communism. The propaganda against the Russian revolution had made such agitation popular and a number of "Bolshevik" style products had turned up in the local markets: Bolshevik sweets, Bolshevik bread, Bolshevik shoes, etc. The two best public speakers of the day, Dr. Salvador Ricardo Merlos and professor Francisco Morán, came, undercover, to the shop and vigorously agitated against the Central American Union, the despotism of the Government, the imperialist exploitation of our country. At the same time, they denounced religious fanaticism and superstitions, and they stressed the need for a scientific conception of the world and of life. So all the big prejudices I had brought with me from Ilopango, my basic conception of the world and things, suffered devastating blows. During my first days working at "La Americana," I swore I had seen the Devil, that the Ciguanaba[1] had scared the hell out of me, and not only did I blindly believe in God, but with the pride of every ignorant person I refused to accept the idea that anybody might not believe in Him. But nevertheless, in the shop I found out that my immediate supervisor, Gumercindo Ramírez, was a total atheist, based on convictions that were powerful for their simple clarity. About the Ciguanaba, for example, I had been so completely conditioned by my social environment that I was positive I had seen it. Although the truth of the matter is years later I had, in this respect, a very strange experience which I'll

80

talk about later. On returning to my village from the shop, my new conversations with old friends caused a certain alarm, and I passed myself off as an unbeliever, a person totally liberated from superstition. The fact is I was beginning to convert myself into a deeply confused liberal and, of course, I was still filled with all sorts of prejudices. But now I was aware that problems such as those dealing with the existence of God, the Devil or the Ciguanaba herself weren't fundamental problems, nor anything like it. And besides, in the end I felt that if God did truly exist, certainly under no circumstances could He be opposed to the struggle of men to be free and happy. More and more, this struggle seemed to me to be the fundamental problem. Although back then I wouldn't have known how to deal with it.

In spite of those who now denounce the struggle of the people as something alien to the basic nature of Salvadorans, I will say that, along with other forms of struggle, including armed struggle, it does have a long history with us. It's enough to relate the events of 1921 and 1922. The fact is, back then the only thing that was talked about was fighting back, though it should be said that a correct conception of the problem didn't exist. Instead there was an eminently *caudillist* idea that was dominating the political struggle, and even more, the armed struggle. Also, the Army and its diverse factions were thought to be the only decisive military force in the country. We youth thrived in that atmosphere, and every day we tried to do something to push the revolution forward. It was during that period that a growing group of revolutionary artisans and students, who'd kept holding conspiratorial meetings, conceived of a plan to infiltrate the Army by enlisting at El Zapote. The idea was to lend inside support for an armed invasion which was supposed to come from Honduras under the command of the progressive landowner Arturo Araujo, an engineer who later had a prominent though sad role in the history of our country, as is well-known. These students and artisans believed they could persuade many soldiers to come

81

over with their guns and everything into the anti-government ranks. A few shoemakers from master Angulo's shop were among them, and that's how I found out about the plot, although when I asked to participate in it, they said no. The plot failed because these comrades were rejected by the commander of the barracks, who either had been conveniently informed, or had smelled something fishy, or had simply applied to the situation a principle that was basic to the thinking of the Salvadoran Army: that of not putting a gun in the hands of the most developed (in the political sense) people, as was the case with those artisans and students. The Salvadoran Army has accepted and accepts into its ranks only those individuals whom it feels it can completely brainwash, both ideologically and politically. The peasant class, because of the ignorance which the dominant classes and the socio-economic conditions of our country have kept it in, has been the primary victim of this historical crime, which, in turn, has turned it into an instrument of its own oppression. But, returning to the idea I was developing, I will say that the following armed uprisings in the name of the people did occur during that short period of time: 1) The uprising at the Polytechnic School. For different reasons the cadets refused to recognize the Government and tried to start a military offensive from Ahuachapán. Faced with reports that the Army was marching against them, they entrenched themselves in some pineapple fields and after a war principally of nerves, though there were a few skirmishes, they retreated into Guatemalan territory where they sought political refuge. The cadets thought that with the news of their uprising the people would spontaneously rise up against the dictatorship. But that's not what happened, because not even the slightest bit of mass political work had been done. 2) The Uprising of the 6th Machine Gun Regiment, led by Oliverio Cromwell Valle. It was also immediately put down without much effort by the government, with hardly any casualties. 3) The uprisings led by Colonel Juan Amaya, who I already referred to when I was talking about my stay in the National Guard. The only thing this military man did was lash out against the government, but he

82

was never able to pull off a decisive action. He incited and threatened insurrection for political gains. 4) The Uprising at the School of Corporals and Sergeants. I almost participated in this rebellion and was very much a part of its preparation, development and failure. It all started when we artisans – we were already calling ourselves revolutionaries – had arranged secret meetings with the cadets at the School who were from our social stratum, who frequented the same places as us and who went out with the same girls, the young working class girls of San Salvador. A cousin of mine, who was bursting with ideas about liberation, decided to get involved in the conspiracy and, with the object of creating a revolutionary foco[2] in the School of Corporals and Sergeants, he enrolled. His name was Antonio Mármol and he was a shoemaker like me. Up until his participation in that revolutionary action, he was working at "La Guatemalteca" shoe factory, owned by the Indian, Gregorio Aguillón, who won an award at the world exposition in Barcelona for his exquisite shoes. It turned out that a revolutionary foco was already functioning in the School, and my cousin did no more than join it. The fact is that conditions were favorable for creating discontent among the soldiers. The director of the School at that time was none other than General Maximiliano Hernández Martínez, who maintained very strict discipline with "bread and water" detentions and brutal beatings as its basis. There was also the problem that the Army pay was incredibly low. The idea of the uprising caught fire in the souls of the students and quickly the conditions existed for fixing a date to carry it out. The man who would be President of El Salvador and who would drown us in our own blood, "Pecuecho" Martínez, with the cunning that must be recognized, sniffed out the situation, as we Salvadorans say. He noticed that something strange was going on among his subordinates, he investigated, he bribed, and soon he had grasped the main threads of that simplistic plot, so marked by the youthful inexperience of its participants. One night, unexpectedly, the troops were made to form outside in the courtyard of the barracks where school was held, and through the access tunnel that led to the Presidential

83

House, President Meléndez himself arrived to flatter the conspirators and persuade them to change their minds. The rebellion was set to begin the next day. Meléndez promised the cadets an important pay increase and better food, a radical change in the way they were treated, and he lashed out against the agitators who had incited their spirits. When Meléndez felt the masses were already sufficiently influenced by him, he ordered those who were still unsatisfied and who still persisted in their spirit of rebelliousness to take one step forward. Only eight corporals and one sergeant stepped forward; the rest had been intimidated and had succumbed to those praises and promises. My cousin was among the eight corporals. They were immediately arrested and subjected to a military process or court martial. The military prosecutor, whose name I don't remember right now, demanded the execution of all the rebels. The progressive lawyer who I already talked about, Dr. Salvador Ricardo Merlos, defended them and succeeded in saving all of them, except for the sergeant who was sentenced to several years in prison. But a few days after the sentencing, this sergeant turned up dead in his cell where he was being held in strict isolation. In the penitentiary, and later all over the country, they said it was President Meléndez himself who murdered him, after presenting himself in front of his cell bars and demanding that the sergeant humiliate himself before him and beg forgiveness on his knees for his revolutionary boldness. I don't remember the name of that courageous soldier but, as far as I'm concerned, he sets one of the most beloved precedents in the development of the popular Salvadoran struggle in this century.

In the 1918-19 elections the popular candidate was Dr. Miguel García Palomo, a prominent professional with a liberal streak. But the Meléndez-Quiñónez dynasty defeated him, imposing its dictatorial victory at gunpoint and with savage acts of terror against the people. Beatings and exile were the principal weapons used to guarantee the outcome of the election. But also there were the murdered and wounded and imprisoned and tortured. By the way, the number of Salvadorans who emigrated during that period to other countries in Central America – especially to Honduras and Mexico – to flee the governmental repression was enormous.It has always been said that the Salvadoran is a "stray dog," who loves to travel around the world because of his adventurous spirit, but that's a lie. The rich Salvadorans travel for pleasure and because they can easily afford it. The poor Salvadorans emigrate because they have been thrown off their plots of land, because the government persecutes them or because they are unemployed and on the brink of starvation. That is a historical fact and whoever says differently is ignorant, either a crook or a coward, which is the same as being a crook. In 1921-22, to continue the thread of my story, the popular opposition concentrated itself around the Constitutional Party or Blue Party, which ran Dr. Miguel Tomás Molina for President of the Republic. He was, as I've told you, a man who enjoyed much prestige as Minister of Interior in the Araujo Government. The Government's candidate was Dr. Alfonso Quiñónez Molina, a big crook. The Blue Party had been formed as a *caudillista* party, which is the traditional form of the Salvadoran political party, I mean, of the bourgeois Salvadoran political party. Within it, though, there was a lot of agitation against the dictatorship of Meléndez, and confusion as much as internal contradictions within the government was widespread. By involving myself in the political campaign, I came to admire the political work of those distinguished bourgeois liberals, civilians and military people, who opposed the dynasty and opted for a democratic government. The name of don Prudencio Alfaro was still famous then. He was truly a legendary political liberal who was always in the ranks of the opposition and who, because of his abilities to disguise himself and outmaneuver, was capable of getting out of any trap his enemies had set for him. Another famous person was General Luis Alonso Barahona who, after being persuaded to return from exile in Honduras with promises of amnesty and peace, was finally poisoned to death by the dictatorship. Also, the actions of General León Bolaños, who

85

had clashed head-on with President Meléndez despite being Chief of Police in Usulután, seemed to me to be exemplary. In the exercise of his office, General Bolaños forced the usurious landowners to give the native peasants back their land deeds which were deceitfully taken away from them as collateral for stupid, outrageous debts. When one of the usurers, the father of Dr. Enrique Córdova, who later became a very famous Salvadoran lawyer and author of the Military Penal Code or Red Code, reverted back to his old ways with the peasants, he was literally forced to dress up like a woman and parade through the whole village like that. They forced him to reform his ways. The Córdova family complained to the President, and he brought the whole matter to the attention of General Bolaños. A few weeks later, Bolaños rounded up all the bootleggers in the zone of Usulután and threw them in jail, including several fat-cats with their capes and their walking canes. President Meléndez intervened, but only on behalf of those distinguished gentlemen. Absolutely furious, General Bolaños then ordered all the prisoners released, rich and poor. All this made him the target of the government, which quickly invoked the classic formula: when he was filling the office of Chief of Police in San Salvador, where he had been transferred because of his run-ins with the feudal lords in Usulután, General Bolaños was poisoned to death. On the basis of all this information and these examples, I decided to join the Constitutional Party of Dr. Miguel Tomás Molina, an old style liberal and a man who upheld a dignity of character until he was over a hundred years old, which is saying a lot for a Salvadoran liberal since most of the creeps in our country have come from the liberal camp. At least most of the traitors, that's for sure. It would be enough to say that don Napoleón Viera Altamirano is a liberal, so the Salvadorans would accept him without a second thought. I had my first experience with organized militant politics in that party. I was named by my contacts in the urban zone of San Salvador as Secretary of the Local Committee of the Constitutional Party in San Martín, the village next to Ilopango. It was the first time in my political career, to describe my life's work

86

that way, that I was called upon to do what was a common enough practice among the revolutionary artisans in San Salvador in the first half of the century: to work among the masses from the villages, towns and cities near the capital, from where a large number of us came. My activities were so fervent and committed to the Molinista cause that I immediately earned the deep hatred of the local authorities. I was no longer nice little Miguel, but the enemy of the Government, the political one with another faction, the antagonist, the seditious one. And that happened overnight. At the same time that the presidential campaign was heating up, I became the victim of all sorts of harassment and, finally, on December 24, 1922, I was advised by the village pharmacist, don Gabriel Ortiz, that the National Guard was arresting all the Molinista leaders, and that I better flee as quickly as possible. What was I going to do? A cousin of my mother had a good sewing accessories business in San Martín, and so I asked him if he could help me get out of the village. My uncle wrapped me up in a straw mat and , along with his bundles of merchandise, I wound up in the back of his cart. One of his daughters sat on the bundle I was in, and like that I was able to escape – though not without a thousand and one sudden, unexpected surprises – right under the very noses of those to who were searching for me with a fine-tooth comb. Every precaution meant next to nothing, since the Government was prepared to commit the worst crimes in order to once again seize power, over the ashes of the opposition. In fact, the next day one of the blackest crimes ever committed by the oligarchy and its ministers occurred in San Salvador: the great massacre of Molinista women in the very center of the capital. The Army and police opened fire with their machine guns on a huge demonstration of women from our Constitutional Party, who were marching through the streets in support of our candidate in an absolutely orderly, peaceful manner. The uniformed criminals went to work on our defenseless women, firing from makeshift machine-gun nests set up at different high vantage points around the capital – on the roofs of the barracks, public buildings, etc. And they finished off the fallen with small arms and rifles. Many women were killed and wounded and, similarly, many men from the village were shot down attempting to defend or rescue their wives or companions. Always the same old rage unleashed against the people, the same murderers who we'd see later in 1932, 1944, 1952, 1960, 1961, 1966, etc. The accounts of that cowardly massacre stood your hair on end and made your heart stop. The Army placed the whole country in a state of alert, and the list of the dead and disappeared stretched out of sight. A feeling of impotence fell over us Molinistas, and the most radical among us started to think that political activity like shouting, "Viva Molina!" and distributing leaflets was pure bullshit when the enemy had rifles and machine guns and the whole Army. It was like a fight between a tethered ass and a lion on the loose. Hidden in my uncle's cart, I'd managed to get as far as San Salvador itself, but after the massacre the persecution became worse there than anywhere else. And on several occasions I was almost arrested by the police who were searching everywhere for opponents, Molinistas, suspicious characters, or whoever happened to come along. After a few endless days I decided to return to San Martín, convinced that the authorities were no longer looking for me, having realized that I had escaped. When I got there, I discovered that my mother had moved to the village, since she'd found work as a cook in no less than the Headquarters of the National Guard in San Martín, leaving my sisters behind with friends in Ilopango. My grandmother, Tomasa, had already died by then. One day, washing her son's and grandson's clothes – that is, my uncle Hilario and my cousin Rafael – she cut her hand and it got infected, and she died practically overnight. That happened in 1920, when both Hilario and Rafael had to go into the Army in a draft that the government put into effect in the face of invasion threats by Arturo Araujo, who I mentioned before. When I was able to get in touch with my mother, the first thing she told me was that my political enemies had tried to harm her, for as soon as they realized she was my mother, and that she was going to be the new cook of the place, they went to tell the Commander that they had heard her say she was going to

88

poison all the staff with a "specially prepared" meal to avenge my persecution. The Commander had her summoned and he told her that she had better watch her step, whereupon he got up and left, probably only a little sick from eating her meal. But because of her irreproachable behavior she earned the Commander's respect, and he changed his tune with her. He was so good to her that he went so far as to say that I was being persecuted for no real reason at all, but simply because of political hatreds for the lowly people, and that through reliable information which he had received, he was convinced I was an honest man and a hard worker, and therefore he wanted to make us both a proposition. The deal was, if it was okay with us, that I would live in the very quarters of the Commander, without any fuss and without being seen by the neighbors, since I'd be very safe there until the wave of persecution passed. When my mother told me about it, I thought it had to be a trap, but she convinced me of the Commander's sincerity, and I decided to accept the offer. After all, it was a matter of extending my stay in San Martín: I was certain that they weren't going to look for me in the mouth of the wolf. It all worked out to a tee. The Commander sheltered me there until the storm passed. And I would say he was a very mature, prudent person, difficult to find at any time in the ranks of our military institutions, which are bursting with the worst of our society, the worst of every social sector, and in which the more inhuman the individual is, the higher he climbs. I remember during my last days under the Commander's protection, when several folks from the village, including some of my enemies, now knew I was taking refuge in his quarters, he gave me yet another example of his fair-minded soul and sense of justice. My enemies sent him word with an old gossipy busybody that I, availing myself of circumstances, was having a love affair with his wife. She was much younger than the Commander, and she was very beautiful, from San Vicente, with long eyelashes and a mouth like a flower, who also lived there in the Commander's quarters. She always used to talk with me because she got bored being around so many crude guardsmen, but we absolutely never had anything more than respectable, innocent talks about the countryside, animals, food, travelling, books by Salvadoran writers, etc. When the Commander got wind of the rumor he didn't fly off the handle, as they say. Carefully thinking it over, he inquired into who the authors of that rumor were, and then he called me into his office. Without saying why, he asked me: "Who do you consider your worst enemies in the village?" Openly, I gave him several names without knowing what he was driving at, and it just so happened that it turned out perfect that my slanderers were among them. "You're absolutely right," he said to me, "they themselves are their own worst enemies." And then he told me the whole trumped-up story, adding that I shouldn't worry because he had no reason to doubt his wife, whom he knew very well; nor me, because he judged me to be an honest and loyal man. "The first chance I get, I'm going to screw those bigmouth sons-of-bitches," he ended up saying, "and I can't wait to do it."

Long before all these troubles, I had quit working at "La Americana." Master Angulo, despite his fatherly streaks about which I've already raved enough, had a violent nature and when he'd get all worked up he was capable of hitting and kicking around his workers. He showed his special feelings for me to the degree that some of the workers who didn't exactly like me were grumbling that I was some kind of stool-pigeon for the boss. I used to get them even angrier by saying that they were incapable of seeing a beautiful girl even if she came right up to them and kissed them, that is, that they were just plain jealous. Reality would prove I was neither a stool-pigeon nor a play-doll for master Angulo. What happened was that on a certain occasion a lady came into the shop to have a pair of dress shoes made. At that time there was a style from France called the "Doree Style," which was causing a sensation with the fashionable ladies in the capital. I took her shoe size, gave the order to the operators, and I myself did all the stitching for the final stage. But somehow in the finishing stage someone had either lost them or had taken them, but in any case they disappeared, and if it had been up to us that lady would've been left with her feet dangling in the air. Master Angulo got angry as hell and since no one seemed to be to blame, he came down on all of us as a whole. I quietly withstood his insults until he called us a bunch of "motherfuckers." That insult is to me like squeezing a tiger's balls, although in El Salvador swear words are on the tip of your tongue from the time you learn to talk (but, of course, the whole thing also depends on the tone in which it is said), and unable to control my anger any longer, I got up on a workbench and started shouting at him: "Okay, Angulo, I'm to blame. Now if you've got business with me, come over here and shut me up!" He stepped forward to hit me. He was very big and strong, and I was surely no match for him, so much so that I went for my work knife. When he saw me armed and ready, he paused, turned pale and went back to his office. Later on, he sent word with his wife that it would be best if I immediately left the premises. So I did. Two days later master Angulo, having thought the incident over, once again sent his wife up to San Martín to propose that we forget the whole matter and that everything return to the way it was before. He even sent me money. But I felt everything had changed now, and I couldn't go back to work there, which is what I told his wife to tell him. At least I'd shown those grumblers that I wasn't a stool-pigeon nor a plaything, not for anybody. And that despite being broke and hungry I had the dignity of a man and a worker. Some time later, late in 1921, poor master Angulo's shop burned down, and I went looking for him to give him my condolences. He cried and we made something to eat together. But I never went back to work for him. He helped me a lot in the future, under truly difficult conditions. I remember him with affection not only for his friendship, but because he was the link to my discovery of revolutionary literature.

What were the major causes of all those political developments in which I started to participate, like a little fish swept away from its home by the river's current? During that period, which erupted in 1914, those who held the financial reins of our country were the British imperialists. El Salvador's foreign debt was more than 20 million dollars, an astronomical amount for that time and for the means and resources of the country. This debt had grown with the construction of the railroad, the introduction of automated gold mining equipment made of aluminum, the construction of government buildings at a huge loss, and the founding of new banks. North American imperialism hadn't yet consolidated itself in our region and, with respect to German imperialism, it has to be said that although it had succeeded in penetrating (with a friendly face) our popular consumer market, which preferred its high quality products, it wasn't at that time a real force in El Salvador, nor would it ever be. That is, as imperialism per se. Then again, you never know about that because in actuality German imperialism, together with Japanese and Israeli, is the second most dangerous enemy of our people, after North American imperialism. I would like to explain that situation in detail. Commercially, the most visible country that we conducted foreign trade with was Germany. Hence the people had a high regard for German products and hence they had developed a genuinely fond acceptance, like jerks, of everything in general that was German. I remember the very popular German sewing needles and thread, work tools, stainless steel items such as scissors and Toledo Solingen razor blades, Bayer medicines like the famous 914 injection against syphilis, known as the "German injection." On the other hand, the people really disliked the gringos because of their despicable actions against Mexico, a country which historically has been considered by Salvadorans as a member of our large household, the land where our ancestors came from. That situation, somewhat undefined in the terrain of foreign domination, began to ride on one internal political fact: the total loss of prestige and bankruptcy of militaristic *caudillismo.* As for internal social forces, the overall bird's eye view was more or less this: the landowners were the second mortgage holders of the State, after the foreign imperialist vultures. When the Meléndez-Quiñonistas rose to power, they were as a group on the outs with the landowning sector, which for its part began to maneuver to turn the State into its own exclusive instrument, fearing the loss of its tax revenues because of the national debt. The anti-nationalist dynasty in power, to defend itself from those long shark-like teeth, compromised with the sea-serpent. After all, the Meléndez-Quiñonistas were but a few outnumbered piranhas. They handed the mines over to North American companies, and they took out several state and private loans with Yankee banks. For sure, the severe and brief exploitation of our miners by the Yankees was almost identical in form to slave exploitation. Someone ought to write up the history of the Salvadoran miners: it would look like a criminology textbook, which is what it is. The United States, for its part, was opposed to El Salvador's declared neutrality during the Great World War of 1914 and, therefore, it decided to prop up the Meléndez-Quiñonistas as political puppets in order to penetrate the country. The upper hierarchy of the Army was solidly pro-German, as was the non-landowning bourgeoisie, the petty bourgeois importers, and the people themselves who, as we've said, sympathized with and believed they had interests in common with the Germans. This whole game, being played out in different directions by the agents of the three imperialist countries, was what was at the bottom of those insurrections and threats of military coups and invasions, which I mentioned before. Arturo Araujo himself was now a pawn of British imperialism. Of course I made this analysis many years later, when I already was a militant worker and close to becoming a communist. In those days, myself and many of my friends and comrades, infused with militant *caudillist* politics, were probably blind instruments of those powerful forces. Hatred toward the Yankees and sympathy for the Germans continued to be a very important tradition in the ideology of the Salvadoran Army for some time. Many Salvadorans probably remember how, at the beginning of the Second World War, President Hernández Martínez would talk about "the rotten democracy of the United

93

States," and it is said that he went so far as to collaborate with Hitler's Germany on a tactical plan to land troops on North American soil. Anyhow, imperialism is fundamentally an economic phenomenon, and from this standpoint the North Americans were going to begin constructing their colossal future exploitation of the world and of our tiny little country. The loan granted to the Meléndez-Quiñónez dynasty (16 million dollars) took care of the British debt and a large part of the internal debt, and paved the way for the dynasty's future partnership with its new gringo bosses who'd paid for that right, dollar after dollar. The Meléndez-Quiñónez dynasty had, in our national history, a pretty good reward, the reward given to sellout countries! Despite this situation, the other foreign imperialist interests continued to have a good old time jousting with each other, until they were completely stripped of any and all influence by the international consolidation of Yankee imperialism in the 1940s. Similarly, Arturo Araujo was going to be the last outstanding representative of the interests of British imperialism, imbued as he was with a Labourite and Cooperativist conception of the State and society, a conception he formed during his years as a student in Liverpool. García Palomo and Miguel Tomás Molina, poor fellows, went against the interests of the ruling dynasty by representing the interests of national capital, and thus shared their quota of blows with the people. To be sure the people are almost exclusively the ones who are beaten and murdered, aside from those two or three generals who were poisoned to death, who I talked about earlier. I want to stress the fact that the Meléndezes had their own armed bastion to stand up against the different factions of the Army in the now very infamous National Guard. This body, which as I said before was for the protection of the citizen during the time of Manuel Enrique Araujo, was converted by Melendism into an instrument of repression. From then on it was an intensely politicized body in a reactionary and anti-popular sense. In fact, it was never an exemplary organism, since it was originally organized and led by a colonel in the Spanish Civil Guard, named Garrido, who sometimes was the

94

bodyguard for the German Emperor when he visited Spain, and who was famous in Spain for his "efficient" repressive methods. From such wood, such splinters. But, by all means, the National Guard was at first essentially committed to combating delinquency, and individual guardsmen were for the most part honest, decent men. Today, as is well-known, the National Guard is one of the principal instruments of Salvadoran reaction, directed by North American intelligence agencies and by the most corrupt, most cruel Salvadoran officers, as is the case with the infamous Chele Medrano[3]. To top it all off, they have officially adopted the title of "The Civil Guard."

What role did the popular masses play by then, and what real benefits did the Salvadoran people draw from all these stratagems and schemes? Clearly, political agitation and various kinds of protests were the first indication of widespread popular discontent. We've already seen how in the Army things were red-hot. In the teaching profession, traditionally so important in El Salvador, the problem of backward salaries had reached a crisis and had given rise to an open attitude about struggling around economic demands that had a deep political basis, with professors Francisco Morán and Rubén H. Dimas leading the way. Actually both were very good agitators, both fiery, militant orators. It's sad now to see how the years of accomodation have brought them to so apathetic, superficial and, in the case of Morán, so opportunist a position. In 1921, roughly the time I'm speaking of, an economic measure by the government unified the small commercial interests in the cities against the conservative, reactionary banks: the introduction of the decimal system as the basis of money exchange, thus eliminating the use of *cuartillos, raciones, medios* and *reales*. That governmental measure, by going against the inveterate custom of usage, was causing the small international trade interests tremendous problems and had repercussions on the lines of banking credit for small commerce. Hence a protest movement broke out in the marketplaces of San Salvador. The con-

95

servative bankers, seeing their usurious interests threatened, incited their pawns to step up their protests, and since the people were opposed to the Government, that isolated activity was very quickly transformed into an organized national movement with demonstrations and other types of protest. They organized political rallies in Santa Ana, Santa Tecla, Sonsonate, and then large protest marches in various cities from the interior of the country to the capital. They even used the railroads and formed caravans of carts to transport the multitudes. At the same time, as we'll see later, economic struggles were unfolding within the trade guilds. On February 28, 1921, Government forces machine-gunned a demonstration of women from the markets in San Salvador. Meléndez-Quiñonism specialized in massacring women. But on this first occasion (unlike what took place in the subsequent massacre of women, that I already mentioned) the women, far from being frightened after picking up their dead and wounded, armed themselves with stones, sticks, and knives, and they counterattacked. They even went so far as to seize the police station in *El Calvario* barrio, the closest one to the markets, and they executed several local police who had participated in the massacre. The butchers were the ones who most distinguished themselves in that very special battle. By coincidence, that very day the shoemakers' General Strike for higher wages and against lay-offs and mistreatment by the bosses had ended victoriously – a strike which had been the culmination of the economic struggle by the artisans of San Salvador. I'd like to amplify a bit on the process of development of this strike. I'm going to go back to 1917 so please be patient with my frequent though necessary flashbacks. Somewhere around 1917 a trade agreement with Honduras, which to a large extent benefited the Salvadoran shoe industry, was in effect. Honduras became the best market for Salvadoran shoes, and shoe shops sprang up like mushrooms in our country. Large shoe factories were built, employing a huge number of guild workers under one roof. The demand for hand labor was enormous and skilled workers started to prosper: well-dressed, money in their pockets,

96

drinking the best rum, a couple of magnolias that cost five pesos in their lapels, smoking legal Havana cigars, strolling through the parks with their capes flapping in the breeze and carrying a mother-of-pearl hand pistol in their belts, etc. On pay day, the workers stuck the biggest bills they'd received on their foreheads. Shoes were separated into distinct classes. First class, second class and retail shoes. The war was over, the era of reconstruction had arrived. North American imperialism had penetrated into every market in the world. Our shoes were slowly but surely eliminated from the Honduran market and our industry collapsed with a bang. Prices toppled and competition between shoe factories was fierce. The factories that were putting up the best fight, which more and more seemed to be a matter of survival, were: "La Ideal," owned by Luis Paz; "Bufalo," owned by Pedro Melendez; "La Moda," owned by Gonzala Funes; "La Americana," owned by master Angulo, which was where I went to work, now that times were bad. The first three of these shops were paying good wages since they made a very fine product. Master Angulo paid less, but he had more work than you could possibly handle. By doing piece-work, you were able to earn much more. And the competition was such that right away there were fights even among workers in the same guild. The salaried workers in general felt they were the best, the pillars of the production process, without whom work was impossible. The wage workers, by far the most numerous, were discriminated against and even among them there were two or three different job categories. Faced with that situation, an intensive worker organizing drive was clandestinely begun on the national level, led at that particular moment by my supervisor, Gumercindo Ramírez, the basis of which was a new salary rate that had everybody excited, from the first-class salaried workers down to the third-class wage workers. The new salary rates were discreetly circulated in the form of a draft. The bones of contention were low wages, hunger, unjustified and more and more lay-offs, mistreatment by the bosses, etc. Slowly a unanimous assessment of the situation was taking shape: to back up the new rate proposal with direct action. The

97

shoemakers even decided to go on a general strike for the following economic demands: salary hikes in accordance with the new rate proposal, a halt to arbitrary lay-offs, and decent treatment by the bosses. The most opportune moment was selected: the time of the year when the shopkeepers are getting ready to stock their display shelves just before Holy Week, when everyone wears their new shoes for the first time in the processions. Several shopkeepers supported our demands and used the situation as a means of competing, hoping to gain a profitable advantage over the other shopkeepers. Master Angulo, on the other hand, was against the strike. The conflict was put for resolution before a commission made up of representatives for the workers, the bosses and the Government. Since the bosses had put up no major resistance, the strike was won, flat out. But the day the agreement was to become effective and both parties were going to sign the contract was the day the women of the markets were massacred, and the governmental repression intensified everywhere, coming down on everyone, including the strike movement. That same February 28th, all the strike leaders were arrested and beaten, and the shopkeepers took advantage of the situation: faced with the new contract, they went nuts and fired half the world, they rolled back wages and chaos took over. The Government had killed two birds with one stone: Terror against the opposition as a whole and terror against the first stammerings of the organized workers' movement in our country. I remember how on that occasion my supervisor, Gumercindo, an outstanding leader of the shoemakers by then, who would later fall in with the anarcho-syndicalists and after that return to being a reformist, together with the famous obstructionist, Dr. Salvador Ricardo Merlos, had to clean the johns in the police station with their bare hands, during the time they had to spend in jail. The effect of these events on the shoe industry was the compartmentalization of the workplaces. From then on, one supervisor and one worker rented one room, purchased the raw materials and produced directly for the consumer market. A backward step was taken in the process of

98

capitalist development. That's why our industry didn't end up with large factories, despite the fact that it had now reached the second phase of development, that is, specialization. Much later, Luis Paz, a shopkeeper, wanted to introduce new automated machinery into his shop, but the guild workers, remembering the time when the workers at the factory in Sagrara had lost their jobs when automated looms were brought in, opposed it, as did the rest of the shopkeepers who didn't have the resources to import new machinery. Unified like that, they successfully got the Government (which was now headed by Pío Romero Bosque) to keep the machinery from entering the country. This strike led by the shoemakers, which I just referred to, wasn't an isolated case. Before it, there was a big strike by the railroad workers in 1919, and another by the tailors in 1920. Work slow-downs and partial strikes had flourished up to then and continued to occur as soon as most of the violent repression had subsided. Another problem where popular discontent grew to an explosive level was the landowners' expropriation of the poor peasants' land in the countryside. It was during that period that the real extent of Salvadoran *latifundism*[4] came into focus. And so, the dispossessed masses in the rural zones started to look for their own solutions to deal with the government, protector of those land-grabbing gluttons. If we add to that the international situation at that time, which greatly inspired the working class and all poor people in general (with the examples of the Great Bourgeois Revolution in Mexico, which had a deep anti-imperialist content in its origin and first phase of development; the Great October Revolution in Russia; the revolution and its variations in Germany; the factory take-overs by the Italian workers; the upsurge of proletarianism in Spain, Great Britain, France, the United States, etc.), you will then see how the country was going to find itself, from then on, in a class conflict of an objective nature and from which there was no escape. But the build up of that tremendous pressure had to, through historical logic, find its release valve much later on, a decade or so later. Clearly, in these questions regarding the development and ripening of a revolutionary situation, you must be aware of the fact that the dominant classes always offer palliatives, apparent solutions that are made only to mask the real solutions, but that in the moment when they are applied cause changes that revolutionaries, without losing sight of the ultimate objective, must take into account. On that occasion the ruling dynasty had the bad luck to be selected by North American imperialism as its springboard so it could plunge into our waters, and in this way the Meléndez-Quiñonistas weathered the storm. Moreover, the post-war era had arrived, and with it the temporary skyrocketing of coffee prices. After the financial disasters that for some industries such as our own were caused by North American imperialism, a trickle of money seemed to flow into the country that was the beginning of a hoped-for avalanche. It ushered in a brief period not of fat-cats, but a period in which the "cats" (or groups of financial speculators) fattened up. New sources of work opened up in the mines and on the roadways, a few small humble schools were built, and even the workers managed to get a few scraps of the bonanza. We workers and artisans once again had gold coins in our pockets, and again we wore magnolias that cost five pesos in our lapels. Very pretentious and genteel, believe me I know, but a fashion nonetheless, and a way of telling how high the standard of living was. On the other hand, in the military the pay was still miserably low, and the soldiers were still going around flat broke. However, the terror against any form of political opposition or against attempts at popular organizing remained intense. Since I'm trying to give but a glimpse of my life, I won't get bogged down in details because it would go on forever. But when I so easily say "terror" or "repression," behind each word there's such a long list of sufferings by our people, that if you stopped to think about it you'd want to cry your eyes out or go into the street and kill someone. Beatings and exile were the typical methods of the Meléndez-Quiñónez dynasty. Yet despite this, already by 1924 the workers' guilds had a membership unprecedented in our national history. Before then, mostly since 1914, some organizing attempts in that sense were made, but without

100

exception they all failed. But now in 1923 and 1924 several guilds had organized into trade unions with a deep class outlook. In the large cities, labor was organized in every shop, attracting all the unemployed workers: shoemakers, bricklayers, carpenters, plumbers, barbers, tailors, tanners, textile workers, bakers, mechanics, etc. In the smaller cities and towns, the trade unions had united into one organization of artisans and workers with different skills and trades, which was called "The Union of Varied Duties." In no time conditions became ripe for the creation of the Regional Federation of Salvadoran Workers, which was going to be an important instrument with which the working class would begin to take its place in Salvadoran history. The creation of similar federations in Guatemala, Honduras and Nicaragua, and the deep Central American spirit during that period created a favorable climate for the formation of the Central American Workers' Federation (COCA), and with it international trade with Salvadoran workers occured for the first time. Among the first worker-functionaries I remember is Raúl B. Monterrosa, who was the Salvadoran delegate to the working class of Honduras, and Dagoberto Contreras who held a similar position in Nicaragua. Monterrosa is still alive and is the leader of a group of little old musicians and singers, called "The General Union of Salvadoran Artists" or something like that, which gets its money from the governments that come and go, in the name of art, or who knows what other gimmicks. As if that wasn't enough, he's also the owner of a supermarket, called "Chinteño." And when he hears communism being discussed, he crosses himself.

Between 1922 and 1924, two extremely important years in the process of development of the Salvadoran working class, I wasn't doing the work I should've been doing, that is, I wasn't doing trade union or revolutionary work. After the political campaign and under the Government of the regrettably celebrated Alfonso Quiñónez Molina, life became very difficult

101

for me as much in Ilopango as in San Salvador, and I had to seek refuge in San Martín so I could eat and clothe myself. At first I worked in the shops owned by Camilo Cerros and Enrique Panameño. Since I'd worked in the big factories in the capital, I had many advantages over my comrades and co-workers, because I was familiar with all the fashionable styles and their variations, plus I was well-acquainted with the new tricks of the trade – very pretty stitching designs or the latest heels that caught the eyes of all the flirts. The girls in the village quickly noticed these talents and skills, and so they always requested that I make them their new party shoes. Thus my wages and extra pay rapidly mounted up, and I made up my mind to become independent as soon as possible and try to set myself up in my own shop, even if I had to start out in a dump of a place. When I had saved a few pesos, I thought I would try to get some loans. I wasn't worried so much about my family now, since my sisters were working in their own separate businesses and were helping my poor mother out – they were even able to help her support herself. So I was free to struggle to become independent, especially since there were thousands of contradictory ideas about politics and social struggle pounding on my brain, and I knew that sooner or later I couldn't rely on my wages from the shops to live on. In my search for a loan to add to my savings I ran across something which is still engraved in my memory. I was advised to get a loan from the ladies of the Mena household, especially from doña Clemencia whose family owned enough silver to pave the streets of Ilopango with. So I went to talk with her about my problem. She was a very shrewd old lady, blond and fair-skinned, apparently from Chalatenango, and different stories were going around about her that I immediately attributed to some loud mouths who were just plain jealous. She received me very warmly and showed me into the living room to hear me out, offering me coffee and sweet rolls. I began to feel a little nervous when she sat down very close to me on the wicker sofa, plus she had perfume all over her. Her skin was soft, divine. She listened to my petitions, all garbled I'm sure, since in those circumstances I get tongue-tied. When I

102

was feeling more relaxed, I suggested we go out into the courtyard where we could talk better. So we went out. The courtyard was huge, full of wonderful mango and plum trees, with a vegetable garden and animals for milking or just for fun. She led me over to the carriage-house, what today we'd call a garage, and there I got the surprise of my life. Inside, radiant in the shadows as in a fantasy film, was the white carriage I saw passing in front of my house when I was a small boy and which had remained etched in my mind like a photograph. The wheels had been removed and it was propped up on some cedar planks in such a way that it looked like some king's throne. There was a small ladder leading up into the carriage and doña Clemencia suggested we go in, that it would be more comfortable inside. So we did: we squeezed in. I felt like I was in a dream and I became even more nervous. I barely remember the details of our conversation, I only know that doña Clemencia took my hand and said she wouldn't simply lend me two or three hundred colones since a young, intelligent and enterprising man like myself could count on a permanent investment on her part, that we could go into business together, but she needed to be certain I was really a serious and responsible person. She wanted guarantees that I wasn't going to run around with other women, or party it up, or take to drinking. She ended by saying that when the business got on its feet, I could have a share of the profits and I could even come live with her. She said she thought it all would work out fine, but, as a word to the wise, I should think it over carefully and I could give her my answer later. I left that house feeling as though I was on a cloud, but it didn't last more than half an hour. On the contrary, from the very first when I naturally felt nervous – as I'm not just a piece of dead wood – I got very angry and was saying to myself: "This doña Clemencia, what she wants is to buy a husband." And I suddenly saw myself tied like a puppy with a gold collar to the petticoats of a mistress who at any moment could throw me out on my ass, and I told myself that that wasn't how I wanted to live my life. I didn't go back to speak with doña Clemencia, who had ruined my dream about the white carriage. Fortunately though I was able to get a few loans from friends and neighbors in Ilopango, and I even managed to get a little help from my older sister, who was doing well in her business affairs, which I used to buy a second-hand sewing machine, tools and leather. So I was able to start my own little shop. Actually it wasn't bad: in no time I had so many customers that I needed to hire some operators since there was no way I could handle all the work alone. Gradually I started hiring my co-workers back in San Salvador who were having a hard time finding work, and when business was good my new shop employed seven operators besides myself. The truth is we never had any bosses. We were all equal, and there was plenty of work and enough money for everyone. Many young communists today say that "the revolutionaries of 1932" were folks with an artisan mentality whose main goal was to own their own shop and work for themselves. Not so: if, for example, I made my living then and at other times by owning my own shop, it was because of the necessity to meet everyday demands – to clothe myself, eat, etc. Besides which the shop as a political organism, so to speak, served on many occasions as a defense against enemy activity since it offered respectability and the opportunity to make many social contacts; it was an excellent cloak behind which to organize revolutionary activity. About the shop, once I felt we had the business on a firm economic footing, I decided to expand out in every direction. First of all, as a basis for broadening our market, we put our shoes in the stores in villages like Tenancingo, Peruulapía, San Pedro Perulapán, which quickly became as good a market for us as the one in San Martín. Secondly, I decided to diversify my social contacts by organizing recreational events. So with that in mind, I showed movies in the backyard of the shop, and began holding sporting events. The films were an enormous success. Using rented equipment, we had programs every night and the place was always jam-packed with people. We charged a few centavos admission to pay for the films and equipment, and we put the money leftover into a common fund for the workers. A small four-piece band livened up the functions and God provided for

104

them too, as we used to say. I remember that the Charlie Chaplin films were the biggest hits, and, if my memory doesn't deceive me, we also had success with some Ramón Novarro films. But the majority were films with people whom you never heard of; I think they were made in Mexico or Honduras with Mexican actors and actresses. In the area of sports, we started by organizing a boxing team. The comrades from the shop and myself were the boxers, and we used to put on four fights a week, alternating partners. It quickly became clear that fights between this one and that one were repeated to the point of weariness and so the public got bored, since in most cases it had already been proven who was the better boxer, and so you knew beforehand who was going to win. Plus the fact that the youngsters in the village didn't really take to boxing, mostly because after the first exchange of punches the boxers got so worked up that they wanted to kill each other and a few even wanted to settle the matter with knives and machetes. I got knocked-out over ten times. Therefore we wound up playing soccer, and we had to sell the boxing gloves and all the rest of the equipment for next to nothing. But there was one positive outcome from all this: each day we met more and more people, and we became directly acquainted with their problems, their pains and their joys. As for me, the brief experience of the last political campaign had shown me that I was pretty ignorant and therefore I felt that I had to study and learn much more before I could devote myself once again to organizing workers and revolutionary activity. So, during this period of my shop in San Martín that I'm talking about, I dedicated myself to reading and reading and reading, realizing that this was my duty at that moment and that in this way I would, in the future, be able to work within the guild with greater responsibility and clarity of purpose. I tried balancing with books my lack of contact with the workers' movement in San Salvador, which was really picking up steam at that time, trying not to get too frustrated over the fact that I wasn't engaged in political practice, since I knew that in time it would inevitably come, and that I shouldn't just plunge ahead half-cocked. That is, like an ignorant fool. I became a lover of poetry because it stimulated my imagination, my fervor. My favorite poets were Rubén Darío, especially when he attacked Roosevelt and the eagle of the North; Don Francisco Gavidia, who wrote poems against the tyrannies in our countries; Vicente Acosta and others. I also liked romantic and sensual poetry, and metaphysical poetry. Here I remember Lydia Valiente, a young woman about whom I wrote some verses that I read to my friends. And I still remember a poem that began with the lines: "To be and to be nothing . . ."[5] I devoured Camilo Flammarion, and I still remember the impression Barreto's book *Religion for Everyone* had on me – this book was severely attacked by the priests. But the writer I loved most then was don Alberto Masferrer.[6] I would buy his book, *Evil Money*, then give it away and buy another copy. There were times when I'd set out down the road with a dozen or more copies of that book, and I'd be giving them away to the cart drivers who I met (and who probably knew how to read), urging them to talk with the people they met on their routes about the book. Similarly, I used to go to the beer and moonshine vendors, accompanied by my comrades from the shop so those jerks wouldn't beat me up, and together we started an anti-alcoholism campaign based on the pronouncements of don Alberto. From that time on, I established a good relationship with the peasants.

On the other hand, the so-called "society" in San Martín had its eyes on me. The rich, the dominant upper class, are monopolizers of men. If someone from the lower class happens to stand out because of his qualities, quickly they try to grab him and place him at their service. So the day came when some of the local fat-cats invited me to become a member of the Local Society, which is a kind of club that exists in every town and city, and which brings together all the so-called "decent people." I kept putting it off since I was positive that my social place wasn't with these people but with the wretched poor, with the people of the village, which was where I was born and where I would die. Nevertheless, those fat-cats didn't feel defeated in the least and they wouldn't let up just like that with their flatteries and subtle bribes. For the Saint's feast-days, they made me steward of the *Centro* barrio, their barrio, and they gave me many dinners. Yet, despite the fact that I was cordial and participated in their celebrations and returned their favors, my ears and heart were only truly open to other voices: those that came from San Salvador and spoke about the successes of the young Regional Federation of Salvadoran Workers, which united the still incipient guild and trade union movement in El Salvador as no other organization had ever done before. A very unexpected incident turned out to be, for me, a way of saying goodbye to that stage of my life that was already too prolonged: my first encounter with love. I mean, of course, my first serious encounter with love. Before, I had brushes with women, but no one had really made a deep impression on me. Despite my youth and the fact that I was popular with the girls, I avoided, though not fanatically, getting mixed up with the ladies. Therefore when I organized a celebration the mothers allowed their daughters to go, entrusting them with me to watch over and take good care of them. Also, I used to go down to the river with a group of girls, and I never gave the gossiping big-mouths, who are in every small village, anything to talk about. They couldn't be more right when they say that the smallness of a village is measured by the length of the tongues of the inhabitants. Among the girls there was one who, for pure family reasons, I knew better than the others: my cousin Carmencita, daughter of my uncle Feliciano, my mother's brother. Since she was young and very cute, with the small body of a deer and lively eyes, dimpled cheeks and a graceful way about her, she had a veritable swarm of admirers, and I, who because I was her cousin had no designs on her and was just whistling in the wind, started to become her confidant. I listened to everything she had to say, and I tried to give her honest, sound advice, though it was the advice of a young man and not of a grumpy old man. There was a period when the new Local Commander, the telegraph operator and three musicians in the village band (the same ones who played at our film showings) were all in love with

107

her at the same time. Carmencita hadn't shown any preference for any one of them and more or less rejected them all, but she was worried because all five were at each other's throats. I was simply advising her of what I thought was right, and that she had to see that any flirtation under those circumstances would be like ordering, "Open Fire!" Seeing how I supported her in that situation, our relationship grew much closer, and since those five suitors saw how she'd joked around with me and trusted me and openly showed her affection for me, they were probably more jealous than a dog in heat. So, either together or separately, they started a malicious rumor about Carmencita and me. In no time it was going around from ear to ear, and when my uncle Feliciano got wind of it, he exploded like a bomb. In a fit of rage and without asking any questions or making any inquiries, which is what he should've done, he accepted the truth that was no more than a rumor: that I was living with Carmencita, that we were lovers. As usual in these kinds of cases, while the matter was being looked into more calmly, they turned me in to the National Guard. To the great happiness of my fiercest rival, the Commander of the Guard, who was head over heels in love with Carmencita, who I supposedly seduced. They arrested me and transferred me to the Court in Tonacatepeque as a rapist. While they were carting me off with my thumbs tied with a rope, beating my ass sore, between a pair of creep guardsmen, Feliciano threw my cousin out of the house, disgraced only by word of mouth. Finally, my father intervened with some lawyers, who obtained an order to set me free on bail, and they liberated me when I was halfway to the Court, in the middle of the road, since they had to catch up with me by horse because the way to Tonacatepeque was over a mountain range. Although free on bail, I remained bitter and disheartened by that experience and I didn't have the least desire to go back to San Martín. I went immediately to San Salvador, sending a note to the workers in my shop that they should liquidate my holdings, bit by bit, and send me the money. In San Salvador I started out by living with friends, but I soon found work in a good shoe factory that enabled me to rent a room of my own. The capital was a boiling pot of political activity with the workers' organization as its most visible focal center. From that time on, I threw myself with all my fervor into the organized Salvadoran workers' movement. Once and for all, forever. Carmencita, for her part, followed me to San Salvador and came looking for me at work in order to talk with me. Because of her father and family, she was sad and disconsolate but she wanted to face a new life with a fresh, optimistic spirit and outlook. She told me that although the rumors back in the village were only rumors when they referred to the innocence of her body, that wasn't so with regard to her feelings for me because it was true that she was in love with me and wanted to be my wife, really, and not just because people said so. I still tried to make her see that life with me would be very hard and miserable, and she was still too young to be taking upon herself so many burdens, that perhaps it'd be better if she went back home and asked her father for forgiveness. But she persisted and persisted, and finally I thought how could such a good stroke of fate turn out bad, and so I made her my woman for real. All of a sudden I was so in love with her as always happens when you are young and have your whole life ahead of you. In spite of the things that happened years later, which you will know if you finish reading my story, which is also the story of the many people around me, who loved me and hated me, I never regretted having loved so much and having had Carmen as my companion and comrade. From then on, she was loyal and self-sacrificing, and at the same time patient and a fighter, a good mother to my children, a good wife to me, who, while enduring life at my side, was the ideal figure who appears in the dreams of every flesh and blood revolutionary.

Before going on with my life story, I'd like to say something about El Salvador's president during the period I've been talking about, namely, Alfonso Quiñónez Molina. From what I just said it's clear that the Meléndez-Quiñónez dynasty managed El Salvador as though it was a plantation, a business. Well, Quiñónez was a lawyer, the broker, the overseer and the muscle of that business. With one hand he held a stick over the people, while the other was deep in bribery and corruption. He had the good fortune of a flourishing coffee market inasmuch as the high coffee prices put some 40 million colones in his pockets each year. He was a corrupt, corrupting man who knew how to corrupt others. He gave grants to his informers in the villages to set up gin mills, and he appointed his lovers tax administrators and even Chiefs of Police in the villages, towns and cities. He was a megalomaniac who loved publicity and who spent millions on propaganda. The big international thieves, gringos and Europeans, made hay bribing him with their paid publicity and propaganda to shape public opinion about foreign intervention. But in their souls the people hated him, and his memory still causes folks to grimace in disgust. Quiñónez was, because of the way he ruled, the Oscar Osorio[7] of the 1920s. And he will go down in history justly portrayed in the little popular verse which they sang to the music of La Cucaracha:

> All the girls have
> two lemons on their chest
> and a little further down
> is the portrait of Quiñónez.

---

[1] *Ciguanaba:* Salvadoran mythological personage, daughter of the god of Rain, adulterous wife of Yeysún, believed to appear before passers-by at night in the form of a beautiful young, abandoned woman in order to test their nobility or their wickedness (translators' note).

[2] *foco:* guerrilla center of operation. Core of revolutionary strategy known as foquismo, first put forth by Regis Debray, where isolated guerrilla actions would incite the workers and peasants to spontaneously rebel against the regime. Hence plays down the importance of political organizing work with new and/or already existing mass organizations (translators' note).

[3] General "Chele" Medrano: founder of the right-wing paramilitary group, ORDEN, and former head of the National Guard.

4 *latifundism:* political economy based on ownership of large tracts of land, plantations, haciendas, etc. by the few rich (translators' note).

5 This line is reminiscent of a line from Rubén Darío's poem "Lo Fatal": "Ser y no saber nada..." (To be and not know anything...) (Translators' note).

6 Alberto Masferrer: prominent Salvadoran intellectual in the 1920s. He attacked the oligarchy for their refusal to share their wealth with the rest of the country. He also reprimanded the poor peasants on the evils of drinking and machete brawls, and his program calling for a "vital minimum" for every Salvadoran became the basis of Aruajo's presidential campaign platform in 1931.

7 Oscar Osorio: El Salvador's first bourgeois-democratic president (1950-56). His term was marked, on the one hand, by economic diversification and reform allowing for the triumph of the capitalistic class over the semi-feudal and feudal oligarchy. It was a period of rapid industrial modernization and expansion with the use of the military as a political vehicle, such as running military officers fo, political office. On the other hand, under Osorio the economic and political situation in the rural sector remained unchanged, and the Government was fiercely anticommunist and showed no tolerance for dissent. By the end of the term Osorio had established a record of suppressing trade unionists and arresting, torturing, exiling, and murdering dissidents.

3

Beginning of the workers' movement in El Salvador. Political activity in the zone of Ilopango. The Ilopango Society of Workers, Peasants and Fishermen. Union organizing in the suburban areas and the first signs of violence.

Pretty soon my activity within the workers' movement in San Salvador took on added dimensions. I was still conscious of my obvious lack of preparation, despite my reading and interest in everything cultural, so I became an active student at what was called the People's University, the education branch of the Regional Federation, which had a strong anti-imperialist and class perspective, and, sympathetic with the struggles of the time, was pro-Sandinista. There's no doubt that in those turbulent years the figure of the great Nicaraguan guerrilla fighter was the human embodiment of all our still-confused political longings because he pointed out the direction which was, and still is, truly for the liberation of our peoples: the struggle against North American imperialism (and not just in any form, but the concrete form in which the best men fight, the armed struggle, the best struggle). It was at the People's University that I personally met Agustin Farabundo Martí, who would be our Party leader during the events of 1932, and it was there that Martí, along with other Salvadoran workers, was democratically elected to go and join General Sandino's guerrillas who were fighting in the Nicaraguan jungles. The lectures were given by many intellectuals and democratic-minded professionals, like Dr. Salvador Ricardo Merlos, and they touched on aspects of such subjects as economics, law and political science. Fortunately, all the professors strongly emphasized North American imperialism as the principal enemy of our people, and in more general terms they characterized the structure of society from the point of view of class divisions. Real proletarian ideology, though, didn't come up more than fragmentarily, shaded with all the ingredients of ignorance, idealism, lack of historical knowledge, and even the malicious distortion of facts that was already occurring by then in certain specific instances. But our enthusiasm wasn't dampened by

115

any of that. We students felt like the man who sees the light at the end of a long, dark and anguishing tunnel. This apprenticeship, along with the propaganda work I began to develop at the same time among the workers of my guild, made me see that under these new circumstances it was stupid for me to keep thinking that San Salvador was going to be just a hiding place, a refuge, from my personal problems back in San Martín, which had grown to the point I've already described. I couldn't just keep holed up within the city. I'd begun to feel like the carrier of a new truth, and I thought my duty was first to bring it to the people of the region where I was born and raised, to my own people. It turned out that when I made a formal commitment to Carmen there was no longer any reason to stay away from San Martín, and even my uncle Feliciano was speaking to me again, convinced that my intentions with his daughter were serious and were now based solidly on mutual love. Plus, when I realized I had to overcome my deep fear of speaking up in class at the university, and that even when I finally did speak up I always stuttered and felt unsure of myself, I realized at the same time that that would never happen to me among the people of San Martín, Ilopango, etc. Because there I knew and loved everyone and everyone respected me and took me seriously, and I'd be sure from the start that my words would have a real influence. So I began dividing my propaganda and organizing work between San Salvador and my native region. Before long I was known for my new work, unheard of for the people of that day: I was hawking and handing out our paper, *The Hammer*, the official organ of the Regional Federation. Little by little that work took on the character of what today we'd call one "street meeting" after another, and from there it was relatively easy to move into holding real meetings, each and every week, where we really could do some propaganda and organizing work. From the first, I'd realized the wonderful possibilities for organizing workers in the entire region of Ilopango, and as a first step I'd integrated several activist comrades from the Regional into the work of selling *The Hammer* and organizing our meetings. In those meetings we explained to workers in the towns and on

116

the farms, to skilled workers and peasants, the many benefits of guild organization, and the economic demands for which it was possible to fight within the legal restrictions of the time. The people talked about their problems too, about the terrible misery in which they lived, the abuse they constantly took from the bosses and authorities. Communication between the masses and us was like hot sparks flying off high-voltage cables: from the beginning we had excellent results, as our words were falling on ground seeded for years and years with suffering, oppression, misery, and lies by conservative politicians. Quickly many saw the light. Within days the intensity of our work mushroomed, which right away made the reactionary authorities prick up their ears and come down on us with a vengeance. But we didn't weaken and the masses didn't lose their spirit. For Christ's sake, we were just beginning a struggle that we still haven't finished. Not yet! One day when I was sort of not looking, the National Guard tried to get me. I was arrested when a local commander in the San Martín zone, an evil bastard by the name of Caballero, denounced me because the Army reservists of the area instead of attending the military parade they held every Sunday, as was their strict duty, had gone for the past few Sundays to our meetings where we sold the paper and discussed the main concepts contained in its lead articles. The commander of the National Guard started in haranguing me, but I always carried a copy of the current Political Constitution in my pocket, and I pulled it out and began to read the pertinent articles to demonstrate that we members of the Workers' Regional were only exercising our constitutional right by holding meetings and, therefore, I should be set free immediately. I convinced that bastard, but before letting me go he told me: "It so happens that by letting you go I'm losing 25 colones since a telegram arrived from the General Office of the Guard announcing that for the arrest of each one of you, there's a reward in that amount." "And who are 'you'," I asked him. "You, the agitators." I got out of there before he had time to regret it and think over those 25 colones. Just in time, since I found out later they were out searching for me again. The problem was

117

there was no way we could abandon that zone. As a matter of honor and principle we'd already taken our organizing work very seriously. The workers in San Salvador for the most part came from the surrounding areas, like Apopa, Nejapa, Quezaltepeque, San Martín, Ilopango, etc., and on Saturdays and Sundays those masses were ready to do political work, not where they worked, but where they lived: so you had to go to them, had to look for them at their homes or where they went to rest up and relax. In spite of everything, that suburban region was less garrisoned by the authorities than the urban region. And also there were a number of population centers isolated from one another by mountains and distance. So when the persecution focused on me in San Martín, I, in turn, focused my political activity in Ilopango, leaving San Martín to other comrades who were not so familiar to the authorities.

In Ilopango we would have one of the most beautiful organizing experiences of that time. My home town was still the same dreamy little village where the quiet hardness of life went on without any major convulsions. The truth is, what seemed real to my child's eyes was only a mask for a dramatic situation, for the broad popular discontent just about ready to explode; a disguise for a tremendous force that only awaited an outlet to become an active, living protest against the injustice and misery. In spite of the highly positive view of things this actual situation offered, and very much in spite of the townspeople's affection for me, it wasn't easy to penetrate Ilopango politically, that is, with my new ideas of liberation. We must always tell things the way they actually were, not looking through rose-colored glasses. It's just that to crack the shell of tradition, fear and suspicion, the first shell is, above all, always the most difficult. At first people rejected me in my new work and threw all kinds of crazy names at me: that I was an evangelist, a Protestant, a Mason, etc. I don't know why, because in our conversations we never spoke out against the Catholic Church or touched on anything having to do with religion, since we knew too well the fanatical atmosphere of the whole country, especially at that time. In the face of that rejection that

118

threatened to sink us from the start, I decided that before initiating a broad organizing campaign among the masses, truly mass work, it was necessary to go to the few really close friends I had in the area and form a select circle, a central nucleus, that could orient, organize and direct the work in the future. So I had, without knowing any revolutionary theory, an idea of Lenin's: to form a select nucleus in order to mobilize the masses. I was very lucky since this first group turned out to be comprised of very talented men. That was when I recruited for the workers' movement and for the world proletarian revolution José Ismael Hernández, a shoemaker, who you'll hear a lot about in the story I'll tell; Vicente Ascensio, who, by the way, just died after remaining a man of principle all his life; Marcelino Hernández, a baker, who would be executed by my side in 1932; and Reyes Presentación and Andrés Marroquín, both fishermen, who would become militants in our Communist Party. These were the firm buttresses, the support group that would serve to help us throw ourselves fully into the work of organizing the people of Ilopango. It must be said, for the sake of historical truth, that ours was not the first organizing attempt there since some other progressive men had tried on other occasions to organize the workers and peasants living around or near the lake. But without exception they had failed in their efforts and, therefore, held a cynical view of our work and were very skeptical about the possibilities for our success. Among others, there were the teacher, Héctor Calero, and a railroad engineer named Benjamín, who was then the stationmaster and who had some influence in town. They both were glued to the idea that it was impossible to do anything there because the people were a herd of ignorant beasts who didn't even realize what was in their own interest. However, we suspected they had always worked outside reality, that they hadn't based their organizing work on the actual problems of the people and, on the contrary, had created an impenetrable barrier between their "enlightenment" and the "backwardness" they ascribed to the people. So we began our work by first finding out what the people thought, what their concerns were, what the point of an

119

organization would be for them, and what kind of organization would best serve their interests. We hit the nail on the head, and the people greeted the organization like rain in May. We avoided abstract slogans, organizing just for the sake of organizing, having an organization based on pure nonsense that didn't mean a thing to anyone. No, first we identified the problems, and only afterwards did we point out that the only method of truly solving them was to organize. The nucleus did intense political agitation work on many different levels, including meeting with people on a one-to-one basis. That was how the climate and conditions were created that would make Ilopango a real focal point for the national workers' movement, for the Revolution in El Salvador. After this first level of political agitation, the next step we took to reach the masses was the creation of a public organization. We named it the Ilopango Society of Workers, Peasants and Fishermen. It was a heterogeneous society, the regional forerunner of the Combined Labor Unions, in which workers were grouped just for being workers, independent of their specific skills and trades. The Society particularly stood out for its large number of fishermen and for their fighting spirit, like a hot volcano, as we'll see in a moment. But the Society's heterogeneity wasn't due only to the mishmash of jobs. We had, for example, problems when a sort of "generation gap" arose within the organization. The older men were opposed to the bold ideas of the young workers, and we had to resolve the question by organizing a Youth Section of the Society with a certain measure of autonomy. The Youth Section definitely was assigned the most important work, that is, the practical task of organizing the rest of the population into our ranks. Another problem in the beginning was that of the women. From the start the local women had been against us. Influenced by the priest, they were the ones who spread around that garbage that we organizers from San Salvador were evangelists or Masons who were prosyletizing against the Catholic Church. Fortunately, we knew perfectly well that the women of Ilopango, as in the rest of the country, had special economic problems, so we made these

120

the starting point for our work organizing them. Most of the women of Ilopango and the surrounding area lived off the sale of fish which, in turn, was bought from the fishermen. That was how my mother supported us. A small group of rich people in town loaned the buyer-vendors the money for their morning purchase of fish at an interest rate of "ten on the peso per day." That is to say, at the "moderate" rate of ten percent per day. A woman who in the morning got a loan of three pesos had to pay the fishermen for the fish, sell it door to door, return to the money-lender three pesos plus thirty centavos in the afternoon, and somehow make a subsistence wage. During the day, the poor women ran around like crazy, going up and down selling their goods, and sometimes they didn't sell anything or what they did sell wasn't enough to pay back the loan plus interest, etc. Unpaid debts were collected by the National Guard. Moreover, the woman who screwed up on the slightest thing today, or who didn't bow to the many caprices of the usurers, would be sure not to get the loan she needed tomorrow. The situation of these women was unbearable, awful. We immediately formed a "peoples fund" into which went every bit of our savings. We wanted to eliminate that criminal form or exploitation at its root, so we lent the fish-sellers money at a rate of "three centavos on the peso per week," that is, at three percent a week. The women saw the light and realized that our society was truly beneficial to them and to all poor people, so they stopped rejecting us and started joining our ranks in large numbers. Again I say that way of organizing was the big secret of how we penetrated so deeply into the Salvadoran masses, which has always been attributed by the reactionaries to some kind of magic formula from Russia or from the Devil. We reached the people through their most immediate and urgent needs, hitting the nail on the head, putting not only a finger on the wound but also medicine. After the success of our fund, we formed the Department of General Welfare to provide social services to everyone in the village who needed them, whether or not they were members of our Society. Among other tasks, the Department provided care for the sick, transporting them to

121

the Hospital in San Salvador when it was necessary (at that time a car for hire, a taxi as they say today, from Ilopango to San Salvador cost 30 colones or more, which was more than most people earned in a month), visiting with them, getting them medicine, etc. Even the most recalcitrant reactionaries in town, namely the Catholics who attacked us the most, joined in this work. The priest couldn't explain just how it was that Protestants and Masons, enemies of God and friends of the Devil, could practice Christian charity in such an organized and exceptional way. As soon as we grew enough to be able to afford a place, we founded our outspoken cultural center which turned out to be an Ilopango version of the People's University in San Salvador. This was truly a forum of democratic thought where every possible subject was discussed: history, literature, natural science, art and public affairs. A parade of the most distinguished speakers of the time passed through the center, among them Dr. Salvador Ricardo Merlos, Professor Chico Morán, Zoila Argentina Jovel, and later even foreign revolutionaries like the Peruvian comrade, Estéban Pavletich, who fought like Martí with Sandino's guerrillas and who still lives in Peru, writing and fighting. On the day of a lecture, as a general rule part of the activities called "Happy Sundays," we'd go down to the local train station to meet the scheduled speaker. That way everyone in town heard about our event and many of them would join our ranks. Some, who really didn't care about the reasons for our work, came out of curiosity. Others, young and old, came out of sheer boredom, wearing dumb looks, sat down quietly, listened to the talks and left without a peep. But they were few. For the most part the masses participated actively in everything. When the subject permitted it, for example, when a professor came to talk about something having to do with botany or mineralogy, we organized trips to the outskirts of town where classes were given in the field, illustrated with practical examples from the environment. They say that's how school was in ancient Greece and that's why the students learned more, because they were always in direct contact with what the professor was talking about. That's why

122

the Greeks were what they were. The people of Ilopango and other villages showed tremendous interest in these lectures, and we did everything possible to encourage it. After the lectures we held raffles with nice prizes and we played dance music on the guitar and mandolin, something that really attracted the young people. I think if it had been necessary to have a circus, none of us would have minded being clowns or acrobats, though we all would have to loosen up a lot. At the same time we also organized a public library. And do you know almost every book–life is full of surprises!–was given to us as a gift by the chief of operations at the Ilopango Barracks, General Antonio Claramount Lucero, who later would be the eternal candidate for President of the Republic of El Salvador, and who sucked in so many people with his purely divisive electoral politics. All of us activists in the Regional who did work in that Society realized that, through it, we were creating the conditions necessary to building a permanent relationship with the people, one based on complete trust. And also the success of our efforts was evident, and that made us stronger. Of course not everything was so rosy. Besides the suspicions of the authorities and the sporadic persecution, there were those infamous and previously mentioned small-town gossipmongers. The rich people in Ilopango spread rumors around that there was something strange about our organization, that nobody did anything good for free and that parents shouldn't let their daughters come to our activities because "They'd wind up pregnant and no one would know by who. "We would answer with Christ's words: "by their deeds ye shall know them," or something like that. We also ran a broad anti-alcoholism campaign. In Ilopango, which as I already explained was a really small town, there were more than half a dozen bars and so many drunks it was scary. The fact of the matter is alcoholism has always been a tremendous problem in our country, unlike in any other country in the world. I think the day there's a revolution in El Salvador the flow of rum will have to be cut off from the very first because otherwise everything that's gained will end up going down the drain. Even a sister of

123

mine on my father's side, Luisa Chicas, was a hardened drunk, poor woman, to the point of sleeping in the street or in the briar brushes, wherever she happened to be when she tied one on. She'd lost all shame and often she was in very bad shape. But anyway, our campaign helped a lot of alcoholics get off the booze, including my poor sister. We also got the authorities to close down four bars. Because of these two successful campaigns of our Society, I earned the respect of my father, at least for the moment. One day he came to see me and he said he was sorry for not having spent more time with me, since I'd shown him I was a good man, a son who would make the most prominent father proud. He asked me if I wanted to live in one of his houses and said that from then on it would be mine, that he was giving it to me as a gift. I accepted the offer, and my wife and I moved in all our stuff. Right away my father wanted to give me a long-term loan of three thousand colones to invest in the coffee trade so I'd have enough to live on. I told him I'd think it over. One week later he came and told me the coffee deal had fallen through, but now he had a plan worked out to invest the money in a drugstore downtown, and he wanted me to run the business. He literally fell all over himself showing me how it was going to be a great deal for the both of us. "But in order for it to be successful," he added in a moment, "there's one condition: that you get out of that crazy political stuff because any investment will fail with the way you are now and we'll lose all the money." I turned down his proposition, telling him I thought he was trying to buy me off and I didn't like it one bit. He left very indignant, particularly because I told him it wasn't the first time I'd been attracted by money and deals, but before the offers had come from sexy women. That night my father's other sons came around with some kids they had picked up and removed all the tiles from the roof of the house. So, that was that, and the next day I left. Because of my father and that house, I thought: "Those who give, then take back, will live to regret it."

Our Society expanded its activity into areas that were actually the responsibility of the municipal and even the central government. For example, we started repairing the old local roads and constructing new ones which were badly needed. To clear a way for the road connecting Ilopango with the highway to San Salvador and San Martín, we managed to get several landowners to give us strips of their property, rights of way, etc. The people rose to the occasion. I remember when a group of men came from Santa María Ostuma in canoes, crossing the lake, in order to work. And families that for good reasons couldn't do physical labor brought water, food and soft drinks for the volunteers. Word of our work reached all the way to the Governor of the Department, who sent down an urgent message to the Ilopango municipal government ordering the immediate start of construction on the road between Ilopango and Apulo, where there was a beautiful beach by the same name, and he said he would personally pay for the entire cost of the project. He interpreted our activity as an attempt by some new political party to win votes, and he wanted to be sure he got something out of it, with or without us. That's why he tried competing with us. But the people were aware that all those improvements and projects were the result of the work of our enthusiastic group and the Society, and therefore they gladly volunteered to work with us, letting the Municipality or the Government carry out what was, after all, their obligation with paid labor. This rudimentary organization built around concrete, collective forms of work would be the germ of future trade unionism in Ilopango and the surrounding region. But the Society's work served as a lesson to people all up and down our small country. I remember a teachers' conference, in Ahuachapán, where professor José María Meléndez said, "While the sun is setting on all of El Salvador's towns and cities, in Ilopango a bright, new sun is dawning." That "new sun" was us, our Society and the prospective organization of the region. Today there are still many people in the Salvadoran revolutionary movement who learned to take their first steps in that school which was so full of life. That's why in the terrible year of 1932 the repressive forces killed so many people and committed so many crimes and barbarities in the region. And I don't think it was a coincidence that that was exactly where they executed me.

Independent of the importance of all this activity about which I'm talking in a very general way, and which was indispensible to our moving forward, where our Society really started sinking roots in fertile proletarian soil was in our work with the fishermen. Having lived with them myself, I knew their problems. They had a miserable existence and many urgent needs, but two fundamental demands were immediately evident. The first was: "Free Beaches." The big landowners fenced off the marshy lake beaches on their property and sent their hired hands to destroy and burn the fishermen's homes, which were built with the crudest of materials. The same thing happened in the rest of the country with the ocean beaches and those on the rivers. We decided to give them our total support, initiating a broad campaign, not just in Ilopango but nationwide, demanding that the government decree freedom of movement on all beaches: a 100-meter zone for marine beaches, 50-meters for lake beaches and 25-meters for the rivers. 900 fishermen from Ilopango, Michapa, Chinamequita, Texacuangos and Candelaria Ostuma signed the initial petition to the President, and practically every nucleus of fishermen in the country communicated to us, by different methods, their allegiance, their total support and their congratulations. All this work began at the end of the 1920s. The campaign caught fire and even the press started to cover it, turning it into a national issue. The women who sold fish unanimously sided with our position. The fact of the matter is, this was the first big demonstration of what a fighting workers' organization could do. Because, in effect, we were already an organized force, although still at a fairly primitive level. The campaign and the struggle didn't end there, later becoming part of the broad struggle of all Salvadoran workers, and it wasn't until the overthrow of the Araujo regime (at the end of 1931) that the historic fight of the Salvadoran fishermen was interrupted. I say this because I remember we had organized a demonstration of more than a thousand fishermen in the streets of San Salvador when the coup that overthrew Araujo struck. By then I was working as a member of the Communist Party within the national worker-peasant movement. The Ilopango Society of Workers, Peasants and Fishermen was overwhelmed by the bold actions of the fishermen, but through them were gained a thousand experiences as well as a broadening of the scope and objectives of our work which up to then had been limited to the local area. But, of course, when the work clearly took on a class character, the authorities intensified their persecution of us. By learning to walk on the spot, we were soon ready to liberate ourselves from the repression and to do extensive mass work in spite of it. The tendency toward organizing trade unions was impossible to suppress. Of course the essential groundwork was done by us, in our region, during the course of the struggle of the fishermen. Because, besides the demand for "free beaches," the guild's other immediate demand was the foundation of a cooperative movement. The impoverished knew that the only way they could help themselves against their misery was to stand united, to try to get better fishing methods, and to oppose fishing with dynamite or with the poisons that killed off the wildlife that sustained them. When, at the beginning, these and other demands appeared as enormous problems with no solution, we took it upon ourselves to suggest forming an organization as an answer. At first, the cooperative was the type of organization best suited to those needs. It responded to the immediate demands of the workers and didn't unnecessarily threaten the bourgeois authorities. Under the slogan, "Build a Cooperative Movement," we organized the fishermen. Many of them later on became self-sacrificing, militant communists: martyrs in the '32 massacre or clandestine activists during the Martínez dictatorship and afterwards. Organizing around the cooperative allowed us to reach out beyond the fishermen, making contacts with workers on the nearby farms. Our propaganda, which though primitive was no less agitational, insurgent and fiery, immediately found an echo in all those proletarians who were miserable to a frightening extreme. I remember our first efforts back then took

127

place on the farms and plantations called "Colombia" (property of the Salazar family), "Alicia," (a small coffee plantation, which if I'm not mistaken was the property of the parents of the man who would become President of El Salvador, the ridiculous dictator, José María Lemus), "Nova," "Escobar," etc. On a farm belonging to a Chilean colonel, who'd been contracted to give Salvadoran officers military training, one of our comrades in the Society worked as a foreman; he was comrade Modesto Ramírez, who later would become an outstanding leader of workers and peasants, and also an outstanding Party leader (and who would go with me to the Soviet Union in 1930). It ought to be clear that the purpose of our work wasn't only to agitate, but principally to organize. And we didn't have to wait long to get some results. The masses of peasants were particularly impressed by the strike we led at the "Colombia" plantation where we won a first-aid station, a wage hike, and improvements in the living conditions for all the workers. As a result of all these events the work of building a cooperative movement became secondary, and all our energy went into union organizing. Just like that, our Ilopango Society of Workers, Peasants and Fishermen became the shining Ilopango Union of Varied Duties. This was work completely run along the lines of the Regional and was part of the broad organizing movement sweeping across the country. It was not predominantly an "Ilopangan" initiative. Of course, that first union wasn't the last. We shortly founded the same kind of unions in Santiago, Texacuangos, Joya Grande, Michapa, and in other places. What's important to note here is that as soon as these organizations were formed, it became obvious that the workers had brought to them their political awareness as well as their reformist, guild demands. Many times, before we could even timidly begin to bring up the future of the union struggle, after better wages or better food and living conditions had been won, the peasants and workers would say we ought to think about how to defend the Union from the persecutions and outrages of the judges, mayors and armed forces, or even better, to plan ways in which the organization could help get

128

workers and peasants themselves into public office in the local area, and if possible, in the Province, and if it could be done, in the whole country. These organizations began to make contact, with or without direction, with similar groups in the rest of the country (already formed or in the building stage), and even with foreign organizations. The mail was still pretty safe to use. The fact that, for example, in El Matazano the union began organized life under the name of Julio Antonio Mella[1] is a reflection, be it small, of the measure of internationalist consciousness that existed. In the central part of the country there were unions with the names of Guadalupe Rodríguez and Hipólito Landero, Mexican revolutionaries and peasant leaders killed in their country by the class enemy. This germ of proletarian internationalism which, at that time, merely honored the memory of those fallen in the struggle against the bourgeoisie and imperialism in Latin America, would later become the basis for the tradition which our Communist Party boasts today. Special mention should be made again about the importance that General Sandino's struggle in Nicaragua had for us in this respect. Anti-imperialist sentiment which greatly supported our organizing work spread into every sector of the Salvadoran populace, and our organization helped to broaden and deepen it. You see, at that moment, even the birthday party of someone's daughter or the processions of the Virgin Mary would end with shouts and slogans supporting the great guerrilla of the Segovias and denouncing the Yankee murderers. I remember that at some kind of social function, I don't remember the occasion, I even got my father to shout out, "Viva Sandino!" And after someone yelled back something, he said: "This jerk has really pissed me off now," though he didn't reach the point of hitting him. Because, despite their popularity, we were dealing with banned slogans: for shouting just one of those slogans they'd throw you in jail without a second thought.

From the moment we began fighting for the basic demands of the fishermen, as I've said, the national and local authorities had fingered us, and they openly stepped up their persecution. With the growth of the cooperative movement, the growing

129

number of strikes and the upsurge of union organizing, the repression got even worse. The government beefed up all the security forces in the area and issued drastic orders to fuck us over. But as I also said, we'd learned a lot in a short period of time, and we were also now surrounded by a considerable mass of people who were rapidly being politicized. At least for a while, we could put up a victorious fight in the face of the authorities' attempts to destroy our base and kick us out. The full support of the Regional Federation was decisive at that point. We could also get very good reinforcements from San Salvador: The Regional assigned new cadre to work in our region, workers who hadn't become known to the authorities and who had distinguished themselves in the capital's union struggle. Among the first cadre who came to work with us, I remember a pureblooded Indian named Facundo López from Santiago Texacuangos, and a young guy called Acevedo. But despite these good auspices, and precisely because of the massive growth of our political organizations, the repressive conditions grew worse day by day. So we had to abandon the town locals and base ourselves exclusively in the rural areas, even going into the mountains where we held our meetings, made our contacts, did our propaganda work, etc. The meetings in the mountains were unforgettable as much for their great attendance as for the fervor of all those present and the conditions, the climate, under which they were held. The huge union organizing meetings we held in the mountains near places such as Chapeltique, Candelaria Ostuma, and Nance Verde made history. The nighttime meeting we called in a place known as Cujuapa caused a sensation too. I remember we went there from Ilopango as delegates from our Union, in fact with Ismael Hernández, and when our arrival was announced the applause resounded all through the darkness. To get to these meetings, which were multiplying all over the country, we had to walk over many roads and paths with Ismael. From Ilopango, we went on foot to the eastern and western provinces, to Atiquizaya, Los Amates, Zacatecoluca, Chalatenango, etc. The delegates from Ilopango were always heartily applauded by

130

everyone at those meetings. In the same way, we could always count on delegates from all over the country to attend our meetings. Around 1931 – I'm jumping ahead now – I especially remember a great meeting held in a ravine called "El Papaturro" on the property of that very plantation, the "Colombia." Among other communist leaders, Farabundo Martí and Max Cuenca were there. The owners had informed the National Guard of the meeting, and the Local Command requested reinforcements so they could surround us. We knew the Guard was coming, we knew how they were coming and from where they were coming because we had posted lookouts everywhere. The fact of the matter is, with the numbers of people we had there, we would have stripped them with our bare hands not only of their rifles but even their pants. There were maybe two hundred armed National Guardsmen. But to avoid bigger problems and unnecessary risks, we agreed to quietly disperse. When the Guard got to the ravine all they found were our red flags.

Everybody brought their own food and provisions to these gatherings. It was moving to see peasant families arrive with all their kids, their bundles of tortillas, coffee, and sometimes even mats to sleep on if necessary. Whenever the Union or the group organizing the meeting had a chance to, a couple of steers or some pigs would be slaughtered beforehand to be shared amongst those attending. Instead of diminishing on account of all the difficulties, our enthusiasm grew and multiplied.

The repression got to be particularly sharp in Ilopango since the authorities figured – and they figured right – that the town had been the source and center of such intense mass activity. Several specific incidents aggravated the situation and it finally became necessary for some of our well-known leaders to leave town and go work in other places. One of those incidents was the following: the workers in Ilopango decided that the feast of our patron saint, St. Christopher, should be celebrated by our Union – whose militants were mostly Catholic – separately from the official celebration organized by the municipality, since it always discriminated against the peasants and workers, only

131

considering the rich landowners or merchants to be of any importance. The priest opposed us, screaming to high heaven that *he* was the one who organized the feast, and as a first step in the name of the Church and the Pope he refused to let us use the statue of the saint in the procession. But a lady who was a friend of mine had a real big statue of St. Christopher in her house, and she let us use it. So we went ahead and organized our ceremonies. The priest was mad as hell and didn't want to be shown up, so he locked the doors of the church with chains. That way our procession couldn't end at the main altar, and, saint and all, we had to stay outside. The feeling of discontent was enormous because nearly everyone in Ilopango had paraded and sung in that workers' procession. But since the priest had called in the Guard to protect himself, we decided to end the procession in front of the church, take our union saint and all go home. But the provocation didn't stop there. That same night, the priest and a few rich people set fire to the main altar of the church and raised a panic, saying that we had been the arsonists. But they didn't dare proceed against us in public. The fire was put out and we all went to sleep. Their plan was to arrest us the next day, one by one, in our homes, charge all the union leaders and put them in the penitentiary in San Salvador. But we were in luck because that very day almost all the union officials had to leave at dawn for Tonacatepeque to attend a trial being held against some Ilopango unionists who had been falsely accused of cattle rustling. Because the repression and harrassment didn't come down exclusively from the National Guard or the Police, but also from the entire State apparatus, such as the courts or the rich landowners and their armed thugs. Anyone could be accused of being a thief and found guilty, and on the farms vigilantes shot at simple firewood gatherers. The bastards killed several people that way. For example, doña Lola de Alfaro owned a lot of property on the outskirts of town, where most of the "water holes" and wells for washing, drinking and bathing were located. Well, just like that the old lady ordered the wells closed and started selling the water, as if she wasn't already rolling in it. In cases like that,

132

friction and problems were naturally going to form between the people and those who so oppressed and ground them down. And like they say, there's the straw that breaks the camel's back. And that's how it is when it comes to the people's patience. At the trial in Tonacatepeque that saved us from being arrested for the altar burning, we were able to get the charges against our comrades dropped. But when we returned in triumph, we found out that the National Guard and the judicial police of San Salvador were waiting on the outskirts of Ilopango to arrest us. The priest had delivered a sermon accusing us, by name, of being sacrilegious arsonists. But we refused to run away, and by eluding the traps of the Guard, we went into town. By that time a large crowd was assembled in the plaza, protesting the priest's accusations and demonstrating loudly that they weren't going to let us be arrested and imprisoned in San Salvador. A good number of the men there had brought their machetes, unsheathed. It was the first time during that period that naked machetes burned against the arbitrary caprices of the authorities. The Guard and the authorities, in spite of the fact that together they were so many of them, when they saw how many we were and how determined we were to fight to the finish, they ran away like cowards. So for the moment we were able to avoid being arrested, but from then on we had to live underground, especially Ismael Hernández and me. But, as those who have suffered say, even the bravest bull can only take so much. The Army troops stationed at the new airfield barracks outside Ilopango, which I mentioned before, also started to harass us. Even the construction of the airfield caused problems and frictions because extensive land belonging to the big, medium, and small landowners had been expropriated, and the discontent was tremendous. And then on top of it, to be fucked-over by those soldiers. I already said that the airfield killed Ilopango slowly, like a cancer. And I say it again now, with more reason. The town's farm economy was severely hurt by the airfield since what were great expanses of corn, rice, beans and sugar cane were now asphalt highways where commercial and military planes could land. And since the

133

people hung on somewhere between subsistence and total misery even when the land was productive, you could imagine what happened when it wasn't. And that sweet little angel, General Claramount, seemed to have given his soldiers free rein to commit all kinds of abuses on the peaceful inhabitants of that place. What had been before our pride and joy, the pretty young girls in our area, became one more misfortune. The soldiers came into town and abducted the women they liked, without asking if they were married or not. Our men and boys did what they had to do, and dead bodies began to turn up. The case that bought the situation to a head was that of a military pilot named Velado, who locked up a little 13-year-old girl in the barracks and brutally raped her. After doing what he wanted with her, he threw her into the street naked, saying that she was nothing more than a whore. The girl, who was well thought of in town, couldn't stand being shamed, and she poisoned herself. She didn't die, but the whole neighborhood was absolutely furious and when that bastard pilot showed his pompous self on the streets of Ilopango, the people captured him and took him to the judge. The charge was pressed on behalf of the family, our Union and the Regional Federation of Salvadoran Workers. General Claramount, in person, showed up with fifty armed soldiers to get the judge to turn the pilot over to him, but while he was testifying we surrounded the courthouse with 200 men, armed with machetes, stones, clubs and a few pistols, prepared to stop anyone from leaving the place even if all hell broke loose. I went into the courthouse as a member of two of the accusing parties and listened to what was being said. General Claramount was insulting the judge, but the latter, who was morally indignant at the pilot's vile act, said he couldn't release the prisoner, that he had to see what his superior, the judge in Tonacatepeque, wanted to do. They spoke on the phone, and happily it turned out that the judge in Tonacatepeque was a ballsy old guy who stuck to the strict letter of the law, because he immediately told the judge to arrest Claramount for obstructing justice and who knows what other crimes, and to put him in jail along with the accused pilot. Of course, that

134

couldn't be done, but General Claramount had to leave with his fifty soldiers with his tail between his legs. The proceedings were begun against the pilot in the name of the regional Federation of Workers, since the girl's family had placed full power of representation in its hands. Then, suddenly, he unleashed his anger against us in a tremendous wave of persecution, and that was when Ismael Hernández and myself had to leave Ilopango. These incidents weren't unique to the Ilopango region. To a greater or lesser degree, similar situations were occurring, for different reasons, all over the country. That's why in 1932, with the discontent and rage of the masses at its height, the insurrectional spark flamed up as violently in the center of the country as it did in Ahuachapán or in Sonsonante. There were superficial differences between the situations from one place to the next, but always the one constant was the horrible misery: salaries in the countryside were thirty-five centavos a day on the average, just to give you a simple fact (14 centavos/dollar). Consequently, with a reality like that, our political agitation work needed no exaggeration, no special emphasis or fancy interpretations. There was no need for demogoguery; that should be said straight out. It was enough to talk about reality just as it was, whether in general terms or citing particular cases, for any decent man to feel deeply wounded and to come to understand the urgent need for change in our country. We might have been gaining revolutionary consciousness in a very elemental and primitive way, but you have to understand that in those days we couldn't rely on the theoretical elaborations nor the lessons of all the practical experience that so many victorious revolutions far and wide all over the world offer us today. I can only speak for myself, but I can say that in those meetings where we talked about working conditions, about the milkmen who died with their kidneys ruptured from riding too much on horseback, about the children with no access to medical attention, who blew up from parasites, about the widespread hunger lashing out in all directions, it wasn't hard to hear, over and again, concepts that sounded to me just like "class struggle," "dictatorship of the proletariat," etc. And I learned to understand the responsibilities of a revolutionary organization and its leadership towards a reality such as ours. The leaders of the FRTS were always where the struggle was taking place, in the best and worst moments. That's why we could rely on the support and respect of the masses. Our motto was: not to leave the masses on their own. If a leader had to go to another place because of the persecution, he had to make sure beforehand that his work would be carried on responsibly by others. Our work in Ilopango, for example, bore fruit even after the original leadership nucleus had to leave for another region. I remember that when General Claramount ran for the Presidency in 1930, he only got one vote from Ilopango: that of Hermógenes Polanco, whose cattle grazed on the General's land.

---

1 Mella was a young, Cuban communist active in the struggle against the Cuban dictator Machado (translators' note).

4

In the nucleus of the young Salvadoran workers' movement. Radicalization of the Regional Federation and its first international ties. The arrival of foreign cadre in the country. The struggle between tendencies within the Regional. Communist ideas and education. The first communist nucleus. The founding of the Communist Party of El Salvador.

The Headquarters of the Regional Federation of Workers of El Salvador was where fervent international propaganda arrived during that period. We received materials from Holland, Argentina, France, Italy, the U.S., Mexico, etc., which reflected the many tendencies and positions influencing the international workers' movement at that time. Thus, reformist, anarcho-syndicalist, anarchist and communist tendencies made their way into the country, tendencies that were vying for hegemony over the international workers' movement. Because of the guild character of the Regional Federation, the tendency which at first met with the best reception was anarcho-syndicalism, although reformism – pushed by the opportunists of the Second International in Amsterdam – also made its way into our ranks. Nevertheless, as time went on a group of us carpenters, weavers, shoemakers, and activists from the Tenants' Union (which had developed parallel to the trade union movement) began consolidating ourselves into communist positions, feeding ourselves with pamphlets by Lossovsky, propaganda from the U.S.S.R., the magazine *El Machete* published by the Mexican Communist Party, the Bulletin of the Caribbean Bureau of the Communist International, the early critiques by comrade Stalin on collectivization, etc. By that point our Regional Federation was already affiliated with the Latin American Trade Union Confederation (CSLA) which also provided us with much moral and material support. With great difficulty, caused mainly by the backwardness of the ideological level of the whole movement, the struggle for leadership of the organized Salvadoran proletariat began. From the standpoint of its actual influence among the masses, the Regional was successful from the start, rapidly striking a chord in the hearts of the unionized mechanics, bus drivers, textile workers, shoemakers, bakers, vendors, carpenters, tailors, masons, barbers, tinsmiths,

139

butchers, railway workers and, what was most important, the unionized workers on the plantations, who, with the exception of a few field hands and the poorest peasants, were proletarians. The Regional also had success in what was called The Trade Union of Various Duties, rural and urban, just like the one started in Ilopango through a process I've already described, that is, unions mixed as much for the different branches of production from which the members originated, as for the fact that urban workers, artisans and agricultural proletarians could join them indiscriminately. Thus, then, we ended up having some 75 thousand members in the Regional (the number of workers we mobilized and influenced was even greater) where nearly sixty-percent were young workers. The ideological struggle, precisely due to its primitive level, became at times very violent and it wasn't a rare union meeting where disagreements were settled with fists. Also, every now and then, someone would pull a knife, and worse, some members carried pistols. I remember in one of those scuffles they were going to stab Dr. Salvador Merlos to death for one of his very sensible mediations, and he was saved only because those of us who already thought of ourselves as communists acted together to protect him and get him out of the place and out of danger. The intense struggle between tendencies within the Regional convinced us of the necessity, for the sake of unity and building the organization, that someone would have to be gotten rid of. We didn't even consider that the idea of compromise, either partial or total, was possible. Therefore, anticipating the coming battles, we made sure to prepare ourselves ideologically in as little time as possible. At that point we started to study comrade Lenin, who was truly the one who opened our eyes to new forms of organization and to new individual and collective attitudes which the Revolution and the workers' movement sorely needed in those early days. We read only a few works by Lenin, what we were able to get our hands on. But as least we had *"Left-Wing" Communism: An Infantile Disorder, Proletarian Revolution and the Renegade Kautsky,* etc. We had various assorted works by Lenin, his speeches and

140

conversations, so to speak. And it's that Lenin is an inexhaustable world of education about which, to repeat, we unfortunately could only know in those days from little pamphlets, articles, fragments, etc. Similarly the International Revolutionary Workers' Movement started paying attention to us by then. Thus comrades with experience and education arrived in our country, such as Jorge Fernández Anaya, from the Mexican Communist Youth League; Ricardo Martínez, from the Communist Party in Venezuela, who they called "Fats" and had been an activist in the reformist trade union movement with ties to Amsterdam, but who later developed into a revolutionary Leninist earning great prestige and authority, that's for sure; Jacobo Jorowics, a Marxist-Aprista from Peru back when the APRA[1] wasn't yet the pisshole which it later became and still is. Comrade Fats helped us a lot to understand the nature of the social composition of the people in the countryside. Jorowics explained political economy, particularly clarifying the concept of surplus-value and its fundamental significance in the process of acquiring revolutionary consciousness about the exploited proletariat. And Jorge Fernández Anaya dealt with problems of organization. The Salvadoran revolution will always have a debt of gratitude to these comrades who, with so much strength of will and self-sacrifice, gave us at the very least the theoretical foundation to confront the class struggle in a scientific way. It's absolutely necessary to make clear and explain that even before the arrival of these courageous comrades, we had attempted on our own to form several communist study groups. The first attempt was organized by Alfredo Díaz Nuila, who had a Bachelor's Degree and some knowledge of Marxism – the fruit of his studies abroad. He taught our group of workers the modest lessons in *The ABC of Communism*, by Bukharin. He was a good friend, a very good person and cordial with all of us, but he could never really understand us proletarians who were suffering so many blows in life. Possibly we expected too much from him. He finally quit teaching because of family pressures, especially from his mother. Then with Francisco Luarca teaching, who we called "Lazy Luarca" and who was half poet

141

and half composer, a follower of Masferrer and a dreamer, we made a second attempt in 1928. But with Luarca, who basically understood us better than Díaz Nuila, there was the problem that he wasn't a Marxist, pure and simple. Worse even: he didn't even know the rudiments of Marxism-Leninism. He was a radical with revolutionary fervor, very honest and sincere, very "Salvadoran," but nothing more. But at least he helped lift the spirits of us young trade unionists who were in his courses, which were but a blend of literature and basic sociology where the central figures were shameless José Vasconcelos and José Enrique Rodó. Alfonso Rochac, who later became the Salvadoran Minister of Economics and who was one of the most intelligent cadre on matters of economic organization used by Yankee imperialism and the oligarchy in our country – render unto Caesar what belongs to Caesar – frequently tried to stick his two cents in our rash attempts at organized study, but he only confused us by making everything so complicated. Again, he was a very intelligent man, about that I've never had the least doubt, but he had a rare knack for making the simplest, clearest things sound so complicated and confusing. He wanted to refine our taste for romantic poetry, for form, leaving aside matters of content. He said that Vasconcelos was better than Rodó because he handled literary form better. And once he gave me a book with a white cover: romantic poetry. It was the perfect opportunity to confront him once and for all with my opposition to his point of view. And not because I didn't like romantic poetry, on the contrary, it always moved me and I was never untouched by a good, inspiring, profound poem, but because what was important at that time was to focus our work in one exclusive direction: that is, to ideologically shape a group of barely literate workers and artisans who were up against great odds and the harshnesses of the social struggle. Anything other than this goal that would steer us away from our basic needs was damaging and had to be fought out in the open – whether it was romantic poetry or discussions about the Spanish Queen's petticoats. A few comrades insisted I was making a big thing out of nothing and were afraid that I was

142

being sectarian, but that confrontation with Rochac served to put things in their proper perspective and prevented us from being manipulated, and it also made Professor Luarca emphasize much more the political, social and organizational aspects of things in his lectures. Precisely from this last standpoint, it can be said without exaggerating that Luarca, even from his literary-sentimental point of view, was able to make us see the power of association, of the forms of organization within society. On trips we used to make into the countryside, a practice begun in Ilopango but which we extended to the militant trade unionists in San Salvador, Lazy Luarca taught us to see the harmony in nature, in the world of the insects and flowers. And he always found a point of comparison using anecdotes to get his point across. Among his many, many anecdotes, I especially remember a couple that have survived the winds of time. For instance, there was the one about the serpent and the mosquitos. Once there was a gigantic serpent who lived in a lagoon and who ate any mosquito that came there to drink or to lay its eggs in the mud. Well, things just couldn't go on like that, Luarca said, so the most intelligent of the mosquitos requested an audience with God and went to beg Him to get rid of the serpent so his mosquito friends could go on living in peace. God didn't like to intervene in the problems of his creatures, but so as not to abandon the mosquitos, He agreed to do something about it. So He threw a rock down from Heaven at the serpent. But the rock barely grazed its tail, and the unwary mosquitos continued going to the lagoon, and kept getting devoured. Then the smart mosquito organized his friends into guerrilla bands. While some mosquitos attacked his eyes, others went for his belly and others for his cock, until the serpent finally had to get the hell out and leave the lagoon, and then, on top of getting fucked over, he caught malaria which killed him, good and dead. The moral of the story was that when there's organized resistance even mosquitos are able to do more than God, who has rocks and everything. Another little story was the one about the frog and the rabbit. What happened was they both decided to have

143

a race for a big prize that the King of the Forest – that is, the puma – was offering. Because of its speed, the rabbit had all the advantages. On the other hand, the poor frog was only able to jump up and down like a grieving old woman. But then the frog spoke to her frog friends and asked them all to gather together along the whole route of the race. Every time the rabbit blinked its eyes one frog would go and hide and a different frog would jump out into the race, saying to the rabbit, "Hurry up, slow poke, I'm way ahead of you," until the vain rabbit quit from exhaustion and the frogs, thinking and acting as one, won the prize. We collected and wrote down these little stories of Luarca's, and we published them in the workers' press of that time. The simple truth is that they helped us a lot to be more creative in our organizing work. Luarca made us sensitive to the spirit of things without needing to make us choose, as Rochac wanted, between what was right and what was practical. But, in any case, that kind of education wasn't what we needed then. So a third study group was organized by professor Juan Campos Bolaños, who was from San Miguel. He'd read some works by Marx, but his guiding star was Gustave Le Bon and others like him. This study group broke up also, as it had to: the more or less instability of these study groups had to do mainly with their weak leadership. Nevertheless, they played an important role and were of great value in bringing those of us workers who now thought of ourselves as communists or who eagerly wanted to be communists together into the common task of creating, in a conscious and organized way, the conditions necessary to be communists. From these primitive and exploratory study groups, we at least became familiar with criticism/self-criticism as a method of discussion among revolutionaries and, therefore, since we also used these meetings to discuss the concrete problems of the workers' movement, many of the trade union lines and directives were framed there, that is, in the "communist" study group. Perfectly aware of our own ideological and political weaknesses, of our inability to make progress even where the necessary education of our new cadre was concerned, we turned our sights to other

144

countries. If the system of oppression and exploitation is international, then why do we workers continue acting like such stupid jerks, never seeing things beyond the national level. First of all, we gave a scholarship to a baker named Calixto so he could go study trade unionism in Mexico, and then, as I already said, cadre from the international movement started to arrive in the country to help us. But this marked the definite end to our improvised trade unionist and revolutionary education which, despite all good intentions, wasn't properly Marxist and even less Leninist. That education had begun for the workers in El Salvador around 1920 with the Workers' Cultural Center, "Joaquin Rodezno." I remember attending there irregularly when it first got going in San Salvador, because my supervisor, Gumercindo, was paying for my classes. There, the principal driving force was professor Francisco Moran, who gave lectures about the Soviets and the brilliant universal perspectives of the Bolshevik Revolution, about what the Russians were going to do with their liberated country. Occasionally – and right now I'm talking about the first half of the 1920s – some well-meaning person in the audience would say to the professor that he should be more careful about what he said, since there might be more than a few undercover cops or informers in the audience. Then don Chico would shout out from the rooftops, "I'm not afraid of lions, so what's a couple of rats."

The international revolutionary watchword within the workers' movement at that time was: smash the reformists and anarcho-syndicalists. By that point my supervisor Gumercindo Ramírez, a guy called Raúl B. Monterrosa, two workers of real merit, both as human beings and as trade unionists, named Tejada and Soriano, and the famous proletarian orator, Joya Peña, had all become unreliable, reckless reformists. We expelled them in 1928. And it was no easy task because, despite their regressive positions, they held prestige from their past deeds and they were still respected by the masses, but with the backing of our suburban organizations, mainly in and around Ilopango, we mopped them up. In 1929 we held the Fifth Congress of our Regional Federation, and those of us who

145

were now communists took responsibility for the regional leadership of the organism. By then, with the reformists having been expelled in the already mentioned way, our central struggle was with the anarcho-syndicalists. With the support of the "communists" and the anarcho-syndicalists, I remained in charge of the Federation's finances, but when they saw I wasn't bending to their positions and wasn't compromising with their line – as had been their hope when they backed me – they took revenge: they decided to stop paying their dues, and they began developing a campaign of economic sabotage among our base in order to cripple our ability to lead. With the Federation in such a precarious financial situation, that sabotage threw us into tremendous debt and was the cause of enormous sacrifices on our part as well as by the masses who were firmly committed to us. The landlord of the place where we had our headquarters evicted us for not paying the rent, and we barely managed to scrape up enough money to move into another place, located opposite Belloso Park. Here the problem took on a different color: since the ideological struggle was so high-pitched and frequently degenerated into loud commotions, it was no time before the new landlord got rid of us. Once again, we found ourselves having to move, only this time we were broke and couldn't afford another place. So, we launched a huge fund-raising campaign where every person gave what they had – out came the cash, personal objects, pets, some inexpensive jewelry from the women, pawn tickets, clothes, used shoes, household items, etc. In one single workday we collected 100 colones which was enough to rent a house that Dr. Enrique Córdoba's father had offered. Amidst all these stresses and strains, we were pushing forward and consolidating the revolutionary line within the Salvadoran workers' movement, making sure that line alone became the motor behind the development of the whole mass movement in our country.

Similarly, during that period our workers' movement started being represented at various international Conferences and Congresses. The worker David Ruiz went to Washington to participate in the Fifth Pan American Workers Congress. Gumercindo Ramírez and Raúl Monterrosa had gone, before their expulsion, to represent us at the CROM Congress in Mexico and came back with a very good impression of the revolutionary and anticlerical movement at that stage of the bourgeois Mexican Revolution. But the most important thing that happened was what we did at the First Conference of Latin American Communist Parties which took place in Montevideo subsequent to a meeting of the CSLA in 1929, if I remember right. The Salvadoran delegates at the CSLA meeting were invited to the Party Conference and were received as the "Salvadoran Communist Group." They were Serafín G. Martínez, a mechanic who was shot at my side in 1932; José Léon Flores, from the Shoemakers Union, who later took up studying economics and became the Salvadoran Consul in New York, and who was a prominent businessman in our country; and Luis Díaz, a carpenter. None were then communists and the only one who would officially become one was Luis Díaz, who, by the way, was elected in his time Secretary General of the first Central Committee of our Party, that is, when it was founded in 1930. In any case, when they came back they had the important job of spreading the watchwords of the Conference in the factories of San Salvador, in the artisan unions and in the Electric Company. But the work didn't go very far because the bulk of the Regional's activity was devoted to organizing work in the countryside and in the suburban areas where, as I've already sketched out, we had penetrated more deeply than ever before in our national history. Around that time I remember there were several land takeovers by the peasants and peons: among others there was the siege of the "Turin" plantation and of several formerly public lands that the Salaverría family had robbed. A Dominican priest, Father Díez, a Spanish mystic and fanatic, denounced the Regional as a Sovietized organization. Thus, we prepared for the Sixth Congress of the Regional in an atmosphere full of polemics and harassment. We still had deep financial problems because of the sabotage by the dissident anarcho-syndicalists and it even

147

turned out that, because it wasn't clear in the minds of important mass sectors who was right in the internal dispute, the unions abstained from paying their dues until they were clearer about the whole thing. Under those conditions, the call for a new Congress was an ambitious act on our part, since, at my insistence, the Regional committed itself to pay room and board for the delegates from the rural zones, who were clearly in the majority. The Sixth Congress was a success. But from that time forward there would be something new in the Salvadoran revolutionary movement: our Communist Party had been born.

Around 1929 the workers in the area of politics were but the naïve playthings of the electoral parties. The university students had become the kind of opposition to the regime which I thought of as being vulgar, destined merely to place the Government in ridicule without delving deep into the fundamental causes of the peoples' problems. It was a satiric opposition, with scoffing cartoons, farcical floats, kidding around and leg-pulling. In sum, that opposition only furthered the Government's social injustice, providing popular discontent with a totally harmless escape valve. Availing themselves of their undeniable influence among the masses, mainly in the big cities, the university students moreover backed candidates in the different electoral parties who they took a sudden fancy to, even though they might be the most unqualified, both politically and morally speaking. The students said they were acting in this way "to fuck things up." Thus, individuals like Dr. Antonio Romero, an alcoholic, and the famous Severo López, nicknamed "Talapa," who was truly an out-and-out bastard, got to be elected mayors of San Salvador. It's no wonder then that in the face of such a shameful spectacle the working class was realizing it had to rely on its own political party, which would defend our class interests on every front. The revolutionary nucleus, those of us who were communists, and to which more and more comrades belonged each day, was much clearer about the whole thing: it realized that that party couldn't just be any party, but, on the contrary, that party alone had to be a Marxist-Leninist party, the Communist Party. This idea was

148

being expressed more and more concretely and the condition for its definitive realization came with the arrival of the young Mexican communist, Jorge Fernández Anaya, who at the same time he came to El Salvador to work on the theoretical-political perspective of the trade union movement, he also became, objectively speaking, our link with the international communist movement.

In March of 1930 the Constitutional Assembly of the Salvadoran Communist Party was convened. Summoned together were the most outstanding, the most committed, the most revolutionary from the workers' and trade union movement during that period. We're not distorting our country's history when we say our Communist Party is the child of the Salvadoran working class, since you won't find any instances, as occurred in other countries, where the CP was primarily organized in the university or among the petty bourgeois intelligentsia. Our CP sprang from the very bowels of our working class, from the trade union movement as a superior form of class organization. The intellectual cadre, whose principal contribution was theoretical, were already educated by the international workers' movement. What could strictly be called the Salvadoran petty bourgeois intelligentsia played a leading role in the Party by spreading some elements of communist ideology, but its direct role in the creation of the Party, in the moment of its founding, was small. Certainly in the immediate future the incorporation of the petty bourgeoisie, at least those who were petty bourgeois by birth, into the Party would be very important, for better or worse. But we'll take a look at this a little further on.

With the help of the fishermen of Lake Ilopango, a suitable, discreet place was found for the Party's Constitutional Assembly: a secluded beach surrounded by trees in the vicinity of Asino. Those attending the Assembly were for sure going to blend in with the groups of strollers who came to those places on hot afternoons to eat and drink, cool off and bathe themselves. The places where we started living as true communists, that is, organized, were very poor: tiny adobe shacks, cheap rooming houses, etc., and they didn't provide a

149

safe site for a gathering as important as that. So among the fig and almond trees, the Constitutional Assembly of our class Party took place.

We were no more than 30 or 35 people, but now I think that was a lot, if, for example, we take into account that our Chinese comrades founded their great Party at a meeting of 50 people. After serious discussions, we resolved to found the Salvadoran Communist Party and proceeded to elect our first Central Committee. I don't remember all the details, but I can say that among the members of the CC elected then there were Luis Díaz, a carpenter who acted as Secretary General; Luis López, a mason; professor Victor Manuel Angulo, Secretary of Organization; professor Juan Campos Bolaños, Secretary of Propaganda, etc. These two professors were the first two intellectuals on the CC, though the truth is, at that point, they were already highly proletarianized and worked as workers, not as academics. Also on the CC there were Secretaries of Finance, Trade Union Affairs, Culture, Peasant Affairs, etc. After the election someone raised the matter of specifically organizing the communist youth and of responding to our international obligations by founding and building the Salvadoran Section of the International Red Aid, the organization for the relief and defense of the world proletariat in the anti-imperialist struggle that resulted in so many victims of different types: the imprisoned, the murdered, the wounded, prosecuted, persecuted, the tortured, the widowed, the abandoned children, the sick, the unemployed, etc. Both proposals passed. The Directorate of the Salvadoran Young Communist League was made up of comrades Belloso and Sorto, both printers; a young shoemaker named Ladislao, whose full name escapes me; the shoemaker José Umaña, who, by the way, is presently a cop, an informer for sure; the carpenter José Centeno, who later we sponsored to go study in the Soviet Union where he stayed a few years, returning after the events of 1932 to Cuba, which was where he decided to stay and live, losing all contact with us. Perhaps someone could ask the Cuban comrades if anyone knew or knows something

150

about him. Myself, I was elected Secretary of Organization of the Young Communist League. José Ismael Hernández, a shoemaker, and Balbino Marroguín, a mason, were responsible for the International Red Aid. Of course, the purpose of founding the Red Aid wasn't just to answer our international responsibility, as I said when the proposal was first put forward at the Assembly, but principally to confront the needs of the struggle which we saw overflowing with victims of the reaction and imperialism. The Red Aid had the responsibility of channeling throughout the country not only our aid and that from the efforts of international solidarity, but, in the first place, aid that the Salvadoran people in general gave to the victims of bourgeois repression, including sectors of the petty bourgeoisie and some less corrupt sectors of the bourgeoisie. For its part, the Young Communist League took on as its immediate objectives penetrating the universities and organizing the young workers. It was, as well, the principal agent of communist penetration into the Army, whose troops were mostly young peasants who were recruited by force.

Neither in the Party nor in the Young Communist League was there at that time a cellular organization. The base organisms were local committees with eight, ten, fifteen and even up to twenty people, but there was practically no limit to the number of people that could be in them. And even if they were subjected to a Departmental and National Directorate, their range of autonomy, particularly in matters of internal organization and in their local work, was wide. We didn't opt for this form of organization because we were ignorant of Leninist principles of party structure, since at that point we were familiar with the cell as a form of organization, both its advantages and disadvantages, mostly through magazines we received from Argentina and even from memory. But because of the actual political level of the Salvadoran working masses, its particular characteristics, the local committee was better suited than the cell to our needs for rapid growth.

From then on, with our Communist Party now constituted, the Salvadoran revolutionary movement got stronger and

151

stronger on every front of the national life, displaying an organic character without precedent, a clarity of viewpoint and purpose, and an elevated spirit of combativeness. But, of course, as a consequence of that popular upsurge, the enemy also intensified the cruelty of its repression. At the same time that political rallies and demonstrations were taking place all over the country, the number of persecuted, jailed, and beaten swelled. The struggle for the freedom of prisoners and the international call for solidarity and justice were new ways of raising the consciousness of the international workers' movement, and formed part of the struggle for world revolution.

The leadership of the Regional Federation was in the hands of "communists," but by the end of March, 1930, it came to be in the hands of Communists. Carlos Castillo, who was a leader in the Party, though I don't remember if he was on the Central Committee, happened to be filling the office of Secretary General of the Federation. There are things about Castillo that ought to be said, and things I'm not so sure about. Even though several of the Federation's nucleuses, which were being influenced by reformism and anarcho-syndicalism, were still waging internal battles, our partisan line managed to get put into action and into the Federation's program. What's more, the thesis and program of the communists started to take root among the broad popular masses and not just within the framework of the organized workers' movement. I think this was due to the fact that we had begun to gear our national political activity to our concrete needs, to the specific conditions of El Salvador, even though our vision was being nurtured more and more each day by a scientific conception of Marxism-Leninism and by the experiences of revolutionary struggles worldwide. Although primitive and still vague, we now had an idea of the importance that a scientific Marxist conception has for the revolution, assimilating what was actually possible in our country into the broad international picture. In keeping with that way of understanding the revolutionary-political organizing task, our Party proposed to lead the people united around one great objective: the realization of bourgeois-democratic revolution. I

152

think that watchword was correct at the time, and that our organizing and agitational steps conformed to it fairly closely. After assuming leadership of the organized workers' movement, we struggled to unify and strengthen it, and only when these conditions were secured, at least to the minimal extent necessary, did we push our revolutionary program whose realization presupposed the inevitable seizing of political power by the Salvadoran people. Those who accuse us of raising the watchword of bourgeois-democratic revolution in a purely mechanical way, following the line of the IC (the Communist International), are wrong. It's true that it was the general watchword of dependent and semi-colonial countries, but in our case it arose from an analysis of our specific, concrete reality. It isn't true that with this plan of action our Party was attempting to mediate a bourgeoisie that didn't exist. We were in a country which had already entered into the second phase of its industrial development, independent of its many after-effects. And back then the power of the socialist camp didn't exist as it does today! We couldn't, without becoming irresponsible, suddenly nationalize the whole economy at one blow, institute agrarian reforms and non-capitalist economic development as is possible now, for example, in Africa. For us the bourgeois-democratic revolution was a pretty limited concept, circumscribed by its most essential characteristics, and even these would have had to be modified in practice to bring about the best results within a weak economic structure and within the different classes of the country. We were sure not to isolate this general watchword from the daily struggle around the most urgent demands of the workers and peasants, with the purpose of awakening the people's confidence in their own forces, which is for me an unbeatable method of forming and shaping revolutionary consciousness. Our errors, including those due to our narrow sectarianism, were not of strategy, not of general watchwords like this one about the nature of revolution. I think all this will become clear when I go into an analysis of the events surrounding the insurrection of 1932. I repeat, we avoided like hell using hollow, empty-headed

153

watchwords, and we weren't above using the most everyday concerns to mobilize the masses. For example, in the countryside we brought the concept of bourgeois-democratic revolution to the peons and hired hands with strike threats against the bosses or with actual strikes for bigger tortillas in the daily meals, more beans all year round, coffee with meals, the abolition of stores owned by the bosses that give credit at high interest rates, wage hikes and better working conditions, the repairing or renovation by the landowners of the thatched huts that the hired hands lived in, etc. We didn't have to wait long to see the fruits of these forms of struggle as far as bringing the masses closer to our general programmatic line. And neither did we have to wait to have our labor demands met, which strengthened the people's confidence in our methods of struggle. On the hacienda "Aguas Frías," for instance, property of the Sol family and located in the vicinity of Santa Tecla, after several days of strike threats the bosses gave in and raised wages from 37 centavos a day to one colon. The same thing happened on the hacienda "Colombia," and on others. There was one strike led by us – as were all the others – against the construction company that was building "La Chacra" baths in San Salvador and the Holland Water Tanks, that had tremendous repercussions. Nine hundred workers ended up walking off the job and a 50% wage hike was won. I remember that Carlos Castillo, who was our comrade then, did brilliant work in that struggle. We lost a very hard-fought strike against the paving company in San Salvador, but we won our demands to lower the rents and electric rates, demands which were backed by large mass campaigns. In Santa Ana we also triumphed, getting a reduction in the electric rates, but the victory was only an apparent one, since the company offset this rate reduction by cutting its hours of service. I tell you, the Salvadoran electric companies have been some of the worst bloodsuckers in our history.

From a personal standpoint, all these struggles represented enormous sacrifices. Our misery was awful, unemployment was rampant. We ate when we could and we went around filthy,

154

just about in rags. The Secretary General of the Party had to have his wife work as a cook in the house of a rich family, and since he barely had enough to eat every day he'd often go and wait by that house so his wife could give him the leftovers they threw out. That is, nothing less than what we Salvadorans call "garbage scraping." Me and my family, and comrade Ismael and his, stayed in a tiny rented room that seemed like a pigpen, since we couldn't afford any better. In all, we were seven: three children and four adults. Our wives sold fruit in the mornings, and in the afternoons they made and sold tamales to relieve our situation and so that we men could devote ourselves completely to organizing and revolutionary work.

With the year 1930, a new period of elections began. The Constitutional Party, which was running Dr. Miguel Tomás Molina for President of the Republic, offered me a job doing propaganda work for 150 colones a month. By the way, it was the mother of the Marín brothers, the ones who would become heroes and martyrs in the civil-military insurrection against Martínez in 1944, who offered me the job in the name of Dr. Molina himself. A different political party, I don't remember which one, made the same kind of offer to Ismael Hernández. We decided, at Ismael's insistence, to consult the Party about how to deal with such offers based on my principled opinion that we shouldn't accept them, because that would mean placing oneself at the service of the electoral power of the bourgeoisie even when more or less decent people were involved, as was probably the case with Molina. The Secretary General of the Party, comrade Luis Díaz, shared my opinion and told us that the primary thing was the reputation of the Party, that we communists had to uphold our honor, above all in a country like El Salvador, where, for example, people all think a girl is honest and decent *until* the moment it becomes public she's screwed up. In this way, Luis Díaz dispelled all of Ismael's doubts.

Of course, alongside the unavoidable misery and our efforts to properly conduct ourselves as communists, there also arose among us various ridiculously extremist and childish attitudes. For example, the wave of what I call "stupid

155

proletarianism" did a lot of damage, both then and later on. The wearing of neckties by communists was practically considered a crime. I had to throw out my dress shirts because you were well-received among your comrades only if you had on a T-shirt. Sneers, wisecracks and even insults were thrown at you if you dressed otherwise. Instead of a leather belt, I started to use a hemp rope to hold up my pants. Naturally our families and many comrades didn't understand all this. There were angry, self-sacrificing militants who expressed strong doubts about these crazy ideas: "For Christ's sake, comrades, do you mean that to be communists we have to be the poorest of the poor and go around looking like we're all fucked up?" The pressure from my sisters (who indeed helped us financially, paying the rent and giving us food) was the most insistent: they didn't understand why, what with us being young, strong and able workers, we lived in so much misery. One day when my mother visited my sister and I was there, my sister said to me in a dramatic and emotional tone of voice: "Mother's here today, and I want you to tell me once and for all in front of her: Which do you love more, this stupid nonsense you're involved in, or Mother?" "I love Mother very much," I answered, looking her right in the eye, "but this stupid nonsense I'm involved in is necessary for everybody and someone's got to face up to it. Mother always spoke with me about great men and she always made the distinction between them and traitors. She also spoke with me about the suffering of the Virgin Mary, mother of that revolutionary, Christ. Here we are, the three of us, and I know we love each other very much, but I'm struggling for millions, who have millions of mothers and millions of children and millions of spouses and millions of brothers and sisters. What would you say if General Sandino came down from Chipotón and gave himself up to the gringos so as to please his mother?" Mother looked into my eyes and then turned to my sister and said: "See, Pilar, I brought him into this world and I know his feelings are good, even if I don't understand a word of what he says." Mother was deeply moved by what my uncle, Feliciano Mármol, her most beloved brother, had recently told her just before he died: "Don't despise little Miguel, I know him. This business he's involved in is going to take him to his grave, but it's a very great and dignified activity, in which only the noblest of men participate."

From time to time my wife would tell me that some relative or close friend of hers advised her to leave me, because there was no future with me. I'd reply that whoever told her such a thing had every reason in the world, and that they probably did it for her own good, that it's true that the life of a soldier of the revolution is a sad life, and I couldn't keep us from being poor without becoming dishonest. She loved me very much, the way a wife loves her husband, and I also loved her very much, the way a husband loves his wife. With youth and love we endured even the hunger, and she didn't take the sensible advice of her close friends and relatives. But I always let her know that if she decided otherwise, she should be sincere and faithful with me, because love is one thing that can leave at any moment. But if trust remains as a bond between two people, it's possible to overcome any circumstances or mutually come to an understanding which is best for both. What fucks up everything is lying.

Don't think that these hardships were the only troubles we revolutionaries had back then. When I said several times that the repression intensified, I wasn't just saying it for the hell of it. You see, I don't like to dwell so much on this aspect of the persecutions, because this isn't an adventure story, but simply notes of my most general recollections in the hope that they will maybe be of some use to today's young revolutionaries. And because I realize true revolutionaries never like to dwell too much on their misfortunes. But the truth is that all the hatred and rage of the bourgeoisie, with the help of their obedient puppets, came down on us more and more each day. During the last months of 1929 and all through 1930, I had to use several hiding places and refuges to avoid the police, and, several times, I even had to disguise myself. My main place of refuge continued to be Ilopango because there the people knew me well and would go all out to protect me. And later on, it

157

turned out that the authorities, above all the National Guard and the police, had agents who were working for both of them. But they didn't last very long and therefore they didn't get to know all there was to know about you. The peasants in the area made me a small underground room and there I worked at all hours typing up leaflets, manifestoes, documents, etc. A few boys, the sons of communists, were my sentinels and warned me if Guardsmen or just some messengers were approaching with a little bell or with some firecrackers I myself had bought them. They had fun and they helped me out a lot. In the large cities, particularly in San Salvador, it was a fact that you had to be on your toes all the time. On one occasion we had an appointment with Carlos Castillo in Centenary Park. We talked a few minutes and then separated. On our way out, we suddenly found ourselves surrounded by the cops. They caught Castillo but I was able to escape. When I saw him again, I asked him what had happened. He told me the cops had released him after an endless interrogation and after they gave him a goddamned hard beating. Afterwards, our wives' houses, I mean Ismael's and mine, were under constant surveillance. The police pretended to be drunks, sleeping it off in the middle of the street, in order to see if they could surprise me. But I was always able to slip by them and I even fixed it so I got to see my babies, who I always had a soft spot for. One time, I came home thinking the house wasn't being watched by those drunks, and my son was screaming like crazy because his diapers were all shitty and his mother wasn't home. While I was changing him, I looked out the window and saw that the cops were surrounding the place, and so, feeling awful, I had to leave my son all shitty and escape through a hole in the ceiling. I ran along the rooftops until I was able to jump onto a train and get lost in the woods. Another time, when I was writing a manifesto attacking Araujo, three cops surprised and captured me. But I had two young, strong comrades with me who made it clear they were ready to beat the shit out of those cops. They ran away to get some help, and we grabbed the chance to get away. A neighbor, who was Guatemalan, and who wasn't even our friend but who figured

158

out what was going on, and he'd witnessed our run-in with the cops, went to our house and took the typewriter and all our papers and put it under the seat of his son's stroller, putting his well-diapered son on top of it. Right away a bunch of cops arrived at the house, but they didn't find a thing. Then afterwards, that Guatemalan, who always took his son around in the stroller, brought the typewriter and documents to the place where we had told him we'd be waiting. Fortunately, there was widespread popular sympathy for us. There was even one time when I escaped from the grasp of the police, leaving a refuge I had near the Army's General Arsenal through a sewer filled with stinking sewage. I came out onto a very busy street, and when the people saw me they thought I was some thief on the run, and they wanted to capture me. But when I told them that I was simply a worker persecuted for political reasons, they let me go, showed me a safe route, and they even gave me money.

And that's to say nothing of our militant members. In the Party as well as in the Young Communist League and also among broad sectors of the trade union movement, there existed a high level of discipline. Maybe we fell into a kind of rigid extremism, but the fact is that on the basis of keeping strict discipline and setting an example, revolutionary and proletarian unity quickly became a reality. Punctual attendance at meetings was a fixed, serious requirement, even if we leaders had to cross tens of kilometers of treacherous mountains. One time I had to lead a meeting of fishermen on the other side of the lake. Since it was pouring cats and dogs, the streams were all overflowing their banks, and there was one that was impossible to cross on foot. I didn't know what to do, and time was passing. First a cart came by driven by some half-wild oxen and the driver was struggling to keep them under control. When I timidly asked him if he could please give me a lift across the river, the man, with his mind glued to those wild oxen, told me to go fuck myself. So when another cart came by, I now told the driver in an authoritative tone of voice, "Stop, right here!" And scared out of his wits, he took me across. Afterwards, from my own embarrassment and because it was all the money I had on me, I gave him a peseta. I got to the meeting at 5 o'clock in the morning and none of the fishermen were there. But when the first ones arrived, positive that there wasn't going to be a meeting, nor anything like it, they were embarrased to see that I was already there, and they ran back to get the others and the meeting was great. So, that goes to show: a leader, come rain or shine, thunder or lightning, must always keep his promises with the masses and always set an example.

It's also clear that we made some mistakes. I already said something about that "stupid proletarianism." I think the worst manifestation of that attitude was the removal from the Directorate of our Communist Party of Luis Díaz, who was always a good communist, and its first Secretary General. It so happened that during a very militant demonstration that took place in Santa Tecla and in which some 12 thousand people participated, there were several people who were killed or wounded at the brutal hands of the police, and many of our comrades fell prisoner fighting the repressive forces. Our Secretary General was one of those who fell prisoner. They were processed and locked up in the local penitentiary. But it so happened that there, in that city, lived a lady by the name of Guirola, doña Violeta I believe, who was a millionaire and who had made a promise to the Virgin of Carmen that if she cured her sick son, she'd perform a yearly act of charity. As the boy got well, the señora felt indebted to the Virgin and every year she'd go to the penitentiary and give each prisoner an envelope with a peso inside. The whole thing was now a tradition and when the day came for doña Violeta's act of charity, the warden of the prison didn't go around asking each prisoner's opinion, but at once had them line up in the courtyard and the old lady handed out the envelopes. On this particular occasion I'm talking about, the Secretary General of the Salvadoran Communist Party took his envelope also. When, without giving it a second thought, he told some of the visiting comrades about it the following Sunday, they got really angry and complained to the Central Committee which, in turn, decided to remove Luis Díaz from the

Directorate of the Party "for having accepted bribes from the oligarchy."[2]

---

[1] APRA: Peru's largest center-left political party. It began as an anti-oligarchic party whose supporters were and are from the middle class, and effectively functions in alliance with the military and ruling reactionary parties (translators' note).

[2] So that readers can make their own comparisons, we reproduce here a fragment of Chapter XXXII from Schlésinger's book, which deals with communist organization. A typical example of simplistic, ultra-rightest, anticommunist literature, mixing half-truths, facts, and documents handled with no rigor or responsibility, this text by Schlésinger is nevertheless of interest in that it deals with questions Mármol's text makes definitively clear: the founding of the CP, the type of initial organization of the party (Chapter 4 of Mármol's text), etc. At the same time, this text is a typically reactionary view of the international aspects of the Central American communist movement. Compared against Mármol's text, Schlésinger's falsehoods emerge so clearly that we feel further commentary to be unnecessary.

THE COMMUNIST ORGANIZATION

Chapter XXXII of the book, *Communist Revolution: Guatemala in Danger?*

The Communist International is made up of the Communist Parties of every nation in the world, and the Party of each country is called a Section of said International. An International Executive Committee which, in brief, is called the "Comintern," has the direction of the International in its charge. The IEC directs all the CPs of the world and has its seat in Moscow, capital of the USSR, ruled by a government of workers, peasants and soldiers who form SOVIETS, which means "Council of Workers, Peasants and Soldiers," led by the Russian CP.

The CP proposes to organize the proletariat, substituting the individualist economic system with Soviet collectivism, a tendency that has met with the most resounding failure and has had to give up ground to State capitalism. In order to implement its doctrines successfully, it has mercilessly smashed capitalism, the aristocracy, the bourgeoisie in the cities and countryside, and the Kulaks, with the end of maintaining the power of the proletarian class, which includes the industrial worker, the peasant, and related elements.

The Salvadoran Section of the Communist International was an organization circumscribed by the geographical boundaries of the Republic of El Salvador. The idea existed that this Section might include the five countries of the former Central American nation, but a

161

diversity of conditions prevented the realization of that design, and a Section of the International was organized in each Republic of the Isthmus. In El Salvador, the Section is called the Communist Party and directed by a Central Committee. The Party, in turn, is divided into subsections directed by Departmental Executive Committees; within these there are, similarly, different local subsections directed by regional Local Executive Committees. Within this apparatus exists a cellular system, which for the most effective organization groups men through factories, farms, or military posts. Every cell in a local area obeys the LEC; the latter, the DEC, and all of them obey the Central Executive Committee, which in turn depends on and obeys the instructions of the Communist International, with its seat in Moscow.

So that the reader can easily grasp the cellular organization, we reproduce the following document:

"FOR THE GREATEST SUCCESS OF THE RECRUITMENT CAMPAIGN UNDERTAKEN BY THE COMMUNIST PARTY OF EL SALVADOR, THE CENTRAL COMMITTEE GIVES THE FOLLOWING INSTRUCTIONS, WHICH MUST BE PUT INTO PRACTICE IMMEDIATELY."

1. The cell is the basic unit of our organization, and gathers together its members of the Party at the place where they work or live. No one can be a member of the CP without being in a Party cell. In the cell, the member of the P exercises the right to participate in the formulation of P policy and in the election of leadership organisms. It is also where all militants give account of and take responsiblity for their activities.

2. Cells are organized in all shops, factories, offices, stores, neighborhoods, streets, farms, plantations, mills, estates, villages, valleys and towns, regiments and barracks.

3. The cell is comprised of at least four comrades, who are in charge of the Executive Committee of the cell, which consists of four secretaries: Secretary General, Secretary of Organization, of Finances, and of Agitation and Propaganda. Recruitment will be done to strengthen already existing cells and to organize new ones.

4. The Executive Committee of the cells depends on the LEC, the latter on the DEC, and the last on the CC of the Party.

5. The neighborhood and street cells organize workers from small shops, store employees, domestic servants, students, etc., who cannot be organized where they work. The cells of farms, estates, mills, and other plantations organize agricultural workers, without fearing to include the most militant poor peasants, among whom there are courageous and truly revolutionary elements.

162

6. It is the Secretary General of the Cell Committee who brings the general work of the cell up to date and establishes contact with the superior organism. The Secretary of Organization is in charge of the task of recruitment for the strengthening of the cell, keeping a registration book with pseudonyms and writing down in said book the comrade's age, wages earned, occupation and place of work. It is the Secretary of Finances who has economic control of the cell, for which a book must also be kept, with lined columns for each of the months. The Secretary of Agitation and Propaganda is in charge of distributing propaganda material in every sector the cell controls, and should direct a group of comrades who will help in the work.

7 The monthly dues are fixed at 0.06 cts. and the membership fee at 0.10 cvs. Taking into account that a comrade who stops paying dues for three months is automatically out of the Party. Only those comrades who are sick, on strike, or unemployed, with proper proof, will be exempted. Out of the amount raised in membership fees, 50% goes to the CC, 25% to the DEC and 25% to the collecting organization, that is, to the cell.

8. The Cell Committee must meet twice a week, at least, and the cell at least once a week. New additions to the cell are proposed to the Central Committee, which is called upon to discuss them and approve them or not. The age of each new comrade, wages earned, occupation, place of work, and previous participation in some of the base organizations must be registered.

9. In order to effect the penetration of the Party's policy and to put its tendencies into practice, COMMUNIST FRACTIONS must be organized in the Trade Unions, Peasant Leagues, Cooperatives, Anticlerical Leagues, Anti-imperialist Leagues, Sports Associations, Congresses, the International Red Aid, Conferences, Municipalities, Parliaments and Assemblies. The COMMUNIST FRACTIONS depend directly on the cells to which the comrades making up the FRACTION belong. The COMMUNIST FRACTION IS THE WEAPON OF THE CELL and is made up of at least two members."

At the Latin American Communist Congress held in June of 1929 in Buenos Aires, the delegate from Guatemala, Villaba (Luis Villagrán), repeated the phrase of another comrade, "the CI discovered Latin America late, especially Central America," where there was great sympathy for Communism. On that occasion, Villaba urged the delegates present to devote more attention to the revolutionary movement in the countries of the Caribbean. He complained about the lack of experience of the Party in Guatemala, where the theses of the CI were almost unknown and the cellular organization wasn't known until 1929. The Salvadoran delegate, Diéguez, who stated that the SCP became organized almost spontaneously, argued the same thing.

163

He whined that the Regional Federation of El Salvador was born on the basis of a cowardly society; that the Council of this group tried to penetrate the masses and effectively organize all the workers, but that the latter themselves had opposed a tenacious struggle against such aims. He praised the labor of a bold worker on the side of the cause and referred "to the intelligent González Aragón, a Nicaraguan national, who knew how to bring his convictions to the soul of the people," maintaining that the Communist Party was born within the trade union organizations. It is undoubtable that this work was aided by public officials, since the delegate himself states that at the beginning the group was viewed with "benevolence" and were only thought to be "exaggerated elements," but when they realized it was a matter of a Communist Party, the officials developed destructive tactics, trying to scare off the workers, which was impossible to do.

The Salvadoran trade unions were in close contact with the Mexican groups in the CROM, directed from official circles by a leader of the Aztec nation: don Luis H. Morones. Salvadoran delegates were at the Fifth Congress of this group, but nothing came of it because the work was in the hands of intellectuals, "to whom the leadership of the unions should never be given, because they always betray our aspirations," as the Salvadoran delegate says in his report to the above-mentioned Communist Congerence in Buenos Aires. He further states, in order to defend this awful thesis, "that in El Salvador all the intellectuals have betrayed the cause, with the sole exception of one student who has known how to stay within eminently revolutionary criteria without defecting."

The Salvadoran trade unions lost quite a bit of prestige, because their funds disappeared from the treasuries, and this, of course, dampened the enthusiasm of those who gave what little they had for the essential expenses of the cause, which is why it didn't progress much. But from the discontent "emerged a new, essentially communist group." Guatemalans as well as Salvadorans sent special delegations to Mexico so they might learn how they ought to develop their activities, because according to their comments they didn't have a plan of action to push forward the work. In Guatemala, it was the "Workers' Unification," transformed into the "Socialist Workers' Unification," that took on definite colors; but persecuted by government officials, it retreated from activity and confined itself to organizing a few trade unions, among which figured that of the Bakers. In 1925, after holding a ceremony in Lenin's memory, they were attacked, their press was destroyed, and the agitator Del Pinal was arrested and spent thirteen months in prison. That same year, a delegation from Mexico arrived that brought instructions to transform the CP of Guatemala into the CP of Central America, as a section of the CI. It was then that delegates from Guatemala, as well as a few from Mexico, went down to El Salvador, and these were the ones who definitely organized the CP within the Unions. The delegates came back satisfied on realizing that El Salvador offered a field "ripe for new ideas." On their return to Guatemala, they organized a women's society called "1st of May," and immediately afterwards the Mexican delegates returned to their country, convinced that they had fulfilled their objective. The functioning of the CP of El Salvador dates from 1925 (Note by R.D.: Schlésinger confuses the founding of the CP in El Salvador, carried out only in March of 1930, with the attempts made in the 20s, above all in Guatemala, to found the Central American CP or CPs in each Central American country, which never got off the ground).

In El Salvador trade unionism didn't have the desired result, and only the effective organization of communism revived the intensity of the social movement. The activity of the latter increased with the election propaganda of 1926...but with obvious confusion...and "the lack of real leaders who could guide the masses through the courses of communism." The CP of El Salvador, as can be gathered from correspondence, was closely tied to the CPs of Guatemala, Honduras, Nicaragua, and Costa Rica, with the Central American Congress, control of each one went to the Secretariat of the Caribbean, with its seat in New York, organized at the request of the Venezuelan Martínez. For Internal Direction, an Executive CC was organized, with its seat in the Salvadoran capital, and Octavio Figueira as its Secretary General. (Note by R.D.: Octavio Figueira was one of the pseudonums of A. Farabundo Martí, who arrived in El Salvador after the founding of the CP, as a representative of the International Red Aid.) This Executive CC was composed of different secretariats: Foreign Affairs, Interior, Finances, and Agitation; and each one gives out orders for their own branch...Jointly with the CI, within the radius of its jurisdiction, another organism with distinct characteristics operates. The CI is the political director of the communist campaign, and the other, a kind of Society for the Protection of the Persecuted, called the "International Red Aid," with its seat in Moscow, but with different secretariats in the large cities of Latin America. The Secretariat of the Caribbean of the SRI has its seat in New York, and that of South America is located in Buenos Aires. This Red Cross of the communist armies develops effective work and raises funds by all means of collection, such as the sale of lapel buttons, literature, and other similar things. The SRI maintains the strictest agreement with the communist groups and acts now and then as an effective propagator of red tendencies. Martí, among others, didn't exercise immediate leadership of the communist forces in El Salvador; he was a direct agent, a kind of spokesman for the CI: an outstanding personality in comparison to the agitators who made up the Central, Departmental, and Local Committees. The SRI was divided into sections. The Salvadoran Section only answers to the Secretariat of the Carribean, ignoring altogether the hierarchical system...

The organization of the Party is much more consistent than a system that tends to amass men with political designs. The communist leaders need men who are convinced, fanatics, who do not question the orders they are given, as crazy or arbitrary as they may be. To swell its ranks, they carry out a number of preliminary tasks, and once the candidates are prepared, they demand their membership into the revolutionary ranks, in order to keep them more bound to the iron-willed discipline instituted as a vital necessity of communism. The preliminary work of setting the atmosphere is the responsibility of peddlers, of the street vendors who slip into every corner of the country, developing their activities within the system that was explained in previous chapters. It is easy to understand how this clever propaganda penetrates the minds of peasants, excites the most sensitive feelings: need and vanity, feelings innate to every social strata and all races. After the street vendor, who has already sown a desire, who has already stirred up a natural tendency in the masses, comes the agitator, proclaiming without hesitation the need to change a regime that doesn't establish social equilibrium, that maintains a state of inequality condemned by all sense of justice, a system of exploitation under cover of which the bourgeoisie expropriates the work, the sweat of the proletariat, while the latter scream under the yoke of the most denigrating economic oppression. Once the field is fertilized and minds are prepared, the indoctrinator turns up, revealing the secrets of the communist system, with a new creed that has abolished completely inequalities and injustices. He talks about Russia and Mexico, where the workers are the masters and owners, where they occupy the houses of the rich, where they are landlords of the valuable estates, of the factories, the shops, warehouses and stores; and finally, he talks about the strong and united communism in El Salvador, that struggles for the prerogatives and well-being of the Salvadoran proletariat. With interest aroused, the red agent expresses himself in very concrete terms, and presents an application for membership into the ranks of the CP. These application forms, that figure in large number among the documents confiscated by the police, read:

"To the CC of the SCP, Section of the CI.

Dear Comrade: I, _____, _____ years old, a worker, with this letter request to be admitted into the CP, submitting myself, of course, to its statutes. For the Central Committee, fraternally, I sign _____. Witness _____ Address _____."

The applicant, once accepted, is enrolled into the ranks, committed to uphold and respect the orders of the Party and the CI. As a prior condition to membership, it is indispensible that the Candidate be submitted to a kind of final interrogation, which amounts to the following questions:

" 1. In which political parties have you been active?
2. Which public offices have you held and how many times?

166

3. Which offices have you held in political parties?

4. How long did you serve in the military and what rank did you attain?

5. Have you been imprisoned because of social issues?

6. Do you have papers for the time you served?

7. To what peasant or worker organization do you belong, or have you been active before in working class union organizations or in peasant organizations?

8. Names of both parents or one of them; only if they are still living. Said names will be noted by the organizing comrade on a separate sheet of paper.

9. Names of your wife and children.

10. What parts of the country do you know? Of Central America or of other countries?

San Salvador, _____ day of 193____.
Witness_____ Pseudonym of applicant_____ "

Simultaneously, registration forms and circulars for instructing the Departmental Committees as to the way in which they should carry out their tasks are sent to different communist groups, and read:

"CP of El Salvador, Section of the CI. CC. Department of Organization.
Comrade Secretary of Organization of the DEC of Santa Ana, of the SCP, Section of the CI.

Dear Comrade:

We enclose with this letter the ballot form for membership in the Party, where the work of organization must be carried out on the following basis:

1. At present, new members to the Party should be admitted by presenting applicants' membership ballots to the DEC.

2. The DEC, through the Office of the Secretary of Organization, will give an account of the applications for membership to the CC, in compliance with point 8 of the Organizational Bulletin, with which you are already familiar.

3. For the CC to consider the membership application, it will suffice to send the names of the applicants, that is, the membership ballots should not be sent to the CC.

4. The membership ballot must be signed by the applicant, who will adopt a pseudonym that will be marked down in the book mentioned in

167

point 6 of the Organizational Bulletin. Only the pseudonym should appear in the book.

5. The membership ballots must be kept in an absolutely secure place.

6. The registration book must not have a title or a heading.

7. As soon as the number of comrades is large enough to form a cell, they must be called to a meeting to establish the cell.

8. Every comrade who knows of one or more comrades who want to join the Party must present them to the Secretary of Organization, so that the latter can give them membership ballots to sign.

9. The Secretary of Organization will inform the Secretary of Finances about the new members.

10. The noting of pseudonyms will be made at the end of each month, so that the admissions will be in dated order, that is, until all membership ballots have been collected. This in the case that the Secretary of Organization does not make the admission himself.

We remain fraternally yours. Proletarians of all countries, unite! For the Department of Organization, the Secretary. AFRE."

5

Trip to the Soviet Union to attend the World Congress of Red Trade Unions. Impressions of the trip there and back through Europe. Impressions of the U.S.S.R. Detention in Cuba. View of Havana in 1930.

Through our Mexican comrade, Jorge Fernández Anaya, it was communicated to our young Party that the Regional Federation was invited to attend the World Congress of Red Trade Unions (PROFINTERN) that was going to take place in Moscow, the capital of the Soviet Union. It was a great joy for the communists and organized workers in the FRTS, that we had barely hatched and already we were being considered for an event of the international proletariat, of the big family of workers who no longer wanted to continue under the yoke of capital. At first, Luis Diáz was selected to make the trip, given his position as Secretary General of the Party, but because he was expelled because of the dumb problem I just went into, a new election had to be held. This time with the votes of the Party Directorate, the Young Communist League and the Red Aid, comrade Modesto Ramírez was chosen to go. But news arrived that in fact two Salvadorans were invited to attend the Congress, and a new election had to be held again. It was then that my name was nominated and I wound up being elected – all in my absence, since I was so involved in my organizing work outside San Salvador and was unable to attend that meeting. The election was hard fought between several candidates, but the peasant representatives in the leadership bodies of the Regional firmly supported me and I was elected. But I really didn't want to go, a little because I was afraid to travel so far away, to the other side of the world – me, who had never even been to Guatemala – also a little because I had so much work to do on the young trade union front, and also because my mother was extremely sick with a bad heart and I was afraid that my leaving might lead to her final collapse. When I raised my doubts and reasons for not wanting to go, Fernández Anaya, who was the one who told me about the decision of the Directorate, gave me the chewing-out of the century and demanded that I respect the

171

mandate of the Directorate and the masses it represented. It wasn't a matter of a vacation, of a pleasure trip, but of a revolutionary task of great responsibility. Finally, he summed up by telling me in no uncertain terms what I had to do: "Listen jerk," he said, "if you go around acting like a sentimental slob, you're going to regret it for the rest of your life because this is no game we're playing. If your comrades have chosen you it's because they have confidence in you, so you better pack your bags, because, if you continue acting like an asshole, I myself am personally going to kick you out of the country." Put that way, I felt I had to muster up the courage and get ready to go around the world alongside Modesto Ramírez. Of course, my golden dream for a long time had been to be able to go to the Soviet Union, but now that it was happening for real, faced with my personal problems and all the work I had to do, my doubts had gotten the better of me. That chewing-out by Fernández Anaya made me more steadfast. There are times when a good chewing-out like that is worth more than all the advice given in the manner of Carreño's etiquette book.

I believe it was during the first days of June, 1930, when we left El Salvador. It couldn't have been more than a few days before then that Agustín Farabundo Martí, who had acquired great prestige in the international workers' and communist movements, at least in Latin America, and who was now an active cadre with the International which assigned him the job of running the Caribbean Bureau of the International Red Aid, arrived in our country to join our movement as a representative of the SRI. Martí had become a legendary figure by joining in our name the guerrilla forces of General Augusto César Sandino in the Nicaraguan mountains, where for his fighting courage he earned the rank of Colonel and later became General Sandino's Private Secretary. He had the reputation of being an armed combatant which, like it or not, is the reputation most accepted by the masses because they know it is earned by risking one's skin. You can place your trust in a man, say the people, who is ready to suffer, to die, and to kill for his ideas. And they are right. Martí split with Sandino for ideological

172

reasons. Though considering Sandino a great anti-imperialist patriot, he broke with the narrow, nationalist ideas of this great, popular *caudillo* who didn't share the revolutionary Marxist-Leninist view of class struggle and proletarian internationalism which was by then deeply rooted in Martí's heart and mind. Also maybe it was that el Negro Martí, who was uncompromising when it came to his principles, wasn't flexible enough to deal with an ally like Sandino, but the fact remains that the rupture happened. The split between Martí and Sandino shattered any chance of linking the Nicaraguan guerrilla offensive with the Marxist oriented workers' movement, which, at that moment, had entered into a period of heightened activity throughout Central America. Were their methods contradictory? Wasn't it the same as the struggle taking place today between guerrilla warfare and mass political struggle? This is what the history students and the theoreticians might say, though I'm here only to relate what was and is now clear to me. And besides, this is a testimony of my past and not a document where I'm raising the problems that our parties face today. Martí quickly became the principal figure in our Party and in the entire revolutionary movement of the masses in El Salvador, and he would become the human symbol of the popular peasant insurrection in 1932, and the most important historical figure of our country's communist movement. Despite the fact that his participation in the Salvadoran struggle lasted for such a brief period of time, the stamp he left on our history was and is profound – although this has not been made at all clear, mainly due to the lack of serious students of Martí's life, which is the fault of us revolutionaries. Within the framework of this conversation, I wouldn't dare presume to expound on the significance of el Negro Martí in our history. That's something for communists who have had the time to go to the University to do. El Negro will come up again during the course of the story because he was the most engaged, the most self-sacrificing, the best – without a doubt – of all of us. But I won't offer an interpretation of his life, which is, nevertheless, an indispensible task of the Party. I think something on it has already been done.

173

Someone's biographical sketch of Martí has been published, but more is needed, delving deep into his personality (talking with the many people still alive who were close to him, his family, friends) and his role in the first stage of our revolutionary workers' movement, his actual role in the organization and activities of the Caribbean Bureau of the International Red Aid, etc. For now I only want to leave the sense that when I left the U.S.S.R., el Negro Martí had just arrived in El Salvador after having lived in Mexico, Nicaragua, etc., dedicating himself to the international revolutionary task. The months I was away were enough so that, on my return, I found Martí had become our indisputable leader, the maximum communist leader of El Salvador.

A few days before leaving, I went to tell my mother about the trip. She pretended to be pleased and despite her being sick and against my wishes, she wanted to go buy me a new shirt for the long journey. She said she didn't know where Russia was, but that you had to go around the world to get there. I didn't want her to buy me clothes but she insisted, saying it would give her a great deal of pleasure. "So that foreigners don't think you're dying of hunger," she said, "and so at least they see you have a second change of clothing." Later on, I found out that every day she was going all the way to the Cathedral to pray for me, crying in front of the Savior of the World, asking him to bring me luck on my long journey and to bring me back home, safe and sound. Four days before our departure, she died. Her heart disease became aggravated by a cerebral infection. Doctor Dionisio Merlos was taking care of her, but all his efforts were in vain. I received the painful news while I was doing propaganda work, defending the rights of the street vendors to organize and have freedom of movement. At the time, they were the favorite targets of the Municipal Police. The news tore me to pieces, I couldn't keep from shaking. Nothing consoled me, and the truth of the matter is I started the trip out of a sheer sense of commitment and duty, combined with a certain inertia and a feeling of being overwhelmed by

174

everything. I'd felt that way one other time in my life, when I lost my first wife. When I lost her for good. My mother not only gave birth to me, she was also very important to my development, to my life as a revolutionary.

At last Modesto Ramírez and I left for Guatemala with the aim of boarding a ship in Puerto Barrios for Europe. In spite of my deep remorse, I remember being really moved by Guatemala's beauty – its mountains, jungles, its rivers filled with leaping fish. And for the first time I realized there were countries more beautiful than my own, and not just because of economic development, since in Guatemala, too, everybody goes around flat broke, but because of its natural beauty, its atmosphere. We spent hardly any time in the capital and other cities except for what was necessary, eating and sleeping. In Puerto Barrios we made some contacts with the organized workers' movement there, and we had the opportunity to exchange experiences and chat for a while – in the strictest secrecy, of course, so the police wouldn't discover us and prevent our departure. I had never seen the ocean. And I had only seen ships in the movies. The only water I knew was my lake back in Ilopango where, despite the misery and harshness of life, I felt like I was king. On the other hand, the immensity of the ocean and the huge ships frightened me, since they made me feel small and powerless. We boarded a German ship, the "Rugia," that was bigger than a building or a whole block of houses. Amidst so many conflicting feelings and thoughts, the huge responsibility that was going to fall on our shoulders at the gathering of the international proletariat, at which we would speak, started to get the better of us. At first sight our mission was simple and concrete enough: to inform the workers' organizations all over the world of the accomplishments of the Salvadoran workers' movement, to collect first-hand the experiences of the international proletariat and to return to El Salvador with that wealth of knowledge. But in practice I felt totally out of place and I was sometimes afraid of how the ideas of poor peasants from such a tiny country would stack up against those of the leaders of the international workers' movement.

175

In the hotel we stayed at in Puerto Barrios, which was only called a hotel since in reality it was a disgusting nest of cockroaches, we met up with a Danish man – a fat, likeable guy, who was a salesman of wholesale eyeglasses, and we ended up becoming friends with him in the way fellow passengers do. Once on board the "Rugia," he invited us to have a few beers with him in the ship's restaurant, and I got so wrapped up talking away that I didn't even realize we'd left port, despite the ship's whistle and the bustle of passengers and the crew. When we went out onto the deck, we were already far out to sea and there was no land anywhere in sight. I was absolutely awestruck by the ocean and the sight of so much water made me feel truly euphoric. Everywhere you looked, in every direction, the ocean touched the firmament. Our Danish friend was explaining to us the technical details of how the ship functioned, since he knew a lot about engines and, moreover, had been himself a sailor for some time. He spoke Spanish as though he was gargling, but we understood it all. Also, you could see he was a good salesman as he had a wonderful gift for gab. After we left El Salvador, and having guidelines from the Party, Modesto and I laid down a strict rule not to get involved in political discussions with anyone, in order to avoid any mishap. Government undercover cops, fascist agents and active reactionaries were going around everywhere looking for whoever they could put the screws to, so you had to be suspicious of everyone. Therefore, with our Danish friend, we only talked about machinery, eyeglasses, microscopes and dumb things like that, all the while putting on those wide-eyed faces of interest that would make you die laughing. However, interest in world affairs, in the big political events of that period were bound to come up at any moment, especially on a voyage where so many people live together in boredom for so many days. And sure enough that's what happened. At the table where Modesto and I ate, there were also two Italian gentlemen and a Mexican who clearly felt contempt for us, laughing under their breath at us poor people from a poor country, who even from a distance smelled like filthy poor workers and peasants. The fact is you can take

176

the man out of the country but you can't take the country out of the man. I just ignored those guys, played dumb and told myself deep down that in the end we two poor, lousy Salvadorans were going to a destination much farther than them. But things weren't left at that. They were looking to talk with us, but only to bust our balls and make fun of us. Passing by the port of Corinto on the Nicaraguan coast, the Mexican asked us in a mocking tone of voice – even though we told him so several times – if we were Salvadorans. After we again said yes, we were Salvadorans, he asked us about General Sandino, about what the Salvadoran people thought of him. Since I felt pissed-off, I really wanted to answer him with something that would piss him off: I told him that we workers in Central America had supported the just struggle of General Sandino against the Yankee invaders, but that right now we were deeply outraged by the meeting the Nicaraguan guerrilla leader had had with the Mexican President, Calles. "And why so angry?" the Mexican asked me. "Because President Calles," I answered, "is nothing but a puppet and watchdog of Yankee imperialism." The man became instantly furious, and I got ready in case he started swinging. He shouted at me to prove it immediately. Then I, who by that time had a lot of facts and figures at my fingertips from all the international propaganda we'd received, came down on him like an avalanche: "It's as clear as day," I said. "What is the basis of the Mexican economy? Who owns the banks, the oil industry, the railroads, mines, electric companies, communications? Tell me, if you'd be so kind . . ." His Italian friends didn't participate directly in the argument, but they started to make fun of him since I'd stuck it to him good. "The Salvadoran has set you up for the kill," they said, laughing. And the Mexican, who had no place to turn, could only end up saying, "It's because you're a communist, that's what's going on." "You're calling the facts by strange names, señor," I said, "but it's just that in El Salvador there are daily newspapers and, if you know how to read, you learn something in spite of all the lies. I didn't know Calles had banned newspapers in Mexico, but since you don't know what kind of country you live in, it proves it to me, I'm sorry." From

177

then on he changed his mocking air with us and became more friendly, and we were able to kill time with small talk. Actually he wasn't a bad guy, just a ball-buster. On arriving in Puerto Límon, we had a friendly chat over a couple of beers. And when we said goodbye to one another in Cartagena de Indias – such a beautiful Colombian port – he was very warm, and when I told him that I was going to Berlin to get treatment for a serious nervous disorder, he hugged me affectionately and said: "I hope you get well quickly in Berlin and are able to continue on farther, perhaps to Moscow." And with both hands holding my head, he added: "This little head of yours should be filled with new knowledge." The Mexican and his Italian friends were going to Colombia to recover the body of a pilot who had perished in a famous accident, a pioneer of interamerican aviation who drifted off course over Colombia and whose name I can't remember right now. It was something like César or Císar.

In Cartagena I noticed a new passenger boarding the ship: a young, dark man with curly hair, rather intense looking and a bit nervous and who gave me the impression of being an intellectual. I discreetly managed to find out that he was from Ecuador and that his name was Quevedo. I'm not sure why he caught my eye and why I wanted to approach him to talk. That very night on deck we struck up a conversation. I asked him what he thought about the Chaco border war and immediately the language I'd been hoping for came out of his mouth like a bright ray of sunlight. He talked with me about monopolies, British imperialism, chauvinism and things along those lines, and I also unpacked my little bag of expressions. Finally, we introduced ourselves and embraced one another. He was a law student and was also going to Moscow, on behalf of the Ecuadoran communist movement. I felt glad and fortunate at having crossed paths so early in the trip with another brother moved by our cause.

Naturally the ship was carrying all sorts of passengers. People of many different nationalities and beliefs. I remember there was a group of Czechs who spoke Spanish, a whole clan of rather disheveled Palestinians, some friendly Guatemalan señoras who were going to Europe for a vacation – a very rare thing to do at that time since you had to be rich even to go to Mexico. Also travelling with us was a German (that is, German by birth, not a German shithead) brewery engineer, who was returning home after building the "Polar" brewery in San Salvador. There was another young German (and this one turned out to be a shithead) who, in order to fight the boredom, organized daily discussions on every possible subject in which all the passengers were invited to participate, either as listeners or as improvised speakers. As for me, I was asked to give a talk on social and workers' issues – I guess I looked the part. Partly because I was a ham and partly because I was obsessed with speaking, I accepted the invitation and gave a talk on the problems that afflicted the world of workers in those days: the worldwide economic crisis, unemployment, forced emigration, repression by the government bosses, etc I even referred to the intense struggles that the German working class was developing, and the German guy who organized the discussions and who was a patron of the German bourgeoisie violently disagreed with me, shouting that if I thought that the German workers were exploited and victimized by the bourgeois regime I shouldn't go to Germany. I told him that I was lucky to have some money and I was simply going to get medical attention. "You're a typical example of the average man from the tropics," he started yelling, "a narrow-minded idiot who goes to Europe for his health but who at the same time feels free to bad-mouth it." I didn't get angry, I just told him that more sickness abounds in exploited societies, but that those who are to blame for the sickness of our peoples and societies were the bosses of international capitalism, where the imperialist German bourgeoisie figured very prominently. We stopped before it got really ugly, but the guy probably ran his mouth off to the German crew members that I was anti-German – because that night the sailors started to get on Modesto's and my nerves. When we went walking on deck, they would make like they were beating tom-toms and howling as if to say they considered us savage Indians. One day I got really pissed-off and was all set to take on

179

a group of Germans who were washing the floors and who even stopped working for a while to throw wisecracks at us, but a Czech passenger held me back and calmed me down. "The whole problem is that someone had told them you're Japanese," he explained to me, "and it turns out that there was a Japanese spy disguised as a Chinese cook working on this ship, which during the last world war was a warship, and it seems he left the Germans with some very bad memories." It wasn't going to be the last time someone would think I was Japanese, but I didn't find that particular occasion amusing in the least. I started to feel like I wanted the days to fly by so I could get out of there as soon as possible, as the whole atmosphere on the ship made me feel tense and powerless. Just as a curious bit of information I'd like to add here that the times I felt best were during the storms. Unlike the rest of the passengers, storms didn't make me run to my cabin, because after all I was a boy who grew up on the lake, a man of the water, and nothing ever made me seasick. The rest, on the other hand, even the sailors, were throwing up their guts from the rolling motion caused by the huge squalls.

Slowly but surely we were getting closer to Europe. The ships of that time were as slow as turtles. We passed by the Azores, and we were able to visit Plymouth and some other port I don't remember. Finally, one overcast, cold and damp morning we put in to Hamburg. Quevedo, the Ecuadoran, was able to help us out a lot since he spoke pretty good English, but even so, since no one was waiting there to meet us, we started to have some difficulties. A black man who sold sweets at the harbor and who spoke English was able to understand Quevedo, and he agreed to be our guide until we found a cheap hotel where we could drop our things and continue looking for our contacts without interruption. But all the crummy hotels were too expensive for us, since we hadn't come to Europe just for a short stay. Finally, the black man took us to a sailor's club that, even though it had a red flag hanging over its door that filled us with high hopes, was full of drunks who were shouting and singing until they couldn't any longer. Nobody paid any attention to us in there, no one could understand us because nobody spoke English much less Spanish. But meanwhile, we began to serve ourselves big pitchers of beer with gin and rum that many of the drunken sailors gave us. It occurred to someone to go look for the young sailor who understood Spanish because he had travelled throughout the Carribean and South America, and who also turned out to be a communist. Two birds with one stone. From then on everything worked out all right. That comrade got in touch with the Party and a few minutes later a comrade named Walter, who was a representative of the Party in the German legislature, arrived to pick us up. After welcoming us on behalf of the German proletariat, he told us why he wasn't waiting for us at the port, since our message hadn't arrived, and then he drove us to a hotel that they'd already reserved for us. It was a modest hotel, but very nice, decorated with photographs of Marx and Lenin. There they gave us 44 marks apiece for pocket money and for which we signed a receipt. In the lobby we met other Latin American delegates to the Congress of the PROFINTERN, who had already arrived or were just arriving. Comrades from Brazil, Argentina (a peasant by the name of Díaz), Uruguay (comrade Suárez). Also a Soviet comrade whose name was Irma and who was going to be our interpreter or *perivochi*, as the Soviets say, came to greet us. She was married to a Mexican and had lived in Guadalajara for several years, so we understood one another right from the first. She said that in her heart and in her ways she'd always be someone from Leningrad, but the truth was she had found life in Mexico very much to her liking.

As a first collective step, all of us who spoke Spanish decided to organize ourselves in order to deal with the everyday problems of life. My fellow comrade, Modesto Ramírez, was named head of the cooking; the Ecuadoran, Quevedo, was in charge of doing the shopping, and the money was in my hands. During the following days, Quevedo and I went and did the shopping.—.we bought sausage, eggs, ham, milk and chocolate. The workers in the shops and markets were very friendly and generous, and they did us many favors. One

181

night, the communist sailor who'd put us in touch with comrade Walter came to take me out to the cafés and cabarets in Hamburg – which turned out to be a completely new experience for me. I'd only seen cabarets in the movies. I really enjoyed all the different types of bands, we put away plenty of beer and I got pretty high. That sailor comrade had a lot of women friends and we danced with them until very late, so late in fact that when I got back to the hotel the concierge – a nice, little old lady – pulled at my ears in fun, joking around, and said in German, "carouser," according to what the sailor translated. The next day Irma, the Soviet interpreter, together with her little daughter, came by to take me to see the churches in the city. I said okay simply for the education, since nothing about churches interested me, but once there I was really impressed and I was glad I'd decided to go, since we saw such imposing cathedrals never imagined by me back in El Salvador. After leaving one of these churches, we walked down a street filled with whores and just like they did with every man who passes by, they grabbed me by my arm and pulled me towards their rooms, and only by pure luck was I able to escape. My Soviet comrade cried, horrified by it all, and I thought to myself: "Strange, here the prostitutes hang out near the churches – since I didn't see any in the cafés and cabarets last night." Although to tell you the truth one never knows about such matters. Perhaps it was because the street prostitutes were poorer and looked more like those in my own country, while those in the cabarets looked like the wives of the rich in El Salvador, only less provincial.

On the first of August, if I'm not mistaken, a very large workers' demonstration took place in Hamburg on the occasion of International Anti-Imperialist Day, in which contingents from every guild and trade union in the city participated. Together with the local labor leaders, we marched at the head of the procession as representatives of Latin American workers. Crowds of people lined up all along our parade route, shouting, "Rot Front" ("red front," I think). Then suddenly mounted police turned up, blocking our way, and they arrested one of the top

182

leaders of the German workers, but the militant response by the masses prevented them from going any further, so they had to let him go and the demonstration proceeded. Then we held a rally in a big square. There, speakers raised in general terms the same demands against unemployment and misery that we were accustomed to raising in El Salvador. Suárez, the Uruguayan, spoke on behalf of the Latin Americans, communicating among other things our admiration for the level of organization of the German working class, and he stated that with that kind of organization in Uruguay we would have already seized power. He also put his foot in his mouth – needlessly, I must say, since we were guests in a foreign country – when he told the German workers that they lacked the enthusiasm and high spirits of Latin American workers in their demonstrations. That is, in one single blow he called the German workers cowards. Comrade Suárez was merely caught up in his revolutionary fervor and he didn't mean any harm. The next day the reactionary press in Hamburg launched an attack against the foreign agitators and it was clear that what deep down had been most offensive were the comments by comrade Suárez.

The time finally arrived to continue our journey. We all agreed not to go through Poland because you had to go by train and, with conditions at the border being what they were, our final destination would've become known and they might have detained us. So we left Germany secretly on board a Soviet freighter, since it was impossible to get a German exit visa to go to the U.S.S.R. In a closed van they took all of us delegates who were in Hamburg to the ship and put us right down into the ship's hold, where we stayed until it was on the high seas. Then a sergeant in the Soviet navy came and led us to the dining hall, communicating to us, through Irma, that in a few minutes we would be officially welcomed. It was the captain of the ship who welcomed us on behalf of the people and Government of the Soviet Union. He was just a young kid, flush in the face and very friendly. They served lunch which was neither great nor lousy, just average, and then they assigned us cabins so we could rest. They weren't fancy but they were

183

better than the cabins on the "Rugia." That night, after dinner, they invited us to a play performed by the crew members themselves. Those comrades, men and women who'd served us dinner and who took care of washing the linens, making up our rooms, etc., played their parts with grace and a natural ease. And the play had great revolutionary content. On another one of those nights we had the opportunity to attend a maritime union meeting. The leaders were the stokers and other workers and communist sailors, and the captain and officers had to sit with the masses on the benches in the back. The Union Committee and the Party cell had political power on the ship, while the captain and officers were only in technical control. Modesto and I and all the rest of the comrades were really moved by these things, since we were well aware (and the experience on the "Rugia" proved it to us "lousy Salvadorans") that on capitalist ships the situation is totally different and hierarchies of exploitation set up definite divisions. On the "Rugia," even the most exploited sailors considered them-selves superior to us, and the captain only showed his whiskers in the dining room for the first-class passengers, and even that was only every now and then. That different relationship among the crew members on the ship that carried us secretly out of Germany was the sign that we'd arrived in the Soviet Union, to the first socialist revolution in human history.

We arrived in Leningrad uneventfully. When we entered the port, to our great surprise, a flotilla of red submarines that had been escorting us on the high seas surfaced. We were so anxious it was incredible. During the quick voyage across Europe, we had the opportunity to see a number of large, exciting and lively ports with all the social contrasts one could want, but generally speaking they were very attractive. When we disembarked in Leningrad, however, the widespread, overall poverty really struck us. Leningrad looked like it was a totally neglected city, with buildings either destroyed or under construction, barren or muddy parks despite the fact that it was the middle of summer, filthy and deserted streets, monuments all twisted up, the people all dirty, etc. And on the piers you saw

184

lots of men, women, children and old people casting their fishing lines into the water and waiting endlessly for the fish to bite. They brought us to the "Hotel English," very close to the enormous church of St. Isaac, which is one of the most beautiful I've seen in my whole damn life. The hotel itself was neglected enough to have a half-somber aspect that would have depressed anyone on the spot. Of course, none of us said anything to the Soviet comrades who'd come to greet us; we just looked at one another with long faces. And we were hoping that something good would happen soon, just to lift our spirits. We ate a little something at the hotel and then we divided up into groups in order to take in the city. As if it was yesterday, I remember that the first good impression I had of the whole place was the sight of a very lively circle of civilians and soldiers who were playing the accordian and a guitar and were dancing and singing all together. It was a very simple thing but very meaningful for me. The day the authorities and the people fraternize like that in my country something drastic would've had to have happened and would have to go on happening. We walked all over the huge city, and Modesto and I ended up getting lost in one of the neighborhoods. The weather was hot and the nights lasted only a few hours, no more than four or five. We came to a place where there were many people going in and out, and we thought we'd be able to get something to eat there. But it turned out to be a peoples' theatre. The people realized right away that we were foreigners and just like that we were surrounded by a large group who, I guess, were asking where we were from. We showed them our PROFINTERN credentials and got them to understand that we were hungry. The word "restaurante" is understood in Russian. They didn't take us anywhere, but right there people pulled out of their bags black bread and sausage, onions and cucumbers, and they fixed us a couple of huge sandwiches. They even gave us tea right there in the middle of the street. Then they took us into the theatre and we saw the play without understanding beans about it, although it was something about smashing capitalism and making world revolution. When that was over, a bunch of

185

citizens accompanied us back to the hotel and on the way they toasted us with several swigs of vodka from a flask one of them was carrying over his shoulder. When we joined all the rest of the Latin Americans, each one had their own story to tell. On the following day we again took in the city, only now in a more organized way, all the delegates going together with interpreters. We could see work being done building and rebuilding the city and cleaning up the streets, but the shortage of asphalt and cement in many of the zones with dirt roads caused the city to be swamped in mud with the least bit of rain. Plus the people weren't disciplined not to throw garbage away just anywhere. It was very strange for us to see only women working on the scaffoldings and operating the cleaning equipment, but also I have to say it was the women who operated the transits and other precision instruments. Comrade Suárez, as always, asked why the women were working, and they themselves answered through interpreters that in the first place because of tradition, and in the second because the men were working on matters of major importance on the production front. Suárez persisted and said that he wanted to know why all the women were working so slowly, and to give an example he asked for a pickax and demonstrated the rhythm that he thought they ought to be working at. They all burst out laughing and said that that pace was proper to the times of the Czars and that now they weren't slaves and they were doing what they were capable of doing.

All the delegates wrote letters home to our Parties, trade union movements, comrades and friends, telling them about our first impressions of the U.S.S.R. Comrade Suárez asked that we let him read the letters as a kind of fraternal supervision. Fact is, I didn't like that one bit and I thought by then that Suárez was full of shit. But so as not to make a big fuss, I agreed and handed over my letter. Suárez became infuriated with the general disillusionment expressed in the letters, but he hugged me in front of everybody since I didn't interpret pessimistically what we'd seen, and in my letter I gave a viewpoint with a future perspective. I had the advantage of having the Soviet Union's figures on economic development at my fingertips, which I got from all the Soviet propaganda that we received in El Salvador, and I knew that behind the picture of apparent poverty there was a positive reality, though still hard and difficult, typical of a country going through a prolonged period of birth. I mailed my letter directly from the U.S.S.R. to El Salvador, positive that the Party would criticize me afterwards for doing that, but it and my later letters got there with no problem.

One day, without any notice, they moved us from our hotel. They transferred us to a very fancy hotel, exclusively for foreign diplomats and high-ranking engineers contracted by the Soviet government to help in the socialist construction. All of these people were arrogant, boring, and they acted – every single one of them – as though they were doing the world proletariat a big favor. The wives of the engineers seemed really irritated by our presence and showed obvious disdain for us, and I felt like I was back on board the "Rugia," although I realized we had simply fallen onto an island of capitalism in the middle of a socialist ocean. You just had to pretend you didn't notice and make yourself swallow it. Fortunately, we were only there two days and then we left by train for Moscow.

Immediately on arriving in the Soviet capital, we went to the offices of the PROFINTERN (World Red Trade Union) to receive our permanent credentials as delegates to the Congress, on presentation of the mandates that verified us as representatives of the working class of our respective countries. At the PROFINTERN headquarters I had a big surprise when, on passing by a room, some guys called out: "There's Miguel Mármol." They were two comrades from Guatemala whom I'd met when they visited our country and for whom we had much affection: Antonio Ovando Sánchez, a carpenter, and Luis Chigüichón, a baker. After authorizing us, the Soviet comrades invited us to a big luncheon in the dining hall of the Palace in which the PROFINTERN was located and which was absolutely luxurious, to such a degree that it had been one of the favorite places of the Czars. I said to Ovando Sánchez that back in our own countries we wouldn't have been able to go into a palace like this without first getting washed up and perfumed. At the luncheon I could see that the reputation the Soviet comrades had in the art of downing shots and not getting drunk was true, because when we were already seeing double from so much vodka, they seemed to be just warming up their engines. We spent the following days routinely, waiting for the opening of the Congress, and we were able to well-acquaint ourselves with the city and do some sightseeing. We went to the opera, the ballet and the circus, which was what I liked most, especially because of the trained animals. The ballet has never really excited me and the Soviet ballet dancers, in spite of everything and though they're Soviets, don't change my mind. For me, to be a ballet dancer means being effeminate and when they come out on stage leaping, shaking their firm little asses, it makes me want to shout out something obscene. I enjoyed the Russian opera a lot, though, because it's louder, less refined than the Italian opera and those that reach us in San Salvador. Those choruses of Cossacks and Boyars sound like a thundering storm. Afterwards, we began to hold preliminary informational meetings in order to familiarize ourselves little by little with the topics that were going to be discussed in the important international gathering. I decided not to miss even one meeting despite that fact that other comrades were going out with the Soviet girls and they were inviting me to do the same, and they were even going around spending their time drinking and partying it up. My conduct earned me the esteem of some delegations. I particularly remember that the Argentine anarchists present at the Congress publicly congratulated me for my responsible behavior.

Since they gave us 16 rubles every four days and we didn't have any major expenses, a few of us wanted to save the money to spend on things our comrades back home could use: for example, a typewriter, a camera or something along those lines. However, on learning of such plans, comrade Suárez, because of his political awareness and training (and also his presumptuousness, let's be frank), took it upon himself to be something like a self-appointed leader of all of us Latin

188

Americans. He called us all together and criticized us harshly, accusing us of having gone so far as to accumulate money in no less than a socialist country, and he even went so far as to demand that we let him check what we had in our pockets. Starting out from a correct position, comrade Suárez always ended up taking things too far, completely missing the point. We explained to him that we wanted the money for a typewriter which would then be used in the revolutionary work back in our own countries and that it wasn't a matter of anyone's personal business nor profit. But we were unable to persuade the majority who were really impressed with Suárez's fiery speech and even the Secretary General of the CSLA, Miguel Contreras, who was present at the discussion, raised the watchword that we had to spend all the money that came into our hands. So then, being the disciplined comrades that we were, we started to spend our stipends on vodka, wine, sweets, fruits. Among those who were present at that discussion, which turned into a political meeting against saving money, I remember comrade Valdez, from Honduras; a black Panamanian whose name escapes me; comrades Sastre and Piedrahita from Colombia, and others. We decided to regularize these meetings of Latin Americans throughout our stay in the U.S.S.R., in order to deal together with all the different kinds of common problems that might come up, and we began to function as one organized group. In these meetings, the problem of a generally negative attitude on the part of the delegates caused by the miserable conditions in the two Soviet cities we had visited would come up all the time. Because of this, even comrade Lossovsky himself, who was the top leader of international trade unionism at that time, had to continually come and provide us with relevant explanations. "A certain Filipino comrade," Lossovsky told us on one occasion, "was of the opinion that it was disturbing to see that they still use animal driven carts and carriages for transportation, when in the Philippines, a very backward country, the means of transportation are modern and efficient. I asked the Filipino comrade," Lossovsky added, "if these carts in Moscow belong to the Soviet working class or to imperialism, and if in the Philippines their modern means of transport are owned by the Filipino working class or by foreign imperialism." I thought then that although Lossovsky's argument was correct and pointed out a fundamental difference, it would have been better to have publicly accepted the backwardness of their means of transportation and other aspects of Soviet life in 1930, problems characteristic of a blockaded country which was inaugurating a new world under tremendous disadvantages, all things about which the Soviet leadership didn't have any reason to be ashamed or embarrassed. Because by taking the position that what's ours is good because it's ours, even if that sounds like pure nonsense, you can go a long way. "A couple of Latin Americans for their part," Lossovsky told us on another occasion, "talk a lot about the fancy display cases in Europe in which the eggs are beautifully packaged in colored cotton, and they add that here in Russia there's nothing in the display windows. I invite you to see with your own eyes the factory movement and to do your shopping in the cooperative stores." No sooner said than done. We went first to the factories: this was an endless line of heavy machinery that arrived day and night to be installed and put into production. Something that by itself spoke for the dynamism and perspective of the Soviet Union. We went next to the cooperatives and we couldn't buy anything due to the long lines of people trying to purchase clothes, shoes, gloves, fabric, canned goods, records and books, household items. Since we put off going shopping until the nighttime hours, when they told us there'd be less people in line, we lost out completely because by then there was nothing left to buy, everything had already been bought up. Lossovsky explained that in Europe the people didn't have money to buy things, that they had no purchasing power, and that's why the bourgeoisie felt it had to stimulate spending through advertising and marketing, having to invest huge sums of money for that purpose, sums that also came from the exploitation of workers. On the other hand, in the Soviet Union the people had money and bought up so much that production in many instances

190

wasn't keeping up with the demand. Comrade Lossovsky was very precise in his facts and he helped all of us to see more profoundly through the thicket of problems facing the construction of socialism. Another piece of advice that the Soviet leader gave us was to not pay attention to the women who came over and propositioned us, since in general the prostitutes who remained in the U.S.S.R. were people who collaborated with the enemy, spies, and they could be used to find out our whereabouts and obtain information about us. The internal and external enemy was watching our every step. From then on, all the comrades who'd been going out carousing around did a complete reverse. The fact is, Lossovsky had our deep respect, he was nearly idealized by all of us. Back in our own countries, we had all learned a great deal, even before we got to know him, from his pamphlet on trade union questions, and we all appreciated the value of his theoretical help in the building of our movements and organizations.

In the following days, formal lectures were organized on different, interesting aspects of Soviet life and economy, given by experts in their fields. For example, for us shoemakers a leading worker in that trade gave the history of the footwear industry in Russia and in the U.S.S.R. In the last stages of Czarism there were 23 thousand shoemakers working in more than 400 shops, with an annual production of 7 million pairs of shoes. The bourgeoisie wore custom-made shoes imported from France, Italy or Austria-Hungary, but there were 193 million people walking around barefoot. And you should understand that in the brutal Russian winter that meant life and death for many people. The Russian shoemakers guild was traditionally revolutionary and its members had participated brilliantly in the insurrectional struggles. For which it paid a high price: its ranks were wiped out, either murdered, tortured or forced to flee the repression. That situation in the guild, together with the post-revolutionary crisis in general, caused even the lousy production of 7 million shoes to fall off drastically. It wasn't until 1924, seven years after seizing power, that production leveled off at the old seven million figure. That year the First Congress of Soviet Shoemakers took place, which approved a new production plan as preparatory to joining in the Five Year Plan of the U.S.S.R. It planned for growth in all areas of production down to the last detail: for so many millions of shoes, so many knives; and so many oxen that would need so many bales of fodder; so much wood for so many shoe molds; so many millions of yards of fabric for linings, etc. The whole basis of the Five Year Plan was set up from preparatory plans such as this one, where an increase in one branch of production requires an increase in all the rest. The results of all this planning were successful, the proof of which was that at the moment we were receiving this information shoe production had increased to 127 million pairs of shoes annually. Nevertheless, given the enormous population of the U.S.S.R. millions still were going barefoot.

Labor leaders from other countries also spoke to us about their struggles. I especially remember what the Italian union leader, comrade Giermanetto, told us about the underground workers' movement against Mussolini. Every one of his answers to our questions was truly a remarkable lecture. The Soviet comrades also answered our very wide-ranging questions in a similar way. It was obvious that they wanted us to return to our countries with the most complete view possible of the U.S.S.R. Well, why were there so many drunks in the U.S.S.R.? What happened was that alcoholism had been a traditional evil in the country, rooted in the people for generations. After seizing power, and against the will of Lenin, a tough Dry Law was enacted which proved to be counterproductive because the only thing it did was increase the rate of clandestine drinking. And, curiously enough, the clergy and other reactionary forces exploited the resentment of the drinkers to their advantage. Afterwards, the Dry Law was abolished and work against alcoholism began among the masses on a medical and cultural basis, and by using drinking substitutes, which were proving effective. All this work was the responsiblity of the Party organizations, the trade unions and the mass organizations.

192

With regard to the living conditions in the U.S.S.R. at that time, I remember the following things: there was rationing of consumer goods and the meals were very modest for the normal adult. You could eat meat and drink milk 5 days a month. The children, elderly and sick had meat and milk every day. But the most important thing was the great spirit and understanding with which the people endured those hardships. Everybody knew the deeper causes for these difficulties and the reasons why they had to bear up and overcome them. From the leaders of the masses down to the school children, they were fully aware of all the problems, all the tasks of socialist construction, all the difficulties and perspectives, because the Soviet Government told the people the exact truth and didn't deceive them with false promises or with dreams far removed from reality, as politicians in the bourgeois state do. Even the youth of today in the U.S.S.R. are not as informed about their country as those I met in 1930. This explained why the people were so united in resolving their problems and lashed out with everything they had against the saboteurs and the enemy. The class struggle was still sharp. The clergy was conspiring against the Revolution and urging sabotage. The Kulaks were killing off the livestock and poisoning the public drinking places. But they all had to watch their step because the people were standing vigilant over their victories. The struggle was even reflected in the type of money used. We delegates received pocket money in the form of bills and everything was okay until we needed to make change, in centavos or kopeks, as they're called there. Since the reactionaries were trafficking in nickel coins which they smuggled into China and Japan, there were practically no coins left in circulation. The return for the bills, the change received, was given by noting down the amount on little pieces of stamped paper. These couldn't be used for the purposes of the reactionaries, but naturally they caused a lot of trouble for petty commerce. That business of waiting in lines was a big pain in the ass, and I personally was driven crazy by it. The Soviet comrades explained to us that controls were necessary and therefore commercial transactions had to take longer than usual, which accounted for the lines. Before controls were established, the reactionaries exploited the people for profit and promoted scarcity. Before controls it was common for the reactionaries to buy up huge quantities of bread and then throw it away or feed it to the pigs. One day we attended – all the delegates to the Congress – a gigantic rally where Marshal Budionney was the main speaker. The great military officer gave a brilliant speech, pointing out various weaknesses in the industrial organization and specifically calling attention to the gaps that still existed in the consciousness of the workers as they faced the sacrifices that the needs of production imposed on them. There were workers, for example, who left their factories in order to find better salaries in other sectors, and thus jeopardized the factory program which depended on its workforce. Budionney conferred on the Young Communist League a large role in the solution of all these problems. Similarly, he lashed out against the saboteurs, by then public enemy number one, especially those saboteurs who destroyed the workers' food supply and the machinery. In that revolutionary vigilance, even the Pioneer children had their role as the eyes of the Party. Indeed, a few days later a large network of saboteurs was uncovered, some of whose leaders were shot with the unanimous approval of the people.

The Congress was a big success. The main moderator was comrade Lossovsky. But there was also a co-moderator, the representative of red trade unionism in China, who informed us about the situation and needs of the workers' movement in the colonial, semi-colonial and dependent countries.

The Congress reflected the broad range of international trade union experience, and I have to say that this made for an atmosphere of criticism/self-criticism such as I've experienced in few of the political congresses I've attended in my life. I gave a report on El Salvador to the world working class represented there. Our report dealt with the existing forms of exploitation in the country, our organizing efforts among the working class and

194

peasantry and their revolutionary struggles, and it was amply substantiated with facts, with details extracted from everyday life. I remember that the exposé on the living conditions that the peons and peasants on the Cangrejera plantation, property of the Guirola family, had to put up with caused a deep impression. The men worked from dawn to dusk for a daily wage of 37 centavos on the colon (15 centavos on the dollar), half-naked and getting only one ration of corn tortillas and a few beans a day, which was exactly the same food they gave to the pigs. The report was generally received with great enthusiasm and interest, and for several days afterwards I was asked many questions by the delegates of many countries and consulted about the Salvadoran experience.

Within the Congress itself, two formal meetings of Latin American red trade unionists were organized. The first meeting dealt exclusively with the problems of organizing in the countryside. There was a long discussion, for example, on whether tenant farmers and poor peasants joining the agricultural unions would benefit the Revolution. The line that won out was the one that would restrict the agricultural unions exclusively to agricultural proletarians. The tenant farmers, poor peasants, etc. could carry out their struggle through other organizations such as the cooperatives, etc., and the unions should continue to be in the countryside what they are or tried to be in the cities: solid nucleuses of the working class. This question had been clear to us from the start, based on our rural organizing experience in El Salvador, and that it was the line that won out in that meeting filled us with pride. It meant we weren't walking on thin ice, nor sowing the sand. Also a lot of effort was spent on leaving clearly established for everyone the basic structures which the Red Trade Union was using at that time to meet head-on the nature of class composition in the countryside and its accompanying economic conditions. The second meeting of Latin Americans concerned itself with political points: the character of revolution in our countries (which were counted among the group called "colonial, semicolonial, dependent," since terms like "underdeveloped countries" or "The Third World" weren't coined yet), legal or illegal forms of organizing, the forms of struggle (armed or peaceful) and their appropriate combination, etc. Comrade Manuilsky, the great Soviet cadre of the International and the Red Aid, was asked by us to clear up some of the theoretical aspects of those discussions that had us baffled for a long time. There was, however, unanimous agreement on the part of our delegations on the most fundamental problems, such as for example the character that the revolution should take in Latin America. We all recognized that the kind of revolution that was imperative at that time was the bourgeois-democratic revolution. However, when I recall the events of 1932 in El Salvador, I realize that we still grasped revolutionary concepts as simple fetishes or images, as abstract entities independent of reality, and not as real guides to practical action. In 1932, we made a communist insurrection in order to struggle for a bourgeois-democratic program, we established soviets in some parts of the country, but in their content they were but municipal bodies of bourgeois origin. Well, we paid dearly for not comprehending the practical applications of those concepts!

In the meeting in Moscow, we even went so far as to formulate a concrete program for the bourgeois-democratic revolution in Latin America: confiscation of lands stolen by the governments, confiscation of lands usurped by the *latifundistas* and its redistribution among the peasants, nationalization of foreign companies, socialization of the properties where unions capable of maintaining an effective administration existed, nationalization of the banks, stimulation of industrial development, etc. Our contribution to the Congress and our reports on our experiences in the meetings of Latin Americans, which were able to provide valuable insights for the worldwide revolutionary workers' movement, gave us deep satisfaction. The treatment we received indicated our international prestige, gained in only a few years: the reputation of our mass movement was without doubt. At our request, the implementation of the thesis, according to which a small yet popular communist party with hegemony of leadership of the masses can start a

196

revolution – the struggle to take power in a direct way, taking into account at all times the objective conditions of each country – was accepted for Latin America. But it's clear that at that time we Salvadorans didn't possess a commanding grasp of the problems of revolutionary strategy and tactics, understood in a strict, scientific way. I think that would have been too much to ask of us. We were truly beginners, beginners in 1930, which isn't the same as being beginners in these modern times, now when there's so much experience within the grasp of revolutionary youth. Neither was our local enemy, the bourgeoisie of El Salvador, the enemy armed to the teeth that it is today. It wasn't disproportionately more powerful than those, such as us, who wanted to rock it to sleep and then smash it over the head. But it's also true that we didn't have the Marxist manuals that exist today, nor the contributions from today's international movement. Martí, Luna and Zapata, the three martyred intellectuals in 1932, read *Capital* in translations from the French, typewritten and even written out by hand. I also said that I read *Capital*. But how could I have possibly understood something like that? What we understood were the theoretical statements made at the level of propaganda and disclosure, the language of resolutions and congresses. That's why we Salvadorans fit right in at the World Congress of Red Trade Unions, which I've been describing here.

Once the sessions of the Congress were over, we went on an extensive trip through the interior of the Soviet countryside. Rostov, Tiflis, and Caucasia were places we stopped at along the way, which we got to by train, car, cart and even by horseback and on foot. The group I was with was mostly comprised of Latin Americans. The only representative from another region was a North American farmer, who spoke no more than a couple of words of Spanish. Within the group, we formed our own internal organization, adopting all kinds of security measures in case the enemy tried to follow our tracks. We even used pseudonyms. Mine was "Guerrero." Similarly, we organized a wall-newspaper which we wrote out completely by hand, called "Hard and Straight," full of criticisms and self-criticisms

197

and which we put up in easily visible places in the trucks we were travelling around in. Each one of the comrades had a responsibility: preparing meals every day, cleaning up the rooms or wherever we happened to be staying temporarily, etc. One fine morning the North American farmer criticized me and the Guatemalan comrade, Chigüichón, for shirking our job of preparing and portioning out the meals. He did it in a letter for "Hard and Straight," which was like an editorial. So we, to get even, started cooking and dishing out huge portions of food for everyone. But then they threw us out of that job for good, because they said we were wasting all the provisions.

One of the places that impressed me most during that trip was a coal mine called Chasplin, near Rostov. For us, workers from countries where there's so little industrial development, it was very enlightening to observe the rhythm of work of the Soviet workers. The work was hard, but equal to the effort required of them, the privileges that they and their families enjoyed were enormous. We fraternized and ate with the miners there. I remember that I stuffed myself on a whole bunch of fruit that made even our Mexican comrade Valentín Campa, who was along with us, start poking fun at me. Afterwards, we arrived in Tiflis, the capital of Georgia, land of comrade Stalin. There, the President of the Republic received us in his yellow palace. We organized an exhausting itinerary of places to visit: we wanted to see everything and the Soviets wanted to show us everything, so we barely got any sleep. On one of those days, I decided to lead a strike so we could rest for at least one day. We won: we slept for more than 20 hours and then we resumed the same exhausting pace. I also remember with fondness our arrival in Bakú, the great oil center. Representatives from the local soviet greeted us and the most striking thing about them was how shabbily they were dressed. Their clothes had patches on top of patches and their shoes were mere shreds. Together with them we placed a wreath of flowers at the tomb of the twenty-six people's representatives who were murdered by the reactionaries and by the troops of foreign imperialism in a famous revolutionary action that shook the world. It was a moving and militant act and we Latin Americans provided a hopeful note with our revolutionary songs: "Red Cavalry," "The International," "Children of the People," and the "Hymn of the Uruguayan Young Communist League."

After the trip we returned to Moscow by the military route from Tiflis. The problems of the long journey home to our own countries had to be raised. Comrade Manuilsky painted a pretty terrible picture of the situation: different police agents in Europe and in Latin America were just waiting to arrest us. In the case of some delegates and a few countries the danger was a matter of life and death. There had been many indiscretions due to our lack of experience in dealing with conspiracies and most of us delegates were known by the authorities. We were returning, as they say in El Salvador, "marked men." In light of these events, the Soviet comrades suggested I ought to stay in the U.S.S.R. for a long time and study, some four years, but I kindly rejected their offer and suggested instead that they should offer several scholarships to Salvadoran comrades in the trade union and revolutionary movements. My idea was immediately accepted and they set up four study scholarships for Salvadoran cadre. Actually, after only a couple of months, two of these scholarships were used. This is how Aquilino Martínez and José Centeno, both from the Young Communist League, went to study in the U.S.S.R. Aquilino Martínez, after finishing his studies, tried to return to El Salvador, but he was captured going through Berlin by the Nazis, who tortured him barbarously and gave him strange injections. Aquilino resisted their torture and didn't give those criminals any information. He even tried to get away by committing suicide: he jumped from the fourth floor when his executioners weren't watching. Finally, they sent him back to El Salvador as a criminal, but when he got there it was obvious he had gone mad and the Salvadoran government put him in an asylum. The other scholarship student, comrade Centeno, in light of Aquilino's ordeal, had to take a different route and he managed to get to Cuba, but given the reigning conditions in El Salvador at that time (1934) he had to stay in Havana. We never heard from him again.

199

We left the U.S.S.R. in November from the port of Leningrad, on board the Soviet freighter "Herzen." The weather was freezing. It was snowing and freezing raining and very depressing. We got off the ship in Kiel and that's where our troubles started. The harbor police had started to make very thorough searches, but we got the surprise of our lives when they searched Suárez and me. Because on opening Suárez's suitcase they found several hammer-and-sickle medals and they just looked at one another, smiled at us and then stamped our baggage "inspected." We went to Hamburg, Cologne, and Liege by train. In Liege, the Belgian police detained me because of my Japanese-looking features and they tried to interrogate me in Japanese. But finally it became clear that I was Latin American, and they released me. It seems that during that period Japanese spies were popping up everywhere. At last we arrived in Paris. Some Venezuelan women comrades, assigned by the Communist International to look after and protect us, were waiting at the station, since according to what they told us, enemy spy activity in Paris was intense. We lived hopping from one hotel to another to elude persecution by the French and International police, and we managed to pass ourselves off as Latin American singers, since those women comrades were walking around disguised as mandolin and guitar players. We were in Paris 26 days under these conditions. And despite our moving around so much, the International was in contact with us and managed to get us a daily newsletter filled with news that was of interest to us. It was through this newsletter that we found out that the ship on which our Brazilian comrades were going home was shelled en route. And about a Mexican comrade named González – the local authorities shot him as soon as he got back to his village. And all at once they fired all the representatives of the German workers from their jobs. One rather young Mexican comrade who was travelling with us became extremely worried and ended up going out of his mind. Comrade Machado, of the Venezuelan Communist Party, who was in Paris and had finished his medical studies, took care of him. As for me, the face of that insane comrade, poor wretch, remained forever engraved in my mind – so weak and pale, and with his jaundiced, bloodshot eyes. One must fear fear itself, I've always said. And personally, it is fear I dread the most: it makes one die before their time.

We Salvadorans were the last ones to leave Paris because of various problems, but mainly because the comrade who was representing the International there, comrade Hercle, who, by the way, was also representing the Soviet trade unions in France, gave us very little money for our trip back home and we had to go looking for the cheapest ship possible to return on. That was because the representative from Honduras, one Valdez, had stolen his delegation's trip money, leaving comrade Hercle holding the bag. As for me, it never would've crossed my mind that there could be thieves within the movement, but because of that experience I say it's better to be cautious because you wind up sounding stupid, saying: "That comrade is irreproachable, but, damn, the money sure is missing." The fact of the matter is that the world they say God made is like a crippled centipede, so say the little old ladies.

After many tries we located a French cargo ship, "The Magdalena," which was going to the Caribbean and taking on passengers in order to turn a profit, not leaving a single spot unoccupied. The staterooms for the passengers were terrible, but no way were we going to get back home swimming. To board the ship we went to Le Havre and waited for the ship to lift anchor. No hotels for us at night now, but sleeping in the parks and surviving on a diet of raw fruit and water and an occasional sweet. Around the docks we made friends with the other prospective passengers on "The Magdalena": small merchants, mostly Palestinian. In light of all this even the lousy cots and the awful food on ship were for us fit for kings. The crossing this time was more boring. The first stop we made was Tenerife, in the Canary Islands, and it was great for me to once again hear Spanish, despite the fact that the first words I heard were those of a Canary Island sailor who was working on a tugboat and who was yelling at our crew to throw him a line: "Jesus Christ, you fucking bastards are a pain in the ass." There we took on several

201

Spanish sailors to join the crew and among them was a socialist from Barcelona who quickly became friends with us. When we told him that we would probably get off in Cuba to try and catch another ship from Havana that would take us to Central America, this comrade warned us that the situation on the island was extremely grave from a political point of view, since Cuba was under Martial Law by the criminal dictator Gerardo Machado and the Cuban police didn't think twice about imprisoning, torturing or murdering revolutionaries, even if they were foreign citizens. We decided to take a series of urgent steps so that we wouldn't arrive in Havana like a bunch of jerks and fall right into the hands of the police. With Modesto Ramírez, we staged mock interrogations trying to cover every possibility that the police might use to trip us up. The sailor from Barcelona offered to carry a bunch of printed material I'd brought with me from the Congress off the ship, since the police didn't search the crew members due to the fact that they were all accomplices in smuggling contraband. But nevertheless, I also decided to make use of my overcoat, sewing my personal notes from the Congress and other very important papers into the lining. So we got ready to arrive in Cuba, with our anxiety mounting mostly from the slow, boring voyage during which, day after long day, we didn't see anything but the ocean. I'd exhausted my poetic enthusiasm for the ocean's immensity on the first crossing, and by now I just wanted to set fire to that mountain of waves.

Other sailors were saying wonderful things about Havana. They said it had the best whores in the world, and cheap; the best rum in the world and the best tobacco in the world. And they told the most incredible adventure stories that made me blush, though I've never been a holy saint. I wasn't interested too much in those siren songs. Imagine going around thinking about whores when in Havana one of the most corrupt and repressive police forces in Latin America was possibly waiting for me!

On arriving in Havana things happened very quickly. The ship anchored in the bay around six in the morning, but Machado's police didn't even let us have breakfast, since

202

immediately a whole bunch of cops boarded the ship and had all the passengers line up in two columns. Just like that: one line for those who were going to pass through Customs normally, comprised entirely of first-class passengers except for one or two who they shoved into the other line, and another line for those who were being detained from that very moment on. No need to tell you which line Modesto Ramírez and I were in. Along with some Italian immigrants, we were put in Tiscornia Prison, where we found Cubans and foreigners by the hundreds being detained for various reasons and who weren't able to enter Cuba legally. Of the third-class passengers who were on the ship, nearly all had to pass through Tiscornia, some only for a few hours while others were kept for days and even after we had left. Sometime after 12 o'clock noon, some mean, hungry looking cops came and searched our suitcases. They didn't find anything because we weren't carrying anything, only our humble change of clothing. They told me to take off my overcoat, that I was going to roast in it because of the heat, but I paid no attention and told them I was freezing, that not only was I sensitive to cold from the time I was born but that I was also carrying a malarial fever that made me tremble with a chill in my insides. "Plus," I told them, "the nervous state that this un-justified detention produces in me makes me feel even colder." When they began to interrogate me, I once again realized they thought I was Japanese and suspect, some kind of spy. I told them they were full of shit and that I spoke Spanish better than them, that I was Salvadoran and that they better not fuck around with me because of my Indian features, that the American Indians had come from Asia and that, therefore, we looked Japanese, and that it wasn't my fault the Cubans couldn't tell the difference between an Indian and Japanese person since the blame was with the Spanish who killed off all the Indians and there was no way left to compare the two. Finally, they told us that we had to leave our suitcases there, so as to inspect them with special, scientific devices and to fumigate them against whatever germs they might carry, and they brought us to some detention sheds, especially built so no one could escape, until

203

our situation was resolved. Fortunately, they swallowed all that about me being so sensitive to cold and they didn't take my overcoat, so even though I was sweating bullets underneath, I saved my papers.

We began, Modesto and I, to see how we could make contact with the outside world, the best plan being to make contact with the Cuban communists who, even though they seemed to be fleeing and hiding because of the repression, would be able to do more than a few things for us. The days were passing, however, and our situation wasn't going anywhere. We were as much prisoners as in any penitentiary. Little by little we became sort of friendly with a young Cuban girl, really very pretty, who spent her day cutting flowers in the Warden'sgarden, who everyone was more afraid of than the bubonic plague and yellow fever put together. We started to make shy small talk, silly things, about films and songs, and then she started bringing us books and newspapers to kill the boredom and she would stay with us a long time talking with us about our countries and our trips across the ocean, etc. Until one time she told us that she was really the Warden's daughter and promised to intercede on our behalf since she was convinced we were decent people, honorable and humble, and that it was all surely a mistake. We also wanted to do something for ourselves and after getting permission to write the outside, we sent a letter to El Salvador, recounting the news in the Havana newspapers which reduced itself to praises for Machado. In our letter we added a few praises for the tyrant, tossing him flowers, positive that the Cuban mail censors would read them. The letter got through easily and when we returned to our country we found out it had been received with no problem. The things one has to do in life . . . Around two days after sending that letter, our friend told us that her father, that dreaded prison Warden, got up early every morning and went out into the garden to trim his shrubs and vines with a sickle and some shears, and that this was the best time to talk with him about our problem because he was always in a good mood then. Like a lion with a full belly. So that's what we did: we got up

204

early to catch him and we approached him as soon as he started to trim his bushes. It worked so well that the man gave us an appointment to see him in his office that very afternoon. When we arrived, he was waiting for us with his secretary, who was going to take down the whole conversation in shorthand. He started to talk with us about El Salvador and it was obvious to me that he still suspected we weren't Salvadorans. With me, it seems that stupid nonsense about me being a Japanese spy was still a problem. He asked me what date the Spanish landed to conquer the country, plus a whole slew of other facts about our history and geography which by then I knew by heart. I talked and talked about El Salvador up to my ears, but little by little I steered the conversation around to the lands of Maceo and Martí, who at one time in their revolutionary lives had been exiled in Central America and had even had lovers, children, good friends and bad enemies, as is usually the case with great men, who after all aren't made of stone. And that was where he, himself, really started talking, because it turned out that he thought himself a fervent follower of Martí, and he delivered a whole lecture on the Apostle of the Cubans. It seems that before the Cuban Revolution, Martí had a number of would-be followers, some of whom were scoundrels. At least that Warden of Tiscornia was a better disciple of Hitler than Martí, and it's also a fact that in El Salvador many crooks have used the Apostle's name in order to profit and keep on profitting, fooling old guys who think they're liberals. Halfway through the conversation, convinced that we were indeed Salvadorans, the Warden ordered that our Consul in Havana be summoned. He was an old Indian from Armenia named Blanco, the father of a Salvadoran journalist who lived in San Salvador, clearly very influenced by Aprismo and by that old faggot Raúl Haya de la Torre. That Consul was off in outer space somewhere, he arrived with his breath reeking rum and not just from three drinks either, so we could easily convince him that we had come from Europe because we were sailors and the shipping company we were working for had left us high and dry, stranded in France, and that with a great deal of effort we had gotten up the money to return to our own country. Right there the Salvadoran Consul himself told the Warden he would take responsibility for us and he asked him in the name of the Salvadoran Government to allow us to continue our trip home. If it hadn't been for him, we wouldn't have been set free until 1959, when Fidel Castro triumphed.

Since we needed a Guatemalan visa in order to enter Central America through Puerto Barrios, we had to go all the way into Havana to pick one up. They sent us from Tiscornia in the custody of an undercover cop, whose sly, crooked face you could spot a mile away. We quickly bribed him with some gifts and some beers, right there at the Havana harbor, to let us take a taxi to the Guatemalan Consulate and browse a while through the streets of Havana. We caught a taxi and headed towards the center of the city, hanging our heads out the windows and asking questions about everything. As it was obvious we were in custody, the taxi driver asked us if we were Cubans. When we told him where we were from, he said in a loud voice: "Oh Salvadorans, and prisoners in Cuba, what times we live in! It's that all these cops and people in the Government are lousy bastards who don't know how to treat decent people because they 've gotten where they are among thieves and criminals. And what's really fucked-up is that the one who gives all the orders is that old son-of-a-bitch named Machado." I got nervous because I could see trouble coming and I didn't know what to think or do. Also there was the possibility that the man might be a provocateur who was just going around looking to use the Law of Caiaphas[1] on us: hit them when they're down. But the cop just muttered to the driver: "Cut it out, pal, it's not so bad." And still the driver came back: "Shut up you, you bastard, you're no better than the other scoundrels." He brought us to the Guatemalan Consulate and waited until they gave us our visas, and then he took us for a drive through Havana. The city didn't seem very happy, the atmosphere was tense. What really made it all worthwhile were the girls: in the parks, the streets and stores, really cute little numbers, Spanish and mulatto, black and Indian. As we passed the Capitol Building, the driver

206

pointed it out and said: "Look at that shit: it's going to cost us a total of more than 18 million dollars and all so that old son-of-a-bitch can dine with the gringos. Cuba is a real disgrace, gentlemen." We just said that we didn't know anything about politics, except that the one thing we could say was that in El Salvador things were worse, there was more misery and you didn't have the consolation of so many pretty women. The cop for his part just acted like he didn't hear the driver and stared out the window at the sky or the horizon. We went to eat lunch at a restaurant and the driver gave us a lot of details about his country that revealed much about the corrupt situation and terror under Machado's regime. "The working class doesn't just keep its mouth shut in Cuba," he said, "but the situation is very critical. The police murder with impunity. You can't congregate in groups on streetcorners because you're immediately fired upon, especially at night and in the barrios. Fines bleed the people to death. The economic crisis is deep, and what the Government wants to squeeze out of the people the rich, who maintain it, take. You pay fines for owning dirty work tools and equipment, a car in my case. You even have to pay a fine for carrying a big pocket watch because it's considered a blunt weapon. In other words, it's all bullshit." Finally, the driver brought us back to the port and, despite the fact that we insisted on paying a fair price since he'd spent the whole day with us, he didn't want one centavo. Maybe it was a question of some communist comrade, but we, despite his kindness and good will, didn't identify ourselves. If fact, it wasn't the first time we heard talk like that against the Cuban government in Cuba itself. In Tiscornia everyone was talking politics and even openly discussing Marxism, running through every subject in this world – and in the other – that came to mind. Since the Cubans are always rather boisterous and rowdy, they always made me think with their arguing that they were going to kill each other over politics or astronomy, but they never raised their fists. Unlike us, who, even before someone shouts at us or raises their voice, have already pulled a knife or a machete to do the talking. But be that as it may, remember that they've never given in to the

207

tyrants and that's why they have been the first Latin Americans to free themselves from the noose of Yankee imperialism.

Afterwards, we didn't have any more trouble. We took another ship bound for Puerto Barrios and when we got there I felt that we had ended our first journey around the world, and that we were returning to our country and to our home, alive and kicking.

---

[1] *Law of Caiaphas:* High priest of the Jews under Tiberius, was Annas' son-in-law. He presided at the trial of Jesus, finding Him guilty of blasphemy, of being a false king.

6

Return to El Salvador. Social agitation increases. Elections and the rise to power of General Maximiliano H. Martínez. Government repression. Internal discussions about popular armed insurrection led by the Communist Party. Miguel Mármol during the days of the insurrection. His capture and execution by firing squad. His escape from the dead and his convalescence.

When we arrived in Puerto Barrios, Guatemala, we somehow miraculously passed through immigration thanks to the good nature of a functionary, who as soon as he saw our Salvadoran passports said we were all Central American brothers and stamped us for entry, no questions asked. They didn't search us or hold us up either. One, two, three, we were on the streets – free and feeling like we were already practically in El Salvador, because from there we could've even walked home. When we made contact with the dock workers' organization, however, they told us that we had passed through immigration by the skin of our teeth because political control was tight and because anyone suspicious was going to get the boot. We blessed that immigration official, who maybe was in a good mood because he'd just finished chatting with some girl for a good long while. May God give you more luck than intelligence, my mother used to say when she was alive. While in Puerto Barrios we managed to do some communist education work. We talked to the banana workers and to groups of friends and sympathizers about revolutionary ideas, but then the local comrades told us that we had gone too far and very probably the police were already going around searching for us. And so we arranged to go to Guatemala City as soon as possible. The comrades of the organized workers' movement in that capital received us enthusiastically. The Guatemalan delegates who had attended the Congress in Moscow, Ovando Sánchez and Chigüichón, still hadn't returned from the U.S.S.R., so it fell on us to provide the workers' nucleuses and Guatemalan revolutionaries with their first details of the Soviet Union and the World Congress of Red Trade Unions. Our compatriot Miguel Angel Vázquez, who was deported from El Salvador for being a communist, was living in the Guatemalan capital at that time. This comrade, together with those who have already been mentioned in their turn, was

211

one of the first to introduce Marxist ideas into Central America and was really a very respected person for his skills and great knowledge. Since he knew different languages, especially French, he read Marxist texts from Europe and translated them to be used by the revolutionary movements in our countries. Someday a well-deserved homage will have to be paid this comrade who, after so many years of hard, self-sacrificing struggle, after years and years of anguish, setbacks and miseries, remains true to the principles of the Revolution. In Guatemala, Miguel Angel Vázquez introduced us to many revolutionaries and it filled us with joy to see how the popular movement was spreading and gaining strength throughout Central America. Vázquez put us up and fed us for most of a month since he had specific instructions from the Salvadoran Party to exercise precaution, because our government had issued arrest orders for Modesto and me all along the border and throughout the country. But the desire to return to our land was burning in our hearts and some days later, in light of the fact that the rest of the Party instructions still hadn't arrived, we decided to run every risk. We put together a plan and a route to get into El Salvador. We decided that Modest Ramírez, who was lesser known than me, should attempt to enter El Salvador normally by train. That Modesto got in easily, but once he reached San Salvador and was busy with his family and comrades he kept putting off contacting me, so that I was left stranded. I waited a few days more and then ended up deciding to take the same route as Modesto. Before leaving, comrade Vázquez warned me that it was known all over El Salvador that I'd gone to the U.S.S.R., since the anarcho-syndicalists had taken it upon themselves to print that fact in their paper, and so the situation looked pretty bad. On arriving at the Salvadoran border, I had my first scare. The police officer at the border checkpoint turned out to be Rosalío Colorado, a neighbor of mine from San Martín, who knew me and who, by the way, had been jealous of me because his wife was friendly and nice to me, and he had misunderstood the whole thing. No way around it, I had to confront him face to face. But to my surprise, after

212

greeting me and asking me how things went on my trip, he processed my papers normally. He added that he didn't have any orders for my arrest and that for his part he wasn't going to start fucking over a neighbor, but he warned me that from then on I'd better watch out because there was absolutely no doubt I was taking a big risk by going into Salvadoran territory, since everybody was saying I was a communist and had returned from Russia with who knows what insurrectionist intentions. At the first station stop, inside El Salvador, I ran into a lady I knew, whose name I didn't remember at the time, who told me exactly the same thing, adding that they might arrest me at any moment. I started to take every precaution, spending long times locked in the john, staying alert every second in case I had to jump off the train. That was how I reached Apopa, a town very near San Salvador. It was December 30, 1930. I jumped off the train when it started heading for the capital, and waited until I found an adequate means of transport to complete my journey. I managed to get a loaded truck, which was going to San Salvador during the night, to take me along as a passenger.

The day after I arrived in San Salvador I got in touch with the Party and was immediately greeted by the Central Committee in order to communicate some of my impressions, the first ones. Already, in Guatemala, I had become aware of several changes in the composition of the Directorate and now, here, I could verify them. Narciso Ruiz, who rose from the Bakers' Union, had replaced Luis Díaz as Secretary General, since the latter had been expelled by the Directorate for that stupid reason I already told you about. Luis Díaz would, by the way, be estranged from the Party for many years, but he returned in 1944 and again later in 1965-66. Another pleasant surprise was finding out that one of the figures who was most prominent in the struggle of the people was Agustín Farabundo Martí, who enjoyed enormous prestige. His strong personality and courage of conviction were supported by his past: an anti-imperialist fighter in Mexico who had suffered imprisonment and torture, after having left his law studies in El Salvador and travelling around the countryside in order to experience the exploitation, the life

213

of the poor, directly. Later on, he participated in the Sandinista struggle, as I already said. Martí, as I also think I mentioned earlier, wasn't a member of the Central Committee of the Party but was working very closely with it, officially representing the International Red Aid in the country. Also I learned that comrades Alfonso Luna, Mario Zapata, Moisés Castro y Morales and Max Ricardo Cuenca, young intellectuals of great value, had joined the Party and were working close with the leadership nucleus.

I made my first contacts with the Party, as you can imagine, clandestinely, but my arrival in San Salvador couldn't be kept a secret for long. In no time groups of workers and peasants from Ilopango and San Martín and even from other places started coming to see me, so that I might tell them about my impressions of the U.S.S.R. A few even brought paper and notebooks to copy down my comments. Interest was wide and varied. They weren't satisfied with general overviews, but solicited detailed information. Was it true that there was hunger and religious persecution in the U.S.S.R.? Was it true that there was no freedom of assembly? I answered each question. What was all that about free love? I explained that it wasn't the immoral act that the bourgeois press hypocritically judged it to be, but that, on the contrary, it was a matter of the ennoblement of relationships between man and woman in the new social relations based on the liberation of humanity from exploitation. And what about slave labor? And what about having their children taken away? I told them about the system of daycare and the attention given to raising children, about how, thanks to all these things, the working woman could be a mother without worrying about problems of a material nature. What do the Soviet workers think about solidarity with the struggle of workers all over the world? I told them about the rally we had had with the workers from the biggest bread factory in the world and what those comrades proved to us: that they were working for us also. Are there Catholics in the U.S.S.R.? I told them about my experience with a woman who had explained it to me like this: "I'm a Catholic and I believe in God, but I say my prayers

214

before going to bed since I don't have time to go to church, after working all day and studying astronomy at night; God understands and is pleased with me, as He blesses me and makes me happy." I fully explained to the peasants who visited how the collective farms operated and what living conditions on them were like, as well as my experiences in the units of the Red Army that we visited. Also I cleared up their doubts about an issue that the reactionary Salvadoran press was stirring up then: the alleged *dumping* that the U.S.S.R. was going to cause by suddenly unloading its products on the international market, a possibility clearly denied by the blockade and the lack of international economic relations, two arms of imperialism being used against the Soviet nation. The whole thing got so big that I had to set aside the whole day and part of the night for speaking about my Soviet experiences, since commission after commission of workers and peasants continued coming to hear me talk. Of course, I didn't talk just about the good things, the rosy picture; I also talked about the tremendous problems facing such an enormous country: food shortages, huge production deficits in the face of the needs of great masses of the population, not enough technicians to develop production as required, sabotage by the enemy, etc. And on top of everything – the good, the difficult and the bad – the titanic struggle of the Soviet people and their Communist Party to surmount that state of things. Similarly, I told them about the comrades we met and with whom we had direct dealings: Lossovsky, Manuilsky, Voroshílov, the legendary Budionney. Lossovsky was the most popular among the Salvadoran proletariat. I told them about when we were with him and his young wife in their house and how Modesto Ramírez had made steak Salvadoran style and how we played 'confessions.' Yes, and how comrade Lossovsky had as his punishment in the game to imitate a dog pissing with its leg raised, and how Modesto had to sing a Salvadoran peasant song.

The people were so interested in what I had to say that the Central Committee of the Party decided we ought to inform the masses at public gatherings. Therefore I wrote a very broad and

215

detailed report (which was later lost, in 1932) and I read it at several massive gatherings, some legal and others clandestine, in different places around Ilopango, Santa Tecla, Ahuachapán and at several secret meetings for peasants, political meetings which we called "ravine meetings." At this kind of gathering we would meet with three or four hundred peasants in a ravine or gorge, under darkness, and we'd talk all night long. All this required precise organization to provide security for the masses and to evade the authorities. The atmosphere in these meetings was truly moving due to the obvious fervor and revolutionary hope that welled up in the people. I remember one particularly well-attended and heated meeting, in a place on the plantation "La Montañita," in Ahuachapán. It would be exactly at that place that the strike after the elections in 1932 would break out, a strike that would become the excuse for the Government of Martínez to unleash massive repression. My propaganda work about the Soviet Union would in practice greatly expand, mixed of course with the immediate political work, until already well into 1931 the authorities started to persecute me fiercely and I had to limit much of my public activity and my long speeches. The half-legitimacy that, according to the watchword of the Party, I had attempted to gain suddenly came down on me and I had to go completely underground to carry out my work. The clandestine work of organizing and agitating had to be deepened and it became the first order of the day. Personally, my duty was organizing and directing the clandestine nucleuses of the Young Communist League, and the local committees of the Party in Soyapango and Ilopango. Time after time, we returned to San Salvador with comrades from these places in order to organize and orient groups of up to fifteen members of the Young Communist League and the Party in the barrios of Candelaria, Concepción, El Calvario, San Estéban and Mejicanos. All these groups had to meet on the outskirts of the city in order to elude persecution by the police. Frequent meeting spots were the fields of Flor Blanca, which were then uncultivated; the outskirts of La Chacra; the mountain near San Jacinto, etc. Modesto Ramírez worked with

216

me in all these places and I remember he was a tireless comrade, who agitated day and night, sleeping two or three hours a day and eating when he could. At the same time as this clandestine organizing activity, the Trade Union organizing work of the Regional was continuing and we communists tried to be the best organizers, the ones who set the example, because the Party cadre came out of those ranks. The fact of the matter was that in the brief amount of time we were in the U.S.S.R., the Salvadoran movement had grown by one hundred percent. Of course, the authorities were going around hungry after us and we had to use more than a thousand tricks to guarantee our safety and the continuity of the work. What times those were. To hold meetings at night we placed oil lamps all around in bordering camps and to guard the meetings even the local children helped out, signalling us with little firecrackers or bells when the National Guard patrols or the Army, etc. were approaching. I'd already been informed in Guatemala that the mass movement in El Salvador had taken on enormous scope and importance, and that what was most needed were cadre capable of leading that gigantic work. The Party, the Young Communist League, and the Regional had made a strong effort that still fell short of what was needed, even though each cadre did many different, exhausting tasks. The Caribbean Bureau of the International sent us information and orientation materials and, to the extent possible, communicated to us the experiences of other parts of the world, but all that was just a drop in the bucket.

Our mass movement had a deep, democratic, anti-imperialist and revolutionary content: the secret organizing work visibly bore fruit in the massive acts of protest and the struggle against the government repression – fighting for the demands of the workers in the countryside and in the cities, for the democratization of the government as much under Pío Romero Bosque as under Araujo, against imperialist intervention in Guatemala through puppet governments, against anti-popular, imperialist repression worldwide. Our mass activity at the time

217

attracted the attention of the international communist and workers' press.

Of course, this work had its price. In spite of everything the enemy was stronger and more organized than us. The prisons started to fill up with political prisoners, and they stayed full, and the International Red Aid increased its activity as an act of solidarity. Similarly, a broad government campaign of deporting all foreign revolutionaries on whom it had information started to be carried out. One particularly talked-about case was the deportation of the Guatemalan comrades Ernesto Juárez, a shoemaker, and Emilio Villagrán, a carpenter, who had won the love of the Salvadoran masses for their self-sacrificing work. Political prisoners were ordered to do forced labor on the road to Cojutepeque, which was being built then, but the massive protest activity mounted by the SRI forced the government, in most cases, to quickly set them free. Romero Bosque had set up a democratic government friendly to the workers for only his first two years in office. After that, the repression came down on us hard.

On another front, the Red Aid took a firm stance in defense of the victims of the government's repression and so its two principal leaders, Agustín Farabundo Martí and Ismael Hernández, were imprisoned by the police in an attempt to check the solidarity movement. Both immediately went on a hunger strike to protest their arrest. Martí was a born fighter who was never shaken, with an aggressiveness that would distress anyone, a spirit that came from his absolute identification with the cause of the humiliated. He used to say that a leader of the poor must be the angriest one, the most outraged in the face of the class enemy. And I think that's right, above all since he was living through a period of revolutionary upsurge in which it was urgent to awaken the consciousness of a people who had been asleep and held down for such a long time. About that arrest of Martí and Hernández (I hadn't yet returned from the U.S.S.R.), they spent four days on a strict hunger strike, at the end of which the Chief of Police, General Leitzelar, had them brought to his office and when they were in his presence he asked them

218

in a friendly and conciliatory tone: "How are you feeling, gentlemen?" And Martí answered him with his voice firm: "As men always feel, you big son-of-a-bitch: strong!" There are comrades in the Party who feel ashamed to talk about these things, because they say Martí was just plain crude and brought up badly. I thought it was a tremendous thing. At the time, Martí was the expression of a popular protest movement, representing the masses, beaten down and vilified by the authorities of every sort. On the crest of a crashing popular wave, one mustn't go around being diplomatic or wishy-washy, much less compromising. Diplomacy is left for when the struggle isn't so explosive and immediately pressing. If General Leitzelar, who probably wasn't the worst military officer El Salvador has had, got punched in the face, congratulations: Of course, at that moment Martí's attitude left the officers who were guarding him with their mouths hanging open. A couple of them drew their pistols and shoved them into el Negro's chest. One of them told him to apologize to General Leitzelar and el Negro responded by kicking him in the shins. Shoving them all the way, they returned them to their cells, convinced that you couldn't do any talking with those kind of men. Two days later, they sent Martí out of the country on board a steamer headed for the United States. On reaching the United States, they suggested that he continue on to the U.S.S.R., with the Salvadoran government paying for the trip. Martí refused to step down on North American territory and didn't want to have anything to do with continuing on to the U.S.S.R. He returned to Central America on the same ship and managed to elude surveillance and to escape in the Nicaraguan port of Corinto, making contact with the revolutionary movement in Nicaragua and immediately making plans for his return to El Salvador, to his combat post. In the meantime, Ismael Hernández had remained a prisoner, enduring the rigors of the hunger strike alone. First of all, he went eleven days without eating, and then the authorities started to move him from prison to prison in order to elude the big protest movement that the organized workers had mounted on his behalf and on a national level. At one point they put him in an insane asylum, in shackles, in a cell where they put the water hose on him all day. Ismael didn't fold for one instant and stood firm, refusing to eat as long as the order for his release wasn't made. While he was in the asylum, the President of the Republic, don Pío Romero Bosque, requested they bring Ismael to his office so he could try to intimidate him and make him give in. They brought Ismael to the Presidential House in shackles and wrapped in a rubber cloak, since his whole body was monstrously swollen from being under the water hose for such a long time. As soon as Ismael was facing President Romero, the President started yelling: "You're a dumb asshole and an outlaw. A heartless, irresponsible child. How can you stand your mother going from prison to prison trying to save you? It would be good for you to disown these rebellious, stupid ideas of yours and return to society. We are prepared to offer you that chance if you demonstrate true repentance." As Ismael started to sweat bullets, don Pío ordered the guards to remove his rubber cloak. So that's what they did, and the horrible sight was revealed. Ismael in shackles and swollen horribly. Don Pío was deeply affected and hesitated, and then Ismael took the offensive: "The immoral ones, the cruel ones, those who produce so much sorrow in the families of the people are you. I serve the interests of the humble and the humiliated, and that's why it doesn't bother me to suffer these trials. I'm a communist who tries to be true to his way of thinking, as comunists do in every part of the world." Don Pío lowered his head and said that he didn't know they were treating political prisoners like this. He added that he was going to order Ismael's immediate release and that he was going to give him money so he could set himself up in business and so he'd forget his revolutionary ideas and not have to go through any more of these terrible trials. Ismael refused to take one centavo, and the only thing he asked was that they give him back his work tools, which they'd confiscated when he was arrested. Don Pío ordered him free under strict surveillance. Ismael returned to the street directly from the Presidential House, and later the Party took him out of San Salvador, to the

220

east, where the police would lose track of him. Ismael then settled in San Miguel. By the way, in those days there was a social conflict of gravest proportions in San Miguel. What was called "the Sotista uprising." The administrator of the millionaire Meardi family in that city, by the name of Soto, was unjustly accused of embezzlement. Soto was a very good-natured and honorable man, known among the people for helping the poor. The judges, bribed with Meardi money, found Soto guilty despite the popular uproar, and the people suddenly rose up with violence against the local authorities. In reality, no one was expecting an uprising like that, but just for that reason the masses exploded into violence. The people looted and smashed up the bodegas and warehouses owned by the Meardis, and they just ignored the local authorities. The President of the Republic declared a state of siege throughout the Department of San Miguel and sent in the Army to control the situation. Various steps were taken, in accordance with the Meardi family, to localize and put down the unrest, and the violence was quickly controlled. Ismael Hernández, despite his shaky physical condition (they very nearly amputated his leg because of the damage done by those shackles and the swelling from the water), managed to take full advantage of that violent situation to organize a good base for the Party and the Red Aid. Out of the "Sotista" struggle, he brought into our ranks many people of weight and with a popular following, who had influence over the peasant masses in the region. Also, at that time he started organizing a clandestine militia that grew to 700 well-chosen members, which, by the way, during the events of January, 1932, was camped in the San Miguel cemetery, waiting for the necessary orders to take the city by force.

As is easy to see from these accounts, today's young communists are wrong when they say – as if they know it all – that we were men with a deeply-rooted artisan mentality. Although, strictly speaking, it's true that most of us (I'm talking about the top cadre) were indeed artisans, we lived the lives of proletarian revolutionaries. What happened was we didn't stay

221

long working in one shop because the demands of the mass work, extensive political work, prevented us from doing so. The bosses didn't have confidence in us as stable workers. And they were right, we weren't going to lose time making a pair of shoes for some lady at the moment when it was necessary to produce a manifesto. That's why we thought of owning our own little shop, in order to earn a living and have some independence. As I remember, during that period of the struggles I've been talking about after leaving master Angulo's shop, I worked in the establishments of Luis Rivas; in "La Elegancia," owned by Cirilo Pérez, next to the First Infantry Regiment; in the shoe factory owned by a gentleman named Prudencio, who was from Zacatecoluca and who, by the way, even cried when I had to go somewhere else to work; and also in the shoe factory of don José Enrique Cañas who was a good boss to me, who on several occasions hid me from the police and who was the one who gave me a pair of shoes for my trip to the U.S.S.R. But between shops, and between the shop and the struggle, I wasn't in an artisan's state of mind, thinking about my own shop for its own sake, about my little sewing machine for the machine's sake. To repeat: if you thought about owning your own little shop it was for the freedom it offered to work without a fixed schedule and to devote yourself to political work at your convenience. If some of us had our own shops at the time, it was for tactical reasons and not because we were petty bourgeois artisans. Such was the case with me, Ismael Hernández or Léon Ponce. Plus there were other reasons aside from the free time it offered: the shop was your cover. As a shopkeeper, one was *maestro don* Miguel Mármol, which was more respected by the general public than just compañero Mármol, or Mármol the shoemaker. And that doesn't mean anyone had it over anyone else. It was a matter of nothing more than taking advantage of the best conditions in order to penetrate the broadest circles. Of course, the time came when the repression became so sharp that our little shops had to be left in the hands of comrades who weren't so well-known, or be shut down for good. The repression wasn't confined to any one place, it was carried out throughout the national territory. I was working hard on perfecting my methods of eluding the actions of the police, to the extent that I fell prisoner only once during that intense stage of persecution. It was early in 1931, during the activities of the electoral campaign in which I participated. It happened on the occasion of a mass rally in Juayúa, and Chico Sánchez (the peasant leader from Izalco who would be executed in 1932) and myself were arrested. The National Guard brought us to the local prison and threatened to kill us, at the request, according to them, of Mayor Emilio Radaelli, who would die, by the way, in the actions of 1932. On that occasion the masses of Juayúa violently protested our arrest and the authorities had to let us go. The people dispersed and went home, and then the authorities arrested us again. But the masses returned and they had to release us once more. It's worth stopping to talk a little on the matter of these elections, since they were very closely connected to the outbreak of the popular insurrection. The elections for the deputies and mayors which I'm now going to talk about took place under the Government of Araujo, who had risen to power with the support of the people, but who then quickly fell out of favor. The electoral process would be interrupted by the coup that overthrew Araujo, planned and immediately headed-up directly by the archcriminal, General Maximiliano Hernández Martínez. These elections signified the end of any chance for a peaceful solution to the Salvadoran political problem of that time. Why did we communists participate in those elections? The fact of the matter is we were only picking up on the unrest of the masses. Conditions all over the country were terrible from the economic point of view, because the worldwide crisis of capitalism that broke in 1929 lashed out at our country in a particularly disturbing way. In the countryside the situation was extremely miserable, there was real starvation and true despair among the peasant masses. These masses began to intensify their political work, channeling their unrest into our ranks. And this first political expression by the peasantry and farm laborers was just enough for the bourgeoisie and the Government, for the

223

landowners and their instruments of power, to start using violence against the people. Actually, the bourgeoisie had organized violence against the working masses of El Salvador since 1930. The landowners were setting fire to the poor peasants' fields, stampeding cattle through the cornfields of the hired hands and tenant farmers, laying-off massive numbers of the rural proletariat as a way of unloading the burden of the crisis onto the backs of the workers, besides creating a climate of physical terror in which the number of individual crimes was endless. The repressive forces of the government collaborated in the creation of this climate, since the least censure of the workers by the landowners was enough to have them punished mercilessly. The worst act of repression took place at the "Asuchillo" plantation in the Department of la Libertad, early in 1931. It so happened that a trade union meeting was called there to discuss the problems of the economic crisis. The owner of the plantation banned the meeting and sent in the National Guard. A detachment arrived which opened fire on the meeting and many people were killed. That's why Farabundo Martí came out of hiding and went to talk about it with President Araujo, but there was no getting through to the laborite politician. Farabundo became furious and insulted the President. They arrested him on the street and put him in prison, but he immediately declared himself on a hunger strike, just like when he was arrested before. For twenty-seven days el Negro Martí was on a hunger strike and for twenty-seven days the Salvadoran people were in the streets fighting for his freedom. There was a big commotion in the press over Martí's imprisonment and the actions by the masses, and the unpopularity of the Araujo government spread. This loss of popularity, unfortunately, was capitalized on by Araujo's bourgeois political enemies and provided the sly and foxy Minister of War of that weakened regime, General Martínez, who had been a presidential candidate in the election that Araujo won, with plenty of room to maneuver. Anyhow, the struggle for Martí's freedom ended successfully since, in the face of the mass pressure, he was ordered released. And to think that

224

more than one revolutionary Salvadoran writer has tried to reduce this fact to an incident provoked by el Negro Martí having one too many, swearing at President Araujo and getting locked up for such ridiculous circumstances! Martí wasn't the only political prisoner in the country. The prisons were overflowing, and exile was the order of the day. The official violence began to cause among the masses a level of response that was ever more appropriate. Large mass confrontations and even clashes with the Army and National Guard occurred in Sonsonate, Santa Ana and other places in the country. For example, on May 17, 1931, there was a popular rally in Sonsonate demanding Martí's freedom. The cavalry in Santa Ana, together with troops from the Sonsonate Regiment, violently broke up the rally and all hell broke loose, resulting in a tremendous massacre. They killed ten or twelve comrades and there were scores of people seriously wounded, beaten and imprisoned. In light of that violence, the masses – and not the Party – began to express through the trade unions and other organizations their desire to challenge the bourgeoisie in the municipal elections. The Communist Party didn't participate in the Presidential elections that Araujo had won, which had the not entirely false reputation of having been the only true free elections held in this century in El Salvador. That's why some people still call that old fox, don Pío, "the father of Salvadoran democracy." Several other candidates had participated in those elections, such as Claramount, Enrique Córdova, Miguel Tomás Molina, General Martínez, etc. The masses had elected Araujo. And despite the coup that you could see was coming, the masses weren't convinced that the electoral road was used up. On the contrary. In those days, City Hall had complete jurisdiction over the local government, the municipal police, judicial functionaries, etc. The masses completely believed that a change of leadership in the administrative apparatus would really solve many problems. It was truly a need of the masses that expressed itself in their rallies in a particularly persistent way. As I see it, we communists didn't understand, despite the ultimate weakness of that expression,that it signified the readiness of the Salvadoran workers to politicize their struggle. Since you mustn't forget that despite the violence with which the struggle of our Party and the organized workers' movement was stamped, it was up to then a fundamentally economic struggle. Even the Central Committee at that point ended up circulating a resolution prohibiting these instigations in the municipal-mayoral elections, reminding the masses that we found ourselves in an economic struggle and that therefore there was no reason to get into politics. In the name of the Young Communist League and the Workers' Regional, the task of quieting down the masses in this area fell on me and many other comrades. The fact of the matter is the masses were very disciplined. But later on, in October, the Party decided to participate in the elections after a prolonged heated internal debate. This discussion was held in an expanded plenum of the CC, with representatives from all the mass organizations, and it took place in secret in the area which today is the Flor Blanca barrio and which was then open countryside. We representatives of the Young Communist League and the Workers' Regional were opposed to participating in the elections, but not for the reasons the Party had brandished, that is, not to confuse political struggle with economic struggle. On the contrary, we said that the economist watchword which had prevailed up to that point had killed the political enthusiasm of the people, but that the hard, concrete reality was the following: the elections were going to be in December and therefore barely a couple of weeks remained in which to do agitational and propaganda work and that, in the extreme case, even assuming that an effective job could be done and we could get a lot of votes that would win us some posts, these were going, no doubt, to be denied us because of the electoral fraud the government was planning or because of the strength of the repressive apparatus, and that such occurrences in the midst of the raging, nationwide class struggle were surely going to spark off generalized violence, to a point that we still weren't prepared to lead and guide in a revolutionary way. The CC was solidly behind its new line about taking part in the elections and its best proponents in that

226

debate were comrades Moisés Castro y Morales and Max Ricardo Cuenca. Moisés Castro said that even though we probably wouldn't win the elections, that campaign would serve us to make contact with the people, in order to make them aware of our position and to organize them politically on the basis of a broad program. In fact his arguments were very persuasive, as have been the arguments of those who continue defending "electoral contact with the masses" these days. Max Ricardo Cuenca stuck by what he called the disciplining of the masses and said that our work ought to consist in consolidating that discipline and channeling the masses in the direction of the long term objectives of the Party. Today I'd say that we should have seriously asked ourselves (and this is a question a party should always ask itself) up to what point were we ourselves capable of guaranteeing a mass line in the face of the organized violence of the bourgeois state. In any case, Farabundo Martí agreed with Castro y Morales and with Cuenca, and finally we all agreed to work in the elections through the Young Communist League and the Workers' Regional, voicing (through me) our reservations in the sense that, at the same time, we ought to be working on preparations for a big coffee plantation workers' strike, organized not only to win substantial wage increases but also that could advance political positions if it was related to an event like the elections. This statement was of utmost importance to us. It was a huge step forward in the area of strikes by Salvadoran workers, since it was a strike conceived at the national level, that moreover included the possibility of gaining the solidarity of workers in other lines of production and went beyond the traditional work of partial strikes. We immediately informed the Caribbean Bureau of the Communist International about this discussion, requesting their opinion and advice. We never did actually receive a reply. Next we named an Electoral Commmittee, attached to the CC, which would be the organism by means of which the Party and the Salvadoran revolutionary movement would direct the campaign. I was made responsible for mobilizing in the Department of San Salvador, the villages and rural zones of the Department.

227

Around that time our then comrade Carlos Castillo, a cabin-etmaker, got out of prison, a cadre who had been picked by the Party to be a member of the Directorate of the Regional, about whom I've already talked several times, and the first thing he did when he met me was to yell at me for not having firmly defended in the expanded Plenum the position of the Regional of having nothing to do with the elections. Castillo had a lot of influence back then and he managed to convene a meeting to reconsider what had already been agreed upon, which also was held in the fields of Flor Blanca. I attended that meeting at the expressed urging of Castillo, but when I arrived I realized that Max Cuenca and other comrades weren't at all pleased by my presence. Again, I brought up the problem of not working in the elections. But everyone there shut me up and said that the problem had already been voted on and settled. Castillo sided with me: the electoral fraud would be fatal and, in the face of it, the people would resort to violence. And he offered concrete evidence. He said, for example, that in Ahauchapán the townspeople had already prepared a plan – that if victory was denied them by fraud, they would attack the barracks and impose the popular will with armed force. Castillo insisted that our Party wasn't capable of leading the people in an insurrection to seize power. Max Cuenca said that the experience of the elections would be an historical precedent and he started in quoting Lenin. The end result of the meeting was that It confirmed the resolution to participate in the elections. My job wound up being, since I was disciplined, one of renewing and raising the electoral, political spirit of the people, even though I was personally opposed to the activity. Time flew by and things were happening fast, hour by hour. The moment came when an urgent meeting was called to consider a series of secret reports that had reached the Directorate of the Party and that made clear that a coup to overthrow the Araujo government was close at hand, probably inspired by the Minister of Defense himself, General Martínez. Several of us comrades pronounced ourselved in favor of rising up in anticipation of the coup, carrying the masses to national insurrection, since it was predictable that a government headed

228

by General Martínez, the individual directly responsible for most of the massacres and repressive measures that I've been talking about, was going to have the character of a brutal, terrorizing, anti-popular dictatorship. I think the prospect of such a dictatorship removed any adventurous appearance to an insurrection planned under those circumstances, and the fact of the matter is we had sufficient popular forces to be optimistic. Later on, it will be shown what it was we were missing. Farabundo Martí, however, was very calm while listening to our proposals and said that it wasn't so important that General Martínez seized power, that in any case our actual chances of avoiding it were very slim and that a nationwide insurrection was too much a price to pay in order to prevent the ascent to power of a dictatorial government. He added that conditions for the success of an insurrection would be even better under a criminal government. Farabundo quoted Lenin profusely and said that the Salvadoran Army still wasn't sufficiently discredited in the eyes of the people and, on the other hand, civil governments like Araujo's were at that point totally discredited. Therefore, it was likely that a coup led by a military officer like Martínez would find support from important sectors. Farabundo said that we shouldn't call for insurrection, but instead take steps to confront the coup positively, safeguarding the organizations, sustaining the influence of the masses under the new circumstances, etc. That same night our candidate for Mayor of Ahauchapán showed up at the meeting, a worker named Contreras. He came in all excited and told us that the barracks in Ahuachapán was under siege by a contingent of 900 peasants who had decided to settle accounts for the arbitrary acts by the authorities, of which they were victims. He said that the urgent pleas of the Commander of the Regiment, Colonel Escobar, hadn't done a thing and that the local leaders of the Communist Party requested a delegate from the Central Committee to come and quiet down the peasants and get them to go back to their homes before it turned into a slaughter. I was assigned to do that job and I left immediately. On arriving in Ahuachapán, I talked with the peasants and was able to persuade them to

229

return to their jobs. Colonel Escobar said: "These sons-of-bitches only understand their own." Eight days later the same situation occurred: seven hundred determined peasants seized the local military Command Post. That is, the people of Ahuachapán and the entire west were morally up in arms. Once again I was the person picked to appease the masses and once again I was successful, but this time the peasants told me it was the last time, that I ought to tell the Party that it better be careful not to keep telling the people to throw water on the fire, because the next delegated pacifier (even if it was me) was going to run the risk of having "to face our machetes even before the class enemy." The people were fired up, they had taken all they could. The Party ordered me to remain in the area of Ahauchapán in order to carry on the pre-electoral work in the countryside. The job was a tremendous amount of work and subject to all kinds of pressures. During the day I worked in the city and at night in the mountains. I ate when I could and slept every third day. And close to the scheduled date of the elections I started to suffer hallucinations, from physical weakness and too much work: I ended up seeing National Guardsmen shooting at me, killing me, and then at one point I collapsed and fainted. The Red Aid brought me to Santa Ana and from there they sent me to San Salvador, but I couldn't lie still and rest, not even for a week, since the local leadership in Ahauchapán demanded my presence there. The prospect of violence breaking out was no longer a far-fetched fantasy, you felt it coming just around the corner. I grew very afraid that widespread violence might break out because I knew the people were going to get the worst of it and, therefore, I tried in my work to channel the popular rage in the direction of a general strike, an intermediate stage between the electoral road and insurrection. The Party didn't know anything about this, it was purely a personal undertaking. And the thing was, that those among us who were working with the masses at that time really knew the development of the struggle, and our opinions had to prevail over the assessments they made back there in the Central Committee in the name of doctrine. I think that our not deepening this work and organizing it better was why we lost the battle of '32 in such a crushing way. Because we were caught, as we Salvadorans say, with our pants down.

A steady flow of very complete information regarding the preparations the enemy was making to massacre the people was coming in every minute to the electoral meetings of the Party. During that period the enemy's counterintelligence apparatus was functioning very badly. Even Army officers who were sympathetic with us came to tell us that the government's plan to fix the elections and to crush the Salvadoran revolutionary movement was essentially a military plan, the physical elimination of our cadre. Of course, the elimination of Araujo by Martínez was going to be the accelerating factor in that plan. Also these officers informed us that in certain sectors of the Army, especially the youngest officers, noncommissioned officers and soldiers, there was a disposition to turn their guns against the commanding officers and Government in support of the people. Under these conditions my position had been becoming more concrete: my thesis was that if there was an electoral fraud, violent provocation had to be avoided and the organized forces restrained, but if the provocations on the part of the Government were so great that they demanded a response, we had to channel the people's violence towards a nationwide, general strike – a general political strike through which it would be possible to slowly develop, under more favorable conditions, the armed insurrection to seize power. On December 2, 1931, I led a big peasant meeting near Ahauchapán. After it was over, I headed back to the city, but on my way I was met by several committees of peasant women who were waiting to speak with me about their problems and the elections. They told me that a rumor was going around that a coup had taken place, that it was ours and that comrade Martí had taken power in the name of the poor of El Salvador. While we were talking, some military planes were flying over the area. On reaching Ahuachapán, I found out that the coup the Party was expecting had happened, that the sinister General Maximiliano H. Martínez had seized power and that he was the strongman who actually ruled behind the facade of a "Government Junta," which had replaced Araujo. In fact, the junta disappeared from the scene in a matter of hours. Already in those moments, an appeal for national unity around the Junta and General Martínez was circulating everywhere, signed in Santa Ana by Cipriano Castro, a well-known bourgeois politician. All propaganda material of this kind that fell into our comrade's hands was burnt according to my instructions. I hurried off to the capital to try and make contact with the Central Committee. When the coup happened the election campaign was already pretty far ahead, and we communists had mayoral and congressional candidates in all of what we called the revolutionary zones of the country, that is, in most of the central and western parts of the Republic. Among our candidates, I remember Marcial Contreras, who we ran for Mayor of Ahauchapán; the driver Joaquín Rivas, a candidate for Mayor in San Salvador, etc. I forget the names of our candidates in Sonsonate and Santa Tecla, who won overwhelmingly when it came time to vote. About our slate of Deputies in San Salvador, I only remember Ismael Hernández. I'd like to say now that we communists indisputably won elections in Sonsonate, Santa Tecla, Ahuachapán (though here, as you'll see, in the end we had to withdraw from voting and declare a strike), Colón, Teotepeque, etc. This didn't surprise us, our estimates in all these places predicted it, it was the perspective we already had when the Martínez coup happened and that's why such an incident didn't intimidate us. On the contrary, in the face of the coup, the Party resolved it would continue our electoral campaign and that open agitation in support of the candidates would be stepped up. All of us who were in relative hiding at once came out into the streets and reactivated the local headquarters of the Party, which was located opposite Centenario Park in San Salvador. We thought that in view of the complex situation, we had to act with boldness. The coup and, above all, the figure of General Martínez had caused uncertainty and doubt, even in some powerful reactionary sectors. Since Martínez was a theosophist, he had been making anticlerical

232

propaganda that upset the Salvadoran Catholic Church, which traditionally has been a very effective unifying force among the diverse tendencies of the Creole reaction. Right away we realized that there were various political sectors that didn't know what to do at the time, and it cleared our way to act openly and with greater intensity. We felt compelled to open local headquarters in Ahauchapán and Sonsonate, and we communists were travelling through the rural zones of these two Departments as if the plantations and haciendas were already the peoples', such was the mass support we were getting from the peasantry. We made open propaganda at every level of the Party's organization: Farabundo Martí, Alfonso Luna, Mario Zapata, I myself, etc. spoke at public rallies. We stepped up our printed propaganda, and our newspaper for the intellectuals in the Party, "Red Star," that had started within the student movement, increased its number of circulation runs. The masses themselves told us that we shouldn't talk so much, that we better be careful because the enemy was watching our every move, just waiting for the right moment to destroy us completely. The oppositionist unrest against the new regime, however, was growing day by day in every sector of the population. In no time there were actions among the high school and university students, the former, especially, protesting the military discipline that the new Minister of Public Education wanted to impose on them. In the midst of so much political agitation, the Government unexpectedly ordered de facto that the elections would have to be held on the 3rd or 5th of January. The bourgeois parties had been advised of this date well in advance so that they'd have a big jump on us. We responded by intensifying our propaganda campaign even more. Our rallies spread into the barrios of the cities, into the villages, on the plantations, at major intersections, on the big roads and even on the beaches. The reactionary propaganda attacked viciously: its basic objective was to frighten the masses away from us, and to that end they raised the threat that the Government was preparing an anti-communist massacre. In this activity the clergy, in spite of their reservations about Martínez,

233

played a truly sinister role. The elections would take place separately. On the first day would be the mayoral races and on the following day, the Deputies.

Election day for the mayors has remained patently engraved in my memory. More than anything, that day seemed like a party, but behind the apparent celebration the tension was torturous. All the contending parties made a big show of it. Everyone was playing marimbas and passing out tamales, coffee, sweets and soft drinks in the voting places, except the Communist Party. The Fraternal Progressive Party of General Antonio Claramount Lucero and the party of Goméz Zárate, which didn't spare any amount of money or effort in their eagerness to bribe the masses, stood out especially for their crudeness. Every one of these candidates essentially played along with Martinismo and, as was clear later, with growing North American intervention in our country. Araujo had been the last Salvadoran pawn of British imperialism. The Communist Party was in no way acting like them, it was our speakers and our choruses with the little daughters of workers and peasants singing revolutionary songs, such as "Red Banner," "The International," and "Red Cavalry," that created a happy, enthusiastic atmosphere. I remember how the tourists who were staying at the "Nuevo Mundo" Hotel applauded our speakers, whose speeches were the only ones that showed any degree of content, and how the people in general brought our team of agitators water, cold drinks and fruit. The greatest block of voters was unquestionably ours. Araujo's Labor Party had been strong until his overthrow. In the face of the Martínez coup, laborism was cut to pieces and its base scattered, bolstering our Party and others. Araujo's ideologue, don Alberto Masferrar, left the country with his tail between his legs and ended up dying of melancholia. The voting for the mayors started at eight in the morning. All the speakers from the other parties, though they attacked us, acknowledged the order and discipline with which the communist voters had turned up at the polling places. It's interesting to know that there wasn't any violence between contending parties. The violence came

234

exclusively from the power of the state which, given the recentness of the Martínez coup, didn't yet have the political instruments needed to participate in the voting effectively, to advance the fraud in its favor, etc. From the interviews of all the candidates by the national and international press, ours came out looking the most calm and clear, the best informed, the most open and the least self-serving. On the voting lines in San Salvador our voters were joined by voters from the nearby villages, who had already voted back there and who went to the center of the city to urge on their comrades. Apart from this whole exciting picture, the tricks of the official apparatus against the communists began right from the start: they nullified our votes using any pretext, they delayed our comrades from voting and tried to confuse them, since voting then wasn't by secret ballot but was done by oral vote. Many of our voters got confused by these maneuverings, being simple workers without political cunning. In the meantime, the Army had set up their machine gun nests on all the high places in the city, on the rooftops, on top of the monuments, barracks, etc. There wasn't, however, the least disturbance during those elections. The military had to forget the idea of mowing down the people. For the time being. One of our basic disadavantages was that most of those who didn't get a chance to vote before the polls closed were communists. After the voting was over, we activists got together with the object of evaluating the day's work and exchanging our experiences. I criticized the kind of agitation that was done in the face of concrete electoral activity, saying that the content of the propaganda and political agitation wasn't geared to winning, that, given the understanding that the principal objective was to communicate our program, we had neglected to create in the masses a spirit of victory. It wasn't enough that we communists were present at the polls like good school children, all washed and dressed up and with our hair neatly combed. On the other hand, I pointed out that through pure sentimentality we had arranged for the rural masses on the outskirts of the city to vote first, so that the nullification of countless votes had slowed down the voting too much, and at

235

the end of the day most of our comrades and sympathizers didn't get to vote. Finally, I pointed out that the party hadn't coordinated all the publicity for the elections in an overall, comprehensive way and that it had spread itself way too thin. All my criticisms were accepted by the leadership of the Party.

The following day the elections for the Deputies took place. From our experiences in the Mayoral elections, the obstacles and restraints to our victory were for the most part eliminated, and from the first hours in the morning it was already abundantly clear that we would probably clobber all the parties nationwide. The Government then decided to go for blood. And citing diverse pretexts which didn't convince anyone, it suspended the voting and announced it would resume in a few days. The bourgeois political parties expressed feeble protests. We protested vigorously but called on our voters to remain calm. You have to understand that back then there weren't any radio stations or television allowing us to communicate with all our loyal supporters quickly. One thing was certain, and we found that out from the telegraph reports that we received during the course of the day: the Salvadoran people had voted for us more than for any other political party up to the moment of the suspension of the elections, and in some places, like the ones I spoke of before, the voting had already ended in our irrefutable victory. The people not only had voted for us, but they also had helped us to organize our participation in the elections and had put up a good fight at our side. This filled us with optimism. But all these facts were purely idyllic events in the midst of the true storm that was about to explode in the bowels of the country. The night after the stalled elections the Central Committee of our Party called a secret and very urgent meeting. It had to do with listening to a report by comrade Clemente Estrada, Nicaraguan by birth, who was nicknamed "Killjoy," who for some time had been assigned by the Party to work in Ahuachapán. He reported that in Ahauchapán the voting began as usual, that the communists had come out forming one crowded line of more than five thousand men, but when the voting was supposed to begin our line had been surrounded by a

236

threatening National Guard, armed with rifles and machine guns. The provocation was carried to such an extreme that the comrades decided not to vote and returned to their workplaces determined to begin immediately a general strike in protest of those outrageous abuses. At the same time, the strike was going to raise some local economic demands. And in fact, the strike started to get organized. The focus was the plantation "La Montañita." The owners of this coffee plantation, confronted with the position of the workers which was communicated to them through the union in an official and respectful way, called in a large detachment of the National Guard. Up until midday the situation was normal, the Guardsmen were even chatting in a friendly way with the strikers. But then, the bosses at "La Montañita" gave the detachment lunch and got all the Guardsmen drunk and convinced them with gifts, flattery and threats to put down the peasants.

The Guardsmen went back to the place where the peasants were gathered and provoked them to the point of gunning down right in front of everybody Alberto Gualán, a peasant leader with the Young Communist League, and seriously wounding other comrades, men, women and even children. The striking comrades became enraged and answered that gratuitous, criminal aggression by executing fourteen National Guardsmen. That incident sounded the alarm for all the landowners in the region, who managed to get the Government to quickly call in the ferocious cavalry from Santa Ana to surround the place and take revenge on the peasants, without distinguishing between those who had participated in the incident at "La Montañita" and the rest of the poor population. They didn't send in the troops from Ahuachapán because they were afraid of leaving the Regiment unarmed. From that moment on, a wave of criminal terror was let loose throughout the entire western part of the country, mainly in Santa Ana, Ahuachapán and Sonsonate. Reports of the murdered, wounded, tortured, beaten and imprisoned began to pour into the Central Committee like a waterfall. We discussed that grave situation in every detail and, to tell you the truth, our spirits were

237

very low. What could we do? The discussion went on for a very long time and I proposed to take the bull by the horns, that is, I proposed no less than trying to negotiate directly with General Maximiliano Hernández Martínez. Martínez had assumed the Presidency of the Republic during the first few days after the coup. That proposal of mine fell like salt on the wound, since it was a matter of talking and dealing with the most hated man in the country. All the comrades went speechless and gave me dirty looks. I remember that that meeting was in a house in the Lourdes barrio and, at that moment, the tension was so great that I had to go out in the backyard for a while to get some air because I felt like I was suffocating. When I went back in, el Negro Martí had a book in his hands, it was in French, and he read it and said that I was right, translating a passage where it said that under certain, given circumstances the Staff of the Proletariat, that is, the Central Committee of the Communist Party, can negotiate with the Staff of the Bourgeoisie, that is, with the Executive Power of the State. Martí swore that the book said that. Who knows. And who knows what that book was. The fact of the matter is that he said I was right. Everybody calmed down and it was decided to solicit an audience. In the name of the Central Committee of the Communist Party of El Salvador an audience was requested with the President of the Republic, General Maximiliano Hernández Martínez. And it was immediately granted by the dictator. We agreed to invite the national press, but they didn't show up. Back then the major newspapers were *La Prensa, Diario Latino, Patria* , etc. *El Diario de Hoy*, owned by the shameless Viera Altamirano – one of the real outlaws in Central America – was founded later with shady money. Among the delegates named by our Party to talk with Martínez were Clemente Estrada and other comrades from Ahuachapán, and Luna and Zapata.

Our objective was to make concrete proposals to the Government. The Communist Party would commit itself to calming down the outraged workers on condition that the repression would be stopped. Naturally all kinds of criticisms about this position can be made from the point of view of the

238

tactics of a Communist Party, but I think that it sufficiently demonstrated our peace loving spirit before the Salvadoran people. The moment for the meeting in the Presidential House arrived. The rest of us stayed behind with lumps in our throats. When the delegates returned, they looked dejected and pale. You can imagine how we wanted to hear what they had to say. In the first place, they reported that they hadn't talked directly with General Martínez, because he had excused himself claiming he had a bad toothache, and in his place he sent the Minister of Defense, General Valdez. While they were speaking with Valdez, so the delegates said, Martínez stuck his head out a big window with a handkerchief tied around his jaw. It was impossible to get anywhere with General Valdez. The comrades destroyed all of his tendentious, slanderous arguments and made it clear that the landowners and the Salvadoran government were directly responsible for the state of violence that the country was going through. They even accused the Government of deliberately creating, on top of the general economic crisis, a situation which would lead to nationwide chaos, to a real slaughter, so as to make the most of those turbulent waters. Only thing is, that water was going to be the peoples' blood. General Valdez, very nervous, hesitant and indecisive, restricted himself to repeating over and over that they couldn't negotiate anything with him, since he wasn't authorized by the Chief Executive. The comrades had to leave without having achieved the slightest result, except for, perhaps, being humiliated. On leaving the room where the meeting had been held, Jacinto Castellanos Rivas, who was at that time President Martínez' Personal Secretary and who in time would become an outstanding member of the Party, and who, by the way, represented us in Cuba after the Revolution, went up to Luna and Zapata to talk with them. Jacinto showed them out in a friendly way, embracing them, and he told them that unfortunately the people in the government were locked into their irresponsible positions and that he thought the only thing to understand was that even if the Army had many rifles to

239

shoot, the Salvadoran workers had many machetes that needed dulling[1].

In that same informational meeting, and in a very firm way, I proposed that we immediately call the Salvadoran masses to armed popular insurrection, led by the Communist Party. I enumerated the favorable conditions which, in my judgement, existed for its triumph and for the seizing of political power for the later realization of a bourgeois-democratic revolution. The meeting at that point was being held with Farabundo Martí as Internal Secretary General, in the absence of the actual Secretary General, Narciso Ruiz, a baker who was at that time doing urgent organizing tasks in Sonsonate. Max Ricardo Cuenca and other intellectuals left the meeting for different reasons and, according to what we later discovered, they had gone looking for a safe place to ride out the storm that was approaching. The discussion was intense and heated. Farabundo Martí finally agreed with my proposal, accepting that the duty of the Party was to take its place as the vanguard of the masses, in order to avoid the greater, imminent danger and disgrace for us of an insurrection that was out of control, spontaneous or provoked by the actions of the government in which the masses would go alone and without leadership onto the battlefield. The meeting lasted all through the night between the 7th and 8th of January, 1932. The carrying out of armed popular insurrection was unanimously accepted (I mean by those present, not the leaders who left). It wasn't a matter of making a hasty, irresponsible decision: within the dizzy whirl of events it was well thought out and planned. I proposed that, given the ripeness of the revolutionary situation, all preparations be taken care of in eight days, at the end of which time we should open fire and attack: that was enough time to prepare all the work and it would allow us to maintain the element of surprise that Lenin required in this case. Thinking over the exact timing of things, that Lenin also demanded, I said that the insurrection should begin not on the 15th of January nor the 17th, but precisely on the 16th, at zero hour. My proposal was accepted in principle and it was resolved that the Central

240

Committee would be the organism responsible for all military matters. Farabundo Martí and other comrades were in charge of finding operatives among friendly officers in the Army, getting arms, preparation of war materials such as explosives, etc., setting up communications with different regions of the country, incorporation of different social and political sectors into the struggle (for example, democratic political personalities, the student movement, etc.), raising money, etc. These same comrades were also responsible for preparing the insurrection's manifesto that would be addressed to the people. Next, the country was divided into zones of operation and each comrade on the Directorate was assigned to one of them. The CC proceeded to name the Red Commanders who would be responsible for the military commissions in the sub-zones, in the work places, in the regiments, in the mass organizations, etc. and who would report back to the CC about their activities. In the actions of the raging insurrection, the Red Commanders would fulfill the military functions of a captain leading his company. But the military commissions had, moreover, as nucleuses of military direction, other duties that went beyond mere combat. These commissions were going to be in charge of doing all the revolutionary organizing within the Army, dividing units into platoons of ten men, getting arms and storing them in distribution centers and distributing them when the CC gave the go ahead, sabotaging lines of communication, pinpointing the public and secret itineraries of the bourgeoisie's Army, forming details of trench diggers (they were actually formed in San Miguel, Usulután, Santa Cruz Michapa, but they never went to work), controlling the railways and other means of transportation, etc. In our calculations, we counted on the barracks in Sonsonate and Ahuachapán, where our penetration was significant, being incorporated into our ranks, and on the support of at least the relatively large number of nucleuses in the barracks in Santa Tecla. We also had in the capital the support of two companies from the Sixth Regiment of Machine Gunners, which was a regiment with a great democratic tradition, that of two cavalry companies, a small cell of soldiers in Zapote

241

(the Artillery Regiment) and all the soldiers from the Air Force garrison in Ilopango. At the last minute, we found out that we also had the support of two companies of soldiers from the Regiment in San Miguel, in the east, and that around them waiting for a joint action more than seven hundred citizens from San Miguel were gathered in the local cemetery, ready to begin military operations. We also had nucleuses of officers in several other barracks, but these contacts were being handled solely and exclusively by Farabundo Martí. In short, we had more than enough strength in the Army, together with the active support of the insurrectionist masses in the countryside and cities, to smash the bourgeois state apparatus. On another front, the unions in the countryside were in the midst of organizing a general strike. From a practical point of view, they were working under conditions favorable to creating a situation in which the agricultural and rural proletariat could lead the peasantry in a revolutionary insurrection.

Sectors of the revolutionary petty bourgeoisie – and these were other contacts that Martí, almost single-handedly, was going to incite – were going to be used to set up the Government: I'm referring to cadre like Dr. Merlos, Dreyfus, radical professionals, etc. In general, the initial unfolding and development of the organization was very effective. Up to that point the repression hadn't undermined the apparatus upon which the insurrection depended, not even putting a dent in its efforts to organize and strengthen itself. The instructions at that point were for each one to take his place and wait for the order to go. However, when we met again with the CC on the 14th of January to discuss the final details, we were greeted with very bad news: it was proposed to put off the insurrection until the 19th. No one present liked that dangerous idea, but Farabundo Martí calmed us down saying that the postponement was necessary in light of the very real possibility of incorporating the officers and troops from the First Infantry Regiment into the revolutionary movement. Already by this time Farabundo was more than an Internal Secretary General: through the force of events and because of his leadership, supreme leadership – as

242

much within the Party as within the organization for the insurrection – remained in his hands. The irreplaceability of el Negro was surely one of our biggest weaknesses. Which makes the position of various intellectual comrades even more serious, intellectual comrades who found in Martí's hegemony the pretext for getting angry, for withdrawing from doing revolutionary work and refusing to make any contribution whatsoever. Martí, himself an intellectual, but very proletarianized, said that they were just vacillators worm-eaten by petty bourgeois ideology. I proposed on behalf of the Young Communist League that the Supreme Military Committee (a new organism that was proposed, based in the membership of the CC) should be organized strictly with workers as a way to get rid of so much vacillation. After the meeting, we dispersed to communicate the proposal to the immediate leadership in the areas of operation to which we had been assigned: no one liked the news. And on returning to San Salvador after this task, we encountered something even worse, another proposal: postponing the start of actions until the 22nd of January. Taking this new plan to the masses was truly a sad, difficult job. With all this, the enemy already had obtained a large amount of intelligence about our intentions and each day, each hour that passed, they were closing in on us more and more. And this in spite of the fact that the enemy's intelligence and counter-intelligence operations were very deficient. Our intelligence operations were worse and we didn't have any counter-intelligence. Above all, the enemy aimed to destroy right off our political and military leaders, our highest level nucleuses. My older sister had a friend who was an undercover agent with the police and who passed her information, since he was one of our sympathizers. Through her we were able to learn that the police had El Negro Martí, Luna and Zapata under surveillance, that they knew the location of the safehouse where they were staying and that they were going to arrest them at any moment. I went to see them immediately to warn them and tell them about the reports coming in from Santa Ana that there was talk of an imminent uprising of Araujistas, for which, they said, huge

243

amounts of arms had come in from Guatemala. Martí, in light of the alarming news, just started laughing and he told me that I shouldn't be afraid – he refused to take seriously the danger of being arrested – and he gave me a package of bombs they had been making in the backyard of the house. He even tried to calm down the owners of the place, who grew alarmed with my news. This was a family friendly to the Party who lived near María Auxiliadora Academy. Martí told me I should go to San Miguel and place myself at the front of the actions in the eastern zone, but I told him that I had already been assigned to direct the actions which were the responsibility of the Air Force garrison in Ilopango and that that was too important a mission to drop just like that. Martí agreed. So I left, and in spite of my persistence they gave no importance to what I had to say. That very night they were all arrested. My sister came to my place crying to tell me and I sought refuge in the house of master José Enrique Cañas, since I figured the next one arrested was going to be me. Immediately a full plenum of the CC was convened to consider the situation. This meeting was called by Max Cuenca, who came out of hiding for it and who was the leading voice at the Plenum. He angrily called for the immediate suspension of the insurrectional work since many comrades had already been taken prisoner, among them the leaders of the movement who had concentrated in their hands our most important military contacts. I opposed that idea and said that the workers of the Republic were now morally up in arms, that we had deceived and misled them a lot and that at this point we couldn't stop them even if we wanted to and even if we made a most desperate effort. Max Cuenca insisted on suspending the insurrection: he said it wasn't possible to go stupidly into an armed uprising about which the Government knew practically everything and knowing damn well that the Army was just waiting for our first move to spring the trap with blood and bullets on the whole nationwide revolutionary and democratic movement. He reported something that we didn't know yet, that the Government had already taken the first steps to institutionalize the repression and had decreed a state of siege

244

throughout the central region of the country, a state of siege which would surely extend to other areas in no time. The majority of us insisted that to vacillate meant the premature death of the insurrection, that it was already too late, that if we put on the brakes now we were going to lose even the ability to defend ourselves against the terrible governmental repression which was going to come down on us, insurrection or no insurrection. We weren't wrong about that. We carried the motion and it was agreed to go all out and step up the insurrectional work, and to make various adjustments and changes in our plan of action. Max Cuenca, despite his opinions, was assigned to reestablish those contacts Farabundo had been working with, and, generally speaking, we decided to fall in line with the call for a nationwide general strike in order to begin mobilizing our forces towards insurrection. We agreed not to attack the Army detachments unless it was unavoidable and we prepared guidelines and teams of cadre to fraternize with the troops who were called out of their barracks. At the same time, we decided to put up roadblocks to stop the flow of government trucks, to cut off from then on the lines of communication, to try to pin the enemy down in the cities, isolating them there and stopping the flow of supplies from the countryside into the city. An Information and Coordination Commission was set up within the CC, which would be responsible for making sure that the dispositions of the Revolutionary Command were circulating at every level of the movement. The CC, however, after the downfall of Martí, Luna and Zapata, found itself lacking information regarding many vital details that were needed to correctly direct the insurrection. It was now the 20th of January and there wasn't one complete report on the material and human resources we had to count on: we didn't know very much about the number and kinds of arms our forces had, we were ignorant of the exact number of red battalions formed and there was hardly any data on the consolidation of commands at every level, on the assigning of concrete responsibilities, etc. We were basically ignorant of the displacement and movements of enemy forces nationwide, and

245

we had only scattered information that had no relation to the overall picture. The little reliable information on which we depended was jealously guarded by a limited number of comrades on the CC and it didn't filter down to whoever among us needed it in order to get results. At the same time, it was a fact that the CC of the Party, due to the arrest of those comrades I just named, had remained very badly integrated from the standpoint of internal unity, the majority being comrades who held opposing points of view, who were immature and more or less sectarian. I believe at that point our Central Committee wasn't capable, in practice, of turning itself into an efficient and indisputable coordinating and directive force for all the revolutionary work. Within the CC, an incredible ignorance of the importance of intelligence and its revolutionary use, as well as a tremendous underestimation of insurrectional military tactics and strategy, abounded. *Up to the very end the Party managed the insurrection simply as a mass political event, without developing a specific military conception of the problem. It simply never saw that the military problems become the fundamental ones once it has been decided to carry out the insurrection and that the military problems are solved with a special technique and science, which has its own laws, etc.* We were working with the masses as if the nationwide uprising was simply a more elevated form of work on the trade union front, on the mass front of the Party. The central military plan almost wasn't a military plan at all, as we'll see later on. As if that wasn't enough, we were relying on next to nothing in material resources: we had no means of transportation and no money, nor were we able to get them. The 22nd, the date fixed for the beginning of the insurrection, I was going around coordinating cells in San Salvador (work prior to the operations with the garrison in Ilopango), on foot, and without even a penknife in my pocket. And what hurts most is that the revolutionary spirit of the masses was incredibly high: a very serious spectacle not just for sociologists to study thirty years later, but that should have been the North of the insurrectional compass of the Party. Already by that awful 22nd of January, the enemy had seized

246

the initiative from us: instead of a party that was on the point of initiating a big insurrection, at least that's how all the cadre in San Salvador talked about it, we had the appearance of a group of desperate, persecuted and harassed revolutionaries. From one moment to the next, the work was in practice abandoned and everyone tried to save themselves from the unrestrained repression. The enemy didn't wait for our famous Zero Hour to begin their counter-revolutionary military actions. Reports about the start of fighting in different places began to reach us few comrades who, in San Salvador, maintained contacts close to the Directorate. When the reports referred to places that weren't considered by us as zones of operation, it was obvious that there had been provocation by the Army which had forced the masses to react with violence, providing an excuse to move ahead and wipe them out completely. Despite the disorganized state of the communications, the insurrectional call of the CC had reached different places in the west and the mass organizations, following orders, had started to go into action. Reports to this effect started coming into San Salvador, especially from the Department of Sonsonate, where the government in retaliation sent in a heavy column commanded by General José Tomás Calderón, a sinister murderer, nicknamed "Turncoat." From the first moment, it was clear that rivers of blood were flowing, that the fighting was completely lopsided and the people were losing, due to the better organization and total superiority of fire power of the government forces. As I was walking through the outskirts of San Salvador, having lost contact with the leadership through the fault of a liaison who failed, I met up with comrade Dimas, a devoted militant, and he told me I'd better hide myself immediately, at least until a way of sending me to the west was found, which was where the real fighting was, and where we had to concentrate our forces. He then told me that he had a good refuge in La Esperanza barrio and that's where we went. We arrived at a run-down house whose owner was distilling contraband rum, and who became very nervous when Dimas explained that I was going to hide out there for a couple of days. While we were

247

working this out, a comrade from the Party named Alberto Monterrosa showed up, who, on seeing me, greeted me with no discretion whatsoever, calling me by my proper name. The owner of the house, hearing my name, gave a start and got even more nervous. His name was Pedro Escobar and he was really an informant for the police, who for two years had been going around following my trail. I had heard about his reports, including the ones he'd signed with the pseudonym "Platero." And so, with my arrival, into the hands of that son-of-a-bitch had fallen a gift from heaven. After a little while he asked if we would excuse him, that he had ought to go out and run an errand. I was on guard, even though I didn't confirm that Escobar was an undercover cop until years later, and I said to Dimas that we'd better get the hell out of there. No sooner said than done. We moved to the home of Regelio Morales, who had been a candidate for I don't know what on the Municipal Ticket of the Party for San Salvador, and who lived in Lourdes barrio. There we had the surprise of our lives when, in like half an hour, that bastard Pedro Escobar showed up. He had hooked his catch and he didn't want to lose it. That really got me jumpy. In order to get rid of him, I gave him some money to go out and buy a bottle of rum, and when he left I asked Morales to give me a change of clothes and I gave him directions to confuse Escobar, and I slipped out of the house immediately. But it turned out that on my way, on reaching the railroad tracks, I could see that some twenty police agents were coming from the opposite direction, with guns in their hands. Without a doubt they were surrounding me. I took off for a strip of woods nearby and gave them the slip without them seeing me, and I managed to come out on Independence Avenue. There I ran into comrade Pineda, a member of the Young Communist League, who invited me to come and stay at his house, but I told him that they were following very close behind me and that I didn't want to compromise him. Pineda still said he wouldn't mind, that for him to die at my side would be a pleasure. A rain of ashes had let loose over San Salvador, apparently originating from an eruption of a volcano in Guatemala whose tremors could be

248

heard in the far-off distance, and it made people say that it was the artillery fire of the Aruajista forces who'd invaded the country from Guatemala and were fighting in the west. Pineda insisted on accompanying me, at least while I was unable to leave the danger zone, and that's what he was starting to do, but I told him that a place I could go to had just occurred to me, very close by. Only in this way could I convince him to go back to his house. Actually I went to comrade Chilano's house, an activist in the Party who lived on Celis Street. Right there was where they cornered me. Unfortunately that little bastard informer, Pedro Escobar, knew the houses of all the communists in the area and he brought the police to all of them searching for me. What happened was, I took too long changing my clothes for a second time, since Chilano had offered me his, and the police caught me with my pants down. I tried fighting but there were too many well-armed police, and I had no choice but to accept my defeat.

It still pains me to think we communists were such idiots that, from the moment it was decided to go ahead with the insurrection, we didn't even guarantee that each cadre at least had a pistol. I don't know what in the hell we were thinking about. That alone explains how the leaders at my level, who assumed we'd seriously risk our lives if arrested, could fall into the claws of the police without firing a shot, without wounding even one lousy informer. Under a shower of blows, my captors brought me to the offices of the Judicial Police, which is what the secret police was called then, located in the house opposite the barracks where the Police Station still is today. No sooner was I there than they placed me under interrogation. A commander named Gregorio Aguillón interrogated me. I knew him very well, but he didn't remember me: he had been a baker and later a National Guardsman in San Vincente and subsequently he became Commander of the post in Soyapango. During the interrogation another person who knew me came into the room, an ex-sergeant in the Guard named Arturo Martínez, who I asked to intervene on my behalf since I'd been unjustly detained, etc. The guy got terrified when I spoke to him and he just stammered that he had always known me as a good man, before rushing out of the room. Aguillón interrogated me about the meeting place of the Party Directorate, about the times and places of the beginning of the insurrection, and about the communist arsenals. Of course I knew very little about all that, but the little I did know I had to swallow, so I began to side-step the questions and answer back along other lines. I even talked with him about his own life. "I know you," I said, "and I know you have been always poor, like us communists, like me. If right now I asked you to lend me two pesos, I know you wouldn't have the money. This is a struggle of the poor against the rich, and it's terrible that it's poor people like you who the rich use to repress other poor people." And that's how I got around him and he couldn't even get me to touch on the things they had ordered him to get out of me. And after an hour, more or less, he ended the interrogation and they took me inside to a dark cell with double bars all the way down in the basement. In this area there were other cells filled with criminals. I remember recognizing Dr. Salvador Ricardo Merlos in one of them. The cops who brought me to my cell warned me that they were going to come back for me soon for another interrogation, but that this time it was going to be really brutal. And in effect, they came back in a few minutes and took me directly to the office of the Chief of Police, in the barracks across the street. The Police Chief himself was waiting for me there, the dreaded Colonel Osmín Aguirre y Salinas; the Deputy Police Chief, a colonel whose name I forget; and a secretary. By the way, the one who tried the hardest to fuck me over in that interrogation was that secretary, since as always happens in these instances, the little runt tried to win merit badges at my expense. First they asked me about my trip to the U.S.S.R. and about my partisan militancy. I avoided saying anything that they might have been able to use against the movement, but I told them about the U.S.S.R. and the hope it signified for the poor people of the world, and I tried to make them see clearly the profound reasons why communists struggle. For a little while the interrogation turned into a discussion, pure and simple. Like when that

Osmín Aguirre solemnly stated that in El Salvador there weren't any social classes. Besides being an evil bastard, the criminal was just plain ignorant. I told him: "That isn't a matter for discussion. It's easy to prove. Even in this room there are different social classes. Between you, who don't work and live like a king, and the secretary who works like a mule and lives on next to nothing there's a difference of social classes. If there was more time I would show you in detail, on a national level." Osmín jumped up furious, pale and infuriated, and he shouted at me: "You don't have time, you wretch, because right here and on this very day you are going to die." "That doesn't frighten me, Colonel," I answered, "we communists are always prepared to die. We don't even need to make confession." The Colonel turned away fuming and the interrogation resumed: the Party plans, description of our funds, where and when we were going to begin our major operations. I told them nothing, but the fact is they weren't very persistent either. I think that even without me they had enough information. In all, I was there over an hour and then I was returned to my cell. In the hallway next to the Police Chief's office, there was a large group of policemen in uniform, with heavy whips in their hands, and when I walked by they started a big commotion and shouted: "Leave him with us, let us take care of him, let us have him for a few minutes and we'll stretch his balls down to his heels." I shot a wad of spit on the floor and they threatened: "Don't try to sleep tonight because we're really going to get you and you're going to eat shit. You're not the first." In my cell, I stayed locked in my own thoughts. I noted that they had emptied the cells of the thieves and only the political prisoners remained. In a few minutes they came once again for me. In a well-lit room they had hooked up a metal chair, a big one like in barber shops, to a number of electrical connections, and they had thrown black curtains over the windows. Inside there were some twenty policemen under the command of a Commander named Balbino Luna, who, by the way, is still alive and has become an evangelist true-believer. They shoved me in and closed the door behind me. They sat me down in front of a small table and started a new

251

interrogation, only this time someone who I never saw before mediated: a lawyer whose function it was to be a notary and witness the official written record of my answers. This pantomime is called a "Court Martial" or military justice, where the criminal never knows anything until he is found guilty, and it has been the formula for legalizing innumerable crimes committed by the military authorities throughout the history of El Salvador. Commander Luna asked the questions. The same old things: the insurrection plans, leaders, meeting places, organization, locales, funds, etc. In the presence of the notary I had to be a lot more careful about my answers. They asked me if I was a communist and painfully – and even though before, with Osmín, I had said yes – I said no, that I was simply a labor leader with the Regional. And my trip to the U.S.S.R.? Well, although the way of life in the U.S.S.R. was socialism, led by the Communist Party, not only communists could go there, and I told them about the many tourists from the capitalist world whom I saw in Leningrad and Moscow. I hadn't been invited by the Comintern, which was the Communist International, but by the Profintern, which was the international organism of the organized workers' movement. Naturally, after all these years and experiences, I realize what a dummy I was back then at the time. How could I have thought that with this kind of defense and these kinds of differentiations I was going to sway my interrogators in my favor? Finally they ended that superficial interrogation and began threatening me with torture. The notary collected his papers and left. The police stripped me, took off my shoes and made me sit down in the metal chair. The interrogation continued there, but in a harsh, jeering tone. That got me angry and made me shout at the police: "You're a bunch of cowards: the thing is you don't have the guts to kill me and that's why you're acting like clowns. Stop these sissy tricks and make me an Indian sacrifice right now." That got to them. "What's this Indian sacrifice?" they asked. "Well, it consists in hooking you up to live electrical wires and then turning the juice on, either slow or fast. It hurts like a bitch." "What poor slobs these communists are." a cop said, "they don't even like them-

252

selves." Later on, I discovered that among the bunch was the agent who had warned my sister about Martí's imminent arrest. Also I found out later that in the cell for the thieves, which was next to the room in which they were interrogating me, was one thief they'd overlooked who heard everything and who went to tell my sister about it when he was let out. After half an hour, they told me to get dressed and they took me out of there. This time they brought me to the cells of the National Police, on the top floor. These, which are many and plenty big, were bursting with workers and peasants – to the degree that everyone was standing up, on top of each other, unable to sit down much less lie down. I began to recognize the faces of comrades in the Party, the Young Communist League, in the Regional, all of them showing signs of torture and beatings. The first one I spoke with in the crammed cell they put me in was Gerardo Elías Rivas, known as "Cafecito," an anarcho-syndicalist leader, very solid and sincere, wrong politically, but a wonderful person. He was educated in Mexico. A group of "Sotistas" from San Miguel, among whom I remember an elegant, gallant man by the name of Fortis. Another was named Virgilio and a third, Humberto Portillo. Two young, very sharp but very sad guys from Chalatenango, who I didn't know, were also there; the famous Araujista leader Neftali Lagos, a fine journalist from Jocoro; and a whole bunch of workers and clerks who I didn't recognize either. The crowded conditions were awful: you defecated and ate in an incredibly small space. The stench from the little latrine was awful. Set facing the door of the cell, pointed right at us, was a machine gun mounted on a tripod, whose operators would from time to time threaten us that they were going to open fire. Night fell. From the nearby watchtowers, machine guns began firing into the night air to frighten and intimidate the population of the capital. Every minute fighter planes flew over, heading west: they were going to drop bombs on the peasants in Armenia, San Julián, Izalco, Sonsonate. That was when I started to realize that nothing had gone right for us, since by that point, according to our original plans, all the military planes of the Salvadoran Government should have been seized or

253

destroyed by our groups who were going to take over the airfield, in collaboration with the very garrison of the place. I myself had coordinated the plan and had developed good contacts, to the degree that my arrest shouldn't have paralysed the operation. The next day, after an anxious and really awful night, the newspaper was brought to the cell with an article in big headlines about the death of Doctor Jacinto Colocho Bosque. The headlines were huge: MURDERED BY THE COMMUNISTS, as if that death had been the first to happen and the Government hadn't already assassinated hundreds of peasants by then. The article talked about how – in terms that would stand your hair on end – a bunch of peasants had murdered this professional after stopping his car on the road from Sonsonate. The language of all the reports on the incident was designed to create hysteria in the urban sectors, presenting communists as wicked criminals, who, with machetes in hand, had launched an orgy of blood and terror. The press, moreover, was attempting to terrify the population with announcements of imminent assaults by the "red hordes" on the capital and plans by the communists to murder all the private property owners, big and small, and to rape all the women – virgins, wives, young and old. That climate of terror served to justify the real crime of the government and the armed forces against the Salvadoran people. The young guys from Chalatenango were the only ones glad to see the newspaper. I asked them why, since those reports were, for sure, part of our death sentence. "That Colocho Bosque received God's punishment," they said to me. "He's the one to blame for our predicament, our being here. For reasons of personal hatred, he accused us of being communists back in Chalatenango, and marked our doors in red as well as the doors of other innocent people. That's why we're in prison. We aren't communists, but if that bastard has passed on already, we don't mind dying. We already took our revenge before, and we're not going to land in Purgatory because of some grudge. Now we can forgive that son-of-a-bitch." By the way, those who murdered Colocho Bosque were some peasants from Colón who were assigned by

254

the Party to monitor traffic on the road going west, and when they stopped that car they recognized the professional who, during the Government of Araujo, had tricked them into working on the road to Chalatenango, and once there, drove them like slaves, abusing them and squeezing everything out of them, and then he had them fired without pay defending himself with the support of the local authorities. Fact is, that car was the only one attacked, something that's inexplainable if it were just a matter of wanton murderers and if you know that, just like Colocho's car, they detained many cars travelling through Colón both before and after the start of the official massacre, inspecting them and letting them go on their way. But what the press wanted was to stir up repression against the people and their reportage analyzed nothing, but rather limited itself to hideous, disgusting distortions. They didn't know when to quit with their "red vandalism" and all the rest of their epithets. And we saw our execution coming as something unavoidable. For that reason, Cafecito grew afraid and started to complain in a whining tone, blaming the Communist Party for the situation we found ourselves in. I argued with him, disgusted, and got violent with him. Señor Fortis calmed us down, saying that if we were going to share the same destiny, it was wrong to be fighting. But as evening approached the fear mounted. When night fell our demoralization was tremendous and even I myself started to feel my moral strength failing me. The collective feeling of being close to death was so thick you could cut it with a knife. Then I decided to take a radical step. I stood up in the middle of the cell and said to everyone in a forceful voice: "If this fear that's killing us all before our time continues, I'm going to start shouting long live the Communist Party, so that they blow us to bits and pieces once and for all with that machine gun they've got aimed at us." This calmed our spirits down some and at least the whining stopped. Even a few jokes got cracked, lightening things up and forcing us to laugh.

But no one in the cell slept. Not because of the crowding, not the heat, nor the anxiety. Around ten o'clock that night a shout resounded, breaking into the silence: "Miguel Mármol, to

255

the courtyard!" Comrade Cafecito whispered to me that I shouldn't answer, that he was positive they were taking people out to shoot them. Poor, poor Cafecito, that was the night he died, too, only up against a different wall. A second shout rang out, very close to the cell, calling me. I answered loudly: "Here I am, asshole!" While the police opened the door, I dished out my food among those who were left, a prison meal of tortillas and beans and some eggs that the families of some criminals managed to get in to us from the street. They took me away, shoving me, grabbing me by the hair and even beating me with their pistols. They didn't let me put on my shirt, tying it to one arm after lashing my wrists together tightly behind my back. Still I said to them, so as not to lose morale: "You don't even know how to tie like the people can, jerks." Then they gave me an elbow in the stomach that knocked the wind out of me and made me see stars. They kicked and beat me down into the courtyard, to the extent that I thought I was going to die right there on the spot. But no, they'd brought me there to put me with the other defendants. In a few minutes 18 of us prisoners were rounded up, almost all comrades from the Party or trade unionists from the Regional. Among them I remember Manuel Bonilla, a union leader with the Hotel Workers' Union, a kid about 25 years old and member of the Young Communist League; Rafael Bondanza, a great comrade with the Party and a machinist with the railroad in Sonsonate; comrade Marcelino Hernández, a baker; Santiago Granillo, my neighbor, a native of Ilopango and particularly hated by the authorities because he had given himself the pleasure of whipping all the military pilots at the airfield one by one, that kid was really hot to knock off the vultures, besides being a wonderful person (that night, by the way, because he was bad-mouthed by the Air Force cadets, they beat him brutally, showing no mercy, and cut off the arms of his corpse); my comrade Dimas, from the Young Communist League, who I already talked about; Serafín G. Martinez, a union leader and worker at Singer, who, by the way, wasn't a member of the Party; Alfonso Navas, a communist tailor and a man very highly regarded in his guild for his honesty and hard work; a

256

Russian and his assistant, etc. This Russian was a foreigner who made a living selling images of the saints in the rural regions and folks said he was a Soviet communist with the International, but the truth is he never had any contact with me nor with the Party, as far as I know. He was young, tall, fair, good looking and he had a Slavic look. And if he wasn't a communist, the truth is he died as if he had been one, with a tremendous serenity. His assistant, a very young boy, from Santa Tecla, didn't want to leave his cell but they kicked him out and smashed him in the head with their rifle butts. When they were lining us up in the courtyard, some Army officers arrived and asked for me. Then they discussed with me superficialities regarding the reasons for the insurrection. Bondanza and Bonilla addressed them and the police in a haranguing tone, telling them that the day would come when they'd be convinced of the rightness of communism and of the crimes that the Government was committing against the people. The officers merely answered that they had already crushed the communist insurrection and that all over the country thousands and thousands were dead. Apart from that they didn't get aggressive or offend us. A couple of great big policemen finished tying my arms with heavy rope, so tight that I started to feel as if the blood was going to gush out of my mouth. My body started to tremble and then they started making fun of me, saying that I was afraid. I snapped back at the insult and told them it was only from the pressure of my blood, that in fact I was less afraid than they were, and that in my place they'd have already shit their pants three times. A big truck drove into the courtyard to take us away. The police started forcing the defendants to climb in, kicking us all the way. I couldn't get in because the bed of the truck was too high and then two policemen grabbed me by the arms and threw me in, as if I was a piece of luggage. I landed all doubled up next to the Russian and I asked him if it was okay to lean my head on his legs. He spoke with a heavy accent, but in correct Spanish, and he replied very warmly: "Lie down, comrade, don't be ashamed." So we sped away from the police station and headed for the outskirts of the city, precisely in the direction of

257

my native region, something that became clear to me when we passed by Casamata, where a squadron of soldiers came to inspect us. Guarding us in the truck were seventeen national policemen with Mauser rifles; the head of the detail, Captain Alvagenga, who rode in the cab with a German hand machine gun called a "Solotur"; and the driver, who also carried a "Solotur." By the way, that Captain Alvarenga died a few weeks later of an intestinal disorder, maybe he was affected by all those many crimes. The man went out covered in shit. On passing through Soyapango, a platoon of National Guardsmen who had set up an ambush, stopped us and asked that we be handed over to them so they could shoot us right there. They said they wanted "to drink our blood." Captain Alvarenga refused, stating that this was his mission and he was going to handle it. It was then that we knew for sure, once and for all, our destiny. The Guardsmen finally agreed to let us pass and told the police that there'd be no problems, since they and three or four military patrols who were making constant rounds had that region under control. I thought that, in spite of everything, I had been lucky because I was going to die close to my village, close to where my umbilical cord is buried. Since on finding out that we had absolutely no hope, we started to raise hell, the police started in with their kicks and insults. What was all that brutality for, if we were all tied up like sweet tamales. They smashed in Serafín G. Martínez' mouth and teeth with the barrel of a rifle. Finally, we stopped in a really dark place that is part of the canton of El Matazano, jurisdiction of Soyapango. Back then there was a local, very dusty, dirt road. Nowadays it's the road to the airfield or Army Boulevard, the part in front of the Royal Motel, a little beyond the ADOC shoe factory. The moon was bright, but the trees kept the place shaded in darkness. They got everybody out of the truck at the point of a barrel. I pulled myself up as much as I could but was planted on the floor. A policeman came over to help me out and then with a slap he knocked off my hat. But I shoved him hard and he backed off and stopped fucking around with me. When I joined the group, they pulled Bonilla and Bondanza out and put them against the

258

wall. Serafín Martínez, with his mouth full of blood and broken teeth, told Captain Alvarenga not to kill Navas because he had five children. Serafín had a big heart. But I, who had always been crude and bad-tempered, yelled at him: "Don't ask anything from these son-of-a-bitches who've brought us here to murder us." The truck's headlights lit up the scene. Fifteen policemen made up the firing squad, while the other two and the driver and the commanding officer were pointing at us. The commanding officer gave the order: "Ready, Aim, Fire" almost in one breath. I'd say he was nervous. But the troops were really nervous too and the first round only slightly wounded our two comrades. The second round wounded them pretty badly but the comrades didn't go down, standing proud and firm, though you could see death in their faces. Sometimes I still dream about the way they looked. Bondanza shouted out: "Long live the Communist Party!" The third round was on target and they went down. Captain Alvarenga asked: "Let's see, which one of you wants to die next?" "Me," I shouted, and I took a step forward. The firing squad was on one side of the road and the wall was on the other. The police were sweating, despite the summer chill. My whole body itched and I couldn't scratch myself because my arms were tied. I started to cross the road when I heard a calm voice: "I will die alongside comrade Mármol." It was the Russian. As best we could, we joined hands behind our backs, uniting us, and we stood against the wall together feeling proud. The commanding officer gave the order and the first round went over our heads. They didn't touch us, and I thought they were just fucking around, to prolong the torture. "You haven't even learned to shoot straight, assholes," I calmly said to them. The police unloaded two more rounds that only grazed us, and Captain Alvarenga started to curse them up and down. With the fourth round they indeed wounded me, in the upper chest, but luckily it didn't go straight through but rather at an angle because of the way I turned when I heard the word, "Fire!" The bullet passed through my left nipple and arm. For me the wound actually felt good, was a relief since the blood gushing out of me relieved the pressure in my arm caused by

259

the rope knots. I didn't think about the saints coming down from heaven or anything like that. My mother, yes, I thought of her. But more than anything, I don't know why, even there and in that situation, I felt I was going to get out of that mess, that I wasn't going to die there. At any rate, I collapsed, both feet kicking, from the force of the impact. The Russian didn't go down, even though he was also wounded in the chest or in one shoulder. When some policemen from the firing squad came over to help me get up, I was already on my feet again. "Fuck it," I said to them, "you'll never put an end to us this way." I don't know where the serenity, the feeling of invulnerability came from. Another round. Here, for sure, they hit me good. I felt several blows on my body and one like a sharp ring, like an electric shock going through my whole head. I was thinking clearly. The Russian's body was over mine and still dripping warm blood. I closed my eyes and did what I could to breathe without making any noise, even though I was bleeding from my nose. I heard the truck's motor warming up, but the worst thing was when I was able to hear that criminal Alvarenga ordering them to put one last "coup de grace" into any corpse that showed signs of life. They found Bonilla and Bondanza still alive. I heard Bondanza's voice: "Kill us once and for all you sons-of-bitches, with one blast of gunfire." Bonilla shouted out: "Long live comrade Stalin, Death to General Martínez!" And Bondanza was repeating it back. I wanted to repeat it also, but I contained myself. The police insulted them and shot them over and over again. Then they came up to where I was stretched out. They lifted up the body of the Russian, who showed no signs of life. A policeman was going to shoot me, I heard him bolt his rifle, but another said: "That's just feeding gunpowder to the vultures, don't you see his brains all over the place? What we can do is see if he has any money." Later on, I realized that a bullet that struck the Russian in the face had blown his brains out and some of the brain matter fell over my head, making it look like it was my brains coming out of the wounds on both my temples. They tore through my pants looking for money. I only had eighty centavos, which is what was left after I gave that

260

traitor Escobar money to go buy some rum. Captain Alvarenga ordered them to cut the ropes from all the corpses, so it'd be easier for the gravediggers to drag them into a common grave the next day. That was when they chopped up Granillo's body with a machete. Then they just went around cutting the ropes, swiping with their machetes. They wounded me badly in the fingers and in the same arm that, in any case, was already dead from the bullet wounds. Finally, they left. For me, centuries had passed and I felt like I'd been reborn. When I heard the truck far enough away, I struggled up and went to see if there wasn't some other comrade alive like me. They were all good and dead. I took Serafín G. Martínez' brand new, tan hat, because I never got used to walking around without a hat.

In great pain and with the sensation of being born again, I started to get out of that place. I crossed through a corn field trying to be very quiet so as not to alarm too much a dog that was barking. Then I reached a railroad line. My head was beginning to spin. When I got up enough strength to climb the embankment, I heard a train coming and I threw myself headfirst back down into the cornfield, fortunately grown and full of brambles. The light from the train was, however, very bright and, just in case, I hid in a muddy ditch that was close-by. I wasn't sorry that I did, in spite of the fact that all that moving about made my wounds hurt tremendously, especially my hands and arms. Actually I didn't know how badly wounded I was. I say I wasn't sorry I went into the ditch because from there I could clearly make out against the sky the silhouettes of soldiers standing alert, with guns, even on top of the locomotive. No doubt they were reinforcements arriving from the east to strengthen the repression in the capital and in the west. When the train disappeared into the darkness, I went on my cautious way. What was on my mind most were the famous search patrols that supposedly infested that region, according to what the National Guardsmen in Soyapango said, the ones that wanted to "drink our blood." Always walking next to the woods, I was heading for the slopes of the San Jacinto mountains. At a bend

261

in a ravine, however, I suddenly came face to face with a group of men who were either resting or lying in ambush, and, on sensing my footsteps, they quickly stood up. My heart dropped to my feet. I stood there in the darkness, thinking I'd fallen once again into the mouth of the wolf, but seeing that they weren't coming at me, and they weren't saying anything, I took a few steps away and ran off in the opposite direction. After running a few yards, I suddenly felt nothing but air under my feet: I fell into a ditch. Because I was so weak from losing so much blood, even though it wasn't a very deep ditch, it was very difficult for me to get out. I was afraid that, with all my stopping and falling down, the blood that was dripping would make a puddle and leave a trail. Very quietly I tried a new roundabout way and thus was able to reach a path that came from the San Jacinto mountains. Just when I started to climb, a dog came barking after me: I could clearly make out a ranch nearby. With the racket the dog was making, the ranch hands came out armed with shotguns and naturally I thought they were a government patrol or the National Guard. There wasn't any place to hide, so I yelled at them not to kill me. They told me to come closer and so I did, all the while explaining that I was sick, from Cojutepeque, and was headed for Rosales Hospital to get help, but on the road to Soyapango I came upon a firing squad shooting some men and that the police, on seeing me, had fired, hitting and wounding me, and that it was a sheer miracle I had escaped. I was a pitiful sight, covered with blood, dirt, mud and leaves. One of the men went inside the house and brought out a kerosene lamp and when he shined it on me they were all shocked and amazed. One said: "Comrades, it's comrade Mármol who we have here." Then many other men came out of the shrubs and from behind the house, some with shotguns, others with machetes. There were some forty comrades who gathered around me. They asked how I felt and if I thought I would live or not. I told them that being in their hands, I would live. But that it was better if we got out of that place because the whole region was dangerous for a group so large and so poorly armed. We left without a specific course or destination. While we were walking, those comrades

262

argued amongst themselves, reproaching each other and reproaching one particular comrade for having squelched the impulse to go ahead and attack the firing squads and thus save the lives of who knows how many comrades. They got especially angry when I told them the police in the squad were more afraid than their victims. When we moved far enough away into the mountains, I took charge of the practical situation of those comrades: it wasn't advisable to go too far out of the region since their homes and families were there, but neither was it possible to stay together and so badly armed, since we were so many. An armed and disciplined group much smaller than ours would be able to tear us to pieces. I recommended to the comrades that they disperse into small groups of four or five, and if they were surprised by patrols or military details, that they simply say they were keeping the peace around their homes. I suggested that they leave me to rest in a nearby abandoned house and come get me in the morning. I hid myself well, in the middle of a thick, leafy bush that hung down like egg yolk. There were a lot of dogs around there and the barking kept me awake all night, not to mention my wounds were killing me. A couple of comrades returned in the morning with their wives, carrying tortillas and eggs for me. I told them what I needed most was a hiding place in order to recuperate, and they said the best thing would be to hide myself in a nearby ravine, called "El Guaje," that was deep and very secluded. I agreed and we headed for it. They slid me down the ravine with some vines and two comrades who went down with me cleared away a place for me to sleep. The ravine was on property owned by the Meléndez family, sugar cane land, for the sugar factories. When I woke up, it was like four in the afternoon and those comrades were cleaning my wounds with sugar water and *chichipince.* They buried my bloodstained T-shirt and helped me put on my outer shirt, which had almost no stains since it was always tied around my arm, the good arm. It was a khaki shirt, heavy, which by the way I'd bought in Hamburg. So I started convalescing thanks to the loving care of those peasant comrades, the best people there are anywhere. They began

263

bringing me news reports despite the fact that the area was being watched like a hawk. I learned that my family had been informed I was alive, but they didn't believe it. What indeed was certain is that the day after the execution the judge in Soyapango, Maximiliano Rodríguez, drew up an affidavit before they buried the corpses of my comrades and he noted that there were only seventeen corpses, and that that of little Miguel Mármol wasn't there. My sisters had been advised that because it was very unlikely I could've escaped and was still alive, they cry over any corpse. So that's what they did. But my father arrived and, not seeing my body anywhere, he thanked God at the top of his voice and the police who were guarding the judge wanted to shoot him right there on the spot. The people who had come to that place to identify their loved ones saved him with their protests. Also, I learned that new orders for my arrest had been issued. They described me with one eye gone and my face disfigured with terrible wounds. The most awful thing for me during those days was the sporadic gunfire you heard as night fell: the lives of comrades and innocent people who weren't going to have my luck. We'd been just some of the first to be shot. The assassinations continued on a broad scale. After a few days in the ravine, they came to warn me that some 20 pairs of National Guardsmen and 4 military patrols, that is, over 100 men in all, were approaching our hide-out looking for me and that surely they had found some tracks because they were machine-gunning the huts and caves. Immediately we organized an escape. It was as hard as anything getting out of there, due to me being so weak, but finally we succeeded. We headed for the top of San Jacinto mountain, climbing all day. We left just in time because every now and then we heard isolated rifle and machine-gun fire behind us, down below. After night fell, we came across a comfortable peasant home, small landowners. The comrades explained our situation, but the head of the family, who fortunately was alone in the house, told us to go to hell. The comrades had no choice but to force him into cooperating, but since he'd shown signs of being totally enraged, we decided to tie him to a tree, just in case. I rested on his bed and ate his watermelon and bananas. I don't know how, but the guy managed to get loose and he tried to get away, bareback on his horse. The comrades succeeded in intercepting him in time. But I declared that the best thing was to get out of there and so that's what we did, after warning the peasant and telling him that if he dencunced us, he was going to find himself in hot water with our comrades in the region. It was difficult to rest in the mountains since there were so many swarming bugs there: between the ants, mosquitos and wasps, sleeping was impossible. Besides which, reconnaissance planes flew over constantly and we were tormented by the sniper fire. From the top of the mountain we'd watch the airfield from time to time, and we saw for ourselves how the planes took turns taking off and landing on their reconnaissance missions. I felt extremely weak and kept fainting all the time. But we stayed hidden in the mountains this way – eating only green fruits and tender roots – for a few days. Until I decided to go back to the city, to San Salvador, risking my life in order to get decent care for my wounds that were growing worse day by day. The comrades didn't want me to go alone and I didn't want them to risk their lives for me. Finally we came to an agreement. I agreed that four of them go with me and as for the rest, I recommended they stay holed up in the mountains a few weeks more, while the worst of the fighting passed, since the safest thing to do was to keep in contact, but clandestinely. Afterwards, if the news reports were good, they could gradually go looking for the way home or for a permanent place in which to work. Keeping in contact with each other in order not to break the chain was my best advice. During the night we went down the mountain in an attempt to enter the city on the La Chacra side. On reaching that place, we found that it was totally under surveillance. Close to fifty soldiers were quartered there, because they were guarding the water pumps that fed the capital. We had to circle around, crossing the river: the comrades carried me across by hand. From the city we could hear outbursts of rifle fire – Martial Law was still being strictly enforced. I decided that my comrades should return from there to their homes or to their refuges, and I entered the city alone. Over my shoulders was a blanket, the last gift of revolutionary fraternity from my life-savers. And I entered the city without imagining the tragic conclusion that that operation would have for them. The four of them hid, waiting for a propitious moment to cross the river again. They went ahead when they considered it safe, but halfway across they were surprise-attacked by a military patrol. They killed two comrades. One escaped. And the fourth was taken prisoner, wounded. Before they murdered him in the police station, he said: "Kill me, it doesn't matter, we already saved the one we wanted to save."

I was very lucky, since no sooner than I started walking up the hills of La Chacra I ran into a detail of armed judicial police. I lowered my head and mumbled "good evening" and they said adíos and passed without stopping. Apparently they confused me with someone they knew, since it was absolutely prohibited for civilians to walk around at that time of night and the authorities fired at anything that moved if there was no answer to their orders to halt and identify themselves. Occasionally, they wouldn't even speak out first, but just like that would start pumping lead. Even dogs and cats turned up dead in the morning, because of Martial Law. It was so bad that a whole generation of drunken night owls in San Salvador disappeared in less than a week under the fire power of the keepers and defenders of law and order. Among them I remember the famous Chumbulún, a resident of La Tiendona, a real boozer, at times very pleasant and at times pretty crude, who turned up one of those mornings singing with the heavenly choir. I also passed in front of an Army detail that had set up their machine guns in front of the Polar Brewery, and the soldiers saw me and a couple even waved to me. I'm sure they were confusing me with some friend in the area, a friend of the police and the soldiers. From a distance I saw that there were a whole lot of National Guardsmen at the eastern station setting up machine guns on tripods, the kind they call "crow's feet." I went around the long way and also eluded the western station, full of high-ranking police officers. I arrived at 24th Avenue North, that street where now there are only whores and perdition: I had to keep ducking into entryways or into public rooming houses so that the patrol cars zooming up and down the streets didn't spot me. Not a soul was out on the streets at that sinister hour. I felt my heart in my mouth from the weariness, weakness, the numbness and swelling caused by my still open and infected wounds, and why not admit it, I was scared stiff. I got to the rooming house where my wife and sister were staying, but there was no one in the room and it was locked from the outside with a padlock: I thought they had fled from there in order to look for a safer hiding place. In spite of the fact that I knew a policeman they called don Amado lived nearby, I stayed in a corner in the courtyard, hoping that by morning some acquaintance or friend would show up. I did the right thing, because what happened was my sister had moved into another room in the same house, and when morning came she and my compañera went out to buy some food and I made my presence known. They had a real shock, since the last thing they expected was that I'd dare return there. Crying, they told me that actually they'd received reports that I was alive, but they didn't know whether to believe them or not, and that they even, because of all their doubts, had made an altar for me in the room where they would say novenas for my soul to rest in peace. I calmed them down, after letting them cry for a bit so they could get it all out, and then I told them that it wasn't prudent to let on that I was alive and therefore they had to go on with and even prolong the praying. Behind the altar, which had some curtains that a sexton friend had given them, they improvised a bed for me to sleep on, and I stayed there even when the neighbors came in to pray for me. Since my wounds were giving off a strong, foul odor, I advised my sister that she should say they had to scatter poison for the rats and that surely some rat had died and was rotting between the walls. I really got a kick out of the praying, since the neighbors, friends, and acquaintances had many memories of me, of both sad and happy times. But my sister, afraid that someone was going to find me out, raced through the prayers so that people wouldn't stay long. After six at night, the hour

267

when under Martial Law it was prohibited to walk on the streets or leave your house, we didn't have to worry about the indiscretion of our neighbors, but, in any case, the place was dangerous for me since everyone knew my sister and wife lived there and at any moment the police could show up and surprise me. A painful report arrived days later that really ripped me apart, to the extent that I nearly forgot the pain I was in and my own sorrows: it had become public knowledge that Farabundo Martí, Alfonso Luna and Mario Zapata had been condemned to death by a military tribunal and that the tyrant Martínez had denied them a pardon. Also it reached my ears that in Izalco the great Indian leader, Feliciano Ama, had been hung and that in Sonsonate they had shot my comrade Francisco Sánchez without a trial. Almost immediately afterwards, these reports were confirmed by the press. The details of Martí, Luna and Zapata tore my communist heart to pieces. They died the way they lived: loyal to their convictions, to the Party and to the people. The newspapers said that Martí refused to defend himself before the Military Tribunal because he didn't want to resort to the laws against which he'd fought all his life, that he refused to confess to a Catholic priest and that before dying he had declared that he considered General Sandino the world's greatest patriot. This has already been written about in our country and I don't think I have to add to it. In any case, later on I'll come back to these very painful, heroic deaths, so full of lessons for us all. Crushed by the sad news and the worsening state of my wounds, I urged my sister to find an old employee of mine, named Pedro Martínez, who hadn't been involved in any political nor union activity and who wasn't on file, an honest person who had my complete trust. Pedro was in the habit of walking home through our neighborhood and we quickly located him. I managed to overcome his fears and resistance, completely logical in such dangerous times, and I had him rent a room for me in the San Sebastián barrio. Fortunately, my sister and wife had some savings. Pedro fulfilled his mission and agreed to go with me to my new room. My wife and sister cleaned my wounds for the last time with spring water and

268

alcohol and wished me luck. We told the landlady that I had suffered a fall while walking around drunk and that I was recuperating after getting out of the hospital. Pedro left me there, on the bare floor, and agreed to come back with a cot. But he never came back: accompanying me under those conditions gave him a case of nervous fever which prevented him from walking. After spending the first night shut up there and unable to sleep (by that point I also had a wicked fever from my wounds), the landlady came to see me and right off the bat she said to me: "Your wounds are not from being drunk and I know that the story your sister told me is a lie: you've got bullet wounds and they're infected, judging from the smell. I can save you because I'm a licensed nurse, but you have to tell me the truth about what happened, because, if you don't, I'll hand you over to the authorities." I stared into her face and asked her: "Do you believe in God?" "Yes," she answered. "Then," I continued, "out of respect for your God, I'm going to tell you the truth. The Government took me away to be shot because my enemies slandered me, accusing me of being a communist. My name is Miguel Mármol, I am a honest man, a shoemaker, and I've fought for the rights of my brothers, the poor." She relaxed and said what a coincidence, she had been at my mother's wake and she'd heard them talking about me there, although she'd never seen me, but she'd thought I was out of the country, in Russia. "Well," she added, "let's hope that the saint you're named for will come through for you. I'm going to treat you and you're going to recover." I was coughing a lot because of the blood that flowed from my nose down my throat whenever I made the slightest move, and she began by asking me to try and control the coughing, since the tenants couldn't be trusted. Living in the other rooms of the house, among others, was an uncle of the good lady who was an orderly in the Presidential House (which, according to her, was both an asset and a liability), and a musician in the Official Government Orchestra ("He's okay," she said, "but he always goes around dying of hunger and he can be bought."). "Moreover," she said to me, "General Mauro Espínola Casto's wife comes here a lot." I gave her my sister's address so she could get some money for the medicines I needed, but I had absolutely forbidden them to visit me. The lady of the house, whose name was Lucía, saved my life. It's true that I don't even like to think about the treatment she used on my torn and stinking chest, a tincture of iodine and alcohol, but the truth is I was in the hands of a saint. In no time my most serious open wounds healed and I was in good enough condition to do exercises to loosen up my muscles and damaged joints. Señora Lucía told me one time that in a little house close to ours another wounded comrade was hiding and that she was also taking care of him. This comrade got well before me and went to another hiding place. I never found out who he was, only that he had showed up like me, renting a room, riddled with bullets and stinking of rotting flesh. And from that time on, I bless that good señora and I hope that if God exists, he will also bless her for her revolutionary charity. And I'm saying that even though I'm a communist and I don't believe in God. And that makes it worth more than if a priest had said it.

---

[1] The anticommunist writer Jorge Schlésinger, in his book *Communist Revolution: Guatemala in Danger?*, refers to the Communist Party-Salvadoran Government interview in the following terms:

"The events referred to (the incident on the La Montañita property. Note by R. D.) occurred on January 7, 1932, and that same day in San Salvador, the Executive of the Central Committee named the comrades Clemente Abel Estrada, Alfonso Luna, Mario Zapata, Rubén Darío Fernández and Joaquín Rivas to make up a delegation that the next day would meet by agreement with the President of the Republic, General Martínez, to protest in his presence, in the most vigorous way, the abuses committed by the authorities in Ahuachapán. In the document naming this delegation, comrade Estrada is ordered to maintain before the President that the strikes are carried out because of the necessity for economic and political demands. The document is signed by Provisional General Secretary Octavio Figueira (Farabundo Martí. Note by R. D.). The delegates request their corresponding audience to speak with the President of the Republic, but General Martínez refuses to see them, under the pretext of a sudden illness, indicating that in his place Colonel Joaquín Valdez, the Minister of War, will receive them. The delegates report that they appeared before

270

the said funcionary, and that upon questioning him about the bloody events in Ahuachapán, the Minister responded that he knew nothing about what had happened, because that was the area of the Minister of Government. The delegates say that they proposed to Colonel Valdez that a prudent path be taken, insinuating in effect that the *hostilities be suspended*, calling back the Guard, and that they—would make sure the strikers would continue their peaceful strike, essentially for economic demands. This was not only absurd, but also perverse, in view of the instructions given by the CC inciting the membership to begin a political strike to confront the authorities. The delegations ends its exposition in this manner: 'The Minister went off on a tangent, stating that he first needed us to give him the moral and political content of communist doctrines, and about if the CP is an organization that aspired only to economic demands or if it aspired to get into political matters. In summary, Colonel Valdez rambled on for a long time about revolutionary doctrine, finally stating that he could not accept an agreement with the CC of the CP, given that the latter was a clandestine organization that has not presented its corresponding statutes for his approval. He got up and left...Such is the result of our official efforts. Unoficially, Jacinto Castellanos Rivas declareed that we could be assured the government would call off its troops in the presence of a peaceful attitude on the part of the striking comrades. We left, stating to Rivas that we denied any further responsibility to the government, and protesting the alluded-to massacres.' This report is signed by all. The signatures of the delegates follow."

Miguel Mármol, contrary to the case of other documents included in Schlésinger's book, gave me no assurance that this report was written by the Party delegation. Nevertheless, its content essentially coincides with the account of the meeting given by Mármol himself.

271

7

Move to the eastern zone to flee the repression. First contacts with the objective of Party reorganization. The meetings in Usulután. First analysis of the reasons for the insurrection and its failure. The facts about the insurrection. The repressive barbarism of the Government. Analysis of the anticommunist "Black Legend" in El Salvador. Military analysis of the insurrection and its defeat.

When I was in good enough shape to return to an active life, señora Lucía offered me a job as administrator on a small plantation in the vicinity of Santa Tecla, but I didn't accept because I was plenty well-known in that region, and a false name, false documents, etc. would've been of no use to me. On the other hand, between April and May, there were strong tremors in Zacatecoluca and it was said you could easily find work there due to the reconstruction and because the work-hands had fled to other regions. I don't know why in El Salvador the great political problems always happen at the same time as earthquakes, floods and other catastrophes. But I decided not to go to Zacatecoluca. A neighbor of mine from Soyapango, comrade Toño, managed to make contact with me and he advised me to leave San Salvador as soon as possible and establish myself in some village in the east, a region where the repression hadn't been so intense. I remember that he offered to go "around the world" with me until I found a desirable and secure situation. My sisters and other family members took up a collection so I could go to the east or, even better, to Honduras. I was getting stronger day by day, but my youthful appearance remained deteriorated: I was emaciated and yellow, like a *ticuriche*, that is, like a consumptive. I decided to leave San Salvador for the eastern region of the country. After all, there in San Salvador I wasn't doing anything and because of the repression I couldn't even think about making contact with the Party, if indeed anyone from the Party was left. I went to see my children to say goodbye properly. I realized in those days that my life was in danger. In fact, now that I'm old I realize I've spent most of my life with my life in danger, but those days in '32 were, without doubt, the worst. I got together with my wife and children in my sister's house and, as other close friends came over, for the first time I was able to hear what people were saying

275

about the things that had befallen the Salvadoran people since January. According to those sources, none of whom were communists, everybody was unanimous in condemning the barbarities of the Government, but no one had an exact idea of what had happened. It was said, of course, that there were thousands and thousands of people dead all over the country and it was clear that who had killed them was the Government, not the communists and not the workers accused of being bandits and murderers. The daily press spewed out its venom about the supposed red barbarism, and the churches and the pulpits were tribunals of agitation where they were asking for tl heads of the surviving communist devils. However, the people weren't fooled by it at all, even though the terror had had the effect of silencing all protest – all questioning. As to the comrades I wanted to know about – public, well-known figures with the Party – no one knew anything. They were given up for dead or disappeared, fled to other countries, jailed, etc. According to what some said, there were no communist prisoners: a communist captured was a dead communist. Later on, we found out that there were indeed many prisoners who were kept for years in Martínez' jails. Some died in them and others managed to survive. The impact of the deaths of Martí, Luna and Zapata was clearly felt among all the townspeople. Several legends were already circulating about the attitude that those three had during the military trial and when they were up against the wall. The Party would succeed after many years in getting the exact version of those deaths through Jacinto Castellanos Rivas, who stayed with Martí on death row all through his last night, and who was with him up until the final moments. By the way, Martí asked Castellanos to stay with him through the critical hours and when he said goodbye to go to the wall, he told him: "Jacinto, you'll be one of us someday." And that's the way it was. Of course, at first glance the only beneficiaries of the situation were members of the National Guard, an outfit that had distinguished itself like none other in repression, murder, rape, etc. Right away the guardsmen were receiving money and cushy jobs from the regime. They began showing off their gold teeth, watch-chains that looked ridiculous on their uniforms, rings, expensive watches, etc., and they started having the money to set up their mistresses, dress their children well and go out for Sunday strolls all decked out, like upstanding middle class citizens with a pistol tucked away under their belts. So when I got to meet with my family, it was very interesting for me to get all that information from friends and relatives. The visit, however, took a turn I wasn't expecting. On seeing the love and the tears with which my children and wife greeted me, and moved by their pleas and persistence, I agreed to let them come away with me. We'd run all the risks together and if we were captured, they'd capture us all and we would all have the same fate. So that's what we did. We arrived in Zacatecoluca on foot, and there we blended in with the many, many people left homeless by the earthquake. But the situation there was worse than we had thought: there was real starvation and no work at all. The picture was the same as you've seen or will see with every earthquake that has struck or will strike within the unjust capitalist system: the poor people made into a miserable lot, sleeping in the streets, sick and hungry, dying from and spreading disease; the shopkeepers raking in their profits, feeding off misfortune; and the rich doing just fine in their beautiful houses that never fall down in earthquakes, attending religious ceremonies to complain to God because He didn't kill us all off, once and for all. We were there one day and one night, and then we took a train to Usulután. The National Guard was in charge of throwing off the earthquake victims, who wanted to go anywhere else but, of course, had no money to pay the fare, hitting them with their rifle butts or machetes. We, fortunately, were able to pay with the few pesos that our relatives and friends had collected for us. But in Usulután the situation, even with no earthquakes, was as tragic as in Zacatecoluca. The lack of work was such that very quickly we had to split up the family again. I sent my wife and sisters to San Salvador before the money for the fares got used up. And I stayed to deal with hunger in Usulután. To keep going east was useless, the situation would continue the same: poor people

277

starving and no work. Alone, I felt like I'd hit rock bottom, and there were moments when I thought about looking for a tree to hang myself on, to once and for all be done with all the misfortunes and sudden fears. All the weight of the defeat of the people fell on top of me like a ton of bricks. That stuff the petty bourgeois say about how misery loves company is just a smokescreen. Because I consider myself just like everybody else and the fact of the matter is, I was always distressed by the misfortunes of others. Among happy people I could never be sad. But in the poor peoples' cemetery that was El Salvador in 1932, I was about ready to die of depression.

After my family left, I stayed on living under the eave of an old run-down house, that I rented for a colón and fifty centavos from a señora named Simona García. Actually, those ruins only served to protect me from the sun during the day, since at night the rain and the cold came right in. Hunger was, however, my worst enemy. What little food there was in Usulután was sky-high. I got up early and started combing the barrios in the city looking for work, but since I was always unsuccessful, I had to go to the mountains to search for something to eat. I spent several days eating in fits and starts, and then only soup made with *chipilín* leaves and ripe bananas that I managed to steal from the plantations nearby. One day, desperate from hunger, I decided to risk going into the center of the city itself to look for work. On passing in front of a house under construction, I bumped into a comrade from the Party, comrade Antonio Palacios, who was up on a ladder plastering a wall. When he saw me, he nearly fell off the ladder from shock, since they all considered me dead and buried. We embraced each other affectionately. Palacios told me he was getting off work for lunch at twelve and he invited me to meet with him to eat then. In fact, at twelve sharp I went looking for him so he could take me out to lunch. He was working for the family of Dr. Córdoba and he brought me to the kitchen of their house to eat. My mouth started to water just thinking about how I was going to stuff myself. We were just starting to eat when the lady of the house came in and, on seeing me and not recognizing me, she got

278

very angry and yelled at Palacios, telling him right in front of me that no one had authorized him to bring vagrants into that house to eat. Sad as it was, I had to go, leaving behind a good piece of pork, which I can still smell. Palacios was dying of embarrassment but I told him that he shouldn't worry himself, that we had to get used to these and other humiliations because we were nothing more than representatives of the defeated proletariat and that besides, the bourgeoisie is always cruel, even without knowing if the one they're offending is actually a communist. For the bourgeoisie it's enough to know that we are poor to insult us and fuck us over. "But we can't let these things be forgotten," Palacios said, almost in tears. I left and didn't go back to look for him. What good would it have done? The only thing that it would have accomplished would have been to make him feel bad. So I continued eating chipilín soup, morning, noon and night. One day I decided to spend my last 18 centavos on a good plate of rice and beans in the city market. In fact, I went there and ate. But on reaching into my pocket to pay, my little centavos had disappeared through a hole. I got very embarrassed, but happily the woman at the foodstand told me not to worry, that I could pay later, when I could. The next day I returned to the mountains, in search for food. But there wasn't a sign of any bananas because they had been cut down to the last bunch, and the chipilín tree that had provided me with soup didn't have a leaf left on it. Evidently, I wasn't the only one who needed to make use of those food mines, free for the taking. So I spent four days without eating, only drinking water. On the fourth day of my abstinence, I met up with a boy in the hills who had cut down some coconuts and I asked him if he'd give me one, that I was starving to death. He got pissed off and told me to go to hell, saying that if I wanted a coconut I should go climb a tree. I didn't have the strength to respond to his insult, much less climb a coconut tree. To spend the time doing something useful and to forget the hunger a little, I decided to go wash my clothes in a nearby river. Washing my muddy pants with just water and reeds, I found in the lining a round object: a centavo. With it I bought three tortillas from a little girl who sold them to the washerwomen. So, I returned from the river with clean clothes and three tortillas, very happy. On the road, I came across a house where there was a woman standing in the doorway staring at me: "Where are you going," she asked me, "with those tortillas?" "To eat them," I said, "but I don't have any salt." "Come over my house and eat them in peace," she said to me, "I'll give you some salt." So I went in and sat down at her table, and she not only gave me salt but a complete meal: rice and beans, fried bananas, eggs and coffee. When I'd finished eating, she told me that I had moved her because I looked like her younger brother. "You look just like my little brother and I thought that maybe he was suffering hunger just like you, because he left months ago for Honduras to look for work." She told me that I was to eat in her house whenever I wished and that she was going to look for a job for me. Her name was doña Ursula Meléndez and she was married to a man named Galea. "My husband also has a good heart," she said. I left really full but I decided not to go back so as not to burden a family that was poor, too, but since my run-down house was very near there, the señora's children found me and at meal times they'd come and say their mother had sent them to tell me the food was on the table. Señor Galea and señora Ursula told me that I ought to move into their house, that my house was going to collapse at any moment and I was going to get crushed, and that I could help them out by doing some household chores as long as I couldn't get paying work. They added that it wouldn't cause them any hardship, that they were okay financially because their grown boys, who were National Guardsmen in Sonsonate, were helping them out. So I agreed to stay a few days, only as long as I was out of work. The night I began living in my new friends' house, I went to hear the Municipal Band in the most central park in Usulután, because I couldn't stand the rigor of my life and I needed to have some distractions. I sat down in a dark, secluded place to listen to the music and ponder my fate. I was lost in my thoughts and hardly noticed that another listener came over and crouched down next to me in that spot. Until he almost shouted at me:

280

"Comrade Mármol!" It was a comrade from the Party, whose name I don't remember, who also was on the run in that region. We shared our experiences and saw that things with us were almost identical: hunger, sudden fears, terror, no work, etc. The comrade told me he would continue his journey the next day, towards San Miguel or La Unión, and he left me a peso, to remember him by. For me it was capital, not a remembrance. The next day I went to ask for a job at the shoe factory of master Humberto Flores, since señor Ursula had found out that the local Regiment had given that shop the commission to make shoes for the soldiers. In fact, this was so and the master gave me a job. The salary would be two colones a month plus a cheque that authorized me to three squares a day at a restaurant close to the shop. For me that was a whole new lease on life! I started working, even though with my maimed and numb hand, I was still kind of one-handed. But my experience making shoes in the capital, in the more advanced and modern shops, gave me certain advantages in spite of everything, and my work was highly valued. As always happens in shoe factories, the conversation among the workers would often have to do with the political topics of the moment. At that time the big uproar in the press, designed in part to make us forget the national situation, was the fierce war in Chaco. Everyone was talking about the hair-raising news in the press – as if there hadn't been something equal or worse in our own country – and I, little by little, started to express my opinions on the matter. Since the records of the civil registry of Usulután had disappeared in a fire, I passed myself off as someone from Usulután named Elías Guevara, who'd left town many years ago. My opinions on the war in Chaco caused the workers to start saying I was intelligent and very knowledgeable. In no time the circle grew with the arrival of progressive intellectuals from the town, since the shop was one of the few places where you could talk about politics without being in great danger. Among them I remember a man named Osegueda, the poet Canelo, etc. One day the subject of the essence of politics was brought up. What is politics? Actually, I was really dumb, I didn't have the least bit

281

of discretion, not even after the terrible experience I had gone through, and I quickly started to give my opinions in depth. "There are those who hold," I told them, "that politics is an economic concentrate." "Well I'll be damned," the poet Canelo said, "this Guevara knows a lot." One day a man from Usulután named Humerto Portillo, who had the reputation of being a communist and who had been in prison in San Miguel as one of the participants of the "Sotista" movement, which I've already discussed, came to the shop looking for me. He didn't find me because I'd gone out with master Flores to buy some leather, but he told the workers that he was aware of my opinions and he was in agreement with them. Later on, I learned that he had spoken very highly of me, even with master Flores, telling him that I was worthy of respect. With friends like that who needs enemies, as they say. Well, the immediate result was that master Flores began to get suspicious of me and the situation got tense. I began to look for a new job. One day I casually ran into a shoemaker I'd known in San Salvador, Nicolás Aguila, who wasn't with the cause but who certainly was a wonderful personal friend. He had established a small shop in Usulután and he put me to work there with him. I thought I'd be safer there. And in fact, I wasn't sorry I made the move. After a couple of days working hard in his shop, Aguila brought me over to his place for a few beers. After two or three beers, very deliberately, like someone who's really thought through what he's going to say, he declared: "Look Miguelito, I know you're still a communist and that you'll be a communist until you die. I don't believe in shit anymore. The only thing I believe in is that humanity is ungrateful and stupid and it's not worth sacrificing yourself for it. The majority of people are stupid jerks only looking to fill their own bellies. I believe you communists are right about almost everything you say and you have to be very dense not to realize it. Very dense or not very Christian. But in this country, Miguelito, people are denser than me, and I assure you I'm pretty dense. And those people who aren't dense are afraid and lazy, and those like you, who always want to fight on the side of the poor are just going to wind up getting your asses

282

kicked good. You can see what's happened these last months, this big massacre. And I don't think it's going to be the last time. Don't count on me for any help in your political work because I've already lost faith in life and it makes me sick to my stomach to think about the political situation that's going to emerge in this country after so much loss of life; since only the rats have stayed alive and free to move around. The only thing I want to say is that here in town there are a few nuts, like you, who are crazy about that communist slop and want to go on being martyrs. That's their business and yours. I'm going to introduce you to them, because I know them from other times when I had illusions. And I hope it's what God wants. But that's the last thing I'm going to do for you. I don't want to get involved in anything." I told Nicolás that I respected his opinions and wishes, but that he couldn't fool me: the fire in his heart wasn't out yet and the proof was in what he was proposing to do for me, since, though it might have been a small thing, it was a revolutionary act. "Think long and hard about yourself," I told him. "If you're an honest man and you understand that our side is right, sooner or later we're going to be in the same trench." And after embracing him, I told him how urgent it was that he introduce me to those other "nuts," communist sympathizers in Usulután.

Nicolás Aguila did what his heart told him, down to the letter, and he put me in touch with Francisco Blanco Martínez, a shoemaker, and with the tailors Luis Dávila and Lorenzo N. He hadn't lied to me. In fact, they were people ready and willing to truly commit themselves. Quickly, they showed the stuff of revolutionaries and I felt the blood once again running through my veins and the mist lifting from my eyes, the fog that had gotten me so down in those last months. The possibility of returning to organizing, to doing, to struggling, was like an injection of life into my poor bones, still hurting right down to my soul. Right away I went to contact Antonio Palacios, who I hadn't seen since that old bitch in the house where he was working sent me packing. We both had experience doing organizing and political work with workers and peasants, and with those three new comrades we founded a cell that, because of us and

283

right in front of our eyes, turned into the central cell of the Communist Party in the Department of Usulután, with headquarters in the departmental capital in order to broaden its influence into the peasant zones. We started meeting to work on plans, to locate friends and sympathizers among the population, to study theory, which, even though we learned it by rote, for us lit up great stretches of the road yet to be traveled. The social terrain, naturally, was extraordinarily fertile and the proof is that within the first week of work we'd already made contact with another three comrades who formed a study circle under my direction, and we had concrete plans to get closer to some fifteen more, well-selected persons, and that was just in the barrio where Aguila's shop was located. Our basic concern was, however, to make contacts and do organizing work with the peasants, and to that end we started going out into the countryside on weekends. Occasionally, we'd leave on Friday night. Very rapidly we wove our urban and rural net between Usulután and Santiago de María. In this last city, we had the luck to meet the Pineda family, the parents, brothers and sisters of the boy by that name, member of the Young Communist League, who had offered me refuge in his house on Independence Avenue almost immediately before they captured me in January. They captured him, too, and they shot him. His parents and siblings filled the void he'd left in our ranks. Once again we saw ourselves surrounded by the love of the peasants, by their caring. The meetings in the countryside started to take place more often; I remember how because of the coastal characteristics of that region we had some giant coconut feasts. The first coconut was for washing our hands with its milk, the second was for drinking the milk and the third was for eating its meat. After that, you could drink the milk and eat the meat of the same coconut. Even in August, we held plantation meetings that attracted up to thirty people each time. The tailor Luis Dávila had a lot of influence among the people in those places, and we depended on him to penetrate many little towns and villages. The fact is, throughout that region there hadn't been any damage from the repression, and the

284

population was practically untouched. But it was also true that in that zone the Party and the Regional had done practically no work at all before. At that time, the outlook there was very favorable, above all because the enemy was relatively unguarded. And the Martínez Government believed, moreover, that it had liquidated communist activity from El Salvador forever.

From the standpoint of content, our first organizational and propaganda meetings were characterized by an attempt to examine critically, using the very little evidence available in the clandestine darkness to which we had been reduced, the correctness of the insurrectional line, the timing of the insurrection, the form in which it was carried out in practice, the results obtained and the reaction by the enemy against the masses, the military defeat and the national situation after the events and, finally, the perspective for revolutionary forces under the conditions of terror imposed by the iron will of the Martinista dictatorship. As a result of the discussions we had in those meetings in Usulután, we wrote up a report of some thirty-five pages entitled "The Whys of the Insurrection and its Failure," one copy of which I later sent to Mexico and another to the U.S.S.R. I don't know which of the copies reached its destination because, sure enough, when they arrested me again, in 1934, in the police station they waved a copy of the same report under my nose. In the report, we came to the conclusion that, at the end of 1931 and in the beginning of 1932, conditions existed to raise with the Salvadoran masses the immediate taking of power by means of armed insurrection by the working classes in the city and countryside, with the aim of installing a bourgeois-democratic revolution that would improve the socio-economic conditions of the working class and be conducive to its development; that would hand over land to the needy peasants and would develop the industry of a newly formed national bourgeoisie, which would see itself freed from imperialist ties. If we had been successful and had had the support of the kind of socialist camp that exists today, the type

285

of revolution to institute would have been, clearly, one to develop a non-capitalist economy based on the most profound agrarian reform, nationalization, gradual socialization and national anti-imperialist liberation. But, at the time . . .

·The conditions that established *the existence of a true revolutionary situation* and that demanded the party's call to action to the masses (which is the point that isn't examined often among us nowadays and which is omitted or diminished by, among others, Dr. David Luna in his analysis, but is without doubt a fundamental point) were the following:

1) The crisis of the worldwide capitalist economy begun in 1929 reached El Salvador and hit the masses with particular cruelty. International coffee prices hit rock bottom. Hunger took hold all over the country and the hopeless desperation of the masses reached an unprecedented level. The bourgeoisie was totally bewildered by the economic crisis and by the new, national political course after the failure of Araujo and his downfall. The economic crisis, moreover, brought the Salvadoran oligarchy, which viewed with horror the mobilization of the masses, to a crucial point: its survival of the crisis and the possibility of its development as a national political power under new world conditions depended on the popular revolutionary movement being crushed.

2) National political crisis. The contained rage of the masses, radicalized by the overthrow of the Araujo Government, a coup carried out by a civil-military faction managed behind the scenes by General Martínez just nine months after assuming power with broad popular support and great ceremonial pomp. Unanimous repudiation of the *golpistas* and the new government.

3) International repudiation of the new Government. For a month and some days after taking power, that is, when the insurrectional possibility was seriously being considered, the Martínez Government didn't have diplomatic recognition from any government in the world.

4) El Salvador was one of the weakest links of imperialism in this part of the world. What's more: El Salvador was a battlefield

286

of various inter-imperialist contradictions, but all the imperialisms were relatively weak with respect to the country. You couldn't say flatly that Yankee imperialism or British imperialism had the Salvadoran bull by the tail at that time. Even General Martínez clearly showed his Germanophile tendencies and was inclined toward Nazifascism. Of course, Yankee imperialism was already preparing its assault on the country and would soon succeed in knocking out the rest of the imperialisms – first after the massacre in '32, when it played its cards with General Martínez, and then, decisively, to the present day, after emerging victorious from the Second World War. It's interesting to see how in history we run across numerous cases where the weakest link of imperialism in a region is strengthened by means of violence: massacres against the people, local wars between sister nations, border conflicts, etc. If the people don't use revolutionary violence to seize control of a favorable situation at a particular historical moment, or, as happened with us, if they use violence badly, sooner or later imperialism makes its move with reactionary violence and strengthens its system of local domination.

5) There was extreme discontent among the state bureaucracy and among the servants and workers of the state in general, because of the radical reduction in their salaries (a fixed reduction of 30%) imposed by the Martinista government.

6) There was tremendous indignation among the peasant masses because of the heightened exploitation and the extreme violence that the boss class and the repressive government forces had been developing against them all over the country: being treated like slaves by slaveholders on plantations and estates, starvation wages, arbitrary and inconsistent wage reductions, massive unjustified firings, evictions of tenant farmers, systematic refusal to lease land, worsening of working conditions of the tenant farmers, destruction of the crops of unruly peasants by burning the sown fields or letting loose all the livestock on them to graze, the closing of all pathways across the plantations and estates – even when the pathway was categorized as a local road, direct

287

and fierce repression by the National Guard in the form of imprisonments, expulsions from homes, burning of houses, rapes, tortures and murder against whoever dared to protest. All this, aggravated by unemployment and hunger and all the rest of the extreme miseries brought on by the economic crisis and by the seizure of the electoral victory of the communists and the rest of the progressive sectors in which the peasants and peons deposited their last hopes, all this, made the rural masses adopt a sharp insurrectional attitude. The urban masses from the central and western parts of the country fundamentally supported the clamor rising from the countryside. The popular masses didn't want to go on living as they had been up to then.

7) Intense political-ideological agitation and social propaganda by different extremist sectors, such as the anarcho-syndicalists, the electoral demagogues, the Araujistas (who had made the promise to parcel out land – later broken – the basis of its propaganda campaign in the presidential election), etc.

8) We had a Communist Party that, though little tested and with big ideological and theoretical gaps, had great discipline and enjoyed enormous popularity and prestige. Its leadership was accepted by the organized workers' movement, the peasant movement (within which its line was truly undisputed) and was very dominant in the student movement and among the petty-bourgeois intelligentsia. Furthermore, our party counted on a good nucleus of communist soldiers and even groups of officers situated in key places in the military organization of the bourgeoisie, as we'll see later on. In this respect I think we can say that we counted on sufficient strength within the Army to initiate a massive insurrection, relying on that strength to deliver the first devastating surprise blow from within the repressive bourgeois apparatus. The SCP had, two years after its founding, the characteristics of a vanguard nucleus that, given the conditions existing in the country at that time, could lead the masses and plan the revolution. In that sense we met all the prerequisites that had been mentioned in the informal meetings among communists at the Red Trade Union Congress in Moscow, that is to say, by

launching ourselves into an insurrection we didn't depart from criteria currently accepted by the international communist movement of the period. That also caused us to believe that, if our insurrection saw itself a success and if the taking of power by the people produced a foreign, counterrevolutionary, imperialist intervention, we'd have the material and moral solidarity of every communist party in the world, of the international workers' movement and of the Soviet Union of Stalin.

9) We also relied on a broad program for a bourgeois-democratic revolution, from which we hoped to have a wide field in which to maneuver in the face of imperialism and be able to incorporate the middle classes into the revolution, neutralizing, at least temporarily, the landowning oligarchy. This program had all the measures necessary to deal with the immediate problems of governing in the first stage of the revolution. Even the person was already designated – el Negro Martí – who would be in charge of coordinating contacts for the integration of the new, broad, democratic government with the participation of professionals on the side of the people, etc. The taking of power by the working class and peasantry in order to make the bourgeois-democratic revolution wasn't a sectarian watchword. The organized workers' movement, though of raw composition, since capitalist development of our country was next to nil, had enormous prestige nationwide and was a truly decisive force. The AGEUS, the professional organizations, the only democratic fronts, didn't exist then. Popular political problems were discussed at length within the workers' movement. As for the rural population, that goes without saying. It comprised (poor peasants and peons or agricultural proletarians) the overwhelming majority of the population (more than 75%) and was as a whole in the most radical position, and was even tending, or starting to tend, toward spontaneous rebellion.

10) The legal roads had been exhausted. In the first place, the great masses no longer believed in bourgeois political parties nor in the bourgeois electoral game. The demagoguery of the Laborite Party of Araujo was what had destroyed faith in

289

the traditional parties, and the electoral fraud against us sank the whole electoral system in the eyes of the masses. The peasant and indigenous masses, for example, had believed that a change of officials would solve their problems (as I already explained), that is, a change of officials that would replace the representatives and mayors with indigenous officials, peasants, etc., with officials from the super-exploited strata. This claim was felt very deeply by the population and that's why our candidates, who came in fact from the masses, got so much support. The fraud did away with those illusions, and the deceived and hurt masses saw that only the armed road could guarantee them anything.

I don't think I sound like a professor, or academic, when I say I believe these aspects of Salvadoran reality at the time are enough to prove that we were facing a typical revolutionary situation, and that it was necessary to take action. I don't think we should be accused of petty-bourgeois adventurism for having done it. But we did it too late, like assholes, we did it after the enemy had begun its repression and had delivered devastating blows to our leadership apparatus, to the basic military nucleuses, putting us totally on the defensive. I think our errors were from the right, not the left. Our errors were, on the other hand, ones of vacillation in the application of a line that was fundamentally correct, which kept us from taking advantage of the right opportunity, of the element of surprise, or maintaining initiative, etc. Our errors were also ones of a tremendous disregard for the material resources of the insurrection: arms, transport, economic resources, communications, etc. And of course, our fundamental and principal errors were ones of the military and organizational type, as I'll have a chance to explain later. We believed we had a party sufficiently qualified to lead the insurrection. This is perhaps one of the matters that can be questioned with respect to the outcome, but only after the fact, that is to say, now. What I want to say is I think we were at the point of what was currently understood at that time, at the international level, as being a party qualified to lead the masses in an action to seize power. In our organizing method and activities, we followed fundamental Leninist norms, trying to adapt them to our situation. Are they going to tell me now that we should have assumed that a classic Leninist party isn't an organism sufficiently qualified to plan the taking of power if it hasn't resolved the military question? Well, that was exactly what we thought. We weren't babes in the woods. As I've already stated, we believed that the strength we were relying on within the Army was enough to start the insurrection and to have high-ranking cadre to lead the masses according to the operational plan we had worked out, and about which I'll talk later. And I want to say that I still personally believe it, even now when I'm able to cite many passages by Lenin on these kinds of problems.

I'd like to pause here, and use it to say once and for all that we didn't receive "orders" nor "watchwords" from the Communist International to "make" the insurrection. The participation of our party in that historical event is the sole responsibility of Salvadoran communists. There is no doubt that during that period a sectarian tendency predominated within the CI which, no doubt, had an important influence on our way of thinking. But the decision, the preliminary analysis and the form in which the actions were embarked upon were exclusively ours, based on local data about our country, and according to our point of view. In this sense, the Communist International didn't have in the events of '32 in El Salvador any other responsibility than that of having been the world-historical proletarian setting within which our Party operated. I say this because the bourgeois publicity seekers and the Salvadoran press have bored themselves silly slandering and lying in the sense that the events of '32 were carried out by following concrete orders originating from Moscow, from the International, from Stalin himself. This is a ridiculous thing to say and just more thievery by the class enemy. Neither is it true that the U.S.S.R. nor the International had set aside substantial economic resources for us in order to make the insurrection. The only, and very small, economic aid we received at any time from foreigners was through the International Red Aid and that was no more than fifty dollars a month, aid destined for the families of those fallen in the repression, for the defense of prisoners, etc. If we had received huge quantities of money from the outside, or arms, etc., without a doubt we would have held the government of Martínez in check for a long time and the reactionary violence wouldn't have come down on us with so much destruction. Of course, it's also necessary to say something publicly that we never denied: we Salvadoran communists in '32 understood that by our revolutionary labor we also helped to strengthen the position of communism in the world and that, concretely, our work directly aided the consolidation and development of the Soviet Union, the only country then where the proletariat had seized power. We communists have always been essentially internationalists and that's precisely why we are the best patriots: because our highest international duty consists of making revolution in each one of our countries. I emphasize this point because it is important and because it is right and because it is true.

Also it's convenient to situate, for many reasons and so as to order the discussion that may come up someday about these incidents, the Leninist character of the activity of the Salvadoran Communist Party from its birth up to the massacre in '32. I think the following facts establish it:

—Our activity was directed principally at the working masses in the city and countryside (artisans and urban workers, clerks, poor peasants, semi-proletarians and agricultural proletarians), that is at the most exploited sector in the country;

—The activity was linked as mass struggle to every sector that could possibly be incorporated, that is: average peasants, poor shopkeepers, fishermen, vendors with small businesses — on the street or otherwise; tenant farmers and renters, students and professionals, progressive merchants, etc. For each sector, our Party worked out programs with specific demands upon which to base its integration into the struggle. The unemployed were organized around the demand for bread and jobs;

—The leadership of the Regional Federation of Salvadoran Workers, the principal mass organization in the country, was won over to our side, wrenching it out of the hands of the

292

reformists and anarcho-syndicalists, which, besides being a concrete need in our own country to develop the revolutionary movement, was a problem worldwide for every communist movement;

–Our international bond with every revolutionary in the world and with all the exploited was firmly proclaimed. We proclaimed among the masses our support for the anti-imperialist struggle of General Sandino in Nicaragua, for revolutionary China, etc., and we proclaimed our solidarity with the international movement of organized workers and peasants and with the Soviet Union;

–We organized and led numerous, broad economic strikes in the cities and countryside and carried out countless, sweeping mass actions (rallies, peasant gatherings – public and secret –, political and trade union demonstrations, political agitation and propaganda, etc.) against social injustice and imperialism, against the repressive policies of the regime, that raised the consciousness of the masses and contributed to deepening the national political crisis;

–We had, similarly, a concrete policy (the bourgeois-democratic revolution, in the terms I've already discussed) and a detailed program. By the way, all the copies of this program disappeared and I haven't been able to look at even one since then. I should ask the Soviet comrades if they've maybe got copies in the Archive of the CI, because we sent them then a whole bunch.

Okay, in order to give a complete picture of things, the pros and cons, I want to say that those inside the Party who flatly rejected the insurrection, gave, as the basis for their point of view, the following reasons:

1)That we only had limited influence in the country and that we couldn't count on support from the eastern region of the Republic. This was false. We even had military support in the eastern region and our political agitation, organizing and propaganda work was broad, though less than in the central and western regions. Moreover, we believed that once all the printing houses and newspapers were seized, we could flood

293

the east with our own propaganda, detaching teams of specialized agitators, etc.

2) That there were many comrades in prison who could be massacred by the Government as soon as we began our operations. What should have been planned was a way of rescuing these comrades. As it turned out, the Government murdered the prisoners who it already had anyway and many thousands more who were walking around "free." At the time this was discussed in the Directorate of the Party, you could count the number of prisoners on one hand: the Mojica brothers from Sonsonate, comrade Zafarrancho, Gabriel Mestica, comrade Erizábal, etc. And later on, Martí, Luna and Zapata.

3) That North American imperialism, regardless of what we were planning, had invaded Nicaragua and wouldn't allow 24 hours to go by before launching a direct military invasion against us in the event that we took power, and that we weren't capable of going up against its well-organized troops, equipped with modern weapons. This thesis was thrown in our face both before and after the insurrection, not only in El Salvador but also within the International. Comrades like Panelón from the Argentine Party, and Siqueiros from the Mexican Party brandished it against us. We, however, didn't believe (and I still think there was good reason in our estimation) that a direct, armed intervention by imperialism would be fatal, or sure of winning. They weren't so strong then that they could just do as they pleased. Even after the massacre, when they wanted to send troops, General Martínez didn't let them land as they wanted. But even in the face of the reality of a Yankee intervention of great importance, General Sandino had already shown us, from the Segovian jungles in Nicaragua, the path: guerrilla warfare in the mountains, national war against the invaders. And in the Salvadoran case (in the event of an insurrectional victory like we're talking about) the Yankees were going to have to confront a mass struggle that by then – that is, when they landed – would have already destroyed the power of the local bourgeoisie. The thing wasn't so simple. Moreover,

294

the program of bourgeois-democratic revolution gave, as I've said, room to maneuver in the face of imperialism. Of course, in this area there were also comrades who went over to the other side, that is to say who completely underestimated the imperialist danger and who simply believed the imperialists were going to stay put with their arms crossed forever, and that they were even going to help us. Of course, that was really like pissing in the wind.

4) That our Party wasn't capable of leading the masses to insurrection — not politically, not organizationally, not militarily, not ideologically. In this respect, I think we have to explain some differences. I think that our Party would have been able to lead an insurrection if it had had and kept the initiative and the element of surprise. But the fact is that, because of vacillations and delays, because of gross violations of the most basic measures of revolutionary security, the insurrection ended up being initiated by us, as I've said more than once, when the Government already had assassinated all the communist officers and soldiers inside the bourgeois Army, had captured and liquidated or was on the point of liquidating most of the leadership of the Party and mass organizations. I think it's best to go into the details of the insurrection so that we don't keep talking into thin air. You have to remember, I'm not trying to get involved in a theoretical discussion.

The start of the insurrection was approved for the 16th of January in a meeting held on the 7th of January, as I already stated. Already by the 14th of January it was evident to all of us that the Government had vital information about our plans. Instead of speeding up the preparations and precipitating events (since there was no chance of turning back, given the fired-up state of the masses who would have risen up spontaneously without the Party, and given the armed provocations by the Government and the Army against the peasant population) the Central Committee approved a new postponement of the first actions, this time for the 19th. This was the day they arrested Farabundo Martí, the best-known and accepted leader of the Party, together with comrades Luna and

295

Zapata, important leaders of the student movement, of the urban masses in San Salvador and of the Party. After long discussions, the insurrection was set for the 22nd of January. By that point, in practice, the repression had begun on a broad scale. On the 16th, for example, our soldier comrades from the Sixth Regiment of Machine Gunners started to prepare their arms for action, since they were following orders issued on the 7th. The officers were very surprised by the activity and, besides, there was a direct denunciation made by a sergeant to whom the comrades had revealed the insurrection plans in order to recruit him. That same day, with troops from other barracks and with the Guard that unexpectedly showed up at the Sixth, they executed almost all the soldier comrades and non-commissioned officers, and the few survivors were locked up in the Penitentiary until they died, as in the case of a sergeant comrade named Merlos, and others. For us, that massive execution meant, in operational terms, the loss of two companies of machine gunners, who would have been decisive if they could've taken part fully in the start of the insurrection. Similarly, our comrades from the Casamata Barracks (First Infantry Regiment) and the Air Force were killed or controlled, virtually made powerless. On top of the massive executions inside the barracks, the Army Command ordered the transfer of troops and officers between all the barracks in the Republic with the aim of disrupting any possible internal plot to revolt. Those most recognized as communists were being murdered in the transfers, including whole platoons and companies who were wiped out in ambushes set by the Army itself. Also, it rapidly conscripted huge numbers of troops from the east, where our propaganda was weak, troops used to repress the western and central zones. We weren't able, under those circumstances, to coordinate the action with the nucleuses we had in the east, in the Army as well as in the population of San Miguel and La Union, which had organized themselves for armed battle, including even companies of engineers, medics, etc.

This initial setback within our nucleuses was terrible for us, decisive in fact, according to our basic military plan that I'll lay out in its general characteristics further on.

In order to understand up to what point the Government took the lead and set the fatal trap for us and the Salvadoran people, you have to know about the fake document attributed to the Secretary General of the Party that, under the title "Instructions to Salvadoran Communists for their General Offensive on the 22nd of January, 1932," began to circulate widely throughout the country, at least beginning on the 20th. This is that document, down to the last dotted "i":

"TO THE DEPARTMENTAL EXECUTIVE COMMITTEES OF THE COMMUNIST PARTY. URGENT GENERAL INSTRUCTIONS.

1) All red commanders must strictly obey the orders of the Departmental Executive Committees of the CP.

2) The 22nd of January, 1932, at midnight sharp, all the contingents of our revolutionary organizations must be mobilized and ready to attack the barracks of the departmental capitals, thus engaging in immediate actions to seize said barracks, as well as the Police and National Guard posts.

3) The actions against the forces of the National Guard must be decisive, not leaving any of those agents alive, seizing all arms and munitions they may have.

4) The revolutionary actions against the bourgeoisie must be as far-reaching as possible with the object, in a short time of merciless terror, of making sure they are reduced to complete impotency, employing against them the appropriate means, that is: immediate execution or death by whatever other means, stopping at nothing.

5) Our forces must go into the houses of the known merchants, proprietors and landowners, killing them all and respecting only the lives of the children, and placing at the disposal of the Departmental Executive Committees of the Communist Party all the money in said houses and everything they keep in their stores and granaries.

297

6) All the warehouses and banks must be opened up, seizing immediately everything found in them and putting everything under the control of the Departmental Executive Committees of the CP.

7) Action must be taken to confiscate all cars and trucks, as well as all gasoline found in stores, warehouses and in private homes.

8) The empty and abandoned houses must be made ready to be occupied to quarter the Red Army and to shelter the families of workers and peasants.

9) Immediately after the taking of the barracks and the other Police and National Guard posts, and having reduced the bourgeoisie to complete impotency through the violent and determined actions of the Red Army, the march on the capital must start, making use of all vehicles held, so that said march will be as rapid as possible.

10) Two of the best cars must be turned over to the Departmental Executive Committees of the CP, which will be driven by absolutely trustworthy comrades.

11) All counterrevolutionaries, the same as with all remaining forces, must be executed, without prior war council, immediately upon being captured.

12) All resistance on the part of the target Army, such as all those who in one form or other are opposed to the course and development of the operations of the Red Army, must be immediately punished under penalty of death.

13) The supplying of the forces of the Red Army must be carried out, naming special commissions who will be in charge of food and clothing.

14) The Red Cross must be organized, in which all comrades must take part, and all vehicles that may be needed must be placed at the disposal of said Red Cross. All professionals, such as doctors, health workers and pharmacists who refuse to lend their services to the revolutionary forces, must be treated as counterrevolutionaries, executing them immediately.

15) The corps of telegraph and telephone operators must be organized, proceeding with the takeover, by means of red troops, of offices that fall into the hands of our forces, shooting the counterrevolutionary employees who betray or refuse to work at the service of the Revolution.

16) The publishing houses must be safeguarded, immediately placing all their employees under the Directorate of the Communist Party, with the understanding that they will take charge of the editing of communist manifestoes, newspapers, magazines, etc. Those who refuse to lend these services must be treated as counterrevolutionaries, executing them immediately.

17) The forces of the Red Army must be treated with the strictest revolutionary discipline, considering as counterrevolutionaries all those who disobey orders and executing them immediately.

18) Instead of Municipalities, Soviets must be proclaimed, which will be made up of Workers' Councils, peasants and soldiers, who will administer and distribute production with sufficient power to proceed independently against counterrevolutionary elements, executing them immediately.

19) A police force must be kept under the orders of the soviets that will inflict on the bourgeoisie the greatest terror, capturing and executing all reactionary and counterrevolutionary elements still alive after the taking of the departmental capitals.

20) The Departmental Executive Committees must remain fully empowered to proceed to take all measures that will guarantee the swift strengthening of our forces and the immediate conquest of power, knowing beforehand that the success of the action will depend on the decision and discipline employed in the moment of struggle, without forgetting that until the taking of the barracks in the capital is established, almost nothing will have been accomplished. Consequently, everyone should know that the principal objective is to seize the barracks in the capital and smash the capitalist big bourgeoisie who reside there.

21) The revolutionary forces will make use of the railroads, treating all employees who refuse to lend their services as counterrevolutionaries, executing them immediately.

22) Preference must be given to the highways for the march on the capital, making use of every car and truck available and establishing a link with the troops in the rearguard by means of mail couriers.

23) Nothing must halt the revolutionary forces. The least vacillation will be fatal. The offensive must be carried out at all costs. The defensive is, as we know, the death of the insurrection. Blows must be dealt against everyone and everything that opposes the course and development of our operations. Every obstacle must be overcome with revolutionary drive and with the greatest of daring.

24) General offensive and maximum terror against the bourgeoisie, smashing it quickly and reducing it to nothing.

25) Long live the troops of the Red Army who will struggle gloriously for the conquest of power! Long live the Red Guard! Long live the valiant soldiers of the Red Army! Long live the Proletarian Revolution! San Salvador, 16th of January, 1932. Secretary General."

As you see, it was a very malicious and underhanded document that circulated widely and did us a lot of damage, since it presented us before the eyes of many simple people as a gang of bloodthirsty murderers, who'd murder for anything without asking any questions or weighing the evidence. Also, this document had the objective of frightening the Army, elements of the National Guard and the Police, making them believe we intended to execute them all. With this, the Government went after getting the troops and security bodies to fight us down to the last shot and not to believe our propaganda that invited them to come over to our ranks, and that was actually getting big results in different barracks, as the enemy itself admits, in Schlésinger,[1] for example. This fake document hurt, especially, because it was written in a language very similar to ours and because it pointed out many activities that doubtless we would have developed in the course of the

300

insurrection (and which had been discussed by the leadership in different meetings), with the taking over and managing of many public services, especially those of transportation and communications. The only thing is, that document gave the insurrectional activities such a bloodstained hand that it turned many people against us, even within our ranks, causing much confusion. It was in documents like this that the repressive forces attempted to base their justification for the mass murder of more than 30 thousand peasants and workers: alleging that it was a matter of a preventive action against the crimes supposedly planned by the communists. That, on top of the rumors that were going around: that we were going to rape women, that we were going to hang all the priests, etc. And later on, based on documents like this, a few fraternal Parties of the International said ours wasn't a real Party, but a party of ignorant machete wielding peons. The enemy succeeded in its objective to create confusion at every level, including some that had never crossed its mind. The truth was different. If our Party had called for slaughter, if it had committed that irresponsible and counterrevolutionary crime, the Salvadoran drama would've been even more catastrophic, because, if the popular masses, above all the peasant masses, listened to any organization, it was our Party, our Central Committee. It's enough to say here, as we'll see later in detail, that the deaths caused by our insurrectional forces were about twenty and in every case they fell in combat, excepting one or two cases where it's true we fell into a reprehensible excessiveness. On the other hand, the Government, I repeat, by unleashing the repression, didn't stop the massacre until it assassinated more than 30 thousand of our brothers, the great majority of them absolutely innocent of any participation in the revolutionary work.

Let's examine now in more detail the events of the thwarted insurrection and its terrible repression.

As is known, the actions of the popular insurrection were carried out principally in the western region of the country. In Tacuba they attacked the National Guard and took over the village for one or two days, establishing a local soviet. In

Ahauchapán the masses besieged the departmental barracks and engaged in fierce combat, but they didn't succeed in controlling the situation. The biggest action was the one in Sonsonate, where the peasants took over the Customs Building and several other strategic points. The barracks of the Departmental Regiment was attacked, but the machine-gun fire hurt us a lot. However, seventeen of our combatants succeeded in penetrating the barracks, by fighting their way in, but because they lacked the support of enough fire power they were isolated from the rest of the masses and killed in action. Sonsonate is the third or fourth most important city in El Salvador. In Juayúa they seized the local barracks, established the soviet and for three days the red flag waved there next to the flag of El Salvador. I don't think any of the members of the soviet in Juayúa survived the subsequent repression. As that guy Pedro Geoffrey says in one of his poems: "As for the first Soviet in America, they shot the shit out of it." That Pedro talked so much shit in his poems that he ended up washing himself in it. In Izalco, similarly, a contingent of some two thousand comrades took over the village for three days and nights and it was only because of the machine-gun fire and aerial bombing that the contingent pulled back and dispersed. Nahuizalco was completely taken over, for an equal amount of time. In Teotepeque, the actions were led by Farabundo Martí's father, who began by seizing City Hall at pistol point. Our forces similarly held, for a brief period of time, Tacuba, Ataco (which was the birthplace of the Cuenca comrades, whose father and younger brothers were later hanged by the Army and the so-called Civic Guard), Salcoatitán, Colón, Sonzacate, Turín, San Julián (which was severely bombed and strafed by the regime's Air Force), and they were prepared to descend on Armenia and Ateos. The intense and well-organized repression by the regime forced us out of all our positions, disrupted our columns and threw our comrades and sympathizers into a mad flight for the countryside and mountains, thus creating the conditions for the massive and practically unanswered annihilation of the people. The assassination of thousands and thousands of

302

Salvadorans was coldly planned by the Martínez Government and the Military High Command, with the total backing of the most powerful nucleuses of the Creole oligarchy and the newborn local bourgeoisie, and was carried out against the people in general, indiscriminately hitting peasants and workers the whole length and breadth of the country and not only in the action zones, although of course in these zones the slaughter was much worse. The idea was to wipe out every vestige of popular organization, eliminating physically the actual and potential militancy of the democratic, popular organizations, including the less radical ones. And the idea was to do it for good, in order to create a desolation that would last years and years. The first days they murdered close to two thousand people a day, and then went on murdering wholesale throughout the Republic for two or three months. And on the level of individual murders, practically for the whole thirteen years of General Martínez' reign. As for the comrades who moved to other regions, they were found by means of the residence lists they compiled in the telegraph and post offices where they received mail, and were immediately ordered to be killed, and as for those who remained close to their villages, they were killed as soon as they were recognized. The extensive communist voting lists used for the elections became the basis for locating and liquidating thousands of persons. Commissions of the National Guard and secret police, dressed as peasant civilians, inspected the plantations in the country on pay days and whoever they recognized as revolutionaries or communist sympathizers, or whoever they thought they recognized, they would immediately kick out of line and kill them right there, in the bushes. The other peasants would hear the shots and screams, and they knew one more communist had fallen. So the terror was tremendous. Moreover, in each locale counterrevolutionary white Guardsmen were organized, called "Civic Guardsmen," made up of bourgeois, opportunist, delinquent or reactionary fanatical elements, who were responsible for locating persons previously classified as communists or progressives and delivering them over to the armed forces, and also for carrying out

303

with their own hands murders, robberies, rapes, tortures, etc. against the humble strata of the population. Even persons who later have passed into the history of our country as democrats, even progressives, formed part of these criminal gangs and participated in the most tremendous crimes against the people. To say nothing of the number of personal hatreds and feuds that were settled in this cowardly way.

It's impossible to relate even approximately the details of the barbarism unleashed throughout the country by the repression of the bourgeois government of General Martínez. Many years have gone by, and now almost unshakable notions about '32 have formed in the minds of the compatriots. Unfortunately, the huge figures leave us cold, too, and they don't communicate the true intensity of those events either. And it's true also that imperialism, in every part of the world, has continued to commit enormous crimes that leave behind the terror that we thought in those days was unsurpassable. But I think the drama of '32 is for El Salvador what the Nazi barbarism was for Europe, the North American barbarism in Vietnam, a phenomenon that changed completely, in the negative sense, the face of a nation. For the Salvadoran people, there were more than 30 thousand killed in the events of '32, which was more than 2.5% of the population at that time. That's not counting the wounded, beaten, tortured, etc., only those killed. Let's remember that each one of those killed wasn't a simple number but a person with hopes, sorrows and emotions; with a first name, a last name, interests, family, friends. It's truly awful. And as I said, the survivors also paid an enormous price: the wounded, tortured, beaten, the prisoners, women raped, children left orphans, families that from then on spent their lives fleeing death and persecution, the starving, the homeless, separated families, persons stripped of all the little they had, etc., etc., not to speak of the thousands and thousands of compatriots who had to leave, fleeing with only the clothes they were wearing, to other countries like Guatemala, Honduras, Nicaragua. It should be said that the biggest mass wave of Salvadoran emigration was produced in 1932. After that damned year all of us are different men and I think that from then on El Salvador is a different country. El Salvador is today, before anything else, a creation of that barbarism, I firmly believe that. All the rest is just make-up, trimmings, candy to keep the people quiet. It's possible that the style of the rulers has changed, but the basic manner of thinking that still governs us today goes back to the slaughterers in 1932. It's enough to think of the many names of civilians and military men who today fill principal posts in public administration and in the repressive forces. I say all this because the truth is that I don't know where to begin to even partially tell about all the crimes committed by the rich and by the Army against the people at that time. I'll just say that the biggest collective massacres were committed in Soyapango (where most of the prisoners captured in San Salvador and in the east were shot), Ilopango, Asino (the same), El Playon (Cujuapa), where they murdered a large contingent of comrades or sympathizers arrested in different parts of the country, and, with one stroke, from pure sadism, murdered all the common prisoners who were doing forced labor on a road that went through there; in Santiago Texacuangos, in Colón, Comasagua, Tacuba, Izalco, Juayúa, Salcoatitán (where also a great group of people who had congregated in the public plaza was machine-gunned), Zaragoza, Teotepeque, Jayaque, the outskirts of Santa Tecla and Ahuachapán. In Armenia, a general named Pinto personally killed 700 peasants after his soldiers forced them to dig their own graves, one by one. General Ochoa, who was the governor of San Miguel, forced the arrested men to crawl on their knees up to where he was sitting in a chair, in the courtyard of the barracks, and he'd tell them: "Come here, smell my pistol." The prisoners begged him in the name of God and their children, crying and pleading with him, since before entering the courtyard they had heard intermittent gunshots. But the barbarian general insisted and convinced them: "If you don't sniff the pistol it's because you're a communist and afraid. The one who has nothing to hide, fears nothing." The peasant sniffed the barrel and right there the general put a bullet in his face. Then he'd say, "Send in the next

305

one." The famous "hero" of the struggle against Martínez in 1944, Colonel Tito Tomás Calvo, was the executioner in Izalco and had another version of General Ochoa's little trick that was a real son-of-a-bitch. When the peasant arrived under arrest and tied up, the general said to him: "Open your mouth and close your eyes, let's see what your teeth are like." They pretended it was a physical exam for forced conscripts. When the man opened his mouth, Tito Calvo shot him through the palate. All these facts are known by loads of people in El Salvador. What happens is that many people are in the habit of forgetting it, to their advantage. This same famous "hero," Tito Tomás Calvo, machine-gunned in the Church of the Conception in Izalco, which was a simple ranch house with a courtyard, more than two hundred persons at one go, the majority women and children. In Chanmico and Las Granadillas, the National Guardsmen burned all the ranches in an area of twenty square kilometers and raped all the women over 10 years old. The Mojica bothers, who were imprisoned in Sonsonate since before the actions, were assassinated after horrible tortures, though of course they hadn't participated in the actions. In Tacuba, as I already said, they hanged the elderly father of the Cuenca comrades, who hadn't participated in the political activities of his sons, together with those others who also hadn't participated, as in the case of Benjamín, who was a child. They hanged one comrade from Nahuizalco in front of his family and then the soldiers threw the body through the air by the arms and legs, and others caught it while it was still in the air, stabbing it with their bayonets. From the barracks in Ahuachapán blood flowed in a river, as if it was water or horse piss. A lieutenant who was on duty there cried as he told about how the peasants, as they were shot in groups in the courtyard, would sing "Holy Spirit You Will Reign," a Catholic song, and that among the pools of blood he and the soldiers in the firing squad had seen the image of Christ real clearly and that they refused to go on killing and protested to their superiors. The protest was made in terms so convincing that the Commander of the Barracks ordered the massacre stopped temporarily. That's how Modesto Ramírez was saved. Seven brothers by the name of Alfaro were falsely accused of being communists on the San José Plantation along with their aging father. In the very entryway of the plantation they shot them all, without even allowing the father to go to his house, which was right there, in order to change his clothes since he asked as a last right to die dressed in white. Terrible scenes like this recurred all over the central and western parts of the country. In Izalco, for the hanging of the respected indigenous leader Feliciano Ama, they brought the school children to watch the spectacle "so they won't forget what happens to communists who dare to rise up against their bosses and the established authorities." The Air Force spent days upon days machine-gunning the rural zones: a person who moved was a person who made the planes spit fire. Filiciano Ama's people on the outskirts of Izalco were massacred in this way and by the punitive infantry. By the way, Ama has remained in the national history as the last great representative of indigenous rebellion, following the tradition of Anastasio Aquino. Ama had joined with communism and the purest of our countrymen had joined our ranks with him. But Ama hadn't joined the struggle as an Indian, but rather as an exploited man. The Regalado family, for example, had stripped him of all his land and beaten him and hung him up by his fingers. I had met him after the events on the 17th of May, when I came to lift the spirits of the masses facing the repression. We met in Sonsonate, I recall. Ama was skinny, his skin the color of copper, with big, healthy teeth. He was totally committed to the struggle and he told me about the abuses he had suffered: he showed me the scars on his fingers from the hanging. He pointed up to a small mountain to show me how far the land he still had went, and it wasn't so small either, and he told me how he was going to allot the land to the Indians who had nothing. He also told me that President Martínez had had someone call him to threaten him and order him to give up the struggle, that they'd told him that "that fruit is rotten and the ants in it will eat you alive," but that he had answered the President that they both had obligations and each had to do what they had to do. Continuing with examples

307

of barbarity, I'll say that all the hamlets in the high regions of the Department of Ahauchapán, absolutely all, were devastated by machine-gun fire. No questions, no arrests, fire and lead were the only argument. In the case of the straw huts, they shot first and then went in to see if there were people inside. A driver who years later joined the Party and who still serves in our ranks, told us a story about how he was working on a coffee plantation in Ahuachapán and that on the 26th or 27th of January he was forced by an Army detachment to drive a truck that had a machine gun mounted in the cab. In the back was a squad of soldiers with automatic arms. They went out to go on patrol, to "maintain the order," and any group of peasants they encountered on their way, whether they were just talking or walking, without any prior warning, from a distance of thirty meters or more, they'd unload their machine guns and smaller arms on them. Afterwards, the captain who was in command, with a .45 in his hand, forced our present comrade to continue driving the truck, running over them, including the dying who were writhing in pain on the ground, screaming. This comrade went mad for nearly two years, left with the impression of how the truck tilted as it passed over the mounds of corpses. "I could just feel it when their bones were breaking or their bodies bursting under the tires," the comrade recalls. In San Salvador, a large group of furiously anticommunist artisans and clerks who went to present themselves at a barracks in order to request arms or to join the Army and fight the communists were politely escorted inside, and once in the courtyard, they shot them all. They were more than a hundred. For years and years the people in the countryside kept being unpleasantly surprised all the time on seeing the skeleton of a hand, a foot, a skull cropping up out of the earth. And every now and then, the domestic animals, pigs, dogs, etc., showed up with a decayed hand or a human rib between their teeth. The dogs made out like bandits digging up corpses whose murderers had barely covered them with a thin layer of dirt, since there was no time to dig deep graves – they had to keep up the killing. The vultures were the best fed creatures of the year in El Salvador, they were fat, with shiny feathers like never before and, fortunately, never since. The National Guard was the most ferocious repressive institution. They'd been deceived a lot and the higher-ups had published our supposed documents, like the one I just explained, where it said we were going to finish off every last Guardsmen after torturing and persecuting them, and that we were going to kill their relatives, etc. With that dread and deception, and with the anticommunist hatred that had been instilled in them in the name of the Nation, the Church, etc., those who one fine day had been honest fighters against delinquency turned into bloodthirsty beasts, without scruples or pity. A typical action by the Guard was, on arriving at any little peasant ranch, to let loose with their machine guns at everything. Then, the survivors, if there were any, were lined up outside the house. The males older than ten or twelve were shot, with or without being tortured, with or without being interrogated. The women older than twelve who weren't little old ladies were raped right there in front of their mothers, fathers, husbands or children. When no survivors were left, they put the corpses on a pitchfork or a stake and they'd attach notices to them warning that that was the fate every communist could expect and that you had better learn from and collaborate with the Guard, or else saying that the family had been abused and murdered by the communists. And don't think I'm exaggerating. Don't think these are just the inventions of the imagination of a communist who seeks to justify himself and to justify his Party. No. The successive oligarchical governments in El Salvador themselves have recognized these facts on more than one occasion, and furthermore, despite that their general line has been that of throwing a heavy smokescreen over those facts, the truth keeps coming out every once in a while to fill the nation with shame. There is, for example, one very important official document, among many others that we have, which appears in *The Military History of El Salvador,* by Colonel Gregorio Bustamente Maceo (who, by the way, is the illegimate son of the Bronze Titan of Cuba, General Antonio Maceo), published by the Salvadoran National Press by order of the

309

Minister of Interior in 1951, under the repressive and anticommunist government of Colonel Oscar Osorio, a great admirer, of course, of General Martínez. Colonel Bustamente, referring to the events of '32, says the following:

"So it was that in December, 1931, large popular uprisings in the western Departments of the Republic took place, organized by the principal leader Farabundo Martí and the students Mario Zapata and Alfonso Luna, who had their headquarters in the suburbs of San Salvador, where they were captured and shot immediately without any kind of trial. And having seized several lists of supporters, among whom were the names of many workers living in San Salvador, all of them were found and shot as they were being arrested. Including innocent workers, who were denounced because of personal grudges. The gossip of an old lady was enough to cause the death of many decent men who were heads of households. Every night trucks would leave loaded with victims of the Chief of Police towards the banks of the Acelhuate River, where they were executed and buried in huge ditches that were dug beforehand. The barbarous executioners didn't even take down the names of those martyrs. General Martínez mobilized his forces and sent them into combat against the rebels, handing down the most drastic orders, with no restrictions, to the commanders of the troops. The machine guns began to sow panic and death in the regions of Juayúa, Nahuizalco, Colón, Santa Tecla, the Santa Ana Volcano, and all the coastal villages from Jiquilisco to Acajutla. There were villages that were left completely razed and the workers in the capital were barbarically decimated. One group of naive men who reported voluntarily to the authorities, offering their services, were taken inside the barracks of the National Guard where every last one of them was mowed down in a line. The panic spread. Several foreign businessmen asked for assistance from their respective nations and the British Government sent warships to the Port of Acajutla, from where they asked President Martínez to allow them to land troops to help their fellow countrymen. But he refused permission, claiming his authority was sufficient to keep

310

the situation under control. And to prove it, he quoted them part of a telegram dated in the city of Santa Ana and sent by General Don José Tomás Calderón, that said: "To this point I have liquidated more than 4 thousand communists." The slaughter was horrifying: children, old people, women, no one escaped; in Juayúa all the decent men who weren't communists were ordered to report to the Town Hall in order to receive safe passage, and when the public plaza was overflowing with men, women and children, they blocked off the streets and machine-gunned down that whole innocent crowd, not leaving alive even the poor dogs who faithfully follow their indigenous masters. A few days later, the commander of that terrible massacre was going around in the parks and streets of San Salvador talking about the gory details, bragging that he was the hero of such an action. The slaughter continued at a wholesale rate, carried out by the famous "Civic Guard," which was set up by General Martínez in every town and comprised of perverse men who committed uncountable abuses against life (of persons), property and the honor of innocent girls. Daily, they reported to the Chief Executive the number of known victims in the last 24 hours, and the looting of goods was such that they even ran out of chickens. The published accounts of different persons claimed that more than 30 thousand were dead, but in fact the number of assassinated was no less than 24 thousand. The fatal months of December, 1931, and January, February and March of 1932 will never be forgotten."

General Bustamente Maceo's document ends here. I don't think there's any need to add anything to it.

The blood of all those thousands and thousands of innocent murdered and wounded cries down for justice from heaven or on earth, though our part as revolutionaries is to see to it that justice is done on earth. Not vengeance. We are not romantic avengers, rather we strive to be scientific revolutionaries who work with the laws of history. To seek simple vengeance would disgrace our dead. But certainly we must seek revolutionary justice in the face of such a disgusting crime. And that justice can be no other than to achieve the ultimate

311

objective that the Salvadoran masses sought when they rose up against injustice: a change in the social order, the triumph of the Revolution. Until that justice comes, our nation, even if the nationalist demagogues get tired of deceiving the people, will never be a part of the civilized world, of free humanity and of the movement towards progress which has now begun in every corner on earth.

But we musn't wait for the revolution to triumph in order to clarify for the people these truths about their recent history. I even think that so long as the events of '32 aren't clear in the minds of Salvadoran workers, the revolutionary vanguard will have a very serious ideological obstacle in the way of its work. Because the systematic slander against Salvadoran communists has been going on for nearly forty years now. At the time the repressive forces fired the first shots against the people, the bourgeois press, radio, Catholic priests, high school and university professors, etc., began a huge campaign (which is still going on and has become worse with the addition of new means of mass communication, such as the radio and TV networks, the cinema, etc.) to distort the facts of the great crime and to throw all the blame for the massacre and the countless offenses on the communists. From that time on, it began to paint us as a horde of heathens who'd enter the cities wielding machetes, making the property owners' heads roll and raping virgins. I remember how, among the lies, it started going around that we communists had distributed to our ranks some passes giving each man the right to spend the night with any woman he chose once the population in question was under our control. The timid petty bourgeoisie were trembling in their homes, worrying about their little savings and the virginity of their daughters. The oligarchs remained calm and pompously ostentatious since they knew perfectly well that the mass murder was to their advantage and that the offenses against the needy classes were committed on their behalf. The facts, on the other hand, tell a different story. Where are the many "affronts" committed by our forces on the populations that fell under our control? The "great abuses" against the women of

312

the bourgeoisie on our part never went beyond one or two cases where, for reasons of extreme necessity, the comrades forced the "distinguished women" to help their servants and the humble women volunteers to prepare meals for our starving troops. The deaths caused by our troops were either in combat or in our own defense, with the exception of one or two cases where, as I already admitted, we fell into a criminal excess that we, or course, would have been the first to judge and punish as soon as we had the chance. But I'm not saying either that a popular insurrection is made with tweezers, cotton swabs, and ceremonies. In an insurrection the least you expect is that there will be many deaths on both sides, and in battle the ways of killing aren't so very pretty. It is constantly pointed out, for example, that our comrades barbarically murdered the customs officers in Sonsonate because they killed them with machetes and their bodies were mutilated. What does the bourgeoisie expect? The customs officers were defending themselves, shooting at us, and we only had machetes. What should we have done? Of course, according to our lying accusers, our dead were "pretty," "civilized," "modern," because they died from machine-gun and rifle shots. That claim and argument is really the limit.

But let's look at the facts of our supposed barbarism starting from the moment when the Party put out the call for the popular insurrection. The facts from the bourgeois and reactionary press itself, and from books and pamphlets written on the subject by the penpushers or institutions of the military regime and even from a few studies done by North American anti-communist scholars, prove that we communists caused the following deaths either in the actions of the insurrection or in our own defense in the face of the rampant repression:

a) Dr. Jacinto Colocho Bosque, his assistant Sr. Víctor Durán and (this is the only one Schlésinger mentions in his venemous book) their driver. They were killed on the road from San Salvador to Sonsonate, in the area of Colón, when some of the members of the red patrol that stopped their car recognized Colocho Bosque as the landowner who'd forced them to do

313

hard labor on the road to Chalatenango and was guilty of a thousand and one acts of violence, as I was able to gather from the stories the comrades in the cell told me before they executed us. If the man hadn't defended himself as he did, the thing wouldn't have gone beyond some roughing up. Of course, killing isn't justified by vengeance and, I repeat, we would have judged the guilty parties and decided their responsibility with the greatest revolutionary rigor. But if it was true that these comrades who killed Colocho Bosque were just a bunch of plain murderers, how do you explain – I already asked this before – that he and his companions were the only ones they killed, when they had power over hundreds of families who passed by that spot in their cars on the way to San Salvador, Santa Ana or toward Sonsonate, and who were also subjected to the communist road inspections?

b) The telegraph operator in Colón, whose name is unknown, and the Local Commander and Municipal Secretary of the same place, Colonel Domingo Campos and Efraín Alvarenga, respectively. The telegraph operator was hated by the local people because he was a police informer, and the Local Commander was such a henchman that he had a heavy machine gun permanently set up in the headquarters pointing toward the plaza where the people would congregate. These three were killed in combat, defending themselves with bullets; they weren't murdered as the bourgeois sources say.

c) The landowner Tobías Salazar in the Department of Ahuachapán, and the plantation owner Juan Germán in the same Department. They were killed when they ran into and fired at communist patrols.

d) Señor Miguel Call, Mayor of Izalco, and Rafael Castro Cárcamo, a resident of the same place, who'd been a candidate for Mayor in Chalchuapa. They were killed in open combat when they tried to stop the communist forces from entering the city.

e) Emilio Radaelli, a merchant and landowner from Juayúa. Colonel Mateo Vaquero, also from Juayúa. With respect to the death of the first there are various versions, some of which say that he was killed by his personal enemies, who made the most

314

of the confusion and robbed him of his famous jewels, which were never heard of again. Others say he died, pistol in hand, defending himself against those who he thought were going to confiscate his goods, etc. Colonel Vaquero died in full combat, attempting to impose his authority with bullets.

f) Those already mentioned customs officers in Sonsonate likewise died, and they were no more than four or five.

g) Lieutenant Francisco Platero, with the repressive forces, who died in the operations.

h) Major Carlos Juaréz, with two of his soldiers, and the retired General Rafael Rivas, who died in combat in the battle to take Tacuba.

i) In Nahuizalco, the civilians Alejandro Martínez, Alejandro García, Antonio Roca and Rafael Ramírez were wounded.

In sum then, 17 dead, plus four or five customs officers in Sonsonate, twenty-one or twenty-two dead, and four wounded. That was the sum total of the bourgeois and reactionary forces fallen in the communist insurrection of 1932 in El Salvador. Twenty-two dead, almost all of them in open combat and the rest in undetermined circumstances, and four wounded are the figures they can pin on us communists in this action. The rest of the thirty thousand deaths that happened are the black and eternal fault of the oligarchy and the Salvadoran bourgeoisie, the Army of the tyrant Martínez, of the capitalist system dependent on North American imperialism that still subsists in our country. As Marx more or less said about the repression carried out against the Paris Communards, "the bourgeoisie avenged itself, in an unheard-of way, of *the mortal fear it had felt*." It didn't avenge itself of the real damage we did it, because we barely did it any.

It's possible there were more losses, but those are the ones the reaction gave and always used, and we all know that it doesn't miss a chance to dump on us as many lying accusations as it can come up with. On the other hand, where are the women raped, the men we tortured, the great sackings we carried out? We had enough time to ravage numerous cities twice over before the repression dislodged us. On the contrary,

315

save for the casualties suffered in battle, save for the few violent unavoidable eruptions that barely drew a scare and caused hardly any damage, the cities that fell into our hands were scrupulously respected, reorganized quickly, incorporated into a new way of living where everyone is equal. In the press of that time and in everything that has been written since then on the matter, only fear, dread, what could have happened, what the merchants imagined, is talked about. But where are our offenses against the population that was completely under our control for three days or more? Of course there'll be rich little daddy's girls who think that helping to make a few corn tortillas for an army of barefoot peasants is an insult greater than death, but there's a criminal difference between that and accepting that the conduct of those communists justified a reprisal so vast that not even the clumsy arrogance of the Salvadoran ruling classes can erase it. Even supposing that our actions might have caused 22 actual and indisputable deaths, there are no words to describe the thirty thousand and more murders that the government of General Martínez committed in the name of the Salvadoran ruling classes. And the real truth, the profound truth, is that those thirty thousand deaths weren't exclusively directed against us, weren't aimed to make way for the destruction of the Communist Party of El Salvador, of the Party that existed in 1932. That great crime was done to traumatize and mutilate the Salvadoran people for years and years to come, in order to secure the conditions necessary for the oligarchical-imperialist domination of the country, to restore "a cemetery of peace" that would be the basis of an iron-willed dictatorship such as Martínez', which, by the way, lasted no less than thirteen years. It was a perfectly planned mass murder, mechanically and coldly executed and its consequences were determining factors in the later history of our people. And they continue being so even now, in my view. Thirty thousand Salvadorans murdered in a couple of weeks is the greatest argument that anticommunism in El Salvador has to date. And its manipulation has been, without a doubt, masterfully handled in the reactionary sense. The years of the Martinista dictatorship, the continuation of the military regime up to the present, the decades of imperialist propaganda, the work of the pulpit, the schools, etc. have managed to throw on our revolutionary honor the terrible burden of that great crime, while the true criminals, the high-ranking officers of the fascist-imperialist Army that passes itself off as the "national Army of El Salvador," the bourgeoisie who assassinated so many people, even for the mere pleasure of trying out their new shotguns within the ranks of the sadly celebrated "Civic Guard," the informers and cowards who made denouncing people a modus vivendi, the instigators, those who paid for the military initiative with hard cash, the priests who blessed the machine guns that decimated our humble people, these are the ones who have held almost uninterrupted national political power these last long years, almost forty years, some being now replaced by young men or by their disciples, others still hanging on tooth and nail despite their age, wearing the faces of little old men that are beginning to make our people forget the fury and cruelty with which they acted in 1932. As for me, I don't like to keep making speeches, but my memories of those terrible days make my blood boil and drive me to the point of tears of rage. If the truth isn't what I'm saying and if the truth is in the hands of the government and the bourgeoisie, in their versions, why is it that it's still practically prohibited to talk about 1932 in El Salvador? Why have even the newspapers of that awful period disappeared from the libraries and newspaper archives, from the files of the newspaper publishers themselves, which are available as a public service? Why do our historians and journalists continue going along with giving young people a schematic, false and criminal view of "the massacre that the communists caused in 1932" and not dare to state the naked truth down to the last detail? Is it that it costs too much to accept that, from then on, we have been governed by a system soaked with the blood of our brothers and sisters, parents and children? It must be said that even we communists have a profoundly negative, incorrect attitude in this respect. Independent of the fact that since 1932 our Party has been extremely weakened,

317

persecuted, suppressed, and has had to work under horrible conditions, the truth is that we haven't done enough to delve deeply into that event that shaped the contemporary history of our country. And one thing is certain: that the communist who doesn't have the problem of '32 clear in his mind, its significance and experiences, cannot be a good communist, a good Salvadoran revolutionary. But it's not just a matter of making it clear for the select ranks of our Party. We have to, once and for all, wipe away our "black legend" from the eyes of the people and put things straight. Including what has to do with our grave political responsibilities as a Party. When these things are put historically in their place, we Salvadoran communists will also be in our proper place, as perhaps we never have been before in this country. Only then will we be able to truly, and with honor, bury our dead. Those who died murdered in the mountains and cities, those who died underground after years of persecutions, humiliations and miseries; those who rotted in the prisons, those who never left the torture rooms, those who were forced to flee, empty-handed, dragging their children against their will, to Guatemala, to Honduras especially, to Nicaragua and even farther looking for a place that would allow them, someday, to forget so much horror.

A few of these things, though certainly not all, were introduced in that preliminary report we worked out in the reorganization meetings held in Usulután, and that we tried to send to foreign countries, as I already noted. I'd like to say that I'm now expressing points of view that have been affected by the ripening of time, with my thoughts over the last thirty odd years, the small raising of political awareness that I may have experienced. Anyway, that report gathered together what was essential, what the international revolutionary movement of the period most needed to know.

I'd like to say a few words now about the strictly military aspects of our ideas back then. Concretely, about the insurrectional plan that the Party proposed to develop, the military plan that was going to be the backbone of the insurrection, of the action to seize power. The plan was

318

extremely simple, as were those who drew it up: members of our Party leadership who didn't have any knowledge of military strategy or tactics, who hadn't read the classics on war and who didn't have, and this has to be emphasized as much as possible, the international experiences of the present to draw on. At that time we didn't know who Mao Tse-Tung was, and the Soviet marshals who won the Second World War were in the academies or were still lieutenants, it seems to me. Che Guevara and Fidel Castro were still kids with baby teeth. That is to say, the theory of anti-imperialist armed struggle by the underdeveloped peoples wasn't yet elaborated and our basic precedent was the uprising of the Russian workers led by Lenin, by means of which they seized power and gave birth to the U.S.S.R. Our Party's plan was based on the central idea, which was detected by the enemy early on, as I already said: to seize the main Army barracks throughout the country with the object of breaking the back of the essential forces of the enemy, using the element of surprise, and of taking possession of the light and heavy armaments in order to hand them over to the popular masses in the countryside and cities, thus forming the Red Army of El Salvador. Once armed, these masses would disperse in such a way as to take control of the whole country, from the military, administrative and political standpoint, in accordance with the guidelines and organizational forms indicated by the Communist Party and the mass organizations, etc. To normalize the country's institutional life after the seizure, power would be placed at the local level into the hands of the Peasants', Workers' and Soldiers' Councils (soviets).

In order to seize the barracks and take possession of the arms, we made two different plans: 1) the seizure of the barracks from within, which would happen in cases where we had a strong enough communist organization of soldiers inside the barracks, as in the Sixth Regiment of Machine-Gunners, the Cavalry, etc. in San Salvador. These contingents had received instructions to go into action before anyone else; they would be the ones responsible for firing the first shots of the insurrection. 2) Seizure of the barracks from the outside, that is, by means of

319

direct mass action. Also, possibilities of an intermediate case were considered: barracks that could be taken by mass action but with limited support from within when the internal forces weren't sufficient to decide the situation alone. Some variations were also taken into account, according to the particularities of a few special contingents within some branches of the bourgeois armed forces, as was the case, for example, with the Air Force. In this case the arrest of all the pilots and their incarceration had been planned, with the exception of the officer pilot Cañas Infante, who had shown himself in his behavior to be an advanced and progressive man. We planned to make use of him to bomb Government positions that resisted the push by the masses or the internal uprising of our comrade soldiers.

Of course, each barracks as a concrete objective had its own plan for assault or uprising that took into account its specific characteristics. This plan also included diverse maneuvers to surprise the enemy, in order to reduce the effectiveness of its forces or render any counter-attack useless.

As for the internal uprisings in the barracks, communist soldiers would have to act in small units, corresponding to the cells organized by the Party under the command of secretly – though democratically – elected Red Commanders. Once the barracks was in the hands of the revolutionary forces and they could proceed to arm the people, each soldier, communist or sympathizer, would have become as a general rule the Red Commander of a group of five civilians, who in turn remained subject to the Military Cell to which their Commander belonged. For its part, the Party had already named civilian Red Commanders who would lead small groups for the operations in the Departments of Sonsonate, La Libertad, Ahuachapán and Santa Ana. Even when it was a matter of large, massive operations (for example, the attack on a large barracks, like the one that housed the Regiment in Sonsonate), our forces would be divided internally into small groups possessing great autonomy of action.

The repression came down before we had finished coordinating this plan on a national level and before we had mounted even a minimum of the necessary organization. That's why, once the Party leadership was arrested and the communist forces within the Army liquidated, the great masses who we counted on to seize power throughout the country remained dispersed, disoriented, subject to contradictory instructions, not knowing what to do. Of course, the lack of organization at the national level was not only caused by the repressive avalanche in January of 1932, but, in general, by the conditions of a climate of fascist terror imposed against every type of popular and democratic organization all during 1931. I want to make it clear: we did have functioning, at great pains, an organization at the national level, but solely for the mobilization of the masses in open, unarmed activities – guild, economist, etc. These circumstances and the broad nature of the mass movement in El Salvador had also caused us to arrive at the pre-insurrectional stage with our ranks deeply infiltrated by the enemy, which allowed the Government to be basically informed of our moves. The fact of the matter is we were much too lax in this, since many times we allowed traitors against whom there was overwhelming evidence, and who it was absolutely necessary to isolate and even execute, to be left in peace and continue as militants.

The lack of coordination, the disappearance of the National Directorate at the most critical moment, the carelessness about methods of providing conspiratorial security, the lack of adequate organization at the national level for the purely military tasks of the insurrection were, I believe, the main causes of the military defeat, the basis of the whole crushing defeat.

One could argue, of course, whether the military plan was itself adequate or not, whether or not it was flexible enough in the face of a possible change in circumstances. Some think that the military plan wasn't really a military plan, but instead a very general outline which was lacking in specific details. I'm inclined at this point to believe that, but anyway it's a problem for the experts on military matters of the Revolution. I don't think it's my job to go into a deep analysis and a whole critique on this subject. I've only wanted to put forth a series of facts for the most part unfamiliar to Salvadorans, so that they can be examined by our youngest comrades and be made use of for an analysis. I don't have the sufficient capacity or knowledge. And I don't think this is the job for any one person alone, no matter how capable, no matter how well-versed in Marxism they may be. The result of an individual analysis of a problem so complex and so deliberately confused and distorted will always be partial. We're talking about a task for a revolutionary organization, for the Party, which we communists haven't yet fulfilled. The real reason? There are many: negligence, too much work, divergent opinions among comrades in the Party leadership, fear of the immediate consequences that the work of exposing such serious truths within a situation still dominated by the class enemy could have, fear that history will discredit us, little mastery of the Marxist instruments of analysis, erroneous criteria that prevent us from studying historical problems and everything that isn't the elaboration of the political line or next week's actions, etc. But nevertheless, I insist that it is an indispensible revolutionary task. As for me, I'm not in any way afraid of it. On the contrary, I believe that I'll only die in peace when my Party and my people demonstrate they have learned the fundamental lessons of the slaughter of '32.

---

[1] About the repression against communist nucleuses within the Salvadoran Army, Schlésinger, in his already cited book, omits several facts denounced by Mármol. If one knows that this author wrote his book with material given to him by the Salvadoran police, and in the capacity of a writer paid by the Guatemalan and Salvadoran oligarchies, it is evident that his version complements Mármol's without detracting from it. Schlésinger's version is the following (pages 176-179):

"The state of effervescence and the progress of Red agitation in El Salvador increase in unusual proportions. Local authorities constantly pursue provocateurs, because since the municipal and delegate elections, the communist leaders have come out and made public their propaganda based on promises for their followers and threats for their adversaries.

In the barracks, news about the progress of indoctrination among the troops has spread. The officers and leaders are uneasy, knowing that the sympathies of the troops towards the comrades—as they began to call them—was getting more visible by the moment and even more enthusiastic. From time to time, isolated groups of soldiers read to one another the bulletins of the SRI or some other piece of the communist literature that was secretly arriving at the very centers of the Army, with the stated purpose of undermining the foundation of the institution that could be an obstacle to the final establishing of the new political order that they planned to impose on the State.

On January 16, 1932, at the Sixth Regiment of Machine-Gunners, a soldier named González presented himself before Sergeant Fernando Hernández, denouncing a conversation held among various soldiers, Corporals Trejo and Merlos, and Sergeant Pérez, in which they insisted that the chiefs and officers of the barracks should be done away with, as they were representatives of the military bourgeois. Sergeant Hernández, losing no time, called on a sergeant he knew in the company under suspicion, to ask him, with a comradely tone that inspired trust of the questioned, about how things were going. The latter answered that everything was arranged; that they were only waiting for definite orders to proceed, and to prove it, he showed him a sheet of paper in which the soldiers urged to declare themselves for communism. Learning these details, Sergeant Hernández gave the Barracks Captain the corresponding material, turning over to him the subversive paper in his possession. The Captain immediately advised the Commander of the Regiment, who woke up all the chiefs and officers (this happened during the night) to hold a secret meeting and try to come to agreement on what should be done, discussing the above-mentioned paper and two others that had been taken from the soldier José Santa Ana.

The night patrols were tightened up directly under the officers, and also commissioned to find out, with the greatest exactness, what was happening in the ranks, setting a certain hour of the following day to learn what information had been obtained. This recommendation was very successful, because the officers, already advised, were able to learn the details of the movement and acquire new evidence: among the latter, that of the approach of an automobile to the barracks on a night previously agreed upon, to signal with its horn the moment to proceed with the arrest or assassination of the chiefs, and to open the doors of the barracks, where the soldiers of the Red Army would equip themselves. With these details of indisputible veracity, the Regiment Command prohibited the chiefs and officers from leaving, while it authorized leave for the troops, at the same time informing the President of the Republic of the situation. The collection of automatic arms was ordered immediately, leaving just those in the guard-towers, and entrusting their custody to the officers.

323

On the day of the 18th, there was an attempted uprising, but it was immediately snuffed out by the Captain of the Barracks in alliance with the three chiefs of the corps.

The General Commander of the Army, through the Minister of War, gave broad powers to the Chief of the Regiment to put down, in any manner, all attempted uprisings. The latter, in view of such orders, came to an accord with the Directors of the National Guard, the Police and the Central Penitentiary, and once they agreed, sent detachments to suspected soldiers from the 2nd Company to the different noted branches, where upon arrival they were arrested, reporting back the casualties to the rest of the aforementioned Company. The barracks was reinforced with cadets from the Military Academy and later with troops from other garrisons.

When the arrested were tried, each declared under questioning their complicity and the existence of a revolutionary movement under the leadership of the Communist Party. The the agitators Joaquín Rivas and Carlos Hernández, the latter a driver for the Regiment, were the ones who put some of the soldiers into contact with Martí. With this information, the arrest of the leader and his deputies Alfonso Luna and Mario Zapata was carried out.

On the day of the communist action, the automobile approached and gave the agreed-upon signals, but when the drivers got out they were met with a long round of machine-gun fire, seconded by the action of the infantry, already in advantageous positions and ready for battle.

The calmness of the Regiment's commander, Colonel Felipe Calderón, and the valor of its officers, saved the situation, snuffing out the projected uprising without the bloodshed of those involved. Subjected to military tribunals, the guilty were sentenced with appropriate punishment, avoiding in this way the disaster that would have come from the loss of a barracks of real military importance.

In the Cavalry Regiment in the capital, evidence of a possible insurrection also began to be noticed. The soldiers seem shy, quiet, but with a certain anxiety, as if grave events were about to happen to them. These conditions bothered the Chiefs, who already knew something about the difficult state of things across the country, and who noticed what little enthusiasm the troops had during the development of events on December 2, when the military coup defeating the engineer Araujo was carried out.

For these reasons, and owing to vague revelations made to him, the barracks chief called in the officers of the corps and some of those by then disbanded. With the pretext of cleaning the weapons, he orders that all automatic arms be distributed to the officers, leaving the troops only ordinary firearms. He takes these measures using the subterfuge that, since they are new arms, he intends to instruct the officers so they in turn can instruct the soldiers. Someone gives a lecture about the mechanics of the new machine guns, reestablishing trust in the soldiers involved, who had thought for a moment they had been discovered.

But these arms are not returned to the stockpile; they are left in the hands of the officers who, when night falls, place themselves at the most strategic points in the barracks; from where they can defend it and at the same time proceed against the troop's quarters upon noticing suspicious movements of the masses. On January 19, at 10:30 p.m., groups of men begin to form at some distance from the barracks, but closely watched by the sentinels, the defense is made ready. It had already been noticed that an entire company had gone to bed with rifles at their side, without checking them as was customary. Surveillance of this company is doubled and several machine guns are put in certain places to sweep over them at the slightest movement. One of the groups hovering about the barracks gets too close to the walls. It is noted that they carry small arms and some rifles. At that point the head sentinel tells them to halt, and since they do not stop, the first shot is fired at them, which was the agreed-upon signal to open fire. They attack violently, and in the noise of the gunfire, the suspicious company starts to move out slowly, as if trying to jump the guard-room; but at this moment, backing up the fire from the opened ramparts against the attackers, the machine-guns in the middle open up on their own against those under suspicion, who, seeing themselves attacked without pity, band together in confusion, thus making extermination easier. The attackers, when they realize that the barracks is not to be handed over as planned, disband and flee, losing themselves in the nearby ravines, but leaving the field littered with corpses."

A superficial analysis would be enough to make more than evident the contradictions in Schlésinger's version, above all in reference to the events in the Sixth Machine-Gunners. It is unbelievable that the chiefs would adopt such a risky procedure for humanitarian reasons ("to give the soldiers leave in order to arrest them later in other barracks") at a time when even those who came to offer their collaboration were being shot in the Salvadoran barracks, as can be seen in the document of Colonel Bustamante Maceo cited above by Mármol. As complimentary information, I should say that on page 179 of the copy of Schlésinger's book I have used, Mármol wrote in the margin, in his own hand, the following explanation in reference to the events in the Cavalry: "This crap about the assaults on January 19 is not true. They sounded the alarm that Neftalí Joya—an Araujist leader—was invading the capital, and they machine-gunned our soldiers in the Cavalry."

325

8

The rebuilding of the Communist Party of El Salvador. The rebirth of the Party in San Salvador. The arrival and departure once again of Miguel Mármol from the capital Marmol is recaptured by the police in 1934.

After all that work of analyzing and discussion, which took up many meetings, we again started our Party organizing work in the Department of Usulután. One of the first tasks was to regroup the comrades or sympathizers dispersed throughout the region, who might be living there without contacts or who might have fled there from the western region. Toño Palacios, originally from San Miguel, helped a lot with that work. That first nucleus in Usulután acted as a leadership nucleus, since we had no contact with the Party leadership, or, to put it better, we didn't know if the Party leadership or any of its remnants were still in the country.

When we had a minimal organization going, we decided to start doing political work aimed at the masses, in the belief that we shouldn't spend too much time underground. On the contrary, it was necessary to show the Government and the masses the vitality of the Communist Party, to give signs of life and activity, to show that neither the massacres nor the wave of terror could completely bury a revolutionary movement inspired by just and human principles. One of our principal tasks, at first, was to protest to the Government and its supporting sectors all the anti-popular repression we were hearing about. We sent our protests by telegram or by mail, always from villages that were far away. We couched the telegrams in business terms or some other kind that the operator would put through, but the people we sent them to – police, executioners, despotic bosses – understood perfectly and suffered their effect. There was no problem with the mail, because back then it wasn't the technical arm of the police it is now. But in any case it was impossible to hide the fact that our political activity was resurfacing, above all in the eastern region of the country. Then we started to write and put out union propaganda, urging the working class of the country to reorganize their trade unions, destroyed by the

329

repression. Once progress was made on that score, we next thought about raising the quality of the new militants in our rural and city cells. I personally prepared organizational outlines until an actual manual of guidelines could be pulled together, which were circulated throughout the cells. At first this was all pretty mechanical, the boys even memorized the workbooks as if they were geometry lessons, but in any case they were of great use to us in bringing along the new militants, teaching them that a communist organization has its rules, its regulations, its specific ways of functioning that, while not rigidly dogmatic (since above all they should adapt to actual circumstances), serve to create a general operative framework. I remember we had great success with my organizational model among the workers at one of the main tanneries in Usulután, the one owned by the Paniagua brothers, where we signed everybody up, including the apprentices. We also, little by little, extended our circle of sympathizers among the petty bourgeois shopkeepers, students, professors. I remember professor Luis García, from Usulután, who without becoming a Party militant was a great help to us in making contacts. By November we felt strong enough to carry out more public, bolder actions. The first opportunity we had was to protest the use of pictures on I.D. papers, a measure that was too costly for the citizens, especially for the poor people in the countryside, and that, tied to the anti-communist need to keep track of and control the people, was going to be the source of many new attacks. We decided to do a "poster campaign" right in the center of Usulután. Professor García painted a bunch of posters on heavy cardboard, with green letters, that denounced the new anti-communist measure. During the night several groups from our cells put the posters up in all the most visible and frequented parts of town, and the next morning all hell broke loose. Some people said the green letters meant it was an action taken by supporters of Dr. Enrique Córdoba, the old bourgeois opposition I've already mentioned. However, the message of the posters alarmed the authorities with its clear class character: it obviously had to do with the communists. The troops of the Usulután Regiment

330

were called up after the commander informed San Salvador and asked for instructions. That very night, after they imposed martial law in the area, the searches and arrests began. Some of the people defended themselves as best they could, and there were even a few deaths. We continued going to work in the shops, and outside of a few isolated cases which had more to do with coincidence, our militants were untouched by the repression, which meant we were handling our clandestine work correctly. My ex-boss, Humberto Flores, got weak knees when he saw the police and army walk into his shop. He started accusing people, and swearing that the posters hadn't been the work of Córdoba's people, but of the communists led by Elías Guevara, that is, by me. A few days went by and the repression didn't slack off. One day, a client came into the shop to try on some shoes, a sort of half-floozy who'd been the lover of a foreign sailor, and she started cracking jokes with me that had more than double meanings. She came over to me, touched my head and said, "I know what's on your mind, Little King without a crown." I just played dumb, whistling and fitting her shoes. In the meantime I'd already found a nearby ditch, covered with brambles, where I could hide in an emergency. The next day, when I was absolutely absorbed in my work, a squad of policemen under a Captain Landaverde showed up at the shop. But it was only a scare, they just took our names and addresses and left. Even so, I started to feel something heavy in the air, and I was very uneasy all the rest of that day. Close to quitting time, Humberto Flores' brother, pale as a ghost, came in and told us that the boss, despite the fact that they were brothers, had denounced him as a communist because of a family argument, and that the police were looking for him. I could smell trouble and something told me Usulután had gotten too dangerous for me. I called Chico Blanco Martínez into the shop and gave him instructions to move into the place where I was staying (by then I'd left Señor Galea's house, because they never wanted to charge me rent and I was ashamed to be a parasite) and to tell the police, if they showed up there, that he lived alone and he'd never heard of me. I offered to come back

331

for him when the danger had passed. With Mr. Flores' brother, who for sure had never seen a communist before in his life, I went off by the mountain paths to Santa Elena Grande. Flores worked now and then at the shoe shop of a certain Captain Colato, in Santa Elena, and he got me work there as a substitute while he continued on to San Miguel or even farther. He could've kept going to the South Pole, he was so scared. The truth is we got out of Usulután just in time, because the same night we'd fled they broke into my house and arrested Chico Blanco, but since he had an excellent alibi – the night of the poster campaign he'd been at a wake and everyone had seen him – they couldn't prove anything and had to let him go. From Santa Elena I continued to concentrate on our clandestine activity. We established a permanent contact by mail for routine matters and a special, personal contact, through Luis Dávila, for the more clandestine work. Luis played a huge role as our contact, covering that whole region which he knew like the back of his hand and where, as I've said, he was much loved and respected. From Santa Elena Grande I finally established contact with San Salvador, but things weren't all that clear, only that there were a few comrades in the capital living by the skin of their teeth, under terrible conditions. We extended our organizational network to Ilobasco and even to La Unión. There was so much correspondence that one day the mailman said to me: "Not even Gómez Zárate gets as much mail as you do." Gómez Zárate was the Chief Justice of the Supreme Court and with so many people in prison, and the whole judicial system in such a mess, he was the one who received more petitions, appeals and letters than anyone else in the country. The poor people thought he was a softy, but he turned out to be a man harder than stone, the guardian of the laws of the rich. That mailman's words made me really think about adopting new security measures. Nevertheless, I depended a lot on the extensive network of personal contacts and friends I had quickly made in the area. As I was a good shoemaker, I made a pretty good living and enjoyed a relatively high economic standard in the midst of the poverty that was all around me. I bought fruit and gave it to

332

the school children and in that way won over their parents and teachers, and I bought little jugs of strong *chicha* and gave them to my friends, since I never was much of a drinker. I often provided coffee, cigarettes or sweet rolls for the prayer meetings organized to honor the saints, for wakes and other occasions, all of which made me pretty well-liked by the people. It wasn't, however, all a bed of roses, and you had to keep your eyes and ears open all the time. As is well-known, the Usulután region is one of the most violent in the country: people shoot and stab each other just for a nasty look, especially when they've had a few. Three times I was almost killed by different drunks who were ready to blow away the first guy who crossed their path. On one of those occasions, the jerk was a great big, mean guy they called "Garitón." In his drunken stupor he got it into his head to kill me, and only due to my agility was I able to duck his machete blows and take off running. So then Garitón, frothing at the mouth, went back to the bar to console himself, put away a couple of more belts, and killed the barmaid with his machete. She was a very fair and buxom woman, from Chalatenango, who was always up for a good time. Another time, there was a bad scene in the shop. What happened was, I was making some dress shoes on order from the Mayor, who had become my friend – he treated me very well and he even gave me an I.D. card so I wouldn't have any problems with the authorities – when suddenly, the same Mayor flew into the shop like a hurricane, falling down drunk. He started in making bad jokes and getting on the workers' nerves, and finally, since he noticed I wasn't laughing or paying him any mind at all, he came over and sat down on my knees and started riding me as if I was a horse. I told him to leave me alone, but when he insisted on continuing, I all of a sudden stood up and dumped him on the floor, poking him in the ass with my knife handle. Everybody let out a big laugh, and the guy got angry as hell and left for City Hall saying he was going to get the police to arrest me. No way around it, I had to take off again. Since I'd spent a prudent amount of time away, I risked going back to Usulután. The comrades met to consider my return and decided that, because of the extreme

333

risk I ran in the region, it was best that I leave for awhile and go to Honduras. The decision was communicated to San Salvador, through a contact we had succeeded in making, in the hope that by then there would be an organized Party leadership that could give us some directions on how to proceed. We didn't receive anything concrete from the Party, but we had a communication from a small group of anarchists who were organizing in the capital and already had international contacts, in which they offered to send me to Spain for some rest. I turned down the invitation since I felt it would take me away from the struggle for who knew how long, for you always know when you leave your country but not when you'll come back. So, after everything, I decided to begin my trip to Honduras. I left Usulután with 18 centavos in my pocket. Surreptitiously, I passed through Santa Elena to collect the 30 colones that Captain Colato owed me in salary, but he couldn't pay me because he had nothing on hand, and I didn't insist because he had been very good to me. I continued my journey. After a few hours I met a man on horseback who'd just dismounted to have some lunch from the provisions he was carrying with him. I greeted him and he said, "Come over here, friend, if you're on a long trip, I don't like eating alone." And he fed me abundantly and in the end, since we had a long talk and I told him that I was as poor as a church mouse, he gave me a peso when we said goodbye. So, finally, I arrived in Jucuapa where Toño Palacios' uncle was my contact. He was a silversmith in town. He received me warmly, but his wife was suspicious and nasty, and since I had a peso and eighteen centavos in my pocket I didn't have to put up with that kind of unfriendly behavior. So I went to eat in the marketplace. I sat down in one of the dining areas and I was ordering my food when a guy came in who I didn't know, but who looked terrified when he saw me and ran out as fast as he could. That put me on my guard and I left. I ate somewhere else, at the establishment of a girl I'd met during my organizing activity in the last few months, who as it turned out didn't want to charge me for the meal. There is some luck in life, I thought to myself, even in the middle of widespread misfortune. I slept in the

334

backyard of the silvershop owned by Palacios' uncle, and the next day at dawn he took me out of town and gave me directions to keep going east. He didn't have one centavo, poor man, but he gave me two gold rings, unbeknownst to his wife, so I could pawn them when the need arose. I took off at a clip, until at a crossroads I met up with two girls. "Good morning," I said in passing, picking up my pace. "Miguelito, dear God," said one of the girls, frightened, "come here." I went back and said to her, "I think you're mistaken, my name isn't Miguelito." "What do you mean," she said to me, "I know you all right. You're Señora Santos Mármol's son, may she rest in God's glory, and I thought you were long dead." I had to give in, I couldn't help it, though I still didn't recognize her. "Do you remember your friend, Pelo de Cuche?" she asked me, "Well, I'm his sister." In fact, Pelo de Cuche was a friend of mine from Ilopango, and so I told her about my misfortune, thinking maybe the encounter could be useful to me. Then, right in the middle of all this, a patrol of Guards showed up carrying their rifles, under the command of a certain Lieutenant Ríos, who I knew well and who had the reputation of being a bloodthirsty bastard. Right on the spot they checked my papers and began tying me up. I told them I was on my way to San Miguel because I'd received a telegram that my brother was deathly sick in the hospital, that I was from Usulután and I was an honest, though poor, person. The girls stuck up for me and finally the Guards let me go, saying, "Okay, go on and see your brother. But be careful, because the next time we see you we'll really do a job on you." After travelling with no other incidents, I reached San Miguel where I hoped to be received in the house of don Abel, Toño Palacios' father. At the police checkpoint into San Miguel, I had another scare: There, on duty in a police uniform, was an ex-shoemaker by the name of Silva who knew me like his own mother. But I mixed in with a group of peasants who were showing their papers to some other cops, and the creep didn't see me. Toño Palacios' father received me warmly, but he advised me not to stay in San Miguel because police surveillance was incredibly tight and he himself was being

335

watched due to his earlier revolutionary activities. I spent a few days there and then decided upon a new destination for myself that seemed safe: a town near Gotera, called Delicias. When we were in Usulután and Santa Elena, we had received some magnificent letters of revolutionary fervor from Delicias, which came from a blacksmith who said he was ready to give his last drop of blood to the revolutionary task of the working class. They were stimulating, burning letters. He also always told us that there was so much political organizing work going on in the region where he was living, that it seemed as if popular power was already in force there. With this buildup, I went to Delicias. My disappointment was enormous. Actually the blacksmith was there, but when I explained who I was and asked him for help, reminding him of his excellent letters, the man wouldn't admit to anything and said he didn't know anything about it. The way he spoke, he seemed like another person from the one who had written those letters. At first I thought he was avoiding the conversation because his wife was there, but afterwards we spoke alone and there was no change. Finally I asked him to do me just one favor: to take me over the Honduran border. The jerk didn't want to do that either, but he told me I could go across with no problem, that the Honduran Governor of the adjoining Department was progressive, etc. I left without saying goodbye, at midnight, since the blacksmith wouldn't even let me sleep inside his house, giving me instead an old mat to lie on in the courtyard, under the stars. He was a total intellectual, the son-of-a-bitch, that is, assuming he really was the one who wrote those stirring letters! At daybreak I met a little old man and I asked him how much further was the Honduran line. He asked me, in turn, if my papers were in order and I said no, that I was fleeing poverty and I hadn't had a centavo to pay for my documents. Then he advised me not to even think about going into Honduras in that area because the border was closely patrolled on both sides and they frequently killed people trying to cross illegally. "As I see you want work," he said, "I'll give you the address of someone who needs people to work on his farm, near San Miguel." What was I going to do? It all seemed so hard

336

and confusing to me and I couldn't make a decision. I decided to return to San Miguel. In spite of the fact that I went back by way of paths and cutting through farms, I was captured by a group of peasants from a hacienda, but I convinced them I was just a lost drifter and not an escaped criminal, and so, after giving me a little bread and milk, they let me go. I walked the whole rest of the day, then night fell together with a hellish hunger. I thought I was dying. I walked a little more and had to sit down to regain my strength. So, like that, falling down and getting up again, I reached the banks of some river. The moon was lovely and the land open and wide, no jungle and hardly any brush. I drank some water but my hunger didn't stop. Since the path I had taken ended at the river, I decided to walk along one of the banks more or less in the direction, I thought, of San Miguel, hoping to find another road or to meet someone who could orient me. As a matter of fact, after walking a ways, I came across a group of fishermen throwing a net into a shallow pool formed by a bend in the river. I greeted them and asked for directions, and when I saw they were friendly, I told them I was dying of hunger and could they give me an extra fish to eat, raw even. One of them answered me, "Oh, Señor, if we had it we'd give you enough to satisfy you and we'd even cook it for you, but the problem is we haven't been able to catch even a guppie tonight. We've never had such bad luck." And they added that if I waited around, maybe something would turn up and, of course, they'd give me at least enough to get my strength back so I could continue on. So I sat down to rest, while they kept throwing in their net. They threw it in two or three times, and nothing, not even one crummy fish. I felt a little sleepy after walking so much, but the hunger pains made it impossible to fall asleep. Then a rather pretty girl appeared out of nowhere, asking us the way to a place called Santa Cruz, or something like that. The fishermen came out of the water and stood looking at her, who, with her sad little face in the middle of the night in that dusty countryside, was the picture of abandonment. The men showed her the way and told her to be careful, that it wasn't good for a girl like her to be walking alone around there so late at

337

night. She just said thank you and continued on her way, disappearing from view behind a stone wall silhouetted on top of a rise. Almost immediately we heard a mad-woman's laugh and a sort of a shriek that made our hair stand on end. The fishermen said, "Holy Mary, it was the Ciguanaba." But then one of them suddenly snapped the terror that had come over everybody, saying, "Look at the net, it's filled with fish." And it was true, the net was moving and the fishermen went into the river to pull it out, full of fish and shrimps. One of them brought out a bottle of booze he had hidden under a rock, and we all had a swallow to calm us down. Right there we made a fire and roasted the shrimp with salt. All the fishermen were saying that the catch was a gift from the Ciguanaba, because none of us made any advances towards her when she appeared looking so pretty, but that the slightest attempt would have been enough for her to have turned into a monster, revealing a face that would have made us raving lunatics for the rest of our lives. When the booze went to my head, I conjured up enough courage to go look for the girl or the Ciguanaba, but I found no signs of anything. I told them it was all a coincidence, that they shouldn't be so easily affected, and that that stuff about the Ciguanaba was just a big yarn, a simple superstition. However, just in case, I decided not to go on in the darkness and to wait until dawn to head for San Miguel. With my belly full of shrimp, I fell asleep on the river bank. The next day, still thinking about the Ciguanaba, I said goodbye to my fishermen friends and continued on my way. That same morning I reached the outskirts of San Miguel, but I couldn't go into town because the police had barricades everywhere. When night fell I managed to slip in and went directly to don Abel Palacios' house, who was moved to hear about my bad times, though he made fun of me when I told him about the Ciguanaba. Ever since then I have kept that experience just to myself. The next day I went looking for work. At the place the old man who'd convinced me not to go to Honduras had told me about, they didn't need workers anymore. On the contrary, there were a lot of people out of work just hanging around there. So I decided once again to run the risk of returning to Usulután by a new route, a road that went over the San Miguel Volcano. The route was a good one, because I never once met up with the authorities. But precisely for that reason, it did have its problems: bandits and no-good types used it. Some ways down the road one of those thugs, who was eating some wild berries, took up with me. He started talking about fighting and bragging about how mean he was. I was scared because he was a big, strong guy, and so I also started talking about brawling, saying I didn't let anybody fuck with me, that I'd committed some bloody crimes and had more than one dead body on my conscience, that as a friend I was a true friend but as an enemy I was real mean, and I even made the National Guard shit in their pants. We came to a house and went in to ask for some food. The people there luckily had food to spare and they happily served us. Once we were finished, the owners of the house told us to take what was left over for the road. Then that bastard got up and threw it all in his bag, leaving me nothing. The owners didn't say anything, figuring that we'd divide up the provisions later on. Once we were on the road again, however, I confronted him about it and he started mouthing off at me, all set to fight. So I told him I thought it'd be better if we split up, because I was really pissed off and I didn't want to do anything I'd be sorry for. I walked on ahead of him, but since the bastard had long legs I couldn't lose him, no matter how fast I walked. Finally, I reached a peasant hut and I went in to ask for a tortilla. But that bastard waited for me to come out. I told the peasants about what had happened and they said, "Be careful, that son-of-a-bitch must be really bad – you can just see it in his face." Fortunately, a cart drove up carrying a load for Batres, and I caught a ride, offering to help out. From Batres I went to Usulután without incident.

I contacted my comrades, and it was decided that I should go completely underground, working at night as a shoemaker to support myself and giving the shoes I made to my co-workers so they could put them into their shops and sell them. Those were

339

days of hunger and scarcity, bitter times. But we never gave up hope, especially since we were receiving news from all over the country about the slow, difficult rebirth of the revolutionary movement. We celebrated May Day of 1933 in hiding, but the countless number of posters and red flags that appeared on the trees and fences in the countryside, on the roadsides and highways, in Usulután, Jiquilisco, Jucuarán, Santiago de María, etc., spoke eloquently of our existence and activity. On August 5, 1933 it was decided that I should return to San Salvador. By then the organization in Usulután was able to control the entire eastern region without me, and it was necessary to establish a higher level of coordination with the leadership in the capital who we thought to be functioning on some level. I'd spent more than a year on the run, but my work had been fruitful from both a political and organizational point of view. Disguised as sick, a bandage wrapped around my head, I took the express train to the capital. In spite of the misfortunes I've talked about and the ones I'll go on to relate, I've always had good memories of Usulután. People were very good to me there, and I was able to recover from my physical and moral wounds, and even to put on a little weight and get a little color in my cheeks. And I also want to say, to end this, that I had a sweet love there. I fell in love with the woman who directed the school in Santa Elena, a beautiful señorita named Guerrero. I don't want to say any more about it because she got married later on out in those parts, and must certainly be living there. She really didn't reciprocate much to speak of, but maybe a little . . . Her being there was a balm for my wounded heart. From that sweet episode I still have a short piece I wrote, very romantic, but I like it a lot among the things I've written. The pretentious things one does sometimes.

Arriving in San Salvador was a disappointment. The capital looked dismal, desolate. You could breathe the fear that was everywhere and even in the bars the drunks were in the dumps and silent, something that's really extreme for a Salvadoran, who when he's had a few thinks he's king of the world, the

340

richest, handsomest and manliest of men. Also, you saw incredible poverty on the streets. The shops, empty. And in the crackdown the police were so obviously everywhere that you could easily avoid them, but for the common people it was fatal. The few surviving comrades were all dispersed. Nevertheless, with the efforts of new comrades from Santa Ana and the other western regions who had escaped the most violent massacres, meetings were held from time to time to take advantage of opportunities to do political work. They had considered the Party reorganized and proceeded to recognize the leadership group that was functioning in San Salvador as the Central Committee. That was the period when the Party work of comrades such as León Ponce, Roca, and others began, comrades from Santa Ana who would come to be central figures of the new era of the Salvadoran Communist Party, the forgers of several generations of communists, who would also share with me the initial work of proletarian and communist organizing in Guatemala, later on, during the time of what was called "The Guatemalan Revolution." I remember that at this time when I rejoined the work of the Party in San Salvador, my first contacts were with comrade Monterrosa; with a comrade named Antonio, nicknamed "The Devil," who I think I spoke of before, and who would die in 1934 from a hacking tuberculosis he developed from the brutal beatings the National Police gave him; comrade Ramón Ríos; the man who'd been renamed Secretary General, comrade Narciso Ruiz; comrade Francisco Morales; comrade Jorge Herrera, a barber by trade, who's still living now in Panama; comrade Dionisio Fernández; the comrade we called "Hoarse Félix"; the then comrade Julio Fausto Fernández, who would become Secretary General of the Party and a more or less international figure, and who would later betray us, going over to the ranks of the enemy, with his gunbelt and everything, where he became Minister of Justice under the criminal Lemus regime (1956-1960), not to mention becoming a Christian philosopher, a university professor, a high-ranking judge, and a diplomat and who knows how many other things. But, in those days, Julio Fausto was certainly an optimistic young man, very

341

active in the struggle, and I was impressed with him from the time I met him in Paleca at a clandestine meeting. He was very intelligent and enthusiastic. He was one of those brilliant fellows whose talent and skills you could see in his hands and eyes. He would always come to meetings telling about modest organizing successes and of great plans for the future. He read, and made us read, everything, he typed up our manifestos after correcting their style, and he had his student friends and petty bourgeois acquaintances distribute them in their respective social circles. His later destiny turned out to be a true shame – his lack of political conviction disguised as a conversion to Christianity that not even the priests have ever believed. But that's life. Or to put it better, that's the class struggle inside the heads of the allies of the proletariat.

Since my political work had grown, I had Toño Palacios come in from the east and together we took responsibility for organizing the delivery of mail between cells all over the country. We were able to organize mail delivery to the east on a daily basis, carried in person by a railroad brakeman who lived in La Unión, whose name I've forgotten but who I know became Secretary General of the Communist Party of Honduras in 1954. Besides being our mail carrier for the organization in the eastern zone, this comrade also used to put leaflets in the mailboxes along his route, protesting the regime and its daily attacks on the people.

In San Salvador I rejoined my poor wife, under extremely difficult circumstances. We never spent more than three days in the same rooming house, so the police wouldn't find and ambush me. And besides this, there wasn't even the slightest bit of work to be found just so you could scrape by, and our hunger was horrible. In comparison I lived like a prince in Usulután. But in spite of the fear, the empty stomachs, the sense of hopelessness with which we worked, the isolation from the masses, our organization steadily grew with new recruits without us having to sacrifice our strict, selective criteria. The Party was alive and developing. It didn't matter that all of us were often close to dying from hunger or from a deep

342

depression. Everything was hard then, and the truth is that where we didn't see any hope, we would put our faith, pride, anger, stubbornness, balls, anything. The dead weighed heavily on us, thousands of pounds, tons. But they also weighed the other way around, picking us up, if I'm getting across what I mean. It was like, how could you accept that you were wrong when you knew that people like el Negro Martí, Luna and Zapata had died for our truth? We were ignorant and we felt ignorant. I'm old now, and I'm still ignorant. But the bourgeoisie won't ever defeat us by knowing more. That's not the issue. It's one of the historical laws. And even if we didn't manage those laws well, we sensed them, smelled them, we felt them on the tip of our tongues. And we survived. And we survive. And we are in the heat of the fight. And we have a socialist world. And Vietnam. And Cuba. But, after all, everybody knows this, no propaganda is needed.

On one occasion, it must have been around 1934, I was advised that a new comrade had been recruited and that I should swear him into the Party. He was comrade Porficio Huiza. The ceremony would be in broad daylight, right in Centenario Park, almost in front of the place where the Party used to have its headquarters. Now it seems like it was a stupid thing, but back then such boldness was great moral support for us, helping us feel that we were at all times defiant before the power of the enemy. At the appointed time, I arrived at the park. Behind me was my security, a group made up of three comrades who acted like they had nothing to do with me, each one walking along by himself. The new comrade arrived punctually. We sat down on a bench and without further ado I asked him: "Do you swear to be loyal, to fulfill the mandate of the working class, to dedicate your life to the cause of the poor and exploited?" And Huiza said, "I swear it, comrade. And right now I swear that if I don't serve the cause, it's better that you kill me." I answered him: "It's not necessary to talk about death, comrade. What the working class needs is the life and work of fighters. In the name of the Central Committee of the Salvadoran Communist Party, section of the Communist

International, I name you an active member of our ranks." I hadn't even finished that sentence when one of the security people passed close by me and said: "Comrades, the police have surrounded us." In fact, a group of seven or eight cops were slowly closing in on us, as they say, and they were now only 30 meters away. "Here's your first task, comrade," I said to Huiza. And when I saw him get up to threaten the police, I ordered him firmly: "Don't be an ass, what we've got to do is run." And with the help of our security we got the hell out of there. The cops were able to capture one of our security people, who couldn't shake them by trying to hide down by the Arenal River, over near what is today the Guatemala or the Bosque barrios.

Our links with the interior of the country improved notably, and once again our principal work began to be directed to the western region. In between ourselves in San Salvador and those living in Santa Ana, we managed to set up a cell in Sonsonate. Julio Fausto Fernández did great work despite the fact that the police had fingered him. In those days I found myself a fantastic refuge in a house in La Barrio Esperanza, a house belonging to a kind of loose woman who had given one of my sisters work as a servant. She was one of humble origin, but because she was pretty and cute she had impressed the Spanish Consul, a guy named Sagrera, who was also a merchant and industrialist, and who made her his woman and set her up in a house. The man was absolutely nuts over her. She had taken a liking to my sister and, besides, she was horrified by the crimes committed by the Civil Guard and the Army, so when my sister asked her to put me up for a couple of days, she said not to worry, that I could live there as long as necessary. So then I sent my wife and the kids, along with my other sister, to a rooming house out in La Garita, and I shut myself up preparing study materials and organizational plans there in the house of the Spanish Consul's great love. So the house wouldn't be discovered by the authorities, I met my Party

344

contacts nearby in a spot hidden among the rocks and brambles, where the Arenal River runs under the Esperanza Bridge. We met our comrades there, at night, despite the dangers of Martial Law, among which the most dangerous was the certainty of getting shot down on sight by the night patrols. On more than one occassion we had to have a light to read messages by, and, I suppose, because of the superstitious old ladies in the neighborhood, a rumor started going around that the souls of the dead came out of the Arenal at night to do penance, because for sure there were bodies in that river of those who were shot and buried by the police. And because maybe they still had accounts to settle in this world, they roamed about still atoning for their sins and appearing before the living. This version even reached the press, and soon the headlines were talking about "The Great Red Ghost of the Esperanza Bridge." Therefore, we had to stop meeting there in order to avoid being shot at, since no matter how "ghostly" it might be, just because it had been called "Red" it was sure to become a target for cops without any questions asked as to whether it was a soul from this life or from the other one. It was during that time that a really terrible storm unleashed its fury, and the Arenal became an angry, dangerous river. It rained and rained without stopping, while I worked at my typewriter. One night the rain was so hard and the winds of such hurricane force that the river started to roar and the water rose up almost to the bridge. The house I was staying in had been built in a gorge above the river, but it was a brick house with a stone foundation, so there was no problem. But I was very worried thinking about what might happen to my children, living as they were in a rooming house with walls made of mud and cane. It was also very close to the river, but in la Garita, about two kilometers from where I was. I was afraid that the place would collapse and bury my family. So I told the ladies of the house, and my sister, that I was going out to see about my children. They were against it, saying that a man alone in the rain would be a target for lurking troops quicker than you could bat an eyelash. But I insisted and told them it wasn't fair for me to be resting comfortably behind

345

these brick walls, with every convenience, while my wife and children could be dead. The river was raging down below and I felt worse and worse. Finally, following my heart, I left the house despite the pleas of the ladies and of the father of the Consul's woman, who happened to be there at the time. Very carefully, walking along the footpaths in the middle of the downpour, I managed without any problems to reach the rooming house where my wife and children were staying. Fortunately, everything was all right and the place was still standing. My wife and kids, along with my sister, were very happy to see me and gave me some coffee. After I'd been there a half an hour or so, there was a loud banging at the door. I thought, given the sound of the knocking, that it was the police or someone running from the police. I took a pistol out of my sister's table drawer – she had bought it for emergencies – and my wife opened the door. Imagine our surprise when we saw my other sister and the Spanish Consul's woman standing there in the doorway, all covered with mud, exhausted and half-naked. Especially the Consul's woman. She'd lost the robe she had been wearing when I left her and only had her underwear on, her legs covered with cuts and scratches. What had happened? Well, just this, that fifteen minutes after I'd left there was a great clap and the walls started to creak, the floor to lean and the whole house started moving. The river's angry current had washed away the section of the bank where the house was sitting and it went sliding down into the river – bricks, stones, and all – where it was destroyed by the uncontrollable waters. The woman's father had been carried away by the current and for sure had drowned in the muddy waters crammed with uprooted tree trunks. The woman's mother was able to get out in time, but she couldn't make it as far as the rooming house, so she stayed behind to rest about halfway down the road, completely drained and exhausted. I went out to find her and bring her back. Fortunately, the two women had a tavern business around the Independence Avenue area, so they went to live there, completely demoralized by the death of the head of their family. The least of it was the house, since the Consul's

346

woman was sure she'd get another one from him. Once again I felt the brush of death. I had to stay on living in the rooming house and from there reorganize my contacts and political work. But, perhaps because my wife had already been seen by the police, we soon began to notice that we were being watched from nearby. The circle around us began to tighten and finally the day came when I couldn't go out of the house anymore. Probably the cops were waiting for nightfall to come and get me without a scandal. And to top it all off, Antonio Palacios came to see me with two new comrades from Santa Ana who he wanted me to meet. I wasn't able to warn them in time and they fell into the police net with me. Then I thought of a plan. Since Toño Palacios looked a lot like me, I proposed that he go buy something down at the nearest store, a place where there were more cops than anywhere else, to see what would happen. And in fact, they did think he was me and they arrested him. They also shot at him when he tried to run away, but fortunately they didn't wound him. While all this was happening, I had tried to escape by the back door, but when I went out into the courtyard I found a line-up of police waiting, guns in hand. So I had to go back and I headed for my room. When I was nearing it, I saw that they were interrogating Toño in there, screaming at him. The loudest voice was that of Commander Campos, a well-known bastard, who also was trying to scare my wife into "cooperating with the authorities." I just kept on walking and the police didn't say anything to me, figuring I was just a neighbor passing by. Right then the rain started to come down really hard, and I went outside through the main entrance, walking as fast as my legs would take me. But at the first corner there were two cops who knew me well, Esquivelon, who was a real pig, and José Rivas, who had even been a member of the Union in Saloneros, part of the Regional. What saved me was that it really started to pour and although the pigs shot at me they couldn't get me. Also, they were older, heavyset men and they didn't dare chase me through all that water. I took a turn through some empty lot and came out somewhere around la Chacre. From there, I took a bus downtown, but when we passed Independence Avenue I remembered that my sister and the ladies from the house that the river had swept away were living near there, so I got off and went to look for them.

When I got to the address they had given me, where I'd never been before, I realized what the true nature of those ladies' business was. It wasn't just an ordinary everyday bar. It was also a still, that is, they made and sold moonshine there, and, on top of everything, it was also a whorehouse, with live-in whores and rooms where women could be brought. But when you're talking about saving your life, even whorehouses start looking like convents. The ladies welcomed me affectionately and said I could stay there with them, although my sister hadn't wanted to stay when she saw what was going on there. But, however, they warned me that if the house in La Esperanza had been all peace and quiet, here I would be in constant danger because military officers always came, as well as civilians, lawyers and doctors, students and cops, and even priests disguised as workers or journalists. So some measures had to be taken. To begin with, I cut my hair really short and let my little moustache grow out, and to justify my presence in the house, above all with the whores, who have big mouths and take bribes from cops, I wound up working for the business: nothing less than making moonshine. But this work kept me out of sight of the public, in a room in the back of the house. Within two or three days I learned my job perfectly and I not only distilled moonshine and *coyolito* in the purest Cojutepeque style, but also brandy flavored with pineapple or *jícara* or other fruits, and I came up with new concoctions yielding subtle differences in the quality, taste, roughness or smoothness of the liquor. I even experimented with some spices and herbs to improve the bouquet of the brandy, learning in the same way about the chemistry of denaturing liquors like anisette or crème de menthe. And these liquors, added a spoonful at a time to the brandy, produced magnificent results. But I especially had great success with the *coyolito*, which was praised to the heights, even by a group of military officers who came one night partying and who got drunk on my stuff, and who even wanted to take

348

me back to the barracks to set up and manage a still for them. The ladies who ran the house used to say that God watched over me in spite of everything, since although He had punished me by making me a communist, He had also given me talents for surviving, among them a good hand for brandy-making, a virtue only one out of a thousand has, like a person who finds buried treasure or an underground spring.

Meanwhile, my comrade had gotten out of jail and had made contact with me and the others, and had put us all in touch with one another, but the surveillance in San Salvador was fierce and paralyzed us for days and days. And then to really fuck things up, a guy named Sanabria, a cop, managed to infiltrate the Party, in spite of the fact that I had personally expressed my conviction that he wasn't to be trusted and I had opposed his membership. This Sanabria found out where I was staying and the ambushes started again, until I was ordered to leave San Salvador and travel to the eastern region and then to come back again, while the Party would circulate the news that I'd left once and for all for Honduras, in the hope that the police would swallow the story and ease up on me. For various reasons, among them that my wife was about to give birth, I had to come back to San Salvador right away. The surveillance hadn't let up any and the police net around my wife, relatives, and friends was as tight as ever. It kept me hopping back and forth from San Salvador to the nearby towns, like Soyapango, Ilopango, Mejicanos, etc. On several occasions my wife or my sisters were detained for short periods of time, and every time the police broke into our rooms they took everything they could get their hands on, plunging us deeper into poverty. The only thing left for me to do was to seek refuge in San Martín, in the house of another woman I had there who I haven't talked about before and who I won't mention again, for reasons I won't go into. She was Adelita Anzora, with whom I had a daughter named Hildita. Adelita welcomed me cordially and didn't refuse me refuge with her, despite the fact that so much time had gone by since we were involved together. But the first thing she told me was that she was glad I'd shown up, because a kind and honest man had asked her to marry him and since I was the father of her daughter, she wanted to know how I felt about it so there wouldn't be any problems afterwards. "I haven't accepted his offer yet," she said, "hoping I could speak with you first." I told her it sounded wonderful to me, that she deserved a good man and my daughter a good father, and that I couldn't be either one for them because of the dangerous and risky life I led, and because of my other commitments. Adelita fed me and let me stay in her house for a few days, after which I went back to the lion's den in San Salvador. When I left she gave me a box of matches. Inside she had put a bunch of folded-up one peso bills.

But even travelling on the highways was getting difficult at that point. By that time they were even searching the ox-carts, and to travel by bus you had to show your papers, since the driver made a list of all the passengers which he handed over to the police at the town checkpoint. I found out from well-informed friends that between San Salvador and Cojutepeque there was a police detail, headed by a certain Hinestroza, which was out searching just for me. I started to think that they had gotten one of my detained relatives to talk under interrogation, because I could see that the persecution was getting worse all the time. I got work for a few days in a shoemaker shop in Cojutepeque, until I found out that they had arrested my wife again, along with my little niece. And by the way, I had dreamt about my wife being in jail three days before I got the news, right down to the last detail. My friends got me out of Cojutepeque and I again said I was going to Honduras, but I stayed in San Rafael Cedros. I went hungry for a few days until I found a good shop owned by a shoemaker by the name of Granillo, who was the Mayor for life of that little town thanks to General Martínez, and I got a job there, passing for a convalescent drunkard. There I had one of the biggest, happiest surprises of my life when I came face to face with none other than comrade Ismael Hernández, my old friend from the workers' movement, from the Red Aid and from the Party! We both held in our emotions until the first shift was over and we could meet in a discreet place and

350

talk about our misfortunes and our thoughts about everything. Ismael told me a lot of things I hadn't known before about just how dangerous it was for me around there. For instance, he told me that the police had distributed throughout the area of Cojutepeque, Ilopango, San Martín, San Rafael Cedros, etc. alone, no less than 700 photographs of me to the bus drivers, local commanders, the National Guard, the rural patrols, etc., and therefore I shouldn't show my face anymore, and that the best thing would be to leave once and for all for Honduras, and, while we tried to make some good contacts, it would be best to go into hiding and live off the little that Ismael earned. I agreed about going to Honduras but I refused to hide. I needed some money for the trip and I could take advantage of the time it would take to establish our contacts. Finding contacts that would allow me to get all the way Honduras was a slow, disheartening process. But at least in the shop everything was going well and I felt I could trust my co-workers, almost all of them from San Rafael, young guys who were honest and respectable. The Mayor and shopkeeper, Sr. Granillo, was rather fatherly and a nice guy. One weekend he invited me to a party and we drank brandy with the local Commander of the Guard, who seemed not to have gotten one of those pictures of me since he was as friendly as could be, telling jokes and singing. His name was Captain Quevedo. The only thing that disturbed me was that I still hadn't received any news about my trip. But little by little the plan took shape: I would leave from Usulután, on horseback, with a guide who would take me by the back roads and footpaths until we reached Honduras. I was scheming and making castles in the air, when one day a guy, whom I had known since childhood, showed up at the shop looking for work. We had been classmates at the little school in Ilopango. His name was Máximo Colorado, and he and I had never liked each other. He got a job, but he didn't do anything and he never took his eyes off me. I acted dumb and made like I didn't know him. But his presence gave me the chills. It was precisely then that they advised me that the next day, November 26, 1934, I would have to go to Usulután to begin my

351

trip to Honduras. In the afternoon, as usual, all of us workers went down to the river to bathe. When we finished bathing, walking back to town joking and kidding around, I had a sudden change of heart and decided to disappear right away and move up my departure for Usulután. I went back to the river pretending I'd forgotten something. That bastard Máximo Colorado was following behind me, saying he'd forgotten something or other too. That really made me suspicious. And with good reason, because I'd only walked back to the river a few meters when I wound up face to face with two old acquaintances: that bastard Esquivelón and a young cop named Cruz, who was nicknamed "Paris." I couldn't even react, because before I was sure who they were, they already had pulled their pistols on me: "So you finally fell, little bird," said Esquivelón. "This little bird has a name," I said, pissed off, "and that name is Miguel Mármol." I said that because I realized that some of the workers had gone back with us and they were in shock watching the scene. They took me back to town, to the shop, everybody surprised. The police told me to change my clothes, that we were going immediately to San Salvador, but I remembered that in my other clothes I had some Party communiqués and so I told them I had on my only change of clothing. I identified myself in front of all the workers in the hope that news of my arrest would get back to my family, friends, and Party comrades, because Ismael was nowhere to be seen and I figured he had fled. In fact, soon enough the story of my capture would be going around the surrounding towns, all the way to the capital. On the way there, I saw Máximo Colorado and in front of everyone I shouted, "You turned me in, you lousy traitor, but the people will make you pay for everything you've done someday." In jail, little Cruz, the young policeman, was very nice to me. He asked me if I wanted to eat, and I answered that if they would give me something good, or a beer with a meal, then they could bring it. Little Cruz came through. Later on, the guards began telling me that the best thing would be to renounce once and for all my communist ideas, that in the end I was wrong and that nobody could go against General Martínez. I

352

explained the reasons for our struggle, and they just kept looking at me, silent. Then a moment later, little Cruz said to me, "Look, Mármol, I'm very sorry that it was me who arrested you. But that's the way life is, that's fate. I'm telling you this because tonight who knows what will happen to you, and I don't want you to think that I have something personal against you. You're a brave man, and I'll tell you straight: tonight, be prepared for anything." After a few hours they came to take me to the train station. The road was dark, and by that time the streets were empty. That bastard Esquivelón wanted to kill me, and he even shoved me around so I'd try to escape and he could then swear that was the reason why he shot me. But I didn't give him the pleasure. Little Cruz, who was along as his subordinate, remained friendly. Nevertheless, when we arrived at the station, the townspeople had started to gather as a show of support for me. That was really moving, because in spite of the fear and repression, in spite of the low level of political consciousness in that area, the people still dared to say farewell to a communist prisoner. In the station they locked me up in the telegraph room. There, I realized that all the letters and telegrams that might be complaints against the regime had been intercepted and inspected, and that they were making a secret hit list of all the signees. So, the telegraph operators all over the country were playing a criminal role in the Martínez repression! Before the train arrived, Captain Quevedo and a squad of Guardsmen came (they had been out of town when I was arrested) and the Captain told Esquivelón and little Cruz to hand me over to him, that he was going to finish me off right then and there. "Give me that son-of-a-bitch if you want to live," he shouted , horrifying the people. But Cruz told him they couldn't turn me over, because I was their prisoner. Captain Quevedo, who at that point wasn't singing songs to me anymore, yelled at me: "You communists keep thinking the Red Army in Russia will come to save you." I got furious and yelled back: "Don't you ever say that heroic name with that filthy mouth of yours." The Captain backed down some and the people started muttering things against him. A lady asked little Cruz if she could bring me a soda.

Paris gave her his permission and then people started bringing me *chilate*[1], cold drinks, and bread. Each time I accepted something from those folks, I said to Captain Quevedo, "So you see, Captain, whose side do you think God is on, yours or mine?" And the old bastard got so angry he was sending off sparks. Finally, the train arrived and Esquivelón and little Cruz put me on board, well-shackled. There were about twenty Guardsmen travelling on the train, so there was no need for Quevedo and his squad to escort me to San Salvador, and at least I was able to travel in peace. A half-crazy girl travelling on the train was singing over and over that one that goes, "tipi-tipi-tín-tipi-tón, tipitipitín-tipi-tón, every morning at your window I sing this same song." And the old ladies were saying the Rosary on their beads of white seeds.

---

[1] chilate: drink made from maize (translators' note).

9

In General Martínez' jails.

When we arrived in San Salvador, a heavy vehicle was waiting at the station to take us immediately to the Police Station – by that time almost familiar to me. My guards unloaded me like a trophy as we arrived, crowing about their victory, and as soon as we entered the doors of that place they all started in on me, threatening me with torture and execution. Only Cruz kept quiet. I was even received by the new Police Chief, Colonel Linares, who covered me with insults from head to toe. They took me to a room inside and made me undress, and when they saw the scars on my chest and arms, on my hands and legs, they said gleefully that there was no doubt about it, I was really the Miguel Mármol they were looking for, and besides which I wasn't a witch or anything like it, because it was obvious that bullets went into me like any other mortal. Commander Balbina Luna came to verify the identification and made a report. Finally they left me alone, with the interrogation room as my cell. When they brought me the prison food to eat, I refused, saying I wasn't hungry. Balbino Luna came and ordered me to eat, but I insisted that I wouldn't. "This bastard has always been a pain in the ass," he said, "he'll never fall into line until we knock his head off." "It's not my bad upbringing, Commander," I answered. "The thing is I'm not hungry because my people gave me plenty to eat. Tomorrow will be another day, and then I'll eat, but from now on I'll ask you to bring me lots of good food, and not that shit crap you've brought me today." I slept as best I could on the floor and didn't wake up until eight o'clock the next morning, when they came to get me for the first interrogation. Pushing and shoving, they took me into an office where two interrogators were waiting for me: Commander Campos and an agent named Monterrosa, known by the nickname "Snake Eyes." Campos began talking to me gently and softly, posing his questions cautiously, as if he wanted to get my trust. From

357

his questions, from the line of his questions, I began to realize that the Government had a lot of information about our activities, about the structure of the Party before and after the insurrection, about the organizational levels with which we started to rebuild, and about our plans for development. Evidently, with as many communist prisoners and sympathizers as had passed through the torture chambers since January 1932, the police files must have had more than a few entries. With me, Campos insisted on talking about my activities of the last two years, my contacts, the secret organizations that I directed and advised. I said only that I admitted I was a communist, that I admitted having participated in activities leading up to the 1932 insurrection according to our Party line, that I declared myself solely responsible for those tasks and that no one else was involved. "If someone still has to pay for all that, I'm the one," I told them, "either with prison or the death penalty, it's all the same to me." "Of course you'll pay," they answered, "but bit by bit, it's not going to be so easy for you, you've got a lot of old accounts past due and just one death would be like a gift." From then on, the tone of the questions changed and the interrogation became harsh and violent. They even went so far as to shout at me: "There's one thing you're going to clear up for us this very second: why have you said that his excellency, General Martínez, is a murderer and a swine?" "You said it, not me," I replied, "my criticism of the regime has always been political, not personal." "Well, we're going to make you prove otherwise, you son-of-a-bitch hypocrite." And they went off to get a file of papers from which they picked out a document that they angrily threw in my face. It was our famous, "Why the Insurrection and its Failure." Campos said that the document was an insult to the President and they knew I had written it. "The document is mine," I said, "but it's a political analysis, not an insult." They persisted: "We want you to tell us right here and now if our General Martínez is a murderer. Yes or no." At that moment three or four more policemen entered the office, all angry. "The only thing I will say is that I take responsibility for the document. You may do what you want. It isn't in my hands to escape."

358

There was a tense moment and then Campos ended the interrogation. I went back to being locked up in the interrogation room. When I was walking towards it, a prisoner who was sweeping the hall was clearly surprised to see me, his eyes nearly popped out of his head. Later on I found out that he was the thief who had played dumb and stayed in the cell where they were going to torture me in January of 1932, the day before they shot me, and who later had informed my family. He was in jail again, it's the cycle for thieves in El Salvador. The first days went by without anything happening, although the worst enemy of a prisoner – uncertainty – started to get to me. They brought me out of the room and stuck me in a tiny cell isolated from the others. One day, the thief who I mentioned managed to find a way to get a little piece of paper to me, telling me that my sister knew about my arrest and she was doing everything possible to help me. By using hiding places in holes, little papers and signals, I communicated regularly with that good thief and showed him how to build a network of prisoners and relatives of prisoners that would allow us to maintain constant contact with the outside. Since thieves were the ones who came and went more than anyone else in prison, the mobility of the network was very good and the number of collaborators large. But even so, communication once outside was difficult and dangerous. My sister, who was my best contact under those circumstances, was constantly watched by the police, and she had to change her house often just to temporarily escape the surveillance. In spite of all the precautions, one day a good thief named Monterrosa, who was taking a letter to my sister, was intercepted, detained and savagely tortured. The network fell apart for a good while, but we were able to put it back together, always with the collaboration of the thieves and pickpockets. Poor Monterrosa, by the way, died a few months later of an attack of colic, in a police lock-up. My sister claimed the body and buried it in "La Beringa," the poor peoples' cemetery. Meanwhile, my friends, family, and the various Party nucleuses in San Salvador never let up in their efforts to free me. They asked the Supreme Court to place me under their custody, offering personal testimonies one after the other. But it was all for nothing. The response of the Police was that I hadn't been arrested, that I wasn't held prisoner in the police jail, or the Guard jail, or in the Penitentiary; that the Government knew I'd died in the events of 1932. The uncertainty was killing me, slowly, and sometimes I thought it'd be better to end it once and for all. Smashing my head open against the wall or the bars, slitting my wrists, or by whatever other possible method. But they were passing crises. I always found the strength to rebound and to tell myself that I had to go on living, that I should be free again to help organize the struggle, to lend my experience – even if it was little and confused – to the Salvadoran workers who sooner or later would have to become conscious of the revolutionary road.

The personal conditions of my detention were incredibly hard. In the first place, I was being held incommunicado, although as I've said I was able to construct a communications network through the thieves who were my fellow inmates. In the second place, and this really was something that fucked me up, I was permanently shackled. At first, I was even shackled both hand and foot. Later on, just my hands. I spent months and months like that, more than a year, to the point where my fingernails grew so long that they were curling up and making little wounds in my hands. They would only unchain me so I could take care of my basic necessities and even for that I had to insist and fight. On more than one occasion they let me shit in my pants and made me stay that way for two or three days. You have to imagine what it is to live, to eat, to think, covered in shit. But, of course, nothing would have made me give in to them or show any weakness. Shit and all, I remained arrogant and proud and not one of those bastards could look me straight in the eye. When they got tired of it all and took me out to wash my clothes, they came into the cells with their heads lowered, or talking about something or other, or whistling, acting dumb. They never let me bathe except on one of those occasions, and they

360

wouldn't permit me to shave or cut my hair, either. So I looked like the Savior of the World, the Hunchback of Notre Dame, but with the long locks of an Indian instead of a hunchback. Death threats were a daily thing and more than once they went through the motions of taking me out to be shot. I think many of those dirty tricks came from the guards who, when they got bored, tried to have some fun at my expense, the sons-of-bitches, and they could be called worse than that, too. However, what tormented me the most was when they'd tell me they had captured one of my comrades and they were going to take me to watch him being tortured. On three or four occasions they brought me to watch whipping and torture sessions. It was horrible. I tried yelling out encouragement to the comrades, but was immediately beaten and taken away. I never recognized the ones being tortured, partly because they didn't let me watch too closely but kept me moving, partly because the prisoners were perhaps new comrades whom I didn't know, and partly because they were already disfigured like monsters from the blows of those pitiless, heartless men. On one occasion, they let me know that, not counting me, there were 34 communists being held incommunicado in the police cells. One day they brought me to watch them from a distance, at lunch time. They made them eat while walking in a circle, and they had to keep walking faster and faster. Whoever slowed down got beaten with a whip. It was a horrifying scene. If you don't think so, just try to eat your lunch running, while someone threatens you with a whip. Despite being far away, I could recongnize comrade Antonio, who they called "El Diablo," and comrade Pedro Sosa. Pedro saw me also, but it was another day when they brought me out to get some medicine for a fever, and he made signals to me from far away. One of the measures the police took to keep my detention a secret was to change my name. That way, according to them, it wouldn't get around that I was Miguel Mármol. Right from the start, they called me Carranza, both when speaking and when writing. I told the policemen that my name was Mármol, but since only the highest ranking, most trusted police had contact with me, my resistance was useless. So, after a

while, almost unconsciously, I let myself be called Carranza.
Besides this, every time a lawyer showed up to file someone's
personal statement on my behalf, they'd move me to one of the
secret cells that have always existed in the interior part of the
Police Station, the torture rooms, until he left. They always
knew ahead of time when a lawyer was coming, because right
from the Supreme Court there would be a telephone call to the
Chief of Police, so the pantomime could be carried out with no
surprises. There were also lawyers who would just arrive at the
Police Chief's office and ask him if I was a prisoner: he'd put on a
dumb face and deny I was there, and then the lawyer would file
a statement and get the hell out of there as soon as possible.
One fine day Colonel Juan Ortiz, Departmental Commander of
Sonsonate, who had made a name for himself in the repression
of the people since 1932, came right up to my cell bars. He
showed up all arrogant, ready to insult me, with hate painted on
his big Indian face. "Now you're acting all humble, you son-of-a-
bitch," he said, "you bandit, murderer of '32. I'm going to order
you taken out of your cell so I can kick your face in." "Who's the
murderer," I answered him, "me or you? Weren't you the
Commander of Arms who directed the May 25th massacre? I
haven't killed anybody, but you and the forces of the Santa Ana
Cavalry are bathed in blood." The guy thought I didn't know who
he was, and he froze. After that, he stopped his fuming and he
couldn't nail me between the eyes with that furious look of his.
"Let's talk about something else," he said, "I can't get anywhere
discussing the Government with you." After a little while he
even stopped using "vos" with me, and changed to "usted."
"Don't you agree with what General Martínez is doing for the
country? Land is being distributed to the peasants, there's farm
credit, seeds for the small landowners, the Moratorium Law,
etc." "Those are just a few of the things we communists have
fought for," I replied, "and in order to deny them, you have
murdered the people. How could I not agree with land reform or
credit? But where we don't agree is with the ways in which the
Government's theoretical measures are carried out in practice:
you allot a few plots of rocky, useless land, where not even

sagebrush can grow; you give credit at high interest rates that poor people can't manage, only those who don't need it so urgently; and you commit yourselves to selling the crops of the small producers at starvation prices." All these arguments were based on real facts and referred to the big deals that President Martínez and his gang made to obtain fraudulent profits and to keep on with their demagogic sermonizing. Colonel Ortiz noted down my answers in a notebook, with a red pencil. "You don't agree with the "cheap housing" either? he grunted. "The problem," I told him, "is that workers and peasants don't live in those houses, just staunch supporters of the regime." While he went on taking notes, another military officer showed up at my cell, a man who at that time was President Martínez' bodyguard, who later rose to be the Chief of Transit and became the terror of the drivers because of his outrageous fines, blackmail to obtain driver's licenses, detentions for the smallest infraction of the law, etc. His name was Captain Colorado and they used to call him "Crazy Ant." It went the same with him: he began to insult me, until of his own accord he calmed down and wound up joining Colonel Ortiz in the questions about the regime's economic measures. He focused on my disagreement with the system of cheap housing or low-cost housing for those employed, and I went on with him about its demagogic nature and what really needed to be done, which would be to extend the system to benefit the workers and peasants and to base rents on a small portion of each worker's wage. I was way ahead of my time in this matter, if you stop to think that a measure like that one has only been possible since the Cuban Revolution, with Urban Reform legislation, and to this day Cuba is the only country in America which has accomplished it. In a little while another officer came over – when it rains it pours, as the saying goes – the Special Police Judge, an evil bastard of a man named Héctor Muñoz Barillas, and he joined the discussion too, but not without first crudely insulting me, saying that all we communists were insolent, arrogant bums who had to have the wind knocked out of us by force. The tone of the discussion heated up, so some other officers and justice officials came

363

over to take part in it. It was really a rough going over, but they couldn't beat down my spirit. In cases like those, the one who blinks first loses, and once you let your pants down you're not worth a hill of beans anymore. "The thing is," said Muñoz Barillas, "that you people are ambitious and you're never satisfied. With strikes and disorder you won a wage of one colon a day on the "Agua Fría" plantation. If things had continued like you wanted, today they'd be asking for ten colones." "And why not, Captain," I answered, "the desire for progress is innate in man. Let's take your own case. First you were a soldier, and when you had the red insignia of a corporal, you wanted the yellow one of a sergeant. Today you're a captain. And if you get to be a general, you'll want to be President. Workers are just the same, the only thing is they've got the right to be, because they want the well-being of the majority, they want to put an end to exploitation." Then he tried to get me by using a different tact: he started attacking the Paris Commune, and accused the French workers of unleashing a bloodbath. "That's right," I told him, "exactly like us. We unleashed a bloodbath, but the blood that ran was our own. You gave up nothing, the only thing you did was squeeze the triggers of your rifles and machine guns." "What the hell do you know about the Paris Commune," he shouted at me, "I suppose you can speak French?" "No," I said, "but, maybe you've been to Paris as I have?" The argument ended there, and of course it had other moments I don't remember now. Muñoz Barillas said we'd continue our chat another day, since I was an obstinate communist who refused to be persuaded with crystal clear truths, and it had gotten so late, and his wife was waiting outside with the car. He promised to send me some books that laid communist doctrine to rest once and for all, telling me I should study them in detail. He wasn't so rude and nasty anymore when we said goodbye. There was even "take care," "eat well," and "nice to have seen you." But that creep sent a terrible report on me to the Military Tribunal, advising that I be considered a highly dangerous prisoner, an incorrigible, unsalvageable communist, and that they look for a way to get me in front of a firing squad, either legally or otherwise.

These visits, although they got on my nerves, kept me alert and pulled me out of my boredom. I welcomed them while the days, one just the same as the next, passed slowly by. One day all the police were feverish with activity. Bustling around, hurrying each other, giving and taking orders, they washed down the musty halls, took brooms to the spider webs on the ceiling, straightened up the office furniture and some of them even washed up and changed their clothes. The excitement was so great that I started to think that maybe General Martínez himself was going to show up and they wanted to make a good impression on him, since the guy was a fanatic for cleanliness and order. I was off by one rank, because indeed the one who did come there was General Tomás Calderón, alias "Turncoat," who had been Chief of Punitive Operations in the entire Western zone in 1932, and now was Minister of Defense. He came right up to my cell, friendly and polite, along with the Police Chief, Linares, who, on the contrary, was never able to get the sour expression off his face. That old Linares always looked like he'd swallowed a scorpion, he seemed so irritated all the time that it made you laugh. A group of policemen accompanied them. General Calderón began asking me about my visit to the U.S.S.R. I still remember the sound of his first words: "You are Señor Mármol, aren't you? You're the one who went to the U.S.S.R.?" He didn't have to ask me twice. I started to tell him about my experiences and managed to embroider them with all the reasons for the struggle of Salvadoran communists. General Calderón made all the police leave while he stayed on, together with Linares. Speaking to Linares, when I'd stopped talking for a bit, "Turncoat" said, "Yes, Colonel, you have to understand Señor Mármol. I don 't think Sr. Mármol is a criminal, I think he's an apostle. But he's an apostle preaching a cause that may well have had its success in Russia – because in Russia misery and the climate there have tormented the people – but that here it could only lead to disaster, like the one that happened so recently. Because among us social differences don't exist. In our country, no one dies of the cold, or the heat, or of hunger and thirst. God has given us an agreeable nature." That statement really burned me up, I refuted it and told him not to come at me with that crap about there not being a horrible situation in our country, that it was a shame the terrible experience of 1932 hadn't taken the blinders from their eyes. "If you want to see people dying from hunger," I told him, "go out of here and walk around the block, just once. Or go at night to the city gates. Or walk in the countryside when there's no coffee harvest. Then tell me about it." He immediately acted dumb. "Let's talk about something else, let's try to understand each other," he said, "I haven't come here to torture you, I want to reason with you. Why do you love war, Sr. Mármol?" "I don't love war, General, I'm not bellicose. I'm a simple, peaceful shoemaker." "But you have proposed revolution, Sr. Mármol?" "Ah, but that's not the same thing. If we've chosen the armed path for the Revolution, it's because the rich people and the Government have closed all the others to us. And you know very well how we came to the Revolution without understanding beans about military matters. You, as a good son of Mars, well know that if the Army was able to put down the people, it was because it dominated in the art of war, and it had the arms and the bombs that the popular masses lacked. And we're not even discussing here the useless massacre of workers and peasants who'd already been defeated militarily and completely crushed." "Sr. Mármol," he told me, solemnly, "God is always on the side of good men. War is decided in favor of those with better strategy and tactics, better machine guns, cannons and bombs. But it's God who decides that better bombs will be in the hands of good men. That's why humanity progresses with a similar balance as that of nature's. Think hard about that, Sr. Mármol." He extended his hand through the bars and said goodbye: "I hope you will soon obtain your freedom and that meanwhile you will be calm and at peace. You are in the hands of a government of order, which is ruled according to the mandate of the law." My treatment improved for a while. The guards didn't particularly want to fuck around with a prisoner visited by colonels and generals, captains and Ministers, and the ones who used to fuck me over on their own decided to think better of it. For my part, I also modified my agressive attitude in order to take advantage of these new conditions as much as possible. Freedom was by then my main objective. Caged up there like an animal, I wasn't any good to the Party, or the Revolution, or to the Virgin of Candelaria either. One day when I was feeling particularly down, the wind blew a piece of newspaper into my cell, and I read in it a phrase of Dr. Enrique Córdoba's: "When a prisoner is defenseless, the best thing he can do is behave well in prison." That confirmed my own ideas, even though the phrase came from my class enemy. Little by little, without losing my dignity I began to follow the logical orders of the guards and to be less bitter with them. Up until then, if a guard told me not to stand in the doorway of my cell and to go sit in the corner, I'd tell him to go to hell a thousand times. But from this point on, when they'd say, "Get inside, Carranza," I'd go in. I didn't bad mouth anybody anymore and began to act cheerful. There was just one time during that period that I blew up. It was the time they took me out of the cell to go take care of my needs in a latrine that was in the courtyard, since they were cleaning the bugs out of the hole I used. It surprised me that nobody went all the way to the latrine with me, as they always did at these times, but instead one of the cops told me in the hall: "Go to the latrine over there." I went and did what I needed to do, but when I came out I realized those bastards had let loose in the courtyard a huge deer that had been given to Colonel Linares as a gift, and it was a wild, crafty animal with big horns and hoofs that made sparks fly off the cobblestone. That animal saw me and charged at me and I felt like I needed to go to the john again. You've got to realize that I was shackled, and that I was incredibly weak because of the lack of enough food, the absence of sunlight, sickness and fevers, etc. Grabbing desperately, I managed to hang on to his horns once I got away from the first attack and I held on with all my body and soul. But he was an incredibly strong animal and he gave me one helluva dragging all over the courtyard, getting me all scraped up and bruised. Finally some policemen came over with ropes and cords, and they got him off me, dying with laughter. "Ain't that something," they said, "this Carranza was just fucking around with us. He wanted to kick out the Government and he can't even take care of a poor little deer." I swore them up and down starting with the bitch that bore them, including the goddamned deer and Colonel Linares. And, by the way, the same Colonel Linares – wherever he may be, in heaven or down below, he must still be the same irritable Indian, as nasty as a viper – had a strange end that wound up benefiting me directly. My sister told me afterwards that during those days she was devoted to the Holy Child of Atocha, praying to him and lighting candles so he'd intercede on my behalf with God and I could be freed. Since the Child of Atocha wasn't catching on and the months were going by without any change in my situation, my sister, who thought the reason for all my troubles was the Police Chief, proposed a deal to the saint of her devotions: "Holy child," she told me she said to him, "since you don't want to give my brother his freedom, I'll ask you for one of two things: either that my brother dies right now so that you can receive him in your holy bosom, or that the one who mistreats him the most dies, so that the obstacles to his freedom will be taken away." My sister says that then she had a dream where an angel came to her and told her: "Don't be afraid, my child, your brother will live a long life, his bones will grow old." So that's why my sister persists in her petitions to the Holy Child of Atocha. Now that I'm old I've given her a hard time about it all, telling her she should have gone to a less tranquil saint since everybody knows that the Child of Atocha has a big nail stuck up his ass and he doesn't even blink. But the truth is that in this case, if he was the one responsible for what happened, it was all done and over quicker than a jack rabbit. It just so happened that at the same time as this with my sister, the mother of comrade Antonio Nuila, from Cojutepeque, who was among the thirty-four communists held by the police, was desperately trying to find out about her son, working for his freedom, making the rounds of all the government offices, even talking with the big shots and the

368

bums on the streets. Since that bandit Colonel Linares refused to see her, she made an appointment with him using another name, supposedly about another case concerning a common prisoner. Linares was fooled and received her in his office. Once inside, the lady told him she was Nuila's mother, that she wanted to know if her son was alive and what condition he was in, and she wanted to see him. Linares got mad as hell and shouted at the poor woman, "Shut up and get the hell out of here, you impudent old woman." And he gave orders to have her taken away. Then he started cursing out the people who had let her get in, and in his rage he came down furiously on his desk with his fist. Right then and there a terrible pain grabbed his hand and it got worse as the hours went by, and it spread up into his arm. A week later he died, with awful pain all over his body. And that's why I say, wherever he is, he must look like some raving little toad, swearing like a son-of-a-bitch.

To take Linares' place, President Martínez named Colonel Juan Francisco Merino Rosales as Chief of Police, a military man with the reputation of being very mean and perverse. Next to him, Linares would have seemed like a meek little nun. The police, the informers, the officers were all shitting their pants with the news of the appointment, and all they had to worry about were his manias for maintaining perfectly the daily functioning of the jail and offices. I thought, "If these creeps are so afraid of this man, then I better be ready for all hell to break loose on my head." One fine day, early, he took over his duties. By the afternoon he was already inspecting the cells. I saw him and heard him from a distance. He was a big, elegant, older man with a great, strong voice. He asked: "Where is that criminal Miguel Mármol?" With a knot in my throat, I answered him calmly, though I was a little nervous: "Here I am, sir, I'm here." My appearance must have moved him. I was filthy, with a mane of hair falling over my shoulders, shackled and with a rubber cloak they'd put around me to make me sweat out a fever I'd had for a few days. "How are they treating you, Mármol?" he asked me.

"You can see for yourself, Colonel," I said. "Have they beaten you?" "No, sir. The ones they've beaten are my comrades, the thirty-four prisoners in the cells below, in the other courtyard." "And why don't they cut your hair?" I smiled. "I'm not like this by choice, Colonel." Then the man yelled at the cops with his volcano of a voice: "Who the hell is in charge here?" "Colonel Grande," they answered, turning deathly pale. "Call Grande here immediately," he ordered. Colonel Grande arrived full of excuses, saying that in the last week there'd been no barber, that he'd been sick, etc. Merino stopped him cold: "Don't tell me this man's hair has grown like this in a few weeks." "Not only that," I stuck in my two cents here, "the barber has been here since they brought me here, he's Commander Balbino's nephew." Merino looked at me without saying a word and then ordered Grande in a forceful tone of voice: "Tomorrow I want this man taken out in the sun, he should have a good bath and his hair better be cut, and if he's sick give him medicine or have the doctor look at him." And he turned and left, followed by his trembling subordinates. "Wow," I thought, "where did all this come from?" The next day, just as he ordered: they took me out to sun myself, to take a bath and they gave me a French-style haircut I can still remember. That night they put a cot in my cell and I stopped sleeping on the cold floor. By then I had lost count of the months spent under such horrible conditions and to sleep all of a sudden in a bed like a real person put me on cloud nine. I even dreamt about women and other pleasant silly things. Colonel Merino Rosales came to see and talk with me a few times. His tone wasn't exactly friendly, but he was respectful, like an old-fashioned military officer with his captured enemy. He stopped coming to my cell when I insisted that they unshackle me. I told him it was a useless measure since it was impossible to escape from the kind of security they had me under. I'm positive the shackles were a torture ordered from the top, by "pecuecho" Martínez himself, and Merino decided not to visit me anymore so he wouldn't have to discuss it with me. Besides that, several times I'd shown him that the food they were giving me was terrible, that I'd spent centuries eating

tortillas and beans both for lunch and dinner and the worst part
was that the police would wolf down their normal meals right in
front of me, and while it was no banquet it made my belly growl
with envy. But in any case, the situation got better after Merino's
visits. The cops chatted with me and even offered a few kind
words. Of course, we're not talking about the beginning of a
honeymoon either. These were relationships between
enemies, that improved because of time and circumstances.
And because I was defenseless. Since the Colonel disappeared without resolving the problems of my shackles and the
food, I decided to try to do something on my own. First I began
to sound out the guards closest by. There were days the
guards were even inside my cell, so there was time and
opportunity to talk with them and persuade them. The two
policemen who were assigned to guard me most often were a
couple of out-and-out villians, but impressionable. One was a
very young, skinny guy who always got what he went after and
who they called "Chicken," and the other was a man about forty,
with a mean face, known as "Captain Suspicion." Chicken had a
weaker character and I began by trying to get friendly with him.
One fine day, when he was shoveling down his lunch in front of
me, I couldn't stand it anymore and I told him to give me some of
his food, that I couldn't take the tortillas and beans any longer.
At first he refused, but I told him he ought to consider that
political situations could change from one moment to the next,
that he should realize his bosses weren't stupid and they came
by now and then to talk with me, and that it wouldn't be at all
strange that someday, with a new situation, I might even get to
be his boss. "If that ends up happening and you've treated me
badly, Chicken," I said, "I'll fuck you over so bad even the dogs
will howl about it. The very least I'll do is make myself a hammock
from your beard. Then you'll know what I'm made of." From then
on, Chicken started giving me some of his food and he
sometimes sent me bread with cheese, or beans, and even
sweets made with donkey milk. Captain Suspicion started giving
me his food on his own, perhaps on the advice of Chicken.
Since all this had gone so well for me, I decided to go one step

371

further. One Saturday when the cops got paid, they were all passing by my cell counting their bills and coins. When another one of my regular guards – Chebito, who was from Guayabal – went by, I called him over, looked him in the eye, and told him: "Chebito, drop five centavos from the dole you've got there, because if you don't give it to me, your whole salary is just going to disappear, either you'll lose it or it won't even buy you one lousy little tamale. I know what I'm saying. Give me the five centavos, for your own good." This got to Chebito and he gave me a tostón.[1] You've got to understand that ever since I didn't die after being executed, among the cops and informers I had gotten the reputation of being a fantastic sorcerer. Their peasant origins and their contact with the underworld make the police very superstitious. But there were other coincidences that contributed to their giving me that aura. Just a few days before I asked Chebito for the five centavos, I had asked another guard, whose name I don't remember, for ten centavos. He was the one who was in charge of feeding Colonel Linares' deer while it was there. This guard was growing a vegetable garden in the courtyard. I told him as a joke that if he wouldn't give me the ten centavos, a chayote plant that was his pride and joy would dry up on him, and he told me to go to hell. I don't know how it happened, because he watered it every day, but don't you know that chayote plant dried up, and once again the rumors about my occult powers started to spread. So that's why when Chebito was upset by what I'd said and he gave me the tostón, it wasn't just out of the blue. From then on, the policemen and the workers in the prison control office came by on pay days and gave me their pesetas and tostónes. They'd say that when they gave me charity, their money stretched enough for everything and they had more, and that it was because I had a pact with the devil and great powers to do good or bad to my friends and enemies. It's a good thing they never connected me with Colonel Linares' sudden death, because then even the Holy Child of Atocha couldn't have helped me. So this is how I began to get enough pesos to order food from the outside and to bribe a new thief here and there, in order to

372

strengthen the communications network with my family. My sister learned of these changes from my messages and she stepped up the intensity and frequency of her activities for my release. The Police and the Government were still denying my arrest, in spite of the fact that many associations, friends, etc. kept on sending appeals with their personal statements, testimonies, etc. on my behalf. The Judges, under pressure from my friends and family, from time to time would become somewhat active and they'd inspect the cells looking for me, but the only thing they accomplished was that my jailers took even stricter measures to hide me. One time, the Judge arrived before he was supposed to and they couldn't get me hidden in the basement torture cells, so they stuck me head-first into an unlit oven in the kitchen and there I was, breathing in ashes, for something like four hours. Meanwhile, it wasn't long before something else new began. In those days, the influx of new prisoners was heavy and varied. New social tensions, flowering in that same deathly peace that the great massacre left, were now emerging in all their force and they were creating diverse conflicts which, in turn, created large numbers of prisoners. Big-shot smugglers, embezzlers, high-class swindlers, opponents of the regime, conspirators who weren't revolutionaries, etc. came and changed for me the routine of all the prior months. I remember them bringing in, all messed up, don Jorge Restrepo, a big-shot in the upper bourgeoisie, all teary and resplendent in his clothes and white shoes, who'd gotten involved in a fraudulent cinnamon business. And I also remember that in one of the cells across from mine, though pretty far back, they put a group of cavalry officers who were charged with plotting against Martínez. The main guy accused was General Antonio Castañeda, better know as General Fritter because of the nose on him. They also put into those cells some young officers accused of being partisans with General Claramount, the eternal candidate for President of the Republic of El Salvador. Of course, university students weren't missing either, but they generally didn't stick around long in the cells. They were brought in one day, given a good beating that night and sent into exile the next day to Honduras or Guatemala, their lives all shattered and ruined. I managed to make contact with the new prisoners, in order to help them morally and to lift their spirits, and also so they'd know I was there and they could get word around when they left. That's why I sent messages to the journalist, Martínez, a great Guatemalan fellow who edited the literary magazine called *Cipactl,* named after an indigenous princess in the time of Atlacatl, who they imprisoned – I mean the kid Martínez, not the princess – for something or other he wrote that really gave it to the dictator. Since I saw he was sad, I sent him comforting notes. Even foreign prisoners wound up among us in those days. I especially remember a Cuban prisoner, a member of the "Young Cuba" organization who was chained up across from my cell for a few weeks. He was elegant, tall, he argued with the police in an arrogant and proud way and wasn't cowed. The police complained that "he shits on our mother's pussies" and they wanted to really give him a going over. There was one day I saw him looking sad, defeated, and it really got to me, and through a thief who was dishing out chow that day I sent him a little note to revive his spirit, the text of which I still remember line by line. It encouraged him and made him strong again, although because of the way the cells were he couldn't see me, I could only see him. But from then on, even when it was time to eat that prison crap he whistled and sang. Journalists interviewed him, but I never found out if his statements appeared anywhere. One day they came to get him, they took him away and I never saw him again. The time for the Central American and Caribbean Olympics arrived, and the weather was beautiful, clear blue skies. The cops came and went all happy, smelling of perfumed soap and talcum powder. As I sometimes recited peasant verses for them, they called me a "poet." Some mockingly, others with respect.

My stomach illness declared itself suddenly and openly in the form of awful pain and constant vomiting. I couldn't keep any food down and I began to lose weight and become extremely

374

weak. I let my sisters know that I thought I was going to die. They spoke to a lawyer, Chino Pinto, who was very well-known because he had broken his leg the first time he jumped from a plane with a parachute over El Salvador, and because he had walked to Panama, and because one time as a publicity stunt for a charity he went into the lion's cage of the Atayde Circus and drank champagne. This Chino Pinto, though he was anti-communist and rather shallow, had given legal help to some comrades during the worst part of the massacre. Through him an urgent request was made to the Supreme Court, but that old bastard, Gómez Zárate, declared publicly that it had been proven I died in 1932 and therefore my case was closed. I think in some part of the world there must be a totally honest lawyer. Within our Party we do have some lawyers who are good people, but what they say about the biggest crooks in the world being lawyers is a truth larger than the San Jacinto mountains. I'm sure it was Gómez Zárate himself who told the Police about the Briefs and Appeals, because with every legal move the surveillance around me got tighter and tighter. The sixth of November, 1935, I almost died of stomach pain. The pain must have been pretty terrible since I still remember the exact date! They gave me a purge of castor oil and I didn't eat at all for more than a day. The situation made me start thinking. It seemed like the Government wasn't too interested in killing me. What they wanted was to wear me down as much as possible in jail, leave me there for who knew how long until I rotted, make sure I didn't return to political work. Such a situation could be exploited by me with a hunger strike that could be backed up with outside pressure from friends and family members. The outcome could be any number of things. Maybe an end to being held incommunicado and a change to the normal routine of those awaiting trial, which would allow me to see my family, work in the Penitentiary shops, try to escape. Maybe even get them to free me. Since my stomach got noticeably better after the purge, I decided to get my strength up a little so I could go on a hunger strike. I ate as well as I could on the eighth, ninth, tenth and eleventh. With a pencil I'd hidden away, I made several copies of a note declaring a hunger strike, with an explanation of my reasons, purposes, conditions and demands. One of the copies was to be for the Chief of Police, Colonel Merino Rosales; for my family so they could make a big stink and not just let me starve for nothing; another, for the comrades imprisoned in the other section of the jail so they'd know that my hunger strike was also to demand their freedom; one more for a secretary who worked in the police offices, who had been kind and respectful to me, with the hope that if it all backfired, he could publicize it in the future; and the final copy which I stuck in a hole in the cell wall, for whoever Fate decided should find it. On the twelfth, the same policeman who had taken part in my arrest, little Cruz, nicknamed "Paris," was the one who brought me that crap for lunch. Since I didn't take the tortillas and beans he was handing me, he said, "Aren't you eating today, Carranza?" "My name isn't Carranza," I answered him, "it's Miguel Mármol, and today, November 12, 1935, I declare myself on a hunger strike for my freedom and that of my comrades, or else to die attempting it. Tell your superiors, please." Paris took away the food and went to call Major Marroquín, Deputy Chief of Police, who came in person to my cell and to whom I gave the note I'd prepared for Merino. Marroquín told me he would deliver it. A couple of hours later some policemen came with wooden boards and nailed them over my cell door so no one could see me from the outside and I was left in total darkness, with no way of communicating at all. I stretched out on my cot and prepared myself to begin a new struggle. A struggle with myself and my jailers, big and small. On the twelfth and thirteenth I didn't eat or drink a thing, not even water. The generally weak state I'd been in had devastated me, I didn't have any reserves of strength at all, and on the third day of the strike I woke up looking like a corpse, so bad it was pathetic. They took me out to the courtyard for some sun, lying down on a lounge chair. There, something really odd happened. After Colonel Linares' deer had been taken away, they'd given Major Marroquín a present of his own, a wild doe that they had christened with the name Chita. They had her tied up in the courtyard until they were ready to barbecue her. This Chita was bigger and fiercer than Linares' deer. I knew that one time she'd dug her hoof into the chest of a cop who was bringing her some hay to eat, and they had to take him to the hospital half dead. Well, as soon as that animal saw them bringing me out into the sun, she reared up in such a way that after pulling for a few minutes she broke her rope and came running and snorting in my direction. I thought to myself, "Out of the frying pan and into the fire, now this goddamned doe is really going to do me in." The police ran over to protect me out of pure pity, since I was no more than skin and bones. But, imagine how surprised they were, and so was I, to see the doe calmly start licking my hands and sniffing my body, lying down next to my chair like a puppy. The cops tried to joke about it: "Carranza's found himself a girl," they laughed, "Chita's in love with Carranza." But out of the corner of my eye I saw that more than one of them was crossing himself and saying, "Hail Mary full of grace, born without sin." It didn't stop there, either. When they came to take me back in and lock me up again, Chita started rearing once more and she really got hopping mad, she leapt and kicked and although they had her under control for a little while, she still managed to kick the boards on my cell door and she stayed there snorting and smelling between the cracks for a good while longer. "Either this Carranza truly has a pact with the devil, or else God is really watching over him," said the cops. Who knows what they did to that Chita, who knows where they took her, she was such a sweetheart. Three more days went by. Each day I only drank a few sips of water and I was on my deathbed. I kept fainting, but I kept telling myself I had to go on. The guards would come and tell me I was crazy, and they'd offer me special meals, chicken, steak. What really got to me was the vomiting that came on with such tremendous force, adding insult to injury on an empty stomach. On the 17th they took me out into the sun again to lie in the lounge, and I, defiant, so they'd see I was still strong, sat up in a chair. From his cell, General Fritter Castañada made signals and applauded my attitude with his thumbnails, which is the secret way of applauding in El Salvador. With other signs he

377

told me, "You've got balls, my friend. Bravo." That afternoon Colonel Merino Rosales came to see me. He was very cordial, talking to me with kind words and in a fatherly way. "My friend," he said, "I've come to see you and to ask you to eat. It's not necessary for you to keep on destroying yourself. I come to assure you that you will get your freedom. But you should stop this hunger strike that isn't doing anyone any good." "How can I know, Colonel, that your offer will be carried out?" I said, with a weak, little voice. "If my word isn't good enough for you, my friend," he said, "what proof do you want?" "I want to see my family," I answered. "That's no problem, we can arrange it," he declared, "the only thing is that I don't want them to see you in this state. So I propose a deal. If you begin to eat and recover, I'll let your family know immediately so they can bring you clothes, and within two weeks I'll free you. All of this is on my word of honor." I thought about it for a moment and it didn't seem like such a bad idea, so I told Merino: "Okay. I think you are an honorable military man, and you won't go back on your word. I accept your proposition. I'll eat." They brought me a special meal of ox-liver broth, chicken with herbed rice and a sage-flavored drink. The Cell Boss, Colonel Grande, had to take the spoon out of my hand because I was devouring it all so fast, he told me that it could cause a lethal colic. I ate bit by bit and even managed to put down half a beer. Afterwards, I slept for 24 hours straight, right through. When I woke up they brought me more food and I pampered myself by picking what I liked best and even asked for treats. "Take that away, it doesn't agree with me," I was telling the cops, "bring me a slice of pineapple, it's good for a weak stomach." One day they brought me new clothes, telling me they were from my family. It seemed the Colonel was coming through on the deal for me. Three or four days later my sister Cordelia came to see me. She started to cry, and said that in a few months I'd aged 20 years. And she said that when they notified her that she could see me, the policeman who did it told her: "A little old man who says he's your brother has shown up at the Police Station." In fact, I'd gotten a lot of grey hairs and my face was yellow and leathery. I

378

consoled my sister and told her I was going to get out any time now, that she should stop worrying because the worst was already over. But the days flew by and the situation didn't change. Once the two-week period was up, I sent Colonel Merino a letter, reminding him of the agreement, and around then I dreamt they were giving away toys and candy for the children in a beautiful park and that I was still a kid and that I went so they'd give me some. A disgusting hateful old lady yanked me out of line and said there weren't any toys for me, but a lovely young girl, like a fairy, showed up to rescue me and she gave me some toys. I interpreted the dream like this: the toys and candy were my freedom, the hateful old lady was General Martínez, the beautiful and good young girl was Colonel Merino. So then I wrote a letter to the Colonel, telling him I was aware that his superior, the President of the Republic, was opposed to setting me free, but I stressed that he'd given his word of honor. Merino didn't send me a reply, but told someone to tell me to have a little more patience, that everything would be worked out. The cop who brought my letter to him told me confidentially that Merino, after reading it, had said, "This Mármol is smart. He's realized that it's General Martínez who's keeping him sewn up under lock and key come hell or high water." On January 7, 1936, I got good news: they had let all the communist prisoners free. But as to me, zero. Another two weeks went by and I really began to get desperate. The 21st of January I sent a new message to Colonel Merino, giving him a specific time limit before I started a new hunger strike. I hadn't had any visitors since I saw my sister. In the afternoon that same day, the 21st, they came to take me out of the cell and told me I could take a bath, as soon as they brought me soap and a scrub brush. While I bathed, they asked for my shoes so they could shine them up a little, since they'd never seen shoe polish. They told me to put on new clothes because I was going to have a visitor. But then they asked me a question that allowed me to see the light at the end of the tunnel. "Those things you've got under the cot, Carranza, are you taking them with you or leaving them for us as a remembrance?" They were just

379

junky things like a clay mug with no handle for drinking coffee, a spoon, a metal pot, a raggedy old shirt and pants, etc. At five in the afternoon they removed my shackles, finally. I'd been in shackles for four months, straight. They told me the Police Chief wanted to see me in his office. And there, indeed, Colonel Merino was waiting for me. We were left alone. After asking me to sit down, he said in a friendly tone, "My friend, you're finally free, you're going home to your family again. I've kept my word, though somewhat late. I wanted your freedom to be unconditional, but it's not up to me to decide. So I'm sorry to inform you that the Government grants you freedom, but imposes on you the meeting of certain requirements. Firstly, you must stay in San Salvador. You may not go outside the city limits. In addition, you will have to show up and report to this Directorate General every Saturday afternoon. Your freedom will be forfeited if you fail to comply with these regulations. Your comrades who were freed already are subject to the same conditions. If you meet them, I'll make you a formal promise: as long as I'm Police Chief, your freedom is assured." I told him I was in agreement with the requirements and added, "I'll make you another promise. So long as you are Police Chief, I'll keep quiet. After that, I won't say." "Wonderful, my friend," said Merino, "we're in agreement." And I left his office. Into the street. Into a new prison. Only a bigger one with more people in it.

---

1 tostón: one coin equal to five centavos; like a nickel (translators' note).

10

Freedom, on parole. The Salvadoran workers' movement under the dictatorship of Martínez: the "National Alliance of Shoemakers." The situation in the Communist Party.

Some freedom: the situation in my family was awful because of the abysmal misery that had sucked the blood of my loved ones. My sister Cordelia lived in a run-down rooming house, her husband out of work for nearly a year and her children barefoot and shirtless. My other sister was even worse off, since she'd gotten sick. My wife and children living in seclusion, holed up with some relatives in San Martín, eating here and there, and enduring a thousand hardships. Nobody would give me a job for fear of getting mixed up in my situation, as it was obvious I was always being tailed, that the police were following me, not even letting me piss in peace. My friends avoided me: they were poor and out of work and afraid I might ask them for money or drop in on them at dinner time. But what really got me angry was that the comrades in the Party were wondering why the government had set me free so fast. That is, they were suspicious of me. They said nothing about the communists who were freed before me, since they were all together in prison and they'd vouch for each other's conduct. The Party harassed and isolated me and my protests weren't worth a thing. I felt desperate and confused and I wanted to hang myself from the nearest tree. My wife, on the other hand, was asking for us to get together, to live together once again even though the hunger would probably get worse. It tore my heart to pieces to see my little ones dirty and barefoot, dressed in rags and getting sick all the time. In order to be together we decided to live as a family always moving around, sleeping in public entryways but also getting some old friend, such as Nicolás Chinchilla or Jesús Menjívar, to give us shelter in their house or room, so we could sleep on the floor. One time we got a moneylender to loan us a few pesos at a "reasonable interest rate" of I don't know how much percent. With that money we bought meat in San Martín, in order to resell it in the suburbs of

383

San Salvador. I'd carry the meat on my back in a big basket bought on credit and my wife would drum up business. But the police harassment threw us out of business. The police chased our customers away, despite the fact that I went to Colonel Merino to protest and remind him of his promises. Nothing: the persecution would stop one day and start up with greater force the next. I got them to give me work in a new shoe factory in San Sebastián, where they didn't know me, but within a week a commission of judicial police arrived to speak with the boss and they fired me immediately. Then in a fit of helpless rage, I wrote a letter to the dictator Martínez, telling him that my freedom was pure bullshit, that they wouldn't let me earn a living for my children and that that was illegal and prejudicial, that for this it'd be better to stick me back in prison or execute me again. Martínez' answer was surprisingly quick. He sent me excuses and his personal card for the Minister of War, who at that time was General Andrés Ignacio Menéndez, whose nickname was "Cement Armor" because of the amount of starch he used on his uniforms and the way he stood up so straight, though he was a little fat toad. The card told "Cement Armor" that he should give me a concession to supply the Army with shoes and that they should provide me with the means to do it. I realized what they were doing. They were harassing and fucking me over in order to frustrate me and force me to accept work with the government. I brought the card to the offices of the Ministry and said I wouldn't agree to furnish the Army with shoes, since I didn't have the means to produce them. Fortunately, I found work in a shoe factory in Santa Tecla which produced for the poor people in the barrios and in the countryside. Besides making the shoes I had to go out selling them. The harassment from the police was less because I was going all the way to the beaches in La Libertad to sell and the cops verified that I wasn't doing political propaganda. And since there's no evil that lasts a hundred years, nor a back that can resist it, things got better. My wife found work, my sister had success in a cheese business and we began to get over that hard period. But there's a dark cloud for every silver lining, since when you're down and out even the pigs piss on you. Bad luck got me from the other end. My wife began to change, she refused to obey me, days passed without her speaking to me, and she seemed very different, carefree, strange, she seemed to be someone else, with a defiance I'd never known. One day, she told me frankly that she no longer wanted anything to do with me. She seemed to have fallen for someone else. I tried to get her to at least leave me the kids, but it was impossible. We separated and I was left completely crushed. I became deeply depressed. I didn't want to eat, not even when I was starving; people got on my nerves, I felt they were aggressive and hostile. I thought about killing myself. Isolated from the Party because of false suspicions, abandoned by my wife just when things were getting better, harassed by the police, alone and sad, I thought – I repeat – about killing myself and putting an end to all the suffering. However, amidst that despair a ray of hope told me I musn't give in, that at least things couldn't get worse and, if they changed, it'd have to be for the better. I didn't even have the comfort of revolutionary literature because I couldn't get my hands on any books or pamphlets that could have inspired me with renewed strength. What, for sure, carried me through was the memory of the struggle – the recent past when I felt useful among the masses of workers and peasants in whose eyes I often saw the confidence they had in me, in a communist leader who had no right to quit living, no matter how great the ingratitudes of life and men. If I was going to do that, I thought, I probably would have moved my feet when they executed me, so they would've delivered that "coup de grace." But if I had been so obstinate about living – Why, for Christ's sake, was I going to commit suicide? With these thoughts in my head, I was bit by bit getting a grip on myself, trying to forget the irreparable problems, like my wife leaving me. I was working only a little, just what was necessary to eat a little something. And I couldn't make any serious plans. One day, a girl commissioned me to make her some cheap sandals, because all she had was a colón and fifty centavos. I made them with very little material and a lot of ingenuity, and she was thrilled, saying if I could make

385

more like that she could sell them to her friends. The thing caught fire and my sandals became very much in demand. So we made only sandals and I had to hire a black guy, José, so that he'd go out selling while I kept producing. Money started to come in, I was able to rent my own room and pay José. Since my sister's cheese business was doing real well, she lent me money to start up a little shop again. We improved on the idea of the sandals and began making them in several styles. In the face of the general misery and the high prices of footwear, the sandals sold like hot cakes. The weeks passed and I had money to expand the shop even more, obtaining credit and in no time the shoe shop was doing better than my sister's cheese business. Within two months of the expansion, I already had 25 people working and five saleswomen. Several comrades came to work with me, among them Ismael Hernández and Pedro Sosa, who had undergone as many miseries as I had. Our shop was very special because the scarcity forced us to make it that way. We cooked our meals in the shop itself, collectively in order to save, and from there we ended up buying our clothes collectively too, in order to get discounts in the stores. We imposed a discipline of living and working that would allow us to progress together and prepare us for whatever might come. We didn't allow any alcoholic beverages and drunkenness was cause for expulsion from the collective. We went on trips to the rivers, the lakes and the beaches, and we even started to study some social problems – very cautiously, since we were afraid the police might have infiltrated us. Despite our cautiousness, on more than one occasion I was called in by the police where they reprimanded me "for having fallen back into my old ways" and organizing a new form of communist group. Nor was there a lack of Party comrades who said I had sold out to the Government, and hence my relative prosperity and freedom to work. Others were saying I had set up a shop in order to exploit a large group of workers with money the Government had given me. The truth is, in that shop the earnings were shared: I earned no more than the majority of the operators. But when people say "This guy is a disgrace," what they're really saying is they won't let up fucking you over for anything in the world. More than one comrade ended up saying I was a police agent, a stool pigeon, and that you had to be careful with me. I explained my situation and the integrity of my conduct, but those who accused me wouldn't listen to reason. And the other comrades, those who knew through experience that I was still a revolutionary, told me that I didn't need to explain anything to anybody, that I must be patient with the slander. I lived with a lot of bitter feelings, but I did no more than show all the comrades in the shop how I managed the money I'd borrowed from my sister and other people, accounting for the expenses, the cost of materials, the selling price of the sandals and the profits, so they could see the fairness with which I handled things. And at last I made contact with what was still functioning of the Party. Comrade Fidel Gutiérrez, a very poor student, got in touch with me through my family. He told me that a group of communists had kept working organizationally and among them he mentioned Alejandro Dagoberto Marroquín, Julio Fausto Fernández and Amparo Casamalhuapa, all three intellectuals. The few surviving communists had done some recruitment, some penetration into the student movement and even had incited some protests against the regime. Gutiérrez told me that during the days when the last communists in prison got out and even during the week I was released, Party propaganda was going to be distributed in the capital, but that such an action had been suspended so as not to get us involved too quickly. The most able cadre in the Party was Dagoberto Marroquín, recently returned from Buenos Aires where he had become politicized and radicalized to the point of joining the Argentine CP. I let those comrades know I wanted to make contact in order to report on my activities since 1932, because, so far, none of the party leadership had heard my accounts and it was causing many misunderstandings. Even though I did party work on my return to San Salvador in 1933 and made contact with a group recognized as the leadership of the Party (Ponce, Roca, etc.), the truth is it was a matter of personal contacts and there was never an organic meeting of self-criticism in order to leave

387

behind the practices of the past and try to move forward. Prison had meant for me a prolonged absence from political activity and when I got out the situation was different, in the country and in the Party. By then, for example, there was already a group of ready intellectuals, who'd read Marxism and had studied in the university. When I was in San Salvador in 1933, the only intellectual was Julio Fausto Fernández. My first petitions to make contact were turned down. Fidel Gutiérrez disappeared on me for awhile and I went around trying to make other contacts. Finally, I was able to find him again and I persisted in my appeal. The only thing I asked was that they hear me out. And similarly that they receive from me a number of links with the eastern zone, to see if they were still operative. After a lot of wavering and doubts, after internal discussions in which the comrades who had confidence in me had put pressure on those who didn't trust me for anything, I was invited to a Party meetIng. The first meeting after my return to so-called freedom. I attended with great emotion and said to myself that all the sacrifices, deprivations and steadfastness had been well worth it, since the Party had survived, had managed to rekindle itself from the ashes and blood, proving to us that an organization is invincible if it has the truth of the moment in its grasp, despite the errors, deviations, shortcomings, etc., and despite the power of the enemy. I didn't know how the survivors were organized, how the new militants had consolidated themselves: it didn't matter to me. The Party survived. That was the main thing. The rest had to become the reason for our daily work, for our lives. I remember the meeting was held in a large house in the San José barrio. Some ten comrades were present, mostly students, new faces. Dagoberto Marroquín, Amparo Casamalhuapa, Antonio Rodríguez Porth, Fernando Basilio Castellanos, Julio Fausto Fernández, etc. They embraced me enthusiastically and told me that my name and my ordeals had inspired a new generation of Salvadoran revolutionaries. Superficially they informed me about the organizing methods they were employing and the activities they were planning. Then a discussion began on how the Party was going to make ties with the people again, how to take it to the streets once more. I expressed the opinion that it was necessary to recognize the severity of damage caused by the enemy, that we had to start out from one reality: the apparatus of the Party had been destroyed. "Before rushing out into the streets," I said, "it's necessary to reconstruct the apparatus, to reorganize the leadership and get it functioning, and to intensify clandestine recruitment. If we take to the streets as we are, we're all going to end up in the same cell or in a common grave." Dagoberto agreed and convinced the rest. Despite the fact he was never a brilliant personality and was really very reserved and cautious, Dagoberto stood out in those days because of his knowledge, far beyond the average level of all the rest of the militants. Many things he said ran counter to what experience and day-to-day work had taught me; but, in general, none of us doubted that with the preparation he'd brought back from Argentina and with the praxis to be developed within the Party, Dagoberto was going to turn into an able and agile leadership cadre, and that, along with Julio Fausto Fernández, he was going to be in charge of a very important task: that of ideologically strengthening the new sprouts of the Party that we were beginning to cultivate. As a first step, we made up a list of names of comrades, ex-comrades who had the political and moral potential to rejoin the Party, sympathizers and progressive thinking people with whom we could talk, in order to have an approximate idea of the sector that could serve us as a starting point. I was able to offer a lot of information because I knew all the survivors all over the country and I knew the conduct of each one in prison, during the repression, etc. The comrades also reported on the organisms created while I was in prison and which I didn't know anything about; for instance, the organisms created almost spontaneously in Santa Ana, which would be the richest mines of proletarian continuity for the Party years later, once the bourgeoisie showed its true traitorous color. Heading up the Santa Ana organisms then were such steadfast and self-sacrificing comrades, shining lights of the communist movement, as Ponce and Roca, whose activity transcended national borders and whose conduct would throughout their lives – and still is now, in old age – an example for the new generation of Latin American revolutionaries. Dagoberto was overflowing with boundless enthusiasm and, from that meeting on, he would do tremendous work. There was no contact he didn't follow up, no door he left unopen in the reorganizing work. Sometimes he was reckless and he had to be controlled. Nobody would recognize him today, aimlessly dabbling in university politics, father of a respectable family, with a bunch of children who aren't just bourgeois but are high-up functionaries in the bourgeoisie. Amparo Casamalhuapa acted as a contact between me and Dagoberto, and she would later become Dagoberto's wife. But, like that tango says, when it comes to women there's nothing to be said. Due to the surveillance, we decided not to hold large meetings and we organized cells of three and up to four persons. The meetings were highly geared to action. No studying long materials or considering the case of comrade A who'd stolen comrade B's wife away. And they were held in places chosen beforehand, for reasons of security, avoiding private houses, except in extreme cases. Our meeting places were the entrance to the cemetery (the one for the area so anti-democratically called "of the Distinguished" when the truth is, it just so happens, that buried there are, with some exceptions, the biggest sons-of-bitches and shameless bastards El Salvador has had), the Candelaria Church, the Modelo plantation and around the Polar Brewery. Months started to pass by with our reorganizing efforts and the first fruits were springing forth. Our people are an inexhaustible source, they possess an innate revolutionary disposition, they are courageous, extroverted especially in politics, bold and optimistic. What you have to have is a correct line, because once our line takes hold among the masses, there's no losing. That the task of reorganizing the Party was successful so soon after the most horrible massacre in our history and under the savage terror of Martinism clearly attests to this fact.

When the work of the Directorate was regularized, I became responsible for drawing up a new report on the insurrection and its defeat. I prepared myself well, studied the facts once again, revised my conclusions, etc. However, when I gave the report in a special, expanded meeting, Dagoberto surprised me with the argumentative level of his criticism. No doubt he was far superior to any of us and his analysis was more profound, his arguments more thorough and clearer, and I have no reason to hide the fact that he overwhelmed me, despite the fact that I was no meek, little dove when it came to arguing. However, he went too far in attacking the backwardness of the Party Directorate that was responsible for the insurrection, which was the same as criticizing a person for being black or skinny. Of course, the level of our development had been low, but that was a real fact. So was the level of social development in El Salvador, and so was the level for the bourgeoisie and the Army. The insurrection was a concrete phenomenon, the result of deep contradictions existing in an archaic, semi-feudal, criminal and unjust society. The popular forces were the victims of a system in full-blown expansion that inaugurated the most savage methods for the domination of the world: the worldwide system of Yankee imperialism. To throw all the blame on the communist leaders who didn't make a successful insurrection was and continues to be a prejudiced point of view, proper to reactionary or petty-bourgeois mentalities, to intellectuals isolated from reality who, after the events, come up with the most intelligent analyses in the world that don't serve anyone to take a step forward. And what history is all about is taking steps forward, big and small. In spite of the fact that Dagoberto won the argument then, and I only defended myself and the Party from his most exaggerated negative criticisms, accepting our objective weaknesses, things were never the same between us. The arguments and differences moved from the historical into the day-to-day work, the organizational methodology, style of work and programmatical aspect. Dagoberto, because of his quiet and shy temperament, wouldn't blow up in front of me, but his

391

future wife, that Amparo Casamalhuapa, made up for him doubly and always spoke up first. I suggested to Dagoberto that he shouldn't make contact with the workers in the factories, since, as a professional, he'd stick out like a sore thumb, that that job was for a worker like me, capable of going unnoticed in the eyes of the enemy. Plus, all of us figured Marroquín was being watched by the police. Well, little Amparo said that that was just one of my sectarian maneuvers, geared to having all the work of recruitment centralized in my hands. Since my recommendations were ignored, the police in no time had the goods on Dagoberto's contacts with the workers, and they harassed him even more. One day, to make matters worse, a judicial policeman who knew us well – a fat, black cop named Cevallos – surprised us in a meeting on the Modelo plantation and we had to run when he took off like a shot for reinforcements. When we were able to see one another again, Dagoberto said they had called him from the Presidential House and told him that he had 8 days to get out of the country and that, if he didn't go, nobody was going to vouch for his life. Dagoberto decided to go to Mexico, though some of us disagreed. In any case, it was agreed that his absence was going to be for some months, until the military would forget all about him. But Martínez wasn't content with Marroquín's leaving the country. The actions taken against us sharpened and provocations started to abound. One time, an ex-comrade named Chico Campos came to see me, I think it must have been on New Year's Eve, 1938, and he told me that José Centeno (who, as I said before, went to study in the U.S.S.R. and had stayed in Cuba) was in San Salvador and wanted to see me. I fell for it like a jerk and told him to bring Centeno the following day to the Candelaria Church, to make contact. I arrived a half hour early and waited for another half hour. They didn't come. Instead, two policemen showed up who checked me over thoroughly. A few days later, Campos came looking for me again, with various excuses, saying he didn't know where Centeno was, that he'd disappeared. I interrupted him and said that what I was going to tell Centeno was he should be extremely careful, that things were really fucked up and that I wouldn't get involved in political matters, even if they paid me in diamonds. Another time, Campos arrived to tell me that a plot against the Government was being organized, inciting me so that I'd participate. I repeated to him that I had no interest in these things, that I already had fought a lot and I was sick and tired of suffering. But, by that time, I was already positive Campos was a provocateur, because the woman who washed his clothes told me she had found a cartridge holder with the official police seal stamped on it in a pair of his pants. Of course, between provocation and provocation, there were actual plots carried out against the Government, as there was a lot of indignation caused by the economic situation, the repression and the fascist whims of Martínez. One day, Julio Acosta came to see me, he'd been among the 34 communists in prison at the same time I was locked up in the Police Station, and he had my complete trust. Julio Acosta was the brother-in-law of comrade Lagos, a young communist who was put in front of a firing squad in 1932, thanks to his mother. This comrade Lagos was arrested by the police in Chalatenango, but there was no proof against him since he'd been very careful about his clandestinity. His undoing was that when his mother went to see him in jail (on the following day they were going to set him free), she started crying, shouting: "I told you not to get mixed up in anything." With those words she decreed her son's death. Well, anyway, Julio Acosta came and told me he was involved in a very serious plot against Martínez, in which high officers in the Army, professionals, students, etc. were taking part. I knew that Acosta had had conspiratorial experience, since I was in his house in '32 and organized activities there with Julio Fausto Fernández; so I took his news seriously and decided to go disguised to one of the meetings. The meeting was in Acosta's house. Several Army officers arrived, some in uniform, and they started by delivering some small semi-automatic arms and ammunition. They said the coup wasn't going to be in the name of parties nor ideologies, that it was necessary to put an end to the tyranny and install a democratic and anti-fascist government. They told us that

393

everything was all set and ready, and they only wanted to speak with us to see if we'd be responsible for a couple of tasks. They wanted "our people" to attack the Police Barracks, or for us to kill Colonel Merino and sow havoc in the center of San Salvador by setting fire to various buildings. I disagreed. In the first place, we couldn't use cadre from our newborn Party, our few revolutionary sympathizers, etc. in an action like attacking the Police Station or killing Merino, which anyhow was the same thing, since to get at Merino you had to attack the Police Station. We couldn't count on enough personnel, and the arms we had couldn't even take the Police Station in Santiago Texacuangos. Nor did I go along with sowing terror among civilians without having a clear political purpose. I admit I also hated to take part in Merino's death, who, given his own limitations, had treated us all decently. We still hadn't come to an agreement when that meeting ended. A few days later, Julio Acosta came to tell me that the officers had been denounced and that Martínez had exiled them to Mexico. We civilians weren't affected by the repression. It seems the denunciation came after a soldier saw how the conspirators stole the arms, and they got them on that, but without being able to find out their contacts on the outside. Otherwise, the rest of us would've all gone to hell. On another occasion, a miner named Chacón came to see me. "Today, for sure, is the day Martínez falls," he said. "He's going to be stormed on his own hacienda, the one on the road to Zacatecoluca." He added that he knew where the arsenal was that was going to be opened up to the people as soon as the death of Martínez was announced, and, if I wanted, he could show it to me. I was very careful. I didn't trust Chacón and I told him I wasn't going to decide anything so long as he didn't know the name of someone among the conspirators I could trust. Chacón said: "Robles, from the National Press, is one of the main leaders. Get in touch with him." But I checked out Robles and it just so happened he was the flesh and blood brother of General Martínez' barber, who was supposed to be a Nazi and always walked around with a golden swastika under the lapel of his jacket or under one of his shirt collars. "Shit, shit," I said to myself, "this really stinks a mile away." So I played dumb with Chacón. It was at that time that a woman with her dying boy arrived at my house looking for shelter. We welcomed her and fed her and gave her a place to sleep, but the boy died and we buried him with money we raised from a collective contribution. She stayed several days and one time she asked me if I had another relative with my name. When I told her the only Miguel Mármol I knew was the one I saw in the water tub every morning, she explained the reason she'd asked me was because she'd been a cook in the Presidential House and she noticed that a group of gentlemen led by a German, whose name she couldn't remember since it was complicated, came often to see General Martínez. What they did together was spiritualism. One day they even went into the kitchen and forced her to be their medium. They hypnotized her and used her to call up the spirit of Miguel Mármol, the communist who had been saved several times from death. "When the spirit of don Miguel Mármol appeared," the woman added, "the President and the other gentlemen fought with it, yelling at it, because it was a violent and arrogant spirit, and it knew many things." By the way, during the period the ex-cook of the Presidential House was talking about, I had suffered from nightmares and the most frequent one was about an encounter with General Martínez that would always end up in verbal clashes. Of course, all this was no more than a coincidence, but even so, it's strange. Like many things that have happened to me in my life to which I've never found a common thread and which I decided to forget, because, on the one hand, their solution doesn't put food on the table and, on the other, why go looking for a tiger without stripes. Being a communist and having an understanding of the problems of society is enough for me. When the people make their revolution, there will be time to delve into the mysteries of nature and death. The only thing is, these eyes that the worms will eat won't be able to see those days.

As the police surveillance became unbearable, I raised with the Party my leaving the country for a few months. And I said to the comrades that it'd be good to go to Mexico and join up with Dagoberto and take advantage of the time in some serious and worthwhile political study. But since that Amparo Casamalhuapa always had it in for me, she said I had the makings of a traitor, that for sure I was working for the police and that my intentions to go after Dagoberto were sinister, for police surveillance and control. We had a tremendous fight. To make matters worse, Carmela, my ex-wife, was going around by then with another man and wanted to find an excuse for her behavior. She went right to Amparo to say that she also believed I was a cop. That Amparo started raising holy hell again and it was impossible to get anywhere. I felt deeply hurt by those lies and, although I received the support and trust from a large sector of workers in the Party, there were moments when, in light of the ingratitude of those who thought so badly of me, I wanted to chuck everything to hell. Furthermore, a new generation of university intellectuals had taken their place in the Party: Tony Vassiliu, Matilde Elena López, Toño Díaz and others. All of them had been influenced by Dagoberto Marroquín and they wouldn't lower themselves to the level of us stupid, ignorant surviving workers of '32. They wouldn't accept anything in our behavior as positive, and so relations between us grew tense and degenerated to the point of rupturing into a mutual split. On the one hand, there were the workers led by Ismael Hernández, Modesto Ramírez and myself, who set about reestablishing contact with the old guard. This work was regarded by the intellectuals as being parallel to theirs and factional, and they accused me of being the one most responsible, the direct instigator. To the degree that the workers' sector of the Party was called "the Marmolista faction." Finally, I was called to a meeting in La Esperanza barrio in order to clarify the situation and future relations within the Party. Present at that meeting I remember Amparo Casamalhuapa, Toño Díaz, Tony Vassiliu, Carlos Alvarado, Manuel González and others. The meeting turned into a tribunal against me. I was interrogated and called on to give an account of the peasant organizing, about which they weren't totally familiar and which had, to tell the truth, advanced little in the last years, about meetings not under the control of the Party leadership, etc. In the end, I was openly accused of factionalism. I made it clear how everything was functioning irregularly, that we didn't have statutes, a program, disciplinary standards; that we hadn't held a congress and that the integration of the leadership was arbitrary. Nominally, I continued to belong to the CC, but the organism really wasn't functioning. There were new members of the CC who I didn't know. Tony Vassiliu agreed with me when some of them began ridiculing me. Someone said that we had to put aside our differences and begin working in harmony, effectively, as befitted a party that should be the vanguard of the working class and of the people of El Salvador. But that Amparo Casamalhuapa started in again, disrupting the peaceful climate by intervening fiercer than a spitting snake, saying I hadn't been summoned to discuss matters of organization and the line, but simply to clear up once and for all whether or not I was a provocateur, an agent with the police. "Because as far as I'm concerned, he's a cop," she ended up saying. I contained my anger and spoke up: "I lost my mother because I couldn't help her or attend to her health, because I was dedicated to the cause of the workers; I've always lived in misery and because of misery I also lost my wife and my children; I had the honor of eating bread made with the blood of the Russian workers; I've spilled my blood and I've suffered the worst imprisonments – how could I be a traitor? If someone has evidence against me, let him show it. But I'll tell you one thing: if you were sure I was a cop, if you weren't sure I'm still – with all my defects and errors – a comrade, you wouldn't have called me to this meeting." Some of them criticized Amparo for the way she raised the issue, but the evil had already been done and an agreement couldn't be reached. So we Salvadoran communists wound up divided into three groups, which were working parallel to one another. One group was led by Toño Díaz – not the doctor, but a worker by that name. One group that kept functioning around Amparo

397

Casamalhuapa. And our group, which the others called the "Marmolista" group. So, many months went by where it was impossible to reestablish unity, a problem we workers never lost sight of, and which we regarded as an objective to be achieved prerequisite to the existence of a true communist party in the country. However, none of the three groups grew sufficiently enough to impose one central line and draw in the rest. After a long process, reality began to impose itself on the minds of everyone: fascism was growing in the world and the unity of revolutionaries was urgent as never before in order to surmount the defects of our backwardness and our infantile stage. It wasn't an easy process, it had zig-zags and backward steps that make me recall those days with anger. A secretary to the Party, the son of don Benjamín Cisneros, who'd been to the U.S.S.R. on a tour with North American workers, made a trip to Mexico and we sent with him a report of our situation to the Mexican CP, asking for help and advice. Cisneros returned with a note for each group, signed by the directorate of the Mexican CP, which called on all divided Salvadoran communists to unite. During this period, the area of work and level of organization of our group was the most advanced of the three. But it was Amparo's group that laid claim to the name of the Communist Party. However, several comrades pulled out of that nucleus and came over to us. We came to an agreement with the Díaz group to carry out a joint action on the San Benito plantation, a strike that didn't happen because the boss gave in. They arrested Toño Díaz because of a manifesto "On Integral Democracy," after the police got hold of a rough draft and did a handwriting analysis that identified Toño. By the way, years later when Toño was out of the Party, among the charges he laid against us communists was that we "Marmolistas" had turned him in to the police in order to carry out our plan to take over the Directorate of the Party, by hook or by crook. The Amparo group continued to keep me under observation, and the comrades responsible for that have continued serving in the Party up to today, and we kid around about those times, like with Pedro Grande, who back then didn't think much of me but then became convinced of my true nature. Tony Vassiliu also started coming around to see me, but his wish really was for unity. One day he brought me a rough draft of a manifesto for the peasantry, to get my opinion, and I objected to one paragraph that seemed to me to be provocative. Tony agreed, but for reasons beyond his control, the manifesto came out with those extremist ideas. The first result was that seven peasants were taken prisoner, brought in on foot from San Miguel for having the manifesto found on them. I went to the police to intercede on their behalf. I spoke with Major Marroquín the day I went in to report, even though I hadn't done so in months and had practically quit paying attention to that rule, and I told him about the rural discontent. He told me that he had seven of my comrades in prison and he showed me the confiscated manifesto. I told him the manifesto had nothing to do with communists and that the peasants were unknown to us, innocent bystanders, not communists. "What the manifesto shows," I said, "is that the discontent in the countryside is again reaching an explosive level. Are you going to keep making the people angrier and angrier? You handle the country like ignoramuses with a rue plant. The one who cuts off a twig of rue just for the hell of it, burns his hands and causes the rue plant to wither; whoever cuts it for medicinal purposes spruces up the plant and cures his illness. It's necessary to make profound reforms in the countryside, if you don't want to burn your hands and kill the plant. And don't keep taking it out on innocent people, which is what gets the people the angriest of all. These seven prisoners have gotten at least 21 relatives furious, who will go on to influence 100 more. Don't you want to understand the lesson of '32? We communists have learned it." Marroquín intervened on behalf of the peasants, who were convicted of disobeying the police and they got out in 4 months. Then they came to see me and thank me for my efforts.

Meanwhile the possibility of unity between the three communist groups had grown. To the point that a proposal was put forth to unify ourselves into one Central Committee with the

399

three factions equally represented, led by a neutral Secretary General, as a preliminary step to the unification of the bases. All three groups agreed on a Honduran comrade, whose name I won't reveal for security reasons, for the position of Secretary General. Similarly, several requirements were approved for the new militants to join, in order to make enemy infiltration difficult. The Honduran comrade who became the interim Secretary General had been trained by Víctor Angulo, a serious Salvadoran student of Marxism, and he was a tenacious, prudent man, with an intellectual bent. My candidate had been Moisés Castro y Morales, but he had the problem of being harassed a lot by the police. We set ourselves to begin working together and I was beside myself with enthusiasm: a new stage was opening up and I was dreaming away a mile a minute. But the following days were like a cold shower: many little things convinced me that I continued to be the object of distrust. In the meetings at which I was present, only the international situation, the war, was talked about, and they wouldn't discuss plans for the everyday work. I'd learn about those plans only when they were put into practice. I protested that such behavior was unsuited to communists, who above all should be frank and direct, but I was just answered with evasions or they would simply ignore what I said. This left me resentful and withdrawing from the work. At a certain point they no longer called me to Party meetings. Then I felt really bitter and I had no strength left to fight off the isolation. I realize that at that time the comrades had some reason to be suspicious. They had just clamped down on us about reporting periodically to the Police Station. We had to do it every two weeks, on Saturday afternoons, which was precisely when they paid the police and the informers. Not only that, but after they recorded our attendance, Major Marroquín would offer to take us home in his car or invite us out for some beers, things we never accepted. It was just a maneuver to discredit us before our comrades. And all this despite the fact that the Party had decided we should report every two weeks, because conditions didn't exist for us to go underground. So we found ourselves in a vicious circle. And as for me, what came down on me was the Law of Caiaphas: keep hitting him harder while he's down. I didn't even have the solace of other brokenhearted Salvadorans, to drink myself to death with rum, because alcohol never was one of my vices. And with women I'd been badly burned. So I martyred myself in spiritual solitude for a period I'll always remember as the darkest in my life. Blows from the enemy had never bothered me. The enemy could do with me whatever they pleased, but it never made me give in, either morally or politically. Neither tortures, nor prisons, nor firing squads, nor threats, nor insults could make me ask for mercy from the class enemy. On the contrary, their blows have only served to make me stronger, angrier, more committed to struggle. However, the blows and misunderstandings from my brothers, my comrades, have always gone straight to my heart. In fact, those wounds are the only ones that left me with scars. The bullet and machete blows are marks that fill me with pride, but these ones I'm talking about are scars deep in my soul and maybe even in my ideology, and that's why I prefer to hide them, to bury them off someplace where no one will see them. Someplace where they can't hurt.

As the days passed, I calmed down and began to think that the situation would clear up in the end. Many revolutionaries have been the victims of misunderstandings, of lies and traps set by the enemy in order to sap their morale. Faith in the justness of the revolutionary cause, confidence in the final triumph of truth, courage of one's convictions, had to continue being the pillars of my life, even if I had to remain isolated from the Party until who knows when. And, anyhow, if within the Party conditions didn't exist for me to lend my support to the struggle, there were other ways and other forms of acting on behalf of the Salvadoran workers. Surely, at one moment or another in my life, if I was on the right path, I'd find myself in the same trench with true communists and true revolutionaries. In the meantime, I could take advantage of the situation in the shoemakers' guild. The whole guild movement became agitated in those days owing to the huge emigration of Salvadoran workers to the Panama Canal Zone, where work was being started on the expansion of military installations to protect that strategic passageway during the Second World War. I made contact with several workers who left for Panama, giving them ideas and ways to begin building democratic and revolutionary organizations in that country, where, despite everything, the political climate was more favorable than in our own. For a long time I helped out, through letters, several Salvadoran comrades who sustained the revolutionary work in Panama among the migrant masses. One day, when I went to buy leather at a tannery, a comrade in the Party with whom I still maintained contact informed me that a leaflet was circulating calling on the shoemakers to organize themselves within a center called "Salvadoran Social Reconstruction," apparently backed by the Official Party that Martínez had established to give himself political legitimacy, which was named "Pro-Patria." "Salvadoran Social Reconstruction" was intended to be the germ of one single, central guild, through which the Government could control the Salvadoran workers' movement in the future. But the important and alarming thing was that the call had aroused enthusiasm among the shoemakers throughout the country – the first guild that had been called – who saw in the "Reconstruction" the first opportunity to organize themselves since '32. I began to investigate and was able to verify that support for the Government's initiatives was tremendous among the masses, even a cause for rejoicing. I tried to show the comrades with whom I could make contact that it was just a maneuver by the regime designed to broaden their base and keep the workers' movement under control, on behalf of the dominant classes. I didn't convince a soul, not even the workers who in the past had been very influenced by the Party. "A hair's-breadth from the wolf," they said, "but we can organize as revolutionaries, we'll organize ourselves even though it'll be with the support of the official apparatus and then we'll see about changing the character of the organization until it serves the workers." That is, one thing was clear: the shoemakers were going to organize themselves under the umbrella of "Social Reconstruction." I felt my duty was to be with the masses, but so as not to commit errors that would be paid for dearly later on, I got comrades Porfirio Huiza, Ismael Hernández and Félix Panameño together so we could adopt a common position with regard to the newborn organism. We decided to attend the first meeting to see with our own eyes the whole picture, to smell with our own noses the climate of the organization. The meeting at which "Reconstruction" was supposedly going to be set up, was held one Sunday afternoon in San Salvador in a place located where the Apollo Cinema is today, and when we arrived the place was packed and on the door was a big sign which read "Salvadoran Social Reconstruction." Inside, there were huge portraits of Martínez and posters with his slogans: "Democracy is Love," "To Work is the Duty of Everyone." A presidential board led the meeting, although nobody had elected them: they just took up their position, saying they were the organizers. Doctor Manuel Escalante Rubio, Martínez' son-in-law, was the convener, and he was seconded by the reformist shoemaker Gumercindo Ramírez, who was my teacher in the trade, and Mijango, a barber for the police, who, if he hadn't tortured any prisoners, it was just because the torturers wouldn't let him, since he was dying to do it. Escalante Rubio opened the meeting with a speech full of demagoguery and nothing convincing, saying that a group of people concerned with social problems had made a call to form "Salvadoran Social Reconstruction," and that this call had been directed first to the shoemakers because it was evident our guild was suffering more than others the consequences of the crisis brought on by the world war. And there really was a crisis. With the bulk of world capitalist production, and particularly that of the United States, going to cover the war needs, a temporary chaos caused a disruption in many very important items needed for consumer production. Our trade, which was fed with imported materials (thread, fine leather, thumbtacks, nails) suffered the impact of a tremendous rise in prices, and therefore diverse reform measures had been put before the Government (price

403

ceilings, salary scales, etc.). Rubio said very solemnly that in light of the new sources of work opening up in Panama, including crafts such as shoemaking and others, the Government could assist whoever wanted to immigrate, in order to secure a better living and working conditions, steady contracts with no strings attached, etc. Gumercindo supported Escalante and, smiling from ear to ear like a Protestant pastor, insisted on hearing the opinions of the guild on the Government's proposal: to send shoemakers to Panama in order to relieve such a tiny market of the surplus of artisans competing with one another. A deep silence fell over the room. I nudged Ismael and whispered to him: "Now our friends are paying the price for their naiveté. This proposal has hit them like a bucket of ice water. How nice, the only solution for Salvadoran workers is to go off to a foreign country!" Gumercindo and Mijango kept on blabbing about waiting for the opinions of the masses. Escalante Rubio, who was getting nervous, asked what was going on with the shoemakers, they were the most outspoken guild, why weren't they saying anything, had the cat got their tongues. Finally, a worker named Vicente, whose last name I don't remember, asked for the floor. He was shy and humble, but he said what we all wanted to hear: "For the first time since 1932 we Salvadoran shoemakers are all meeting together," he said. "And what kind of state are we in? Well, just look around at each and every one of us. Filthy, poorly clothed, some even barefoot, all miserable and with hungry faces. I thought we were going to discuss how to improve our situation, which is desperate. And what do they come out with – that we have to go to Panama! I think we shoemakers won't have anything to do in Panama. What they need there are bricklayers, electricians, carpenters, mechanics, plumbers, foremen. I'm just a simple guy, and I don't have anything more to say. I'd like to ask the comrades who have a way with words and who are familiar with our problems to come up and speak for us." I asked for the floor. Gumercindo tried to prevent me, but the masses protested, fired up all of a sudden. I went up on the platform and there was applause, but Escalante rang a bell asking for silence. I was moderate. "No doubt the intentions of "Reconstruction" are honorable and good," I said, "but they don't solve the problems of the guild. The crisis that the war has brought to branches of production such as ours – worse in countries like El Salvador where footwear is produced by artisans – is catastrophic. Our problems will only be solved by our organization. So if the Government wants to help us, then it should begin by granting us the freedom to organize, without telling us how to do it!" The applause was tremendous: I'd hit the nail on the head! We hadn't been wrong: even within an official maneuver by the Government, political conditions together with economic conditions made it possible to do work with a revolutionary perspective. Porfirio Huiza spoke next. He was more forceful than me, less cautious. The enthusiasm of the masses was tremendous and the guys on the presidential board were going crazy. Too bad about Porfirio Huiza, because the truth is he was a great orator. I say too bad, because in good time he left the Party and, there's no fool like an old fool, he ended up a prudista.[1] Then Ismael Hernández spoke. "Hoarse Felix" was worried and said we shouldn't talk more, that we were going to get the fucking over of the century. I went back up on the platform and declared that the decision to form a free organization had been launched, that the Government could only bear witness to what had happened, and that as a start we were all called to meet again next Sunday, to continue deliberating. From then on, that "Reconstruction" didn't have a leg to stand on, since it was left discredited in the eyes of the honest workers. Even though it survived for a little while, it was always a clearly tainted organism, that would never deceive anybody ever again. Our strength was such that the following Sunday they didn't deny us the same meeting place, though they knew we were meeting to found an independent organization. On that occasion the attendance was even greater and more enthusiastic. In one week the idea of an independent guild organization had taken hold and already by the second meeting we had its name: "The National Alliance of Shoemakers." This "Alliance" brought shopkeepers and workers together, something which wasn't counterproductive to the interests of the majority, because it was necessary to begin by defending the interests of the trade, leaving for later the demands of the shoemakers proper. In this same meeting a Board of Directors was elected by unanimous vote. The speed of this was notable. I was named President, as the owner of a small shop. Secretary of Organization, Porfirio Huiza, owner of the *chinchero*. Secretary of Propaganda, Felícito (Licho) Martínez, worker. Secretary of Social Affairs, Ismael Hernández, worker. As for the Treasurer, I only remember he was a worker. We fixed the times for General Assemblies, to be held on Sunday afternoons. The atmosphere was so favorable that in two months we had set up the Alliance on a national level. The police were very cautious with us: they kept surveillance on our meetings but wouldn't take direct repressive measures. We were protected by the fact that we'd meet in the same place as "Reconstruction," an organism that wanted to keep up appearances in order to try and attract the other guilds. Escalante Rubio and Gumercindo were going around with their tails between their legs, but they were speeding up their contacts with the other sectors in order to reduce our influence. For my part, I became the main lecturer for the shoemakers of El Salvador. In the meeting place of the Alliance (that is, the "Reconstruction") I related the history of the national workers' movement, its flourishing and its decline. I had to be careful to be mild for the benefit of the police, and at the same time give the comrades a real picture of the tradition we had behind us, of the sacrifices and struggles to which we had to respond with our actions. International conditions had changed a lot and that was reflected in the new opportunities that had opened up in our country. The victory of fascism had stopped being a quickly realized dream in the mind of Martínez and he started flirting with the North Americans. For our part, we advised the workers about the perspectives that the defeat of fascism by the Allies would open up for the international working class, especially on the eastern front, where the most dangerous threat was the Red Army. Similarly, we began to take advantage of the anti-fascist euphoria in order to reorganize our contacts with the

406

working classes in our country. And the contradictions that that situation produced in the regime started to be felt in many tangible facts. For example, on the occasion of the evacuation at Dunkirk, we sent greetings to the English workers. The British Embassy sent our message and from London they answered, thanking us for our solidarity in the name of the King, and communicating to us that the Prime Minister would send a British flag for our headquarters. When he learned about that, Escalante Rubio arranged it so that the workers who were going to Panama, among whom "Reconstruction" had managed to enlist a few shoemakers, would be the ones to receive the flag, shutting us out. Imagine my surprise when Major Marroquín called me to his office in the Police Station to tell me about the scheme and to advise me that we ought to attend the ceremony en masse and take for ourselves, even if it had to be by force, the flag which after all was ours. Whose interests did Marroquín represent? The fact is that, later on, Martínez had to get rid of Colonel Merino and Major Marroquín, since they were accused of fascist and anti-Northamerican leanings. And you can't forget that Marroquín probably acted at times on our behalf out of guilt, since he was the brother-in-law of Serafín G. Martínez, the comrade who was shot with me in 1932, the one whose hat I took. Personally, I still think that those strange attitudes were manifestations of the internal antagonisms within the regime in the face of a worldwide struggle between fascism and democracy. On the appointed night, the British Ambassador and military attaché arrived to deliver the flag at our head-quarters, and the shoemakers who were going to Panama intervened in an attempt to get it for themselves. But since we had been warned, we quickly ran them out and the whole thing happened with just a little pushing and shoving. However, the comrade who received the flag was very nervous and it slipped out of his hands, with everything – flag, flagpole – toppling down. The diplomats didn't conceal their anger, even though they acted all polite with their white handkerchiefs and everything, but even so the ceremony was a success and we were able to show the Government that we had excellent

407

relations with the British Embassy. Escalante Rubio went to inform the American Embassy that the British were supporting Salvadoran communists.

We members of the Alliance took a step forward by proposing the organization of a Cooperative, needed to assist the poorest shoemakers and those who were unemployed, whose number was growing all the time. This reached the ears of the Police, and Marroquín summoned me immediately. He received me in private and said he'd heard about the Cooperative, that it seemed like work worthy of support and that he wanted to take part in it, since it was a matter of benefiting the needy. "I'd like to contribute," he added, "with 500 colones, which I'll hand over to you free and clear, no receipt, no papers, right here just between the two of us. Then the neediest can use the money and pay it back if they can, and if they can't, they won't." I felt between a rock and a hard place, even though I'd personally gotten used to eluding the traps of the Police. It's just that at that point I was representing a legal mass front and had to look at the pros and cons of each situation, like it or not. I told Marroquín that I needed the opinions of my comrades before I could accept any money, that it didn't matter that there were no obligations or who was giving it. I added that if the rest of the comrades agreed, we'd take the money as a loan, that the transaction had to be made in front of Ismael Hernández, Porfirio Huiza and others, and that it would be put down on paper. The document would have to say that the loan was for social purposes and would be paid back in payments of 30 colones every month. Marroquín persisted. "Why so many people? We'll arrange everything just between us. Don't suspect any trap." But I didn't budge an inch. I put the proposal to the comrades and they agreed to accept the loan with the conditions I established. The comrades said that to not accept that money could be used by the Government to accuse us before the masses of not protecting their interests and creating frictions. Huiza, myself and five workers went to sign the paper

408

and pick up the money, which was apportioned among the neediest shoemakers, so they could work with it. This transaction, which we didn't hide, reached the ears of the Party and was severely criticized. The comrades sent me word that they thought it was worse than bad, that it was taking alms from the enemy. I think they were right, the only thing is they weren't the ones standing before the masses, but were holed up cut off from society in excessive clandestinity. I had to face the masses and police harassment. I do not think that trap of Marroquín's was serious, that it had many negative aspects, but at that time we were in no condition to categorically reject the offer, it would've opened up a new front against the toughest sector of the enemy: the direct instrument of repression, the police. But I don't want to overdo it. I admit that transaction was an error, a dumb mistake. But I also say that if there was dishonesty on the part of someone, there's no question about it, the dishonest one was Marroquín for his corrupt intentions. I wasn't going to dirty my hands for a lousy 500 colones. I've always been proud, I value myself too much to have ever let it cross my mind that everything was going to get straightened out between me and the enemy for a handful of colones. For that favor, I'd have sold out when I was a kid, without subjecting myself so many times to death and suffering. And if I keep talking about these things and go on and on about them, it's so you'll see that in the life of a revolutionary there's not only heroism, stories of great battles, epic actions, but that very often the character of a communist must be defended fiercely in the face of the sinister, miserable blows of daily life, in the face of vile deeds and muddy entanglements which circumstances put in front of you along the way. The possibility of being bribed, of getting yourself up to your ears in shit, is planned by the class enemy and has to be evaluated by us with all honesty and soberness. Not because of petty egoism and the petty-bourgeois vice of always being immaculately clean, but because it is a measurable factor which plays its role in the struggle and on which the advances and retreats of an organization, of a Party, often depend. Especially in the case of a people like ours, where the individual

409

personality continues being such a determining force, owing to our lasting organizational weakness. Especially in the case of masses like ours, who have been duped so many times by so much demogoguery. Yes, during the last years of Martinism everything was mucked-up and foul smelling, like mud or shit. For me, it was a relief that that period, in which the dictatorship was toying with us with their stupid, lying promises, their fantastic plans, their offers of unlimited credit in word but nonexistent in reality, came to an end. I'm not going to bore anyone by relating our endless meetings with representatives from the importing houses, the City Hall of San Salvador, the Mortgage Bank, the Credit Offices, etc. The Government itself, with its perennial anti-worker and anti-popular conduct, took care of putting an end to any illusions that arose in those meetings. I repeat, for me, it was a relief that that conciliatory stage came to an end, because, among other things, the Party despite everything and the fact that they kept me marginalized, wouldn't let up putting pressure on me every time it was said that the Bank or the Government or the bourgeoisie was going to give money for one cooperative. Which, of course, was correct. The only excuse for our vacillations in the face of that situation was the historical moment in which they occurred. We were survivors, but more than that, the defeated. We were traumatized and only by means of unheard-of efforts and an incredible faith in our revolutionary destiny did we get through that stage without irreparable errors, without truly disgraceful conciliations. But often we made too many concessions, we lowered our heads too much, we conciliated with the class enemy even though it might have just been on things of procedure and form. In my case, the attitude of my Party, a "wishy-washy" attitude, as we Salvadorans say, contributed to that demoralization which made me serve only marginally and which filled me with confusion and resentments.

The Alliance was, in spite of everything, a positive experience. In the first place, it could be organized at a national level, as I already said, and it became very strong in San Salvador, Santa Ana, San Miguel, San Vincente and Zacatecoluca. It was the first independent organizing experience by Salvadoran workers since '32, it dispelled the fears of the guilds and gave perspective to the trade union front. Out of that experience, disguised and open workers' organizations were founded: artisan societies, associations of mutual aid, neighborhood and workers' councils. Even a National Congress of the Workers' Societies was held, in Usulután, that alarmed the regime a lot. The Alliance didn't participate in this congress out of caution, since we were regarded as the most politicized and communist-influenced guild. The barbers created their own society and won a price increase and Sundays off. The workers in the "Martínez y Saprissa" textile factory organized themselves to form a collective fund, but uppermost in their minds was the idea of evolving into a trade union. I worked with them. In the end, many revived organizations profited from the Alliance experience. But the more we made our presence and strength felt by the Government, so it renewed its treatment – each day harsher and harsher – against us and against the workers in general. The threats, pressures, bribe attempts gave way to false accusations, detentions, mistreatments. Yet, in spite of all this, some who were communists then, including some who later betrayed us and ended up active in the trade unions of the ORIT,[2] continued provoking us and accusing us of the greatest treachery. There was within the Party (independent of the majority who had us marginalized, but didn't interfere with us) a group which I've called "reactionary," led by comrade Pérez and a student of economics, Gilberto Lara, that didn't let up in their accusations. It was made up of people who neither do work nor let others work. Now, that bastard Lara has spent over twenty years at the service of the Government and the reaction. Pérez no, old Pérez is still in the Party, he's a good comrade but he's more sectarian than me–and that's saying a lot.

With me in particular the thing got even worse. The reaction just wouldn't forgive me for surviving. The bourgeoisie knew I was going to continue being a witness to their crimes and that times could change and I could once again become dangerous. And so all its artillery was aimed at me. Escalante Rubio, aware

411

that the international situation prevented the government from liquidating me, started to deliver bad reports about me to the American Embassy, which was by now a kind of super-government in our country. The landowners in Santa Ana asked Martínez straight out that they take drastic measures against me, immediately. The thing is that in this area the dominant classes and the governments in their service rarely make a mistake: they can forgive the most outspoken revolutionaries, they can completely forgive a certain type of revolutionary if he repents, but what they can never forgive is having precedents that tie a person to armed activity, nor having a personality that might become a factor in mobilizing the masses. This explains why even today there are communists who are persecuted and others who aren't. The fact is, there are truly dangerous communists and others who aren't. The amusing thing about that new outbreak of bourgeois attacks against me was that, the more the enemy fucked me over, the more the reactionary comrades fucked me over. They insisted on my being a collaborator, a coward and a lousy disrupter. And since I wasn't being criticized within the Party in a proper way, I felt even more deceived and confused. It got to the point of getting the new people in the Party to turn against me, to the degree that for some young communists I scared them as much as the cops did. For my part, I always tried to be straight with the Party and to understand the problems of our very meagre political development. I can even say I was respecting a party decision when I got the Alliance to withdraw from the umbrella "Social Reconstruction." It happened like this: the Party, over the attacks by the "reactionary" sector and unfounded suspicions, summoned me in order to talk. I remember that comrades Ponce and Roca received me and informed me that the Party had decided that the shoemakers' guild had to withdraw from the Martinista group and they gave me a two month time limit in which to do it, adding that if by the end of that time I hadn't gotten results, I'd be expelled from the Party once and for all. For that task they offered me the collaboration of the communists in the capital. I accepted and began figuring out a

412

way to get the Alliance out of the "Reconstruction" group without disrupting the continuity of the struggle of the shoemakers. Fortunately, a suitable opportunity presented itself. Since the Alliance had had great success in Santa Ana, we called an Assembly in order to inform the shoemakers in San Salvador. Our successes had been such that even General Martínez sent us a telegram congratulating us on our social work. That theosophist Saint Matthew was a hypocrite and a cynic. Representatives from other guilds also attended the Assembly, invited by the shoemakers. Due to the intentionally agitative tone of the speeches, Dr. Rubio, an honorary member of the Board of Directors, halted the meeting and declared it suspended in a violent and threatening tone of voice. I, who also was on the Board, as President of the Alliance, objected and between Dr. Escalante Rubio and myself an incredible brawl broke out. He accused me to high heaven of being a communist, a dangerous agitator, a red murderer; and I didn't keep my mouth shut, I accused him of being a fascist Nazi and brought up his new duties as honorary Consul of the bloodthirsty dictatorship in Paraguay. The thing reached such a level that the guy tried to punch me in the face, but my comrades were quick and restrained him. For its part, the delegation of women textile workers from the "Martínez y Saprissa" factory started to attack the doctor with their umbrellas and one of them broke her umbrella over the doctor's back. The police came and the Assembly broke up. But the outcry of the workers was unanimous: The Alliance will have nothing more to do with "Social Reconstruction"! So I accomplished the assignment of the Party in my own way and with the help of the guild. The Party didn't provide the help it offered; on the contrary, once we were out of the Martinista group the Party withheld all support of the Alliance, which then didn't even have a place to meet any more and started to weaken until it almost died. All this occurred towards the end of the Martinista dictatorship, and it was intertwined with diverse conspiracies that were organized to put an end to the evil life of that 13-year anticommunist regime.

413

1 prudista: member of PRUD: Revolutionary Party of Democratic Unification. Founded by Colonel Osorio in the early '50s, it was the political vehicle for an emergency bureaucracy and middle class, running military officers for President and legitimizing the anticommunist, repressive apparatus.

2 ORIT: Inter-American Regional Workers' Organization. Reformist workers' organization in the 1950s backed by the AFL-CIO (trans - lators' note).

11

The campaigns of April and May, 1944: the defeat of the thirteen-year dictatorship. The National Workers' Union and "Romerism." The restoration of terror: Osmín Aguirre Salinas' military coup. Mármol within the Guatemalan "revolution." Final reflections.

The civil-military rebellion of April 2, 1944, against the Martínez dictatorship surprised Salvadorans. The conspiracy which planned those actions had been an underground one, the necessary response to the conditions of supersurveillance, terror and fear that existed in El Salvador during the open period of 1932, along with the graves of thirty thousand workers and peasants. When the first shots of the "stuttering" rebels rang out in San Salvador on the afternoon of the 2nd, the Alliance militants, neighbors and friends ran to me looking for information, but I was completely out of it. I didn't know what to say. I didn't know if this was a revolutionary movement, or a government ploy, or if what was going on was a shoot-out between military factions. The CP had had information about the conspiracy, and had helped the various participating groups with advice, recommendations, and guaranteeing contacts, but they kept me in the dark, they hadn't told me anything. So I decided to be careful and not put my foot in it. To those I saw crying in the streets because "freedom had come," I recommended that they not show so much feeling, that it wasn't all so clear, that they shouldn't get carried away. However, many positive facts quickly surfaced. I had a real rush of joy when Matilde Elena López, a progressive intellectual who is now a professor at the University, announced General Martínez' fall from power on a local radio station that was in the hands of the rebels. We also listened to the comic Chencho Castellanos Rivas saying the same thing. This Chencho was an announcer on Radio Mejoral who thought he was an artist: he wound up being a real creep, an informer, who even sold out, for money, a clandestine, mobile radio station during the period of resistance to Lemus (1960). Everyone was talking on the radio back then, on the YSP, as if the revolution was already in power. I even heard two comrades from the Shoemakers' Alliance, Luis Felipe

417

Cativo and Antonio Garay, urge the people to support the rebellion, in the name of the guild and the Alliance. Meanwhile, the combat in the capital was growing. There was a terrific shoot-out between the First Infantry Regiment and the Police barracks, and between the Sixth Machine-Gunners' and the El Zapote barracks. The Air Force was with the rebels and the fighter planes tried to bomb the Police, but they botched it up and the bombs fell two blocks away from the target, setting on fire two city blocks of downtown San Salvador. In that fire, the department store "Ballete y Llovera," other businesses, and the Colón Theater went up in smoke; that theater reeked of piss more than any other in the world. The Salvadoran Casino was untouched among the ashes, like a symbol that the April "revolution" wasn't going to touch the oligarchy. The wounded and the dead from the bullets that were flying all over the place filled the streets, and there weren't enough Red Cross ambulances to take care of so many people. The telephones and electrical power were cut. As you can imagine, the number of rumors going around was tremendous, but nobody knew anything for certain: they said the rebels had taken over the communications and had almost all the country's barracks on their side, that only the Police and El Zapote – that is, the First Artillery Regiment – were resisting. The drunks got bold again and were yelling at every street corner, "Death to the tyrant Martínez, death to that son-of-a-bitch 'Pecuecho,' death to all the representatives, long live the Revolution." Everyone wanted to help bring down Martínez, but no one knew how to or who to ask. That guy Chencho Castellanos announced that Martínez was dead, tried and executed on the road to La Libertad. The police had been contained in their barracks and the thieves had a field-day. The same night of the 2nd of April, full of doubts and hopes and under the whizzing bullets, I went to Centenary Park, where the "conscious citizenry" had been called – no one knows by who even now – to arms from the rebel barracks and to enter into combat. Five to six hundred of us men gathered there, willing to fight against the forces of Martinism. In perfect order, we went to the rebel barracks to pick

418

up arms and ammunition. But it would all be for nothing. We went to the First Infantry Regiment that was still going at it with the Police, and then to the Cavalry, to Casa Mata, but the result was the same: zero. It wasn't true that the barracks wanted to arm the people, and that gave the "revolution" a very limited character. But it wasn't the moment to start in denouncing such issues, above all because we had no contact with the masses in the capital. Anxious for instructions and leadership, we went to the YSP, where the call for rebellion had come from, and where they said Dr. Arturo Romero, named as the chief civil leader of the rebellion, was located. When we got to the YSP, we were by now about a thousand fired-up men. But we couldn't get any answer, and everyone had to go on home with a long, disappointed face. The gunfire was still going on, and at any corner you could meet up with a machine gun or bomb blast. From then on, I knew that rebellion was going to end up a total failure. It was known by then that among the rebellion's military leaders was Tito Calvo, the author of the 1932 massacres in Sonsonate and Izalco. It was soon learned that Martínez wasn't dead and that he'd taken charge of organizing the counter-attack against the rebels. The latter were shitting in their pants, because they hadn't counted on coming face to face with the dictator. The plan to kill Martínez had failed, stupidly. The old guy went every Sunday to relax at the port city of La Libertad, and the rebels had planned to blow him away when he returned to San Salvador, right on the road. But Martínez was warned by telephone that gunfire had started in San Salvador, and he simply changed cars and zoomed on into the capital. He went right through the ambush without anyone seeing him. And on sheer balls, he took over all the vacillators who wanted to give up to the "revolution," he organized the resistance and, by telephone, he demoralized the "heroic" Calvo, Alfonso Marroquín, etc. The St. Matthew Sorcerer, as Martínez was also called, had real balls, and a mystical, magical aura that helped him terribly. There's no doubt that he had a good time through the whole rebellion, he played ping-pong with it. Confusion grew in the rebel ranks: the anti-democratic character of the

419

military men kept them from turning to the only force that could have decided the situation in their favor, that is, to the people, the masses in the capital, and Martínez simply put himself in the center of the spider web, positive that everyone was going to wind up in his clutches. It was all just a question of a few hours, more or less. On April 3rd a sergeant from the airport garrison came to see me at my house (where several Alliance members and some Party comrades, all like me with no precise orientation, were gathered) to tell us that at the airport there was a possibility of support for the rebellion, that all the soldiers and ranked officers were in agreement and that the only thing they didn't know was whose orders to follow. The sergeant had come looking for instructions and direction. We decided to pass the information to Dr. Romero. Francisco Pineda Coto, the cartoonist who would become nationally famous as the creator of the character "Juan Pueblo," was the carrier who took the written information. He came back more than discouraged. He had contacted Dr. Romero himself, who read the message and started to cry, saying that it was all impossible now, that the help came too late, that everyone was disbanded and that the military leaders wanted to give up and save their own skins. With a leader like that, the Salvadoran people were really going to be helped! I was beside myself with anger, but what could we do, without contacts with the conspiracy, without arms, etc.? What I don't understand is how the leaders of April 2nd had imagined they were going to receive the people's support. They didn't have the courage to arm them, and even rejected help from those sectors of the army who wanted to fight for real. The leaders of April 2nd hadn't been prepared to fight for real, they thought they were going to overthrow the government by phone, just by bumping off Martínez. It's true that we failed in '32 for lack of an adequate plan, among other things, but that was a matter of class insurrection, not just the overthrow of one hated government in order to replace it with another that wouldn't be as bad, within bourgeois law. The Air Force garrison, despite lacking rebel leadership, rose up and stopped the advance of troops loyal to Martínez who were advancing

420

from Cojutepeque to San Salvador, but, in the end, it was cut off and trapped by a strong infantry nucleus from Zacatecoluca, and there was a bloodbath. Martínez addressed the public, saying he had the situation under control, that a small group of criminals had rebelled against the law and that he was going to proceed with all rigor to completely reestablish order. He decreed a State of Siege and Martial Law throughout the country. The last rebel bastions were giving up little by little. The "heroic" military leader of the rebellion, Colonel Tito Calvo, who was going all over in a tank, ran to the American Embassy to ask for asylum, but the Ambassador denied it to him. As he came out, before he could get to his tank, they arrested him. A few days later he was executed. The embassies filled up with political refugees, especially the Peruvian one, since the most sought after one, the Mexican Embassy, locked and barred its doors because the ambassador, Méndez Plancarte, was fast friends with the dictator. The little drunks stopped yelling about death to Martínez, after the cops killed a few of them who, walking around in a daze, hadn't realized that the rebellion had been defeated. Martínez announced the installation of Military Tribunals that would take charge of prescribing lead for every other person. The executed began to fall. Martínez would have gone down in history as the only man in El Salvador with balls in April of 1944, if it hadn't been for the attitude of some of the rebels in the face of torture and death, especially the civilian Víctor Marín. To try and get lists of conspirators out of him, the police gouged out one of his eyes and burned his arms and legs, pulled out the nails from his hands and feet and crushed his testicles. When they shot him they had to hold him up with a wooden sawhorse. And what a man he was; when a priest came over to him, up against the wall, and said he'd come to comfort his spirit, Marín answered: "It's my body that's weak, Father, not my spirit . . ." That was the man who most raised the honor of Salvadorans in the April "revolution." The other leaders (with a few exceptions who aren't anything to scream about either, as in the case of Colonel Cola de Mico Aguilar, Chief of the Sixth Machine-Gunners, who did fight like he meant it) were all

421

cowards, traitors, wimps, innocents or assholes. And that's the truth, though there may still be some reluctance in El Salvador to accept it. The people would show later, in the campaigns of May and in the resistance to Osmín, that what was lacking wasn't courage, but clarity in the face of national problems. But in the meantime, Martínez reacted like a wounded lion. That little round of executions was awesome. And that the cowardly officers had shit bricks didn't do the ones who were captured or who turned themselves in any good. Martínez had a heart made of lizard skin.

In the midst of this bloodbath, I was ordered to report to the Chief of Police. Rudecindo Monterrosa, the director, was mad as hell but at the same time he seemed nervous and hesitant. The tension was intense for the executioners, too, since behind the murderers' screen, you could begin to see the symptoms of the decline of the dictatorship. The interrogation was to find out what had been the participation of the Shoemakers' Alliance in the uprising. I denied any connection with that event, which was simply telling the truth, independent of my own intentions and adherence on the day of the gunfire. I swore to Monterrosa that those who had spoken on the radio in the name of the Alliance hadn't been Cativo and Garay, that it had all been a logical maneuver on the part of the rebels to try and take advantage of the prestige of our organization. "You people are ingrates," the Police Chief said to me with a bitter tone in his voice, "we've given you guarantees of work and organization, we've given you financial credit, and you pay us back by supporting the anarchists. I summoned you, Mármol, because the government wants the Alliance to pay back the money you were loaned." I really blew up and told him how the loan had been forced on us against our will, to try to bribe and discredit us, and I pointed out that it was being paid back religiously in agreement with what we had signed. "But if you want the rest of the money right now, I'm going home and I'm going to sell everything I own to cancel the shoemakers' debt to the regime," I ended up saying. It seems he didn't expect that reply, because he told me it was okay, to forget everything, not to pay any more installments. "I'm just going to ask you people for one thing," he added, "that you not be ungrateful, that you not keep being against the Government of General Martínez." My blood was boiling, remembering Farabundo Martí, Luna, Zapata, Feliciano Ama, our thirty thousand dead from '32, myself and my own suffering all through Martinism. And they were still telling us not to be "ungrateful" to the regime! Monterrosa told me that he could guarantee Cativo and Garay would not be persecuted, since my explanation had cleared the matter up. It seemed that the government was going crazy beating up on the petty bourgeoisie, and was trying to get control over the working class, to not provoke it. And as for the people, everyone acted like idiots: the workers, on the one hand, in the clouds; the radical sectors of the petty bourgeoisie on the other, suffering bullets and blows, but rooted in their fear of mixing with the people. But it wasn't my explanations that saved me from jails or exile. The government knew perfectly well that as leader of the Alliance, I'd entered into good relations with the British and United States ambassadors, at that time allies of the worldwide working class in the task of defeating Nazifascism.

Perhaps it's worth telling here how I entered into relations with the American Ambassador, who would play such a decisive role in the downfall of Martínez. As I said before, Escalante Rubio had spoken badly of me in the American Embassy, accusing me of being communist, anti-American, etc. The Ambassador invited me one day to chat alone. After consulting with the Alliance leadership I went to see him, and, in a friendly but deliberate manner, the first thing he asked me was why was I an enemy of the United States. "On the contrary," I answered, "I'm on the side of the United States, because shoulder to shoulder with the Soviet Union, it's fighting public enemy number one for humanity – German, Italian, and Japanese

423

Nazifascist imperialism." The Ambassador was a shrewd fox and he didn't stop there. Little by little he led me into national issues, and he began asking me about various people in the Martínez government, the contradictions in the national political atmosphere, etc. When he asked me for my political opinion of Martínez and his government, I laid out for him without hesitation what I thought and knew: I denounced the practice of nonexistent plebiscites, with which Martínez got himself reelected and made it look legal; I spoke of Martínez' Nazifascist sympathies; about how at various times, groups of Japanese pilots and military men had been seen at the military airport in Ilopango, and how the Salvadoran police were hiding a clandestine radio station installed by the Nazis in Villa Delgado, which would begin to operate when the time was right for them, though for the moment it was used for secret communications; about how Martínez had sent to the High Command of the Axis a tactical plan for the landing of troops on North American shores, and that it was also thought that Japanese submarines were supplied with fuel at the natural Salvadoran port of Mizata. All of this extremely interested the Ambassador. Before I said goodbye to him, I told him how I had a problem with the Martinist police tailing me, that they followed me closer than my own shadow, and then he said that if anything happened to me I should personally notify him, and that he would intervene on my behalf. I think I was somewhat favored by this situation, which today is even laughable for being so incredible, but which reflected the terrifically complex political and social contradictions of the time.

The repression unleashed by the dictatorship was counterproductive to its interest in continuing. Martínez did not calculate correctly the state of mind of the masses who had had it up to here with oppression, and who had awakened from the heavy lethargy into which they'd sank after the horror of '32 through the diffusion of world antifascist thinking. The advances of the Red Army had struck the collective imagination

424

positively, and Stalin was respected and loved. The people, incited by the crimes and abuses of the Police and the National Guard, were prepared to face off with Martinism. Sadly, the lack of leadership was almost absolute, at least in the first moments. The rebels were falling daily before firing squads and the military courts were handing down new death sentences and long prison terms. And by the way, Captain and Doctor Héctor Muñoz Barillas, who would so damage me during my last stay in prison, took part in the Tribunals as General Military Prosecutor of the Republic, as did a certain Dr. Paredes, who was a judge for the War Ministry, though he wasn't, they tell me, a lawyer, but rather a pediatrician, that is, a children's doctor. That's why they nicknamed him "Herod." And Martial Law didn't discriminate: everything that moved was shot. The guild organisms stopped functioning, the leaders from every sector were strictly controlled. And the Communist Party was a small group with no ties to the people. But even so, something had to be done so that the people's fury wouldn't be set loose. So, under this persecution and terror, a group of communists met at Pedro Grande's house to consider the situation, the needs that had to be answered with something more than just worrying. After intense debate, we came to the unanimous understanding that we had to create an adequate instrument for channeling popular action against the tyranny, that is, a mass political party with a broad democratic orientation, that could organize into its ranks the majority of the country's workers. It would be a nonsectarian, antifascist and antidictatorial party. The moment was a good one, because other social sectors were talking about organizing to fight, especially the students, the urban petty bourgeoisie, etc., and it was prudent to try and build, with a long-term perspective, a party that would have the organized working class at the front ranks. It was clear that such an organization could only begin to be built clandestinely. In that first meeting, we even came up with the name of the projected party: The National Workers' Union (UNT). At later meetings, the usefulness of people like Luis Díaz or myself participating in the organizing work of the UNT was discussed, since some said we

425

were too well known and would give it all a sectarian aspect, and others, on the contrary, said our presence would guarantee the trust of the organized workers. Luis Díaz, who was the First Secretary General of the Party, had returned to revolutionary work after disappearing for a number of years. A national organizational commission of the UNT was named, made up of the student Amílcar Martínez, at the time one of the most radicalized young men of that sector; the journalist Benjamín Guzmán, who later after his anti-Martinist period wound up an alcoholic, embracing each successive government; and the workers Pedro Grande, Luis Díaz, and myself, Miguel Mármol. The situation was heating up minute by minute. The students called for a national general strike, called the "Huelga de los Caidos." Standing out in its leadership were Reinaldo Galindo Pohl, Minister of Education under Osorio; our present comrade, Raúl Castellanos Figueroa; Dr. Fabia Castillo, and others. The whole country was paralyzed. Businesses closed, banks closed, schools, restaurants, whorehouses, churches and food stores, everything. Martínez sent trucks crammed full of police with machine guns to bring public employees into work by force, but they hid in other people's houses and it was impossible to find them. A lot has been written on this, it's not necessary for me to go into detail. I only want to give a sketchy idea here of our work to provide some organized revolutionary continuity, a sense of our limited communist work in the midst of the huge confusion during the final struggle against Martínez. From within the clandestine UNT being formed, we spurred on the working class in the country's principal cities with the following watchword: "National unity of all the popular and democratic forces of the country against the Martinist tyranny based on the national general strike, until the dictatorship is defeated. Workers: organize politically into the ranks of the UNT." The national strike dealt the death blow to the dictatorship, it left it with no points of support. Even the Americans realized they weren't going any place with Martínez and withdrew their support from him. The excuse was the death of a Salvadoran-North American student named Chepe Wright,

426

murdered at his own front door by a cop. It was evident that Martínez had to get the hell out and the American Ambassador went to the Presidential House to tell him so. May 9, 1944, the theosophist machine-gunner abandoned the Presidency and left for Guatemala, leaving in his place the Minister of War, the weak and pusillanimous General Andrés Ignacio Menéndez, nicknamed "Cement Armor." That was how the thirteen blackest years of Salvadoran history in this century ended.

General Maximiliano Hernández Martínez had a strange and complicated personality. A monster of our backward and contradictory society, a criminal and a mystic at the same time. An ignorant mountain man and a student of philosophy; an adorer of discipline and order, who wouldn't stop at the worst crimes to attain his ends. A Nazi sorcerer. A resentful Indian with complexes, who in spite of always having been scorned by the oligarchs was their ideal instrument for massacring and oppressing our people. An animal, a cross between a snake and a coyote. The anecdotes about his life are endless. He was a vegetarian, he wouldn't touch meat and he ate vegetables, eggs and milk. He would never accept medicine from the pharmacy, only herbs, fruits, seeds, and his famous "blue waters." These waters were just ordinary waters that Martínez kept out in the sun on the patio of the Presidential House in different colored bottles, and to which he attributed magical curative powers. His flunkies drank those waters devotedly, so the "Maestro" would think well of them. The old guy preferred that they call him "Maestro" rather than President or General or Your Excellency. And he thought he was such a master that every Sunday he gave speeches on the radio from the Auditorium of the University, directed at the entire Republic, about whatever topic occurred to him, about democracy, intestinal parasites, theosophy, black magic, sports, fruit trees, body hygiene, world war, kidney stones, the internal peace of mankind, etc. He would prescribe cures to his friends for any illness, saying that his knowledge of medicine came from the

427

great court of invisible doctors with whom he communicated in spiritualist sessions. One time when an epidemic of smallpox broke out in San Salvador, he refused to apply modern methods of prevention and instead ordered that the streetlamps be covered with cellophane in different colors, since the rays of colored light would be enough to clean the air of the malignant plague. Naturally, more people died than should have. When his youngest son got sick with appendicitis, he refused to let a doctor see him, and started treating him with "blue waters." Peritonitis set in and the child died in terrible pain. The "Maestro" simply said that he had to accept it because the invisible doctors hadn't wanted to help. But he didn't play around with his own health: there was always an assistant to test his food so he wouldn't be poisoned. He said that it wasn't as serious a sin to kill a man as an ant, because the man is reincarnated in another life cycle, but the ant disappears forever. That's why the thirty thousand Salvadorans he had killed in 1932 never kept him up at night. According to him, they would all be immediately reincarnated. On the other hand, the General never put down liquor or any kind of alcoholic drink, and he was never known to have mistresses or wild parties. His wife was a vulgar woman, doña Concha, and she was the butt of obscene jokes and stories of the time, which especially showed her as ignorant and stupid. Martínez was a military man of the old school, who had come from the ranks, not the Military Academy; crude, bitter, bilious, it was hard to make him laugh and he was feared for his uncontrollable rages. He never had friends, only unconditional adulators. Stingy and mean, ridiculous and nasty, it's hard to think he was the dictator who had us Salvadorans by the tail for longer than any other. But in reality, the oligarchy and imperialism never needed brilliant geniuses in order to dominate the people, simply bastards without scruples, pitiless and capable of anything. His vengeful spirit brought him to ruin in April and May of 1944, since instead of maneuvering politically on the basis of an indisputable military victory, he let himself get carried away with another bloodbath, which broke the dam of the people's patience. And then neither the invisible

428

doctors nor his communication with the spirits could help him; the gringos took away his authority, the oligarchy realized he wasn't the best instrument anymore for the protection of their interests, and the regime stood alone before the people. The fall of Martínez would mark the beginning of the overthrow of the dictatorships in Guatemala and Honduras. Only Somoza, in Nicaragua, would survive that hopeful period of 1944. North American imperialism had succeeded in displacing English, French, German, and other imperialisms, and it was able to impose new methods of local domination. In the case of El Salvador, maintaining the military dictatorship meant a change of the characters. Martínez wasn't needed anymore.

With Martínez gone, the reactionary forces, their organization and power intact, maneuvered in all directions to subdue the popular triumph and maintain the system of exploitation. The UNT, for its part, called a National Plenary as a way of coming out in the open to consult with the masses. The objective of the Plenary was to examine in detail the situation that had been created in the country and to agree on the line to follow in order to unify the people around a democratic program. Representatives attended from all the UNT committees that we'd been able to organize around the country. However, the Plenary suffered various problems and weaknesses. Thirteen years of dictatorship, thirteen years of zero political practice, had marked us all. Inactivity always takes a heavy toll. That's why the Plenary wasn't capable of analyzing what happened in the process that culminated in April and May of 1944. Either the entire action was credited to two or three heroes, who very soon would show their true colors, or it was accepted that everything had followed the spontaneous activity of the Salvadoran people. It couldn't be determined what had been the elements that built the solid national unity that ended the regime, how the process of unification of diverse social sectors had operated, which sector had contributed most to the struggle. A profound analysis of the military aspects of the April

429

defeat was not done. It wasn't enough to say that Martínez had balls and the rebels were wimps. On the part of the communists, neither did we study in depth our role in the conspiracy, whether the Party participated as an organization or if some communists had just participated individually; what had been the conditions for the participation of the Party or of individual communists as compared to other sectors; what had been their responsibility in the defeat; what role that had played in the May strike, in detail. The UNT began to move forward, but with blinders on, without knowing the elements of the process that was unfolding in the country, the full-blown perspective. Walking like the blind, feeling walls and windows, because of the lack of clarity about the facts we have at hand as a prior necessity for taking the first step, has always been the infantile disease of the Salvadoran left and still seems to be. At that Plenary, the multiple contradictions produced by the force that was channeled into the strike were not examined. How were we supposed to find the correct path through the mist of the future? The Martínez Government was held as something abstract, the incarnation of the evils of Hell, but its social origins weren't analyzed, nor how it created, from the beginning, the worst of contradictions within Salvadoran society and itself. The intellectuals that took over the debate filled the meetings with verbal diarrhea, with worn-out idealism, with heroic poses in front of the microphone, and they spent rivers of saliva praising democracy, the future, the fraternity of all men, without distinction; freedom, an end to the darkness of tyranny, the blue and white flag, the heroes, Alfredo Espino, the Izalco volcano and the *maquilishuat* flower. Nobody asked why the country's revolutionaries had lost thirteen years of history, disunified, hating each other, accusing each other of cowardice, of deviating from the correct line, of betrayal and immorality; suspecting one another, conspiring against one another, without realizing, or wanting to realize, the possibilities for working collectively that always open up for true revolutionaries under the worst of circumstances. It would have been another story if the UNT had recognized that the Martínez

430

government wasn't just a "great national stain" but rather a haunt where the most opposing kinds of social forces ran into each other, producing situations that, although in a limited way, could have been taken advantage of by the popular interests. That sly fox, Martínez, with his craftiness disguised by his Indian face, had sharpened the class struggle ever since he was Minister of War, provoking the people on a thousand and one occasions. Once in power he massacred peasants and workers, to make himself the strongman that the oligarchy and imperialism were looking for. But since he lost control in the repression, he went for a long time without diplomatic recognition from the gringos themselves, something that created tension and great personal resentment for Martínez. The General never succeeded in achieving the permanent unity of the Army, either. In February of '32, Osmín Aguirre y Salinas, the sinister "Peche" Osmín, was replaced as Police Director, accused of conspiracy. In 1934, the secret services discovered the plot led up by their own Minister of the Interior, General Salvador Castañeda Castro, who was also dismissed. On that occasion a Mexican by the name of Vargas was the one who paid the piper, executed in the Penitentiary. In 1935 there were two attempted insurrections: the one led by General Antonio Claramount, the eternal candidate for the Presidency, who had the support of the Guatemalan dictator, Jorge Ubico; and the one by General "Fritter" Castañeda, which I already talked about. Later on, there was an uprising led by Lieutenant Baños Ramírez, who was executed. Colonel Ascensio Menéndez, known as "Crazy Goat," was exiled to France for conspiracy, when he was no less than the Undersecretary of War. The rebellion of '44 was the last of the military actions against Martínez. And what had we done in the meantime? The UNT didn't want to examine that. And that's not even to mention other contradictions which always existed in the Army. The contradictions between the old and the young, between the officers from the ranks and those from the Academy, etc. Martínez also went over the heads of the top Church hierarchy by maneuvering the Vatican's naming of a humble little lay priest, who only officiated at the Church of La Merced, as Archbishop of El Salvador: skinny Luis Chávez y González, who still continues as head of the Salvadoran Church. Martínez had great political sense, and he managed to push the little priest into the Archdiocese, who, for his part, became one of the cleverest politicians in Salvadoran history, one of the best cadre – in spite of seeming hypocritical and back-stabbing – upon whom the oligarchy and imperialists in our country have been able to rely. But all the other bishops who were pissing on themselves to get to be Archbishop became the enemies of the dictator and began to denounce his theosophy. Important sectors of the emerging merchants went head to head with Martínez. For example, the powerful textile merchants, who got hurt by the competition from the State when Martínez set up the "Social Improvement" factories. Martínez also went against the industrial sector because he always tried to limit industrial development with the excuse of protecting guild crafts, but it was really to take care of the feudal interests of the landowning oligarchy. But even the big coffee growers who put Martínez in power fought with him, because he tried on more than one occasion to seize control of the coffee industry. These were contradictions between sharks, but they had the effect of depth-charges. The popular sectors didn't take advantage of them in any sense: they didn't even notice they existed. The National Bank and big business interests lost patience with Martínez when price controls remained in force, and the freeze on salaries sank workers even deeper. This measure made the peasants, artisans and state workers equally unhappy. The people detested the method of governing against the law and against human rights, which began to be talked about a lot in attacking Hitler and world fascism. The United States distrusted Martínez' fascism. The campaigns of April and May brought all these elements together against the regime and brought it down. But this analysis wasn't made in the May Plenary of the UNT: therefore it was natural that we began to trip up. The same thing happened to the Party. It wasn't until long after, for example, that I found out that Dr. Arturo Romero had been a

432

Party member, charged by the CC to locate and unify the groups of the conspiracy; that the Party had decided concretely that the comrades should participate in the anti-Martinist rebellion as individuals, not as communist militants; that in spite of the wishes of the Party, our organization as such had been given the task of printing and dispersing propaganda by the leaders of the April 2nd, a fact that negatively influenced the military conspirators who were most reactionary, ambitious, and fearful of the people, and who speeded up the coup and steered it under conditions that weren't, it seems, the best. In any case, groping and pushing our way along, we communists tried to organize for ourselves an idea of what we would need to do, once the UNT was functioning publicly. The Party met and made urgent resolutions: 1) To actively push the policy of "national unity" with all the forces in the country who aspired to democratization, a policy we supposed would permit the development of the class struggle and the growth of our Party. This supposed a double line: one open, mass line; and another clandestine line, secretly militant, with an organizational apparatus. 2) To give the UNT a flexible line, responding to the political moment, characterized by the reawakening of the masses and the need for growth of the CP, and based on a program of demands that would interest the rural and city workers. 3) To collaborate with the radical petty bourgeoisie in the creation and orientation of a progressive bourgeois party, whose Presidential Candidate would be Dr. Arturo Romero. 4) To normalize the relationship between the UNT and the progressive bourgeois party, to successively develop the electoral campaign. 5) To heed the strike movement's demands for the firing of hostile bosses and foremen who were tied to the dictatorship. 6) To reorganize the rural and city union movement on revolutionary criteria. 7) To begin an intensive campaign of clandestine recruitment for the CP, which would bring into its ranks the bravest fighters from the national mass movement, and to create party organisms where none existed.

With the overthrow of the dictatorship and the appearance of a provisional government dominated by the reaction but subject to pressure from the people and progressive sectors, all the political exiles returned from the country, among them many revolutionaries and some communists. Our policy of "national unity" excited the majority of comrades who came back. We decided to reorganize the leadership board of the UNT, incorporating the most capable of comrades who had returned into positions of responsibility. The new leadership was made up like this: Secretary General, Alejandro Dagoberto Marroquín (communist); Agitation and Propaganda, Darlos Alvarado (comunist); Finance, Luis Díaz (communist); Administration and Organization, Miguel Mármol (communist); Editor of the "Vanguard" newspaper, Abel Cuenca (revolutionary, not a Party militant). The work of the UNT in the five months of relative freedom that began with the fall of Martínez was great.

Within our ranks there was tremendous confusion about the nature of the UNT. Was it a political party or a workers' central? A broad, autonomous workers' party, or a mass front of the Salvadoran Communist Party? A Honduran comrade, Medardo Mejía, who in those days was a militant in the Salvadoran democratic movement, insisted on pointing out this situation, but the problem got worse by bringing it up: he said the UNT wasn't fish nor fowl, neither a party nor a unique central. And then another source of confusion surfaced. The petty bourgeoisie and some sectors of the progressive bourgeoisie who had pushed the April 2nd insurrection organized the Democratic Union Party (PUD) to back the presidential candidacy of Dr. Romero. All this had first been the idea of the communists, but those sectors, though they had received some influence from us, went off on their own and got the jump on us in that work. Dr. Romero was the "man and symbol" of the April rebellion and without a doubt the most popular leader in El Salvador. He had suffered a lot after the initial defeat in April when he was captured and cut up by a Martinist patrol, and he had been at the point of execution. These experiences, his fame as a generous person, a poor

434

peoples' doctor, made him the idol of a people that expected miracles. Romero maintained that aura for many years, in spite of having left the country and abandoned the struggle, until he proved with his actions (when he refused to be Rector of the University in 1958, after a great battle waged by university leftists to elect him) that he wasn't a leader up to the needs of the Salvadoran people. It seems he was personally honest all his life, but as a popular leader all he had was a reputation, the good will of the masses based on the hopes inspired by the struggle of April and May of '44. His militancy in the Communist Party is something I still can't understand. I know he served in the French Communist Youth when he studied medicine over there. And then I found out the fact that he also served in El Salvador and was given by the Party the task of coordinating the anti-Martinist conspiracy groups, as I already said. Possibly that was the only Party task he carried out, because later during the PUD period it's really hard for me to see how he could have been a Party militant. In any case, with the methods at hand for the UNT, we communists contributed decisively in elevating Dr. Romero's prestige with the masses. But the creation of the PUD as a bourgeois democratic organization that immediately had massive political backing, increased the confusion as to the nature and specific role of the UNT and favored the different types of opportunism. Miguel Angel Orellana, for example, an unscrupulous railroad workers' leader, made himself the boss of his union (UTF), which had fundamental importance and decisive influence in the UNT, and he tried to create "Democratic Union Party unions," which was the equivalent of making the workers' movement follow behind the Romerist bourgeois leadership. We communists from the beginning put various comrades into the ranks of the PUD, but they turned out to be weak, they didn't respond to the Party's policy and wound up meek followers of Romerism, without fighting to give that popular movement, so stained with bourgeois and petty bourgeois ideology, the firmness of proletarian positions, at least to the extent possible. We were clear that the comrades shouldn't try to sectarianize the PUD, but that they definitely

435

should be a vanguard element within it, struggling so that working class positions would be radicalizing Romerism. But our comrades never said boo in the PUD and actually reached the point of opposing Party and UNT positions in internal discussions, supporting the most reactionary sectors of the PUD movement. For their part, the reactionary sectors of the PUD unleashed their own maneuvers against the democratic forces that were consistent with their party and with the rest of the country. They sent a rumor around that the UNT had a "card up its sleeve," a secret candidate for President of the Republic who would be revealed at the last minute to divide Romerism and the people. It was even going around that this candidate would be Dagoberto Marroquín, which was false. Within a caudillist political atmosphere like the Salvadoran one, this was an accusation of betraying the people. The contradictions between the UNT and the PUD, caused by these maneuvers, became so great that we decided on having a joint meeting to make what agreement was possible. That was where I got into a terrific polemic with the coffee grower, don Agustín Alfaro Morán. Nothing concrete was accomplished. And by that time, the fascist extreme right had come pretty well along with their plot to return to power and liquidate the whole popular movement, of the workers, petty bourgeoisie and bourgeoisie.

In Guatemala on the 20th of October, the last bastion of the Ubiquista dictatorship was overthrown. Jubilation reigned throughout all Central America and "revolution" was the word of the day. For this reason the fascist Salvadoran reaction, with its power apparatus intact, didn't have to wait any longer to pull out its claws. At the UNT we received information that a coup against the provisional government was being planned for the 25th of October. Unified by that danger, the UNT and the PUD alerted the government and the people in every possible way. But on the night of October 21, when the people of San Salvador were together in Libertad Park celebrating the Guatemalan triumph, the international and Salvadoran reaction,

436

represented by the criminal Colonel Osmín Aguirre who had been renamed Police Director (he had held the post in '32), carried out with great ease the announced coup. This ease can be explained by the complicity of the Menéndez government, which let the reaction do what they wanted. "Cement Armor" passed into history as an example of a shit-in-his-pants president, weak, wimpy and objectively a traitor. The first measure that announced the change of government was the machine-gunning of the pro-Guatemala demonstration in Libertad Park, leaving a large number of dead and wounded. The massacre was followed by persecution of all the Romeristas of the UNT and PUD across the country, without making any distinction as to social class or ideological position. It was a lesson, though unfortunately not a profitable one, for the progressive bourgeoisie, the radical petty bourgeoisie, and the workers. The murdered, imprisoned, tortured and exiled once again became the order of the day. Osmín Aguirre showed the people the hate of the oligarchy and the Yankees in the most merciless way. The fact that a bastard like that is going to die in his sleep will say a lot about how irresponsible we Salvadorans are. It's true he had a throat cancer that's left him only able to talk with a pencil and paper, but if that's punishment, it's a punishment from God and the people shouldn't wait for God to tell them what to do. I myself escaped by a hair. A cordon of National Guardsmen surrounded the place where I was living, but with the help of my neighbors I tricked them and got through the trap. I almost went out shooting, because one of the neighbors had two .45s in his room and he told me if I wanted, he'd attack them by my side. But that wasn't necessary. That night I slept in "La Bermeja" cemetery. Then I went to Pedro Sosa, who wasn't under surveillance, and made contacts there to go into the countryside. I went out of San Salvador by footpaths, crossed Santa Tecla driving an ox-cart that a peasant comrade had waiting for me, and settled in a place called Los Achiotes, in Los Amates canton. There, I received news and got a whole perspective of the national situation. Democratic organizations had been rapidly dismantled, the PUD and the

437

UNT banned. A "national general strike" was attempted, but it didn't get anywhere. Based on the most absolute terror, the Osminist regime was dominating the situation and consolidating itself. Osmín declared that his government would only try to rid the country of communists and then there would be free elections. Dr. Romero had left before the coup for the United States to have an operation on his facial scars from the machete blows he'd gotten under Martínez, for which the reactionaries nicknamed him "Chajazo." Salvadoran exiles went to Guatemala and received support from the newly installed Government there. A Salvadoran government in exile was formed, led by Dr. Miguel Tomás Molina. The panorama was one of absolute disorganization: once again they'd caught us with our pants down, arguing over bullshit. In Los Achiotes I had to live in a cave that the peasants in the Party had made for me and comrade Valiente, who led that base, brought me paper and a typewriter from the last century that he must have gotten from some museum, so I could reorganize my contacts with the masses. On Saturday nights I met with the peasants in the bush fields far from my cave, and we discussed the news, plans for agitation, and pushed forward with our contacts with the clandestine national movement that was slowly reorganizing under the terror. Comrade Valiente's little children brought me food and the newspaper, and they were the only ones who knew where my cave was besides the men who built it. My life in the cave was hard because of the cold and damp, until I learned how to make a fire without getting everything smoky and choking. But the surrounding nature comforted me in my solitude. The birds kept me company, woodpeckers, chiltotas, doves and magpies. Some of these birds stopped being afraid of me and came to my cave looking for crumbs. I wrote a lot during this period: memoirs and other materials that I gave to the Party and that wound up getting lost. One day Ismael Hernández, from the CC, came to see me to give me instructions regarding propaganda. What I was doing from the cave was effective, and it was reaching the masses, but the Party thought I should correct some aspects of the line. For

438

example, I was ordered to stop propaganda in favor of Dr. Miguel Tomás Molina, president in exile. Ismael told me that some of the Party leadership were in diplomatic exile, and that the decision about the corrections of my work had been made by the comrades who were refugees in the Peruvian Embassy. This had been communicated to Ismael by Dr. Antonio Díaz. The few PUD Romerists who had stayed in the interior, the most advanced sectors of the worker and student movements, for their part clearly understood that there was no possibility of legal struggle against Osmín and that it was necessary to begin making armed struggle.

At first, that armed struggle took the form of individual terrorism. A bomb here, a bomb there, a dead policeman here and another there. Romero arived in Guatemala and those in exile joined together to attempt a major armed action against the dictatorship, which the Guatemalan government junta supported, providing rapid training and arms. The anti-Martinist military officers that Osmín had exiled to Guatemala took over the operative leadership, as "experts," of what was to be an invasion of El Salvador from the Ahuachapán side. The thing was chaos from the beginning. In the first place, the Salvadoran government had plenty of information about what the exiles in Guatemala were planning, and it took measures way ahead of time to crush the invasion. In the second place, the great majority of the Salvadoran exiles had no idea of what combat was, and the political level was rock bottom. In the third place, the Salvadoran officials who led the action were a bunch of cowardly incompetents, the cat's meow for planning an action on paper (and not even that, because they say that Colonel Félix Osegueda measured distances on the map without taking surface curves into account). Magnificent for quoting Clausewitz, but zero when it came to leading a hundred men on a one-kilometer march. In the fourth place, there was total lack of coordination between the invaders and the clandestine resistance. In the fifth place, Guatemalan support was withdrawn before the end because of fear of international complications. In the sixth place, the invasion was expecting too much from the Ahuachapán bourgeoisie: this bourgeoisie turned its back on the students and professionals who came from Guatemala with rifles and who "smelled like communists." The invasion was a failure and a slaughter. The National Guard once again went about target practicing against an inexpert enemy. The survivors returned to Guatemala dying of hunger and thirst. In San Salvador the actions were limited to an exchange of shots in one neighborhood. Which doesn't mean that those that died there don't deserve our respect and feelings On the contrary. I think we Salvadorans owe a debt to Dr. Paco Chávez Galeano, who battled alone against a contingent of police and picked off more than fifteen before he fell, shot full of holes. Men like him sustained the Salvadoran people's faith in the struggle. And men who today want that faith to serve for something, should be like Paco Chávez Galeano, at least like Paco Chávez the day he died. Let's be different from Chávez because we're Marxists, and let's be like Chávez for the balls he showed. Marxism and balls: that's the formula for revolution. At least for the Salvadoran revolution, I don't know about the others. As the last fucked-up straw, Romero left for Costa Rica and sent out a manifesto renouncing his candidacy. People became demoralized because, although PUD was banned, they expected its leader to keep up the fight. Romero played the part of a decoy. Poor little fellow, it wasn't his fault he was so weak. But it would've been better if he'd thought it all through before getting involved in things for real men.

The first meeting we communists were able to hold after the Osmín coup was on March 30, 1945. Julio Fausto Fernández presided, along with the comrade who had been General Secretary of the unified CC. I left my refuge and attended the meeting well-armed with propositions. I'd had a lot of time to think. By then the new "Constitutional" government of the Republic had taken power, presided over by General

440

Castañeda Castro, "Ground Glass," who stood alone in the election, for which in all cases votes were obtained at gunpoint, though the situation was sweetened up when they handed out liquor, food and drink at the polling places. At the Party meeting a report of the leadership nucleus was read, the situation and the perspective were studied, and various resolutions were made. In the report, there was an extensive analysis of the relationship between the UNT and the PUD, and of the role played by the Party. The fundamental error of letting the party work slide, of having neglected the growth and organic strengthening of the Party, was pointed out. This had caused us to get wrapped up exclusively in mass work, in the ivory tower of the electoral campaign and in the problems that came up between the PUD and the UNT. The independent task of the working class within the emerging popular front couldn't be guaranteed like that. There's no doubt that the mass work was important, but it's also true that it wasn't the only thing, and that by neglecting the Party's own work we had foregone the permanent harvest of the fruits of our enormous labor. We shouldn't have seen the mass work as an end in itself, but rather as a means to build revolutionary tools. I'm talking concretely about the conditions that existed in 1944-45, when we didn't have a party or organizations or anything. Also criticized was having put off for too long after the coup the meeting for self-criticism, analysis and account-taking of the situation, which meant that each person had been off on his own in an absolutely liberal kind of way. It was also said that not all the comrades had come up to the requirements of the circumstances. Some, because they were into a game of mutual accusation, without obtaining any results whatsoever. Others, for proposing to the people slogans and watchwords, organizational projects, political opinions, etc., that were absolutely incorrect, that confused the masses, that were taken advantage of by the enemy, that didn't convince anyone but that instead made people think that we communists were maneuvering in who knows what kind of way, right under their noses. Still others, for refusing any type of collaboration, such as Julio

Fausto Fernández, who we didn't see hide nor hair or until the March 30th meeting, in spite of repeated convocations. I guess by then he'd already started shitting in his pants from the cowardice that would later make him a traitor. The attitudes of Moisés Castro, Matilde Elena López and Tony Vassiliu were also criticized, for not defending the line of the UNT within the PUD, where they were sent by us as militants. The three of them were sheepish and accomodating to the bourgeois leadership within Romerism. The report classified as opportunistic the attitude of Valladares, the railroad workers' leader, for his having separated the union from the UNT. Also harshly criticized was the provocative, anarchistic and petty-bourgeois activity of Pedro Geoffroy Rivas, who in the newspaper "Free Tribune" let loose a raging anti-clerical campaign, a juicy opportunity the reaction took full advantage of. Geoffroy's anti-clericalism was attributed to a UNT watchword, although that poet wasn't a member of our Party and never had been. We communists are not anti-clerical in principle, and in El Salvador we didn't even make a campaign against the priests in 1932, when we were attacked from the pulpits so criminally. Also cited were provocative activities with the student group, especially in the sector that edited the paper "The Leader," which went about rashly insulting all military officers indiscriminately. The resolutions passed in that meeting were: a) To reorganize the Party; to prepare for and hold a new Congress in order to choose leadership organisms and to concretize the new organic structure at a national level. b) To regroup the labor union movement that had been dispersed by Osmín's coup. c) To publish a union newspaper in support of the latter resolution. d) To put out a document analyzing what happened in the last months in order to set the people straight, in the face of the contrivances by the rightists in the PUD, which blamed the communists for the Osminist coup. e) To suspend the activity of the UNT. f) To give economic assistance to Dagoberto Marroquín and Carlos Alvarado, who were living in exile under difficult conditions.

442

The Salvadoran people had to swallow a bitter pill with the Osmín government. Not only because of the lack of freedom, the murders, the torture, the massacres waged against students, the insecurity of knowing that the most unscrupulous, savage, uncultured and soulless men in the country had the bull by the tail, but also because of the terrible economic situation. A pound of sugar shot up to costing a colon, that is, forty cents on the dollar. Different grains went sky-high. And while the freedom aspect of things got somewhat better when the new "constitutional" government of General "Ground Glass" was installed, as I've said, the economic aspect stayed the same. A feeling of being fooled on top of being beaten was spreading among the people. In effect, the hard hand of Osmín had carried out the role assigned to it by the oligarchy and imperialism: to dissolve the Romerist party and eliminate all democratic opposition. Castañeda Castro got to the finish line of the elections alone, and his triumph didn't please the least bit a people that was still Romerist, only hungrier. Before and after the elections, all day long the radio stations were playing a song that gave you a headache: "Casteñeda is the man who should govern us. . . ." Corn, rice and beans filled the storehouses of the big monopolizing businessmen, who put millions of colons in their pockets from fraudulent speculation with the complicity of both regimes: the one going out and the one coming in. Even the peasants of Usulután, the department that would have been known as "the granary of the Republic," were crying from the scarcity. And anyone who knows anything about the way of life of a Salvadoran can understand what the lack of corn, rice and beans means for us. Lacking those products, the only thing left to eat is, pure and simply, shit. The scarcity was such that, in spite of the conditions of waning terror, in the countryside there began to be talk of the possibility of assaulting the haciendas of the rich to find provisions. I managed to place a couple of articles in the newspaper "Pueblo," and even in "La Prensa Gráfica," owned by the Dutriz brothers (surpassed only by Viera Altamirano as bastards) which has been one of El Salvador's most reactionary papers, financed by the American Embassy, guilty of instigating more than one direct repression against the people, and therefore having its own history of blood and crime. In those articles I assailed the landowners who were monopolizing grain, and the ineffectiveness of the Government's opposition to them. The articles attracted the attention of the authorities and once again, a period of intense persecution began against me. The forces of the repression found me in Santa Ana, where the paper "Pueblo" was located, edited by Efraín Ríos. They couldn't capture me because I was warned in time. But the Party received information that there were official instructions to murder me, and because of that, and in view of the scarce resources on hand to support the clandestine cadre, the CC and the Union Front decided I should leave the country for an extended time, and to carry out that objective I was named Salvadoran delegate to the Founding Congress of the General Federation of Guatemalan Workers (CGTG). In our sister country, the process known as the "Guatemalan revolution" was starting, and the Salvadoran communists exiled there were playing a vanguard role in it. In those days, comrade Amílcar Martínez was living in the Guatemalan capital and he had gotten together all the exiles to inform them of the Salvadorn situation and Party activities. There, Amílcar announced that the Party had decided to send me to Guatemala and to name me delegate to the CGTG Congress. Then Amílcar himself came to El Salvador to transfer me to Guatemala by the clandestine route. That black guy was really active and gutsy in those days, though at times a little reckless.

When the moment came, we left San Salvador and crossed the border. That is, Amílcar showed me where to cross and he entered Guatemala legally, agreeing to wait for me at a certain place in Guatemalan territory. As soon as I crossed the dividing line the sudden scares started. When I jumped a sort of mud-

444

wall there, that showed where the line was, a rifle shot sounded close by. I threw myself down head first. A few minutes before, it had started raining, and it was coming down harder and harder. Since nothing else happened, very carefully and quietly I got up from the swampy ground and little by little went off into the Guatemalan interior, crawling on all fours. I went into the undergrowth and climbed up on a hill that looked down over a river, like a wall. The river was down there, about fifteen meters below, and the whole area was rocky, pure stone. I took refuge from the rain under one of those trees they call "papelillos," nice and leafy. Exhausted (I hadn't eaten or slept since the day before because of my quick exit) I fell asleep. I only woke up, suddenly surprised, when a big yellow cow came over to sniff my feet. The cow got scared and she hid in the bushes, mooing scandalously loud. A little later four or five furious bulls appeared where the cow had disappeared, as if they were looking for someone to string up on their horns. They dug the ground with their horns, snorted with snot and saliva and pawed with their hooves, looking at me and coming towards me like they were crazy. I thought: "Isn't this something. Me, who's saved myself from reactionary terror in several countries, I'm going to die here, mauled by five bulls or thrown into a river that doesn't even have a name." I couldn't climb the tree, because those kind have a smooth trunk and the branches start to grow high up. Not even if I'd been a cat. I stood there paralyzed, in a cold sweat, and the bulls were getting closer. The only thing I could think of was to pray to St. Francis of Assisi. And I don't know if the saint saved me or if my trembling made the bulls laugh, but what's for sure is that they stopped, turned around and went the hell away, tossing their horns and yanking up shrubs. I took a deep breath, gave thanks just in case to St. Francis and, deciding to put off the nap until later, set off for the place where Amílcar had told me to meet him. About ten minutes after I started walking, I ran smack into a Guatemalan border patrol. I was arrested. I told them that I'd just crossed over the border clandestinely because the dictatorship in El Salvador had tried to stop me from attending the Congress of

445

Guatemalan workers, to which I was a delegate, and that I expected better treatment from the new Guatemalan authorities. The patrol chief was a rube of an Indian, an old-style rural policeman, and he wanted to hand me over to the Salvadoran Guard, but a sergeant said to him: "Chief, let's not commit a serious error. This man is honest and he's going to a Congress sponsored by the Government." The chief agreed and they let me go, showing me the road to Asunción Mita, where the authorities could help me continue my trip to Guatemala City. After getting out of that danger, I met up with the black guy Amílcar, waiting for me on the banks of a river, on a skinny horse. I mounted behind, under a torrential rain. At midnight we reached Asunción Mita drenched to the bone. We didn't look for any of those authorities and the next day left for Guatemala City on a bus.

From the moment I arrived in the Guatemalan capital I was absorbed in the feverish organizing activity of the working class. The perspective was so good that I didn't put up much resistance when I was told I would have to stay there. The Congress was a success, in spite of the low political level that the reaction used to its advantage for maneuvering. After the Congress, I began collaborating at the "Claridad" School, a center for political and union education founded and directed by Salvadoran comrades, where the most advanced Guatemalan revolutionaries were formed into nucleuses. The school had its own paper, also called "Claridad," for which I started to write regularly. Many comrades who have gone on to be leaders in the Party and in the Guatemalan workers' movement received their first orientation in that school. The Salvadoran comrades who began that work were Virgilio Guerra, Daniel Castañeda, Graciela García, Moisés Castro y Morales, Matilde Elena López and others, although there wasn't necessarily unanimous agreement between them. But it would be a long story to tell about those contradictions. I also want to make it clear that I'm going to limit my story about this phase of my life in Guatemala to

446

things that happened to me, without judging or going into detail about Guatemalan phenomena. That, by itself, would be enough for a huge book, and is principally a task for the Guatemalan comrades. You also have to take into account the present situation in Guatemala, in which many of the people I could mention still participate or have influence, and to be careful not to give useful information to the enemies of the people in Guatemala, who from 1954 have been on top in power and have been intoxicating themselves ever since on the most awful orgy of blood.

The Guatemalan situation was ambiguous. The Government had permitted a series of democratic freedoms that weren't even dreamed about under the previous regime. The radicalized forces of the petty bourgeoisie, the students, intellectuals, etc., were the leading voices in power, but towards the workers' movement, and towards Marxism and communism, there was reservation and rejection in official circles, where the reactionary ideology and dictatorial tradition left by General Ubico were still uppermost. Besides which, there were pressures from the oligarchic sectors, and the imperialists, who, though they didn't want a return to Ubicism, did at least want a government that would faithfully protect their interests in accordance with the present times. On the part of the people, there was almost total innocence and ingenuousness. The lack of political practice made it difficult to make clear for the workers and popular masses the most obvious maneuverings by the reaction and the gringos. An organizational consciousness got through the heads of the workers very slowly. But in any case, the perspective for revolutionary work was excellent. Guatemala had become the vanguard of Central America, though it may have been a case of the blind leading the blind. Nevertheless, the working conditions were, for us, very difficult. Activity among the working masses demanded experienced cadre, and these could be counted on the fingers of both hands. This meant that each cadre had to take care of a daily work load that was truly enormous, between appointments with unionists, with individual workers, with political nucleuses, etc. The number of appointments I had to go to, for example, made it impossible for me to work at my job. In any case, what I could earn under those conditions was very little. But if I didn't work at all, what was going to put food on the table? The movement was too new to be able to pay professional cadre, there was no money for anything, much less to feed us activists. So I began eating on the run, when I could, where I could, and what I could. There was one point when my only food was a cup of cornmeal gruel that I drank before going to bed. I became yellowish and really thin. One day, I went into the room where Daniel Castañeda was living and realized that a group of comrades were talking about me. Before they knew I was present, I was able to hear how Daniel was saying sadly: "I'm afraid that one of these days Miguel Mármol's going to fall down dead from hunger on the streets of Guatemala." But Daniel himself and Virgilio Guerra, Moisés Castro and all the rest were living under extremely difficult conditions. Bourgeois democracy does not feed revolutionary workers. One night, after a long meeting, the Guatemalan comrade Samuel Saravia invited me out to dinner at the "Noche Buena" restaurant, where I stuffed myself like an absolute pig. I ate a steak with onions, some lettuce and tomato, a dark beer, fried rice and a pile of tortillas as high as my forehead. Years later, Saravia would say that he'd invited me out to eat that night from worry about the constant hiccups I was going around with, hiccups that he thought were from pure physical fatigue. And it was true. The textile worker Amanda de León told her comrades – something that I'd kept quiet – that when I'd passed by the Colón Theater, I'd fainted from hunger and she'd tried to revive me by rubbing my head and neck, and had felt then all the lumps I had under my skin, products of malnutrition. From then on, fruit, sweets, beer, dinners and lunches and even flowers started arriving at my room, sent by the workers who refused to let me die of hunger. But in any case, I was resigned to struggle without letting the hardships matter. Along with Antonio Sierra González and another comrade educated at the "Claridad" school whose name escapes me, I was designated special adviser to the textile workers, a very important sector within the growing workers' movement in Guatemala. Right away we were able to see the disastrous work conditions those workers lived under. Subjected to intense exploitation, without any effective help from the little social legislation granted by the law at that time, with no class consciousness and no idea of ways to struggle legally, those masses nevertheless reacted positively to our first sermons. From the very first moment we tried to influence them on the basis of actual experience, real life, that would put out in the open the class struggle and unmask the boss sector. Above all, we underlined the importance of organizing, of creating a tool that would leave the defense of workers' interests in their own hands. We outlined and detailed the concept of labor conflicts, tactics to win victories in those conflicts and the various maneuvers used by the bosses to defeat us. In this sense the experience of the Salvadoran workers' movement was very useful to us. I illustrated all my propositions with examples from the struggles waged in El Salvador, especially since the workers' movements in both countries had had pretty similar developments, while keeping of course their national peculiarities, in that they both had begun around the time of the First World War, had had great strength in the twenties and thirties, had been destroyed and submerged in the blackness of the long dictatorships, and had resurfaced in 1944. I remember that the Guatemalan workers really laughed when I told them the story of a conflict in the cloth factory "Martínez y Saprissa," in El Salvador, shortly after Martínez' fall. The workers in that factory went out on strike for higher salaries under the advisement of our UNT. The conflict was practically won and the factory owner, a Spaniard, asked to speak to the masses who were gathered at the looms, waiting for the agreement to be signed.We recommended to the workers that when the boss arrived no one say a word, not for anything, and that they let us, their representatives and advisers from the UNT, speak. It was decided that the masses would speak only if they felt we weren't carrying out our duty to them. All the workers expressed their agreement: "Fine, fine." But what happened was, when the boss arrived, he spoke to the masses in a paternal way and asked that they allow him to speak, to give a speech, without intermediaries. And the workers answered: "Yes, don Paco. Of course, don Paco, speak." The old guy, who was a miserly exploiter, talked real sweet: "My dear workers, men and women, my dear girls and boys: I want you to tell me right here if I'm good or bad to you, if I treat you badly or don't respect you. Tell me if I'm ungrateful to you, you who are part of my family." The women workers spoke right up: "You are very good, don Paco." And the boss went on saying to them: "Tell me, is it true or not that I always welcome you gladly in my office to hear any problem you want to discuss with me?" And the women workers: "Yes, don Paco, you always welcome us kindly." The outcome was that don Paco got the masses, made up mostly of women, in his pocket, and then he took the offensive to denounce the agitators who advised the workers against their dear bosses. Because of all that mealy-mouthed stuff, the conflict was lost and there were no raises for anybody, only firings and a heavy hand. The Guatemalan workers, in their own turn, told stories of other similar experiences.

Guatemalan textiles advanced greatly in all aspects and by '46 the sector was capable of carrying out an important strike at "La Estrella" fabric mill, property of the Palestinian Encarnación Abullarach. This strike was a total success from every standpoint. Well planned, organized and led, the bosses couldn't break it. And that was despite the fact that the government put pressure against us, bringing out that old one about how the climate produced by the strike played into the hands of the extreme right, which feverishly conspired to over-throw Arévalo, the "spiritualist socialist." The so-called "revolu-tionary" political parties (since the Arévalo government was "the government of the October Revolution") criticized us harshly and even the General Federation of Workers refused to support us. As for the bourgeois press, forget it, they insulted us and beat on us, screaming for repression, denouncing those of us who weren't Guatemalan so the government would expel us from the country. In spite of everything, we carried the movement through to the end, maintaining the criteria of the independent interests of the working class under the conditions of Arévalo's regime. Our strike won and the workers of "La Estrella" got a 25% raise. But the Arévalo government counterattacked immediately, afraid that the strikes would spread because of the success we had had. The repression was let loose, undoing much of what had been gained up until then. Some comrades were expelled to El Salvador. Comrade Sierra González, who had stood out in the conflict, was confined in a concentration camp in the middle of the jungle of Petén. I had to go underground. Lombardo Toledano, from Mexico, addressed Arévalo in the name of the Workers' Federation of Latin America (CTAL), asking if I was imprisoned, dead, or being sought, and requesting guarantees for me. The other Salvadoran revolutionaries were pursued and some were captured and expelled from the country, though not for very long, because they turned around and came back in again. In any case, that first slap on the head from Arévalo was the culmination of a positive experience, worth analyzing. I wrote about it, but the material was lost on the occasion of another Arevalist repression, that of 1947. Clandestinity was painful, but it ended before too long. The progressive sectors of the government succeeded in getting a looser climate with greater opportunity, at least temporarily, for the activities of the workers' movement. To legalize my open organizing activity, and to have the necessary guarantees, the Trade Union of Guatemalan Shoemakers elected me Organizational Secretary. So in that way I was able to double my work. I ran the newspaper "The Unionist," advised the unions in the shoe factories "Incatecu" and "Cobán," which were the biggest in Central America, and I also advised the unions in such industries as candle and soap making, the bakers, the dressmakers, etc. During that period there were no big strikes in those sectors, but partisan conflicts abounded in the face of the demands the workers had put to the bosses. One very significant conflict that had national

451

repercussions was the struggle to reinstate comrade Concepción Castro in her job at the textile factory "Nueva York," owned by Salvador Abullarach, from which she had been unjustly fired. The conflict was long and hard-fought and served to raise the feeling of solidarity among all the workers in the country, as well as being a factor which stressed that the labor laws passed under the new political conditions needed to function in reality, not just on paper. It's a shame there's no written record of that campaign, because it was a brilliant page in the history of the Guatemalan workers' movement. Also very interesting was the work developed by my union in defending the shoe industry, which was an example for all the other trades. In that activity, the union was able to unify the shop owners, the tanners and the skinners, and succeeded in getting the government to enact protectionary measures that in the end benefited the workers, for example raising the duty on imported footwear. We also stopped the "Incatecu" company from producing leather shoes and limited it to the manufacture of rubber and vulcanized shoes, which protected 1500 shoemakers who would have been left jobless by the production of leather shoes at the "Incatecu," since by extending their production into leather the company would have only employed a hundred workers. Arévalo intervened to declare that the Government felt our position in that case to be inadequate, since it contradicted the need to industrialize the country, a basic question of national development. And if you look at it on the surface, it would be easy to say that the government was right, that it was progressive and we were retrograde. Our union answered Arévalo that the measure demanded at the moment as the basis for Guatemala's progressive industrial development was Agrarian Reform. And by the way, this problem, which would wind up deciding the fate of the "Guatemalan Revolution," was proposed publicly for the first time on that occasion. As long as the peasant masses have no means to consume goods (we were saying in our manifestos) industry will have no chance to prosper, because it will be dependent on too small a market. Just to look at the issue from the industry's point of view, what hopes could it have in a market where only 6% of the population wore shoes? The campaign we made around that problem was a big one and it attracted the attention of the entire country. In the midst of this hullaballoo, my situation had improved a lot and my work conditions were more normal. I became a professional cadre for the Union with a salary of thirty dollars a month. It wasn't a salary to rave about, but at least it saved me from total hunger.

In spite of all that union activity around organization, propaganda and reclamation, we didn't lose sight of the fact that we were planning a broader task: the creation of the Communist Party of Guatemala, which would be able to lead the workers in that national process which was so interesting and so full of positive prospects. In recent years, there had been two frustrated attempts by Guatemalan and Salvadoran comrades to found the Party and get it going. Sierra González and myself joined in a third attempt. We named an executive committee, began to hold meetings, and raised some funds through raffles, auctions, etc. I was the Recording Secretary. But this attempt failed also. In the face of this new defeat, I remember that Moisés Castro y Morales and the Honduran, Amador, said that it was impossible to creat the Communist Party in Guatemala, that the political level was too low, that it was necessary to wait a few years and in the meantime we should just develop union activity. On the opposite side, myself and other comrades, in the face of that third failure, decided to insist more strongly on the creation of the Party, using different methods. We had on hand a small nucleus of experienced, self-denying Salvadoran communists, some survivors of the Guatemalan communist organization of the 20's, but we understood that the Guate- malan unions, because of reasons that had to do with the structure of the country's working class, weren't sufficient for the creation of the Communist Party. That was what the voice of experience was saying, if you just perked up your ears and put aside your sectarianism. So we decided to proselytize very cautiously among the political parties within the "Guatemalan revolution," parties of the radical petty bourgeoisie, and also in progressive nucleuses of the bourgeoisie, the student movement, white-collar workers, the state bureaucracy, etc. Castañeda, Efraín Ríos, Sierra González and myself made up the generative group for that work. We were right on target. In the political movement, we found the fruit of what the "Claridad" school had sown, since many of the militants in the "revolutionary parties" had gotten their first political insights at that educational center. Our work was especially intense with the parties called "Renewed Action" (PAR), led by José Manuel Fortuny, a journalist and law student; and the "National Renovation" (PRN), led by José Orozco Posada, a lawyer. From these political groups and the advanced group that emerged within the CGTG, came the base that, with time, would become the skeleton of the Guatemalan Workers Party (Communist). In those circumstances, little by little, we recruited comrades like Mario Silva Jonama, Alfredo Guerra Borges, Méndez Zabadúa, Hugo Barrion Klee, Bernardo Alvarado Monzón and José Manuel Fortuny. As the work of communist organizing became less cautious and more successful, the attack against us sharpened. The bourgeois press, the priests, the reactionary radio stations vomited out accusations and insults. Anticommunism became the fashion and we Salvadoran comrades were the favorite target of the rightest reaction. Soon enough the flag of the "black legend of communism in El Salvador in '32" started flying. It was then that Schlésinger's slanderous book came out, meant to isolate us and to get the hesitant Arévalo government to take measures to expel us from the country or put us in jail. The campaign took on a sharply chauvinist, anti-Salvadoran character, and even some union leaders participated in it, confused by their low political level or bought off by the reaction. It got to the point where the content of the campaign was so absurd that it was being said publicly that all the problems affecting Guatemala had come from El Salvador. For the leaders of that campaign, prostitution in Guatemala was "Salvadoran," the same as vagrancy, theft, alcoholism, bedbugs and fleas. It's not hard to weaken under such circumstances, and especially not to react with equally chauvinist positions. We were urged by the Ministry of Public Education to close down the "Claridad" School in order to avoid extreme provocations, but we rejected that suggestion. A few weeks later, the school was closed by force. The Arévalo government made serious concessions to the reaction and even went so far as to suspend unionizing rights for rural workers, without a doubt a real regression. The well-known bourgeois politician Mario Méndez Montenegro, who would become a loyal cadre of imperialism but would nevertheless end up a "suicide" because of it, was at the time the Director of the Civil Guard (the Guatemalan police). He called the Salvadoran activists to his office and offered us good jobs with the condition that we abandon the struggle. He said there were no problems with the Honduran, Nicaraguan and Costa Rican exiles in Guatemala, because they just set themselves to working for a living, which was correct and revolutionary. He added matter-of-factly that if we didn't accept his propositions we'd be expelled from the country. We answered that we had come to Guatemala not to earn a living, but as revolutionaries, and that whatever the cost might be we were going to keep on being revolutionaries. And that between the job-bribe and expulsion, we preferred to be expelled. We left, but soon found out that his threats were no joke. Moisés Castro y Morales was expelled to Honduras in a cruel, humiliating way, since even though he had a bad leg and was lame he had to leave the country on foot. The Honduran government, which wasn't revolutionary and had no pretentions of being so, picked Moisés up at the border and took him to Tegucigalpa by plane. Daniel Castañeda and Virgilio Guerra were arrested and were in prison for several weeks, without being charged legally. Graciela García, the heart and soul of the "Claridad" School, pioneer of revolutionary struggles in Central America, was pressured and harassed to an unbearable degree and we decided she should go to Mexico. I managed it so that the repression couldn't reach me, integrating myself into the legal apparatus of the workers'

455

movement, which put me ipso facto under the protection of the law and made it harder to lay a hand on me. When the CGTG decided to create its Political Action Commission (CAP), I was elected General Secretary. And, by means of that organism, I was able to come into contact with the highest Government authorities, with Arévalo himself, who met with us to try to find a formula that would avoid creating a deep conflict between government policies and the workers' struggle. At those meetings, we realized the complexities of Guatemalan politics and the difficult conditions under which the balance of powers, that the government's survival depended on, was maintained. Arévalo himself told us that 47% of the Army was against him and made clear his reservations about the attacks by the reactionary forces, who took advantage of the religious fanaticism and backwardness of the great majority of Guatemalans. Arévalo said he didn't accept the open support of the working class so as not to frighten the landowners or the gringos. "It would be like frightening them with a paper tiger," he said, "because the revolution still doesn't have enough strength." Because of our demands, Arévalo promised to give us a Work Code, which didn't exist in Guatemala, by May 1, 1947. And he promised us that its promulgation would be announced in a radical way, as a basic measure for the broadening of the social base of the regime, as a revolutionary measure, and we committed ourselves to supporting it with the greatest of enthusiasm at the same May 1st demonstration where Arévalo would announce the Code as part of the closing ceremony. Arévalo insisted that he was willing to go as far as the people demanded in the adoption of revolutionary measures, but that it was better not to talk about the class struggle because the reaction within the Army was a serious obstacle. He told us that the anti-national and pro-oligarchy forces in the Armed Forces were led by Colonel Francisco Javier Arana, and that he, Arévalo, had plans to send him on a diplomatic mission to Chile, so the Chilean military, more socially and politically advanced, would be his "finishing school" and would make him less of a big macho. Arévalo needed our support in the internal struggle, that was clear. But May 1st came, with its demonstration and its political meeting, and the Work Code still wasn't promulgated. It all developed like this: in April of 1947, along with Hortensia Hernández Rojas, Antonio Sierra González, and Victor Manuel Gutiérrez, a prestigious teacher who had become a Marxist at the "Claridad" School and who would come to be one of the greatest leaders of the Guatemalan working class before falling, assassinated, in the anticommunist repression unleashed by the gorilla regime that still oppresses Guatemala, I was in Mexico and Cuba, as a delegate of the CGTG to the congresses of the Federation of Mexican Workers and the Federation of Cuban Workers. Although the repression of Prío Socarrás prevented the celebration of the latter, we were able to spend a few days in Cuba and return to Guatemala to inform our comrades about the Cuban workers' movement. The Cuban workers' movement was a strong, combative and enterprising movement, loyal to the principles of proletarian internationalism; fraternal and hospitable. I compared the Havana at that time with the one I had seen in 1930; the corruption was the same, but the workers' movement had advanced a great deal. We delegates of the Guatemalan working class realized the great respect that the Cuban workers had for leadership cadre such as Jesús Menéndez, Blas Roca, and others. Always thinking about the place I was born, both in Mexico and Cuba, I took some steps to arrange for training for communist and union cadre from El Salvador. Thanks to those efforts, the bakers' leader Salvador Cayetano Carpio was able to go to Cuba and take a class in unionizing. We returned to Guatemala to celebrate May 1st expecting the main course to be the promulgation of the Work Code. But the moment we entered the country, we got another kind of surprise: Victor Manuel Gutiérrez and myself were being tried in absentia, accused of preparing an uprising of the peasants on the "Cerro Redondo" farm. The charge turned out to be false and insupportable, but I was left hanging, pending the investigation of the Court in Cuilapa.

457

The first of May, 1947, was impressive for the number of workers who participated in the demonstration in the capital, and it left us organizers who had busted our chops working on it completely exhausted. The whole country mobilized and sent delegations to Guatemala City, without counting the different local celebrations that extended from one border to the other. From Escuintla came 15,000 agricultural workers, voluntarily on foot, carrying their placards on a 60 kilometer trip. There were 11,000 Chiquimula workers, and they carried placards that said: "Only a few of us came because the rest stayed behind tending the corn." In total, the CGTG concentrated more than 100,000 urban and agricultural workers from all over the country in the capital. That day the CGTG handed out to the workers a little pamphlet of mine entitled "Union Orientation." But the Work Code wasn't promulgated on that occasion. After the first of May we met with Arévalo again, in an atmosphere that wasn't at all cordial. He started out by calling us up on the fact that our slogans in the parade had been sectarian, extremist and counterproductive. He told us that the secret services of the Yankee Embassy were more powerful than the Guatemalan police, and they had informed the Ambassador that two things were going to happen in the parade: the surprise announcement of the Work Code and the support of the masses of workers for that measure, from a radical left position. Because of this, he declined to attend the ceremony, though he, like the entire Diplomatic Corps, had been invited by the President. "Colonel Arana," Arévalo told us, "on seeing the Ambassador's seat empty, became extremely frightened when he read the signs of the workers in the parade." The meeting with Arévalo ended on an icy note: he blamed us for having let out his "clever" maneuver, when in reality, the only thing we'd done was to keep a commitment made with him. Arévalo was a bourgeois politician, a confirmed anticommunist, and the only thing he wanted was to be on the good side of both God and the Devil, all the time and in all cases. After that meeting, Arévalo maneuvered to exclude the most advanced leaders from the parties that supported him. He tried to do the same

458

thing in the CGTG, but we blocked him. He created a political crisis for José Manuel Fortuny in the PAR, but we supported Fortuny, reelecting him to the office we'd given him in the Political Action Committee of the CGTG, which signified a vote of confidence from the working class, and he was able to make it through the crisis in his party, whose rightest, Arevalist wing didn't think it prudent to run up against the union movement. Arévalo's later career confirmed what I'm saying: today he's an unmasked flunkie of North American imperialism, of the shark that he went around denouncing while he tried to get the sardines to sleep. Given the conditions of the struggle in Guatemala, and given the weakness of the organized revolutionary forces, the CGTG had to adopt a more and more traditional political role, even entering the partisan game itself. In accordance with the conversations held with the Government, it was resolved that the organized working class would have the right to be represented at the National Congress. The CAP of the CGTG proposed four candidates for deputies to that end. This was discussed at a special meeting held in the National Palace, with all the government sectors participating, and led by the Defense Minister, Colonel Jacobo Arbenz. At that meeting, the reactionary Colonel Arana, Chief of the Armed Forces, said it wasn't the unions that needed deputies to the Congress, it was the Army. And without beating around the bush, he proposed that the seats the workers' movement claimed as its own be given to the Army. That Colonel Arana had no heart. He said all this so calmly it was disconcerting. In the name of the CGTG, I answered him that the Army was precisely the social sector and the institution that needed the least guarantees, because it had arms at hand, and with its tanks, cannons and planes it had been created to guarantee the rights of the people as well as the democratic institutions of the Republic. Fortuny, the representatives of the revolutionary Parties, the Chilean union adviser Pinto Usaga and even Sierra González, from the CAP, were shitting their pants with fright and wanted to shut me up, so great was the fear that weakling Arana inspired. Sierra González gave me a few elbows in the ribs so I'd soften

459

up the tone of what I was saying or shut my trap. Colonel Arbenz, very cleverly, proposed another meeting in order to come to an agreement. From the Palace, the members of the "Revolutionary Block" went to the offices of the Popular Front (a coalition of parties that supported the regime). The unanimous opinion of the party representatives was for the contested seats in the Congress to go to the Army. I intervened to say that was fine, that they could do whatever they damn well pleased, but that I'd inform the CGTG of everything and would denounce the attitude of the political parties, and from then on they could be sure they'd never get even one worker's vote in the whole country. That made them change their minds, and they finally committed themselves to supporting the workers' candidacies. But there was always maneuvering and tricks going on. The elections came and the revolution won, but the CGTG only got one deputy, there was only one lousy seat for the Guatemalan working class in that so "revolutionary" Congress. And the labor union issue was going to be one of the first problems brought up in the Congress of the Republic, since after the ceremonies and taking over their seats, the deputies considered a bill sent by the Executive to normalize unionization in the country. The Congress asked for the opinion of the organized workers, for which the congressional commission charged with forming an opinion about that bill met with representatives of the two workers' centrals of Guatemala, at the roomy local of the Union for Railroad Workers' Action and Improvement (SAMF). Because at that time, the Guatemalan workers' movement was already divided into two centrals: the General Federation of Guatemalan Workers (CGTG), revolutionary, within which different political and ideological currents met, but in which revolutionary and socialist positions prevailed; and the Unionist Federation of Guatemala (FSG), reactionary, pro-imperialist, pro-oligarchic, counterrevolutionary, fierce enemy of the CGTG. On that occasion the FSG declared itself in favor of a law that would impose mandatory unionization for all Guatemalan workers, and stuck to that position tooth and nail. My comrade and compatriot Virgilio Guerra really put his foot into it in this case, supporting

460

mandatory unionization. That method pretty well fit his authoritarian character, and he didn't notice that the FSG's proposition was a reactionary maneuver that was meant to create friction between the State and the union movement. When, in the name of the CGTG, Antonio Sierra and I declared ourselves in favor of voluntary unionization, for the free and independent organization of the proletariat, the whistles and boos from our adversaries were tremendous, but they didn't succeed in silencing us. José Manuel Fortuny, by then a deputy who I personally met in conversation only that evening, since before then I only knew him by sight, and who was part of the Congressional Commission, energetically demanded respect for us representatives of the CGTG and called for moderation and intelligence, warning the members of the FSG that the Commission would leave if they didn't compose themselves. Since the reactionary disorder continued, Fortuny adjourned the meeting. Afterwards, Fortuny invited me to his party's headquarters and there I explained to him the reasons for our position, telling him among other things, that under the conditions in Guatemala where the bosses still controlled some 70% of the workers on their side, and we barely influenced 30%, mandatory unionization was going to permit the bosses to control the entire workers' movement and even swallow us up in the name of a supposedly democratic majority. Voluntary unionization – I said to Fortuny – is the only means that will permit us to capture the working people on the basis of their consciousness. In the system of free unionization, the union is a classroom that teaches, educates and cultures, that raises the political and revolutionary levels of the worker, that truly liberates him. Fortuny was in agreement and finally, within the Congress, the battle was won in favor of voluntary unionization, which restricted the field for the reaction's maneuvers.

On another front, we continued the work of organizing a Marxist-Leninist party. The communist group kept on growing and came to have its own name: "Vanguard." Aiming to raise the

461

quality of its ranks, we always tried to recruit the best men being produced by the process of the "Guatemalan revolution."

During the first days of September, 1947, we met at the home of the Salvadoran poet Pedro Geoffroy, who back then was a sharp Marxist, an extremist even at breakfast; the Guatemalans Mario Silva Joname and Méndez Zabudúa, and the Salvadorans Daniel Castañeda, Efraín Ríos and myself, to set the date for the formal founding of the communist group, which was already functioning informally with the name "Vanguard." We decided on the 15th of September, Independence Day from Spanish domination in Central America. It was agreed that two reports would be presented on that day, a political report about the national and international situation, and a report about union work in Guatemala. I had to write the union report. It was also agreed upon to invite Fortuny to join the new communist organization, since he was one of the most advanced political elements in the country. However, the meeting was never held. Let's look at what happened. Rumors started to go around that on the 13th of September there was going to be a reactionary coup against Arévalo, and that one of the first measures the reaction would take when they took power would be to liquidate all Salvadoran revolutionaries. The CAP of the CGTG made all these rumors and facts known to the government, and Arévalo took steps to defend his regime, using the repressive means at his disposal. The bad thing was that he didn't only use them against the rightest conspirators, but also against the democratic workers' movement. The very day of the 13th, five Guatemalan and five of us Salvadoran comrades were jailed. The government's conduct confused the working class and public opinion. I understood that the regime felt obligated to make concessions under strong pressure from the right, but it wasn't all that serious. What was going on was that Arévalo played his own hand, like the anticommunist he was, like the class enemy he was and still is. On the third day of being locked up incommunicado and with no legal charge against me, I started to protest violently. The guard told his superiors. The Government

462

permitted Fortuny and Gutiérrez, in their role as deputies, to visit us. We told them that we Salvadorans were still friends of the Government, that we didn't want to make a scene about our situation and that we felt any public demonstrations on our behalf should be avoided, since that would play into the hands of the reaction. The Executive Power asked its members to consider whether or not we should be expelled from the country. It was resolved to expel us. The only one opposed to this measure – according to comrade Fortuny – was Colonel Jacobo Arbenz, who said in reference to me that I didn't deserve the treatment I was getting in Guatemala for the intrigues of the Aranista faction, that what I really deserved was a statue made of the same material as my name, that is, a marble statue, for my work of contributing to the awakening of the working class. Arbenz proposed that we be expelled, with all expenses paid by the Government, for four months, so that we could rest up from so much activity and running around. All the Ministers agreed with Arbenz, and even Colonel Arana himself, so as not to wind up totally beaten, supported the measure. We agreed to go to Mexico for four months. From then on, the affection of the workers for Arbenz grew greatly. That stay in Mexico was perhaps the only rest I've had in my life. When the four months were up, I was the first of the Salvadorans to return to Guatemala from "exile," despite the delays the Guatemalan embassy put in my way. Upon returning, CGTG directed me to work on the peasant front. For a time, I became the one hearing the complaints of the indigenous people, attending to four or five delegations at once, and even speaking different dialects. At first it was difficult to understand the Indians, because though they may speak Spanish their way of thinking is different from that of ladinos, and their interests aren't the same as those of other Guatemalans. But I worked it out, using interpreters, maps, drawings, hand signs, etc., to break down that barrier. I can say that soon I became a man trusted by the indigenous Guatemalan peasantry. I remember the people of San Rafael Petzal and those of Rabinal with special revolutionary affection. After that task, I returned to El Salvador, summoned by the

463

Party. I served there for two years and in '51 I returned to Guatemala, and didn't leave until Arbenz fell in 1954. But I won't talk about that period in these memoirs of mine. Maybe some day, later on, if my life gives me such an opportunity. That's a matter of a well-known period, about which the Guatemalan comrades have given definitive accounts. My contribution wouldn't be anything new, and besides, it would have to touch on people and facts that are still part of the Guatemalan reality, and I wouldn't want the enemy to be able to apply to current problems the type of focus that I've permitted myself to take throughout this discussion of issues from the now distant past, which can now be exposed to a critical, autocratic eye without risk, and, on the contrary, to the great advantage of revolutionaries. For the same reason, I won't talk about these last years of my life as a revolutionary in my own country. My Party is still clandestine, and it has to suffer persecution from the forces of the military regime and the CIA. About Guatemala, I just want to add that for the time I remained in that territory, I gave all my strength and activity to the immortal cause of the proletariat, without asking anything in return. The highest up I got in rank was doorman at a bank, with a salary of fifty quetzels a month.

Well, I think it's time to finish this up. To tell you the truth, I've never liked "hogging the guitar," as we say in El Salvador. And it's also true that this has only been half a disclosure, because as I repeat, there are things that still can't be said publicly, though I'm dying to tell them. Above all, a bunch of things about my most recent life. More than one person will write them or tell them when I'm dead.

Reflecting on my life, especially the part of it that I've examined in the most general terms; looking back and contemplating my youth, my political activity, my joys and miseries, a kind of strange feeling of dissatisfaction and happiness at the same time fills my head. Dissatisfaction, for the things our limited strength and capacity did not permit me to do

464

in furthering the popular struggle, for my being partly to blame for the defeats caused by the enemy who still gets fat on the blood and sweat of our workers; happiness, because in spite of the weaknesses of each individual, our group of ignorant amateurs fought the battle of the working class in El Salvador and outside El Salvador, we were the pioneers of the revolution that will inevitably come to transform our countries once and for all. On the personal side, I feel that for me the end of the campaign is near, though I hope that end will last twenty years. I feel tired and beaten up inside, and the years weigh on me heavily. And it's not because I'm so old. It's because I lived every day with all my strength, and didn't give myself time to rest. And the anguish and the hunger have left their mark, too. So, I think the time for me to be relieved has come. A tired and beaten leader becomes dead weight for the revolutionary movement if he doesn't have the courage and integrity to recognize that reality in time. Not just a dead weight, but an obstacle, a ridiculous obstacle. In the middle of a current, a wet tree trunk doesn't help you float, it sinks you. It doesn't hurt me to recognize that, because I've never thought of leadership as power, or militancy at the leadership level as a "power struggle." When leaders understand that their position is not one of privilege, but of greater obligation, sacrifice and responsibility, many internal problems disappear. Besides, I've always thought that youth should occupy the front ranks in the struggle. A party of old men would have to make the revolution at the old folks' home. And in my country, there are enough fervent and trained young people who can take over and surpass all their grandpas. And all this happens as a natural thing, a rule of life, not as a "generational struggle" that sometimes takes the place of the class struggle in some peoples' minds. But this isn't my swan song, as Rubén Darío would say, or my farewell. More than one person wishes it were, and not just the police, the National Guard and the union movement in the ORIT. I'm not saying that I'm going to abandon the revolutionary struggle because of my age or fatigue. I just think that these circumstances demand of me another, less prominent role in the organization that directs my country's popular strength. I only resign my role as leader, taking a step back into the ranks to share my experience there, my few certain conclusions as an old militant and my last energies. Against the class enemy, for the interests of the Salvadoran people and the international working class.

El Salvador has changed a lot since 1925 or 1932. So why, then, have we survived as leaders until now? Why is it that the shoemakers and bricklayers and bakers have kept on leading the new industrial proletariat of El Salvador? I think this has followed, more than anything else, from the fact that we began as leaders during a historical stage that has not ended, or, as the professors in the cadre schools say, a stage that has not closed. This is the stage prior to and after 1932, the stage of the long Martinist dictatorship, the stage of the Guatemalan defeat, the stage of the Osorista-Lemusista demagoguery and of the PRUD (which I haven't discussed in these pages), etc. This stage merges, with all its twists and turns, with the new stage that began for Latin America with the Cuban Revolution. In the world situation, it was undoubtedly a pre-revolutionary stage. But what's befallen us recently is a tremendous confusion that's been reflected in the line of our Party regarding our country's fundamental problems, in our own vacillation and shortsightedness. I think it's more necessary than ever to differentiate between the old and the new, what has been overtaken by reality, which never sleeps, and what still lives and can benefit from the experience of the last forty years of Salvadoran revolutionary history. I've expounded here on the facts and on some of my opinions, but that's not enough. A profound partisan analysis must be made, with Marxism-Leninism in our hands, in our eyes, in our hearts. Only in this way will we know at each moment if we're on the right path, only in this way can we begin to untangle the thread of our failures and our erroneous concepts. Because the truth is we're not on the right path, not by a long shot, and in some aspects we're going backwards, like crabs. What's happened is that we misuse the "propoganda of self-criticism" and we don't like to put salt on the wound too often. And this isn't solely a defect of us ignorant

Salvadorans: it's an international disease. Profound self-criticism isn't always well received, and in the publications it seems the one who says everything is going along just fine is the preferred one. It has to be accepted that this way of proceeding isn't exclusive to us old guys, who can easily be accused of being conservatives and who in the majority of cases truly are. Many new sectors, young ones, in the world revolutionary movement continue to refuse to delve deeply into historical experience using their own heads and simply want to receive readymade recipes for revolutionary action. These comrades came in the wrong door, they shouldn't have joined the Party or revolutionary organizations but rather a seminary or a convent. They'd be excellent priests. Many young people of great talent get lost in the mental, political and moral laziness of wanting to be revolutionaries without living as revolutionaries, without sacrifice, without paying life for its experiences, without taking the risk of going in all the way, without using their heads before getting involved where they don't belong, heads that ought to be used for more than making a hat fit on tight or withstanding the blows of the police. To eat shrimp you've got to get your ass wet, as the saying goes. And that's the truth, at least for the people, since the rich eat shrimp without going to any trouble and it's the others who get wet for them. Only life, hard practice, gives the capacity for independent thinking and makes true revolutionaries. The easy life, comfort, and political lines that are just good for vegetating, for covering up with a babble of words the betrayal of the revolution, only serve to make a man get sloppy and weak. And even practice alone isn't enough. Pushing yourself to the limit applies to theory, too. To be a Marxist, you've got to really get Marx, Lenin, Stalin, and Mao Tse-Tung into your head, not simply read some magazine or other once a year and go around cackling, like a hen who's laid an egg, about discovering some attractive slogan, some new little work to hook dummies. The "Marxists" of magazines and stupid little newspapers abound. What you have to do is study hard and serve the cause hard and open your eyes to reality. And even more so now, when there's such a rich

467

historical experience of socialist revolution and when useful books are coming off the presses by the ton. With all that literature and a little bit of present-day experience, things in '32 would have been different for us. And this isn't an excuse, nor whining. It's putting things into their proper place. For myself, I don't even argue. But for the comrades of my generation, I do demand respect, and the best treatment they can be given is to situate them in the time and circumstances in which they were called on to act. The Salvadoran communists of my generation were men who engaged themselves in historical events that were beyond their capacity, and nevertheless acted with honor, pushed forward the revolution, and knew how to die for their principles with serenity. The communists of my generation were forged in a completely enemy atmosphere, not in a nice period like today's, when you can smell socialism anywhere you stick your nose. They were forged in struggle with a cruel and savage enemy, and in the struggle against our low political level, against our infantile conceptions of organization and militancy, against our poor interpretations of reality, in the struggle against the extreme sectarianism, as much on the individual level as that of the Party and even the Communist International. It shouldn't be forgotten that when we founded the Party, the International was prisoner to sectarian line, whose order was to pit "class against class," scorning alliances and tactical maneuvers. The communists of my generation were formed in permanent struggle against ourselves, against our ignorance and ideological weaknesses. And it has to be said that we didn't win the fight in all cases. But in spite of everything, no matter what they say, I think that generation of communists was better than today's, because it fought with all the disadvantages and without nearly any of the advantages of today, and even so it was able to have the strength to place the red flag of revolution in the hands of today's youth, who have no reason to be ashamed of accepting it. That flag is stained and torn, it's true, but the stains are our blood and the tears are our defeats. That's on the national side. On the international, I want this to be heard and well understood once and for all: ours was a generation of communists that made

468

sacrifices, fully conscious, with absolute clarity about what it was doing, in honor of the strengthening, development, and consolidation of the first proletarian state on earth, of the glorious Union of Soviet Socialist Republics, the beginning of the socialist world and the basis for gradual worldwide revolution. We went into battle with the bourgeoisies of each of our countries to prevent the international class enemy, the world system of imperialism, from being able to concentrate its forces against the homeland of Lenin. The bourgeoisies amused themselves with us, murdered us, beat us, jailed us, became enraged with our parties, but the Soviet Union turned into the dominant power in the worldwide panorama. Each class knows how it makes war, and if imperialism has its strategy, that sometimes leads many who think themselves revolutionaries to suck on their thumbs, we, the proletarians of the world, also have ours. Only those who have bourgeois nationalist concepts firmly stuck in their minds could think that this was "putting ourselves at the service of a foreign power." The issue isn't one of nations, of Russians and Salvadorans, but of classes, of proletarian internationalism, of the universal fraternity of the exploited against the exploiters. That's what makes us know that a Japanese worker is more our brother than a Salvadoran millionaire. When they executed me, it wasn't Alfonso Rochac who was at my side, or don Rafáil Guirola or don Tomás Regalado, as Salvadoran as they may have been, but it was a Russian comrade, a Soviet worker whose name we didn't even know. Maybe he was Polish. Or Hungarian. But for us, he keeps the name he had when he died: "the Russian." So there's very little they can tell me about this area. The sacrifice for the USSR, made by all the communists of the world, was worth it, although the petty bourgeoisie and the social chauvinists, both old and new, may frown and try to laugh at us. They can keep on laughing for another hundred years and stick their frowns up their asses if they like, as far as I'm concerned. World revolution is a task of many years, not work for a single generation. If it was such a simple thing, it wouldn't have been Stalin who would have gone to share Lenin's mausoleum, but Trotsky. And everyone knows that in the end, comrade Stalin himself had to leave that sacred place because in spite of his enormous merits, he committed serious errors that stained his hands and mortified all us communists of the world. Of course it's much simpler to yell "Long live world revolution by the end of this week" than to organize a cell in a new neighborhood. With sweat and tears, we carried out our task, which was ambitious and bold. That's why I think that in every Sputnik, in every victorious economic plan, in every anniversary of a glorious date for the USSR are also present the contributions of our Salvadoran and Guatemalan and Chinese and African and French and our comrades all over the world, who fought and died for the ideal of communism. And, in the reverse, every one of those victories of the USSR should be one more added force, which at the right time will be put to use by the Salvadoran or Guatemalan or African revolution (like it was put to use by the Chinese or in the Cuban revolution) and by every country in the world. This is a question of principle that admits no discussion and that goes beyond any tactics of the moment. And in practice, we can see how it functions: yesterday Ho Chi Minh was an Asian bastion of solidarity with the USSR within the Communist International and on the battlefields of Indochina, and today the USSR supplies the people of Vietnam with the arms necessary to face North American agression; Julio Antonio Mello gave his life for communism, after having been the standard-bearer of the Cuban people in solidarity with the young USSR that tightened its belt and had millions of problems, and now the strength of the USSR is the greatest international support of the revolution that happened on the Island of Liberty. Of course, in all this there are also very complicated problems, crossed lines, more or less temporary but contradictory interests between brothers in struggle themselves, momentary confusions and disagreements, goofups, obstacles, but this is the basis for progress. Socialism has not gone back one inch in its world conquests, though it may still have a thousand or more problems. Little by little, but steadily it advances. I wouldn't want to go on to any other topics

470

without saying I believe that in the task of effecting the concrete, militant solidarity of the worldwide working class, a first-class role was played by the Communist International, the Third International founded by Lenin in order to leave behind the knavish liquidationists and lily-livers of the Second International. This truth is bigger than a house. Honestly, I don't know what would have become of the USSR in the 20's and 30's without the contribution of the Third International. The International helped, in large measure, to make it possible for the USSR to build up the essential forces for the great battle that would be waged against Nazifascism in such a heroic and positive way for humankind. The combative spirit that incited the heroic era of the Third International, its discipline, its proletarian-internationalist consciousness, its elevated spirit of struggle, has not died and will be reborn every time it is necessary. Today we see it in Vietnam, to cite just one example. Although it's also necessary to say that there are some symptoms of accomodation in some regions of the world revolutionary movement. Many errors could be ascribed, on the other hand, to the communists in the era of the Third International, and even in the USSR this period has by now been harshly criticized; but what we can't be accused of is having fallen into divisiveness on the international level, having lost revolutionary vigilance before the enemy, having wavered in the face of difficulties or having renounced the proletarian viewpoint as to the revolution and the world. Comrade Lenin himself considered all these things to be the eyesight of communism, that is, as the questions we should take care of the same way we take care of our own eyesight. They'll tell me I'm sectarian and old-fashioned, but I say that one of the biggest sicknesses of the world communist and revolutionary movement is its weakening centralist concept that today eats away at the ranks of the world proletariat. Nationalist concepts have taken some proletarian countries prisoner, and some parties aspire to make the interests of particular regions or groups prevail. All this is the direct result of the influence of bourgeois or petty-bourgeois ideas in our vanguard detachments. And this, in spite of the fact that

471

imperialism itself could give us a few lessons in how the unification of thought at the level of international leadership should be pursued at all costs, as the battle gets bigger and bigger. Of course, I'm not sucking on my thumb, either, I'm not a baby at the breast and my ignorance about things isn't so great that I don't know times change. I know that the excesses of bureaucratic centralism led comrade Stalin and the USSR into grave violations of socialist legality, into historical errors of a seriousness that is still incalculable. Many, many exemplary communists suffered bodily for all of that, and paid for it with their blood, and it's not something to poke fun at, to dismiss with a joke or blow hot air about. I also understand that the independence of parties grows as each one develops, and that today international problems are too complicated for the idea of the Communist International to be maintained just exactly like it was conceived in 1930. Many things had to change in the international communist movement as time went on, even if you just think of the mess that comrade Stalin's deviation left us in. But, I don't know why, sometimes it seems to me like we're going too far the other way. And that's because, in my opinion – and I'm no genius but I've got a forehead a few fingers wide, just like everyone else – there has never been an exclusively pro-letarian critique of Stalinism. Even the critique that comrade Khrushchev made seems to me personally to be inadequate in a whole lot of aspects: it complied with the requirements of a political critique necessary, above all, to liberate a series of internal social and political forces in the Soviet Union, as several comrades I've spoken with here in Prague have said, but almost everyone is in agreement that it would have been good to have gone deeper into it. No serious and sincere communist was going to be able to throw off dozens of years of his life, his way of thinking, like someone who takes off a shirt that got dirty at work and has to be washed. And what's been left in the air, what's gone around in our countries especially – and this isn't the fault of comrade Khrushchev or the Soviet comrades, but of all the communists of the world – is a petty bourgeois critique of Stalinism, though some may not like to hear it. The critique of

472

Stalinism has been forsaken as something for writers and artists, for university types, for professors. And this doesn't serve the revolution, which has never gotten anywhere by feeding itself on legends, either positive or negative. Just as the revolution isn't served either by continuing the exaggerated veneration of comrade Stalin, as if nothing ever happened at all, which is what is done at present on this subject by some sectors influenced by the Chinese comrades. And this has brought on a series of more and more fucked-up results. Because with petty bourgeois positions, what happens is you never know where they're going to stop. When they begin to develop, they take off on flights of fancy that never hit the mark. As a result of all this, what has suffered most, in my opinion, and I don't think I'm too wrong, is the general principle of criticism and self-criticism at the level of the party and parties, and without that principle it's better just to go bury yourself once and for all. There are many examples of this abnormal, unhealthy situation. As one case, the principle of "non-intervention" in the internal affairs of fraternal parties is exaggerated. And for lack of this mutual criticism, the differences grow uncontrollably and when they become publicly known, it's because there's already a split and then you aren't talking about mutual criticism, but mutual attack. Independent of who's right or wrong or who threw the first stone (and in this sense I maintain the position of my party, which has severely criticized, on repeated occasions, the Chinese positions). As a communist, what's happening between the USSR and China hurts me. It's come to that point, and there's no guarantee that it's the last example we'll see of this sort of situation. If mutual criticism had been carried out correctly, possibly it wouldn't have gone so far. But the fear that they'll say we're fighting amongst one another makes us end up shooting it out. That stuff about one communist party not being able to deeply criticize another is to me a notion for associations of nice little Catholic girls. Some say that this is best because if the bigger parties start criticizing left and right, the ones that are going to wind up losing will be the small parties. Who knows? Even accepting that this danger may exist, I think that in the face

473

of the problems of international revolution, there are no little opinions or big opinions, only just or correct opinions and unjust, incorrect opinions. There are parties that have more means than others to spread those opinions and make them more effective, but sooner or later the truth wins out. We shouldn't lost sight of the constructive role of criticism. A communist organization is built and developed on the basis of criticism, or it is built and developed badly, or it simply doesn't develop. And parties are like men, who are born, learn to walk, grow and develop, and become independent. A consistent criticism should know how to tell the difference between the cases of a party that's still nursing, an adolescent party, a party that can leave the protection of its parents and make its own home, get married and be an independent man. But in the same way that no one would be so criminal as to let a child who was barely nine months old go out into the street alone, because it'd be run over by the cars, neither should the international communist movement permit itself the luxury of abandoning, of not criticizing, newly born parties, who are still sucking their thumbs, like some around. And the worst thing is this has nothing to do with the physical age of the party, because there are some that, unfortunately, are more than thirty or forty years old, but ideologically and organizationally are still crawling on all fours and shitting in diapers. Mutual criticism at the international level between communist parties must be reestablished. It is an urgent necessity for reestablishing international proletarian discipline. And of course, these critiques should be made at the appropriate moment, in a fitting manner, and through appropriate channels: it's not a question of opening up the channel of common criticism for the pleasure of the enemy. Criticism between parties isn't a topic that should be necessarily printed, not even in the communist press. But this practice has got to be revived, in the most urgent way. Among other measures, this would avoid the continuing generation of the splits that so badly afflict us in the present world panorama. Or that mutual criticism should only be a problem just for the occasion of each congress of communist parties. Imperialism is

474

leveling serious blows at us and it seems like we're staying just as calm as you please. We continue to renounce, for the most part, the tool of criticism and self-criticism, which is the same thing as renouncing the great historical experience of world communism from Marx to our own day. I remember, myself, that my old comrades were really hard in their criticism. They even made me cry on more than one occasion. But one thing was law: the comrades who were toughest in their criticism and self-criticism were the ones most zealous for the cause; the comrades who bore up best under adverse criticism and got the best experiences out of it were the comrades most loyal to our cause. And we all advanced together, not at the rhythm of the slowest, but of the fastest, even with our weaknesses. This should function again, on the party level, with all the modifications that have to be made, in accordance with the changes of the times, and in the face of the enemy's maneuvers. You ask who am I to talk this way, like I'm giving a lesson to the whole world? Well, simply and humbly, one old communist among millions of communists, who's risked his skin, and not just once, for the revolution, for the communist movement, and who's not talking at the moment for philosophers, for deep intellectuals, but only and exclusively for everyday revolutionaries, plain and simple. No one in particular owns the international communist movement, just as no one, in particular, owns Marxism. And communist ideas aren't a vine of pretty roses, or a box of bottles of delicate perfumes, or a cage of foreign birds that need spoiling and pampering. On the contrary, communist ideas are born and grow within hard social struggle, and they can only, exclusively, live in constant struggle. If this isn't dialectics, I must be on the moon someplace. I think that moment is past when to be a conscious communist you had to hang on to the idea that we are perfect, that everything on the field of revolution is just rosy, that there aren't any problems of any sort amongst us and that all the shit is on the enemy's side. Thinking that way serves nothing. Because then you don't understand anything when things go wrong, when you come smack up against the hard reality. And above all, it doesn't serve anything in countries where things seem to be as black as night, and that's the case in El Salvador and in the vast majority of countries in Latin America. From going around just making poems about socialism, our parties have had difficulty in truly joining, as parts of the same flesh, with the great masses of our peoples. Us, off to one side, with our speeches about the future, and the people all around, thinking about other things. I don't doubt it's important that the people know how in one workers' state the Five-Year Plan was met by 200%, but the most important thing is that they know how to organize themselves in their own country, and why, and for what. And we have to begin with what we have at hand, not to have excessive illusions about the level of revolutionary consciousness of our popular strata. The level in El Salvador is relatively good, despite everything, but don't imagine, for example, that Marx is more popular or respected than Our Lady of Perpetual Help. It shouldn't be forgotten, because of bourgeois nationalist prejudices, that the average Salvadoran is an individualist, firmly tied to the principle of small personal property – even though he may only have a doghouse and a stool – fucked-up and weighed down from all the inferiority complexes that hammer our brains and fill our heads with stuff about being "real machos" and useless fits of anger. We have to accept that the primary field for the ideological struggle of a party is the hearts and minds of its countrymen, but just as they are, not as the books say they are. The enemy knows this perfectly well, and that's why it works so hard in the University, the schools, the churches, in the official, cowardly unions, the newspapers, television, books, the radio, in religious processions, in sporting events that are used as a means to distract people from real problems, like a party or a spectacle scheduled to take place at the same time as the large political actions that need the attendance of the people; in judicial proceedings against militant revolutionaries, in speeches, the Peace Corps, foreign missionaries, the "paquines," etc. This battle, naturally, can only be fought to advantage from a position of power. Today, the enemy fights this battle with the advantage. Our burden is that we have to fight from a disadvantage, with the

476

goal of getting closer and closer to gaining power, to seizing power. The question that comes to mind, like it's come up for me at various times in my life as a militant, is: isn't it time to be thinking about changing our methods for making ties with the people? Let's not forget that by now imperialism and the Latin American oligarchies have learned by heart the lessons of getting burned by the Cuban Revolution. They won't be fooled again. But in the case of our country, the matter is complicated and the question of methods of struggle has to be sweated over: participation in the elections, for example, hasn't gotten us one meter closer to power up to this point, and our work in petty bourgeois and bourgeois organizations has generally ended up bringing our grist to the mill of the ones we least expected. The aspect of martyrdom, that is, or martyrdom alone, is no argument for our permanently martyred masses. We have right on our side, but we don't have the necessary popular backing. Independent of the apparatus of force and repression of the ruling classes of El Salvador, which is well concentrated, independent of the means imperialism uses to exploit us, what are our greatest weaknesses that allow this situation to still exist? What's been the matter with us, and keeps on being the matter? Why is it that the Cubans, on the contrary, had such success and keep on having it? I'm not just talking about the problem of armed struggle versus mass struggle. It's more complicated than that. But despite the time that's gone by, we communists should be thinking much more about the fact that in Latin America, the first socialist revolution has been carried out by revolutionaries who weren't communists, at least during the struggle that brought them to power, and that it has been brought to the socialist stage by a party or an organization that wasn't like other Latin American communist parties. Could what the young people are saying be true, that we "traditional communists" aren't any good for taking power? Those who say this add that a "traditional party" has never been able to take power, since even Lenin's Russian party stopped being a traditional social-democratic party when it based itself on a peasant-worker alliance in order to lead the victorious insur-

477

rection and make socialism in a backward country. And I repeat, I don't think it's all a matter of involving the Party in armed struggle, or dissolving the Party into guerrillas, or in doing political work solely with an eye on the insurrection. Of course, for myself I feel I'm much too old to go running around again agitating for an insurrection, much less as a guerrilla in the mountains. I know personally that I'm no good anymore for taking power. But, aren't there enough young communists in this country? I've already said that there are. What happens is that national conditions in El Salvador are very narrow, and they contribute slow development. In this sense, I think the viewpoints of some young comrades in El Salvador, who propose an anti-imperialist and anti-oligarchic struggle on the Central American level, are very interesting. It's true that we have a regional organism, which is the Conference of Communist Parties of Central America and Mexico, but up to now its activities have been purely formal and a little strained, an exchange of information between representatives once a year or maybe when San Juan beckons. Our Central Americanist tradition is a fact, and although the bourgeoisies and the gringos have always stirred up divisions, the truth is we're one sole nation, cut into five pieces by exploitative interests. In my heart, for example, I don't feel any difference between Guatemala and El Salvador. I fought in both countries as if they were one. Maybe that's the way out, who knows. Especially now when in Guatemala and Nicaragua, things are about to burn up. This is the task of youth, about that I don't have the least doubt. And if by one means or another our youth take political power in any Central American country, I wouldn't stand by without doing my part, no way. Even if now I maybe can't shoot or get into machete fights with the police. What I could give is my experience, in the struggle and after the struggle. Not to lead those who are really out there battling, but so they'll have points of comparison with the past and won't commit the tremendous errors that we committed. In Cuba there are old communists who've been able to do that, above all because no one could deny they'd lived a life truly dedicated to the revolutionary

478

struggle, that it wasn't just a matter of a pretty new face, of opportunists who would have tried to get on the winner's bandwagon once the first hard hours were over. So you shouldn't start in crying because you can't grab a rifle and go running around the mountains anymore. The ones who should scream are those who can and ought to do it, but stay behind like lazy cows watching the train go by. And what I'm saying about the "struggle with rifle in hand" is true for legal struggle. There is no revolutionary political work unworthy of a communist, even it it's sweeping and mopping the place where the cell is going to meet. Now, let's go back to what we were talking about. There's no need to fool ourselves, the isolated communist doesn't exist. The work of a communist is done within a party. We can't deal with all these problems individually, but on the contrary, as party problems. And if that causes us to make changes in the party, we shouldn't be afraid to do so. Within the Leninist concept of a party, there is much room for adapting to each national reality, to changes, etc. But almost everyone talks about transforming the party, and the practical steps that get taken are few. What we do have to avoid is having the transformations of the Party of the proletariat be made with the idea of pleasing the bourgeoisie or the petty bourgeoisie, who always find a way to get themselves into our ranks and, right from the start, babble to us with their endless empty words. That's to say, I'm not talking about a revisionist transformation of the party. It's a matter of a hard and difficult task, developed under the direct action of the enemy, which brings us back to our lack of preparation, our ideological inadequacies, our great backwardness. What happens is that sometimes we Latin American communist leaders are communists with influential opinions just because we're leaders, not because we're real Marxists. There are those of us Latin American communists who aren't Marxists in the strict sense of the word. Which isn't something to be ashamed of, perhaps just the opposite, in terms of the role we have played, are playing and will play in our history. We adhere to Marxism, we accept the political line of the Party, we embody the line of the international communist

479

movement (and because of all these things, we're capable of giving our lives, dying of laughter), but we don't have the adequate theoretical preparation. Many times we call common sense or simple acuteness for solving a problem Marxism. And because of this, we get so messed up when we face problems that should first be resolved in the head, like this one I've been talking about, the one about possible transformations in our parties in order to deal with today's times. I know they can tell me: "But, comrade, then we workers are going to be fucked-up forever, because according to what you're saying, only theoreticians are Marxists and then the Party is going to be a problem for the intellectuals." That's not the way it is, clearly. Marxism-Lenism is the union of theory and practice. But it's not too much for us to recognize that we're missing the theoretical part, and that it's a problem the workers should claim as theirs, because theirs too is the communist party. Let's take my case, so as not to go too far astray. Why do I say I'm a Marxist? Because with the few fundamental truths of Marxism-Leninism in my head, I do political work as a cadre of a party that tries to base its action and its political line on the principles of Marxism-Leninism. My party is my great bond with Marxism-Leninism, and if my party deviates from those principles, I'm left hanging, because my personal knowledge of Marxism is very general and it doesn't cover all the aspects of life and the world that concern me. Of course, there are some aspects of life and the world that I do know. Of course, there are some aspects I know better than others. For example, the problems referring to the organization of an urban and rural union movement. But I haven't read *Capital,* except in summaries circulating out there. I haven't read even 20% of what Lenin wrote. I don't know much about world history. Naturally, you have to figure that forty-odd years of experience in revolutionary organizational practice have left a lot of things in my head. But I know that's not enough. I understood that as clear as day a few years ago, when my party sent me to take a course in revolutionary union leadership training. That is to say: I'm a Marxist-Leninist who knows he's not familiar with most of Marxism-Leninism, and who's got inside his head many problems that the comrades say don't fit in with Marxism-Leninism, many approaches and viewpoints that the comrades say are incredible in a communist of my age, like for example certain apparent superstitions, bad habits that seem to be religious, etc. I think that in this case in particular, however, we're talking about another sort of problem. I don't believe in God or the saints or the devil or in the Cadejo[1] or the Ciguanaba, but like the Salvadoran I am, I've got them on the tip of my tongue, and every now and then they come out of me. I don't think this is so important. In El Salvador, one says, "Holy Virgin Mary" just to joke around, just like you say "What a lot of crap," or "Shove it," or "I'm getting my ass out of here." It doesn't have anything to do with your ideology. And as far as the things one can call supernatural, I already gave my opinion on that subject. Practice is the mother of truth, and I only talk about what I saw, about what happened to me, about what this witness had as proof to his eyes and ears, as they say in the legal courts. If someone thinks this is magic or supersition, what we've got to do is make the revolution, and afterwards we can talk about it. And this hasn't got much to do with my case being one of a worker, of a laborer. Everyone knows intellectual shining lights who are more conservative than a holy woman, more superstitious than a sorcerer. We workers are the ones who need most to be clear about Marxism. So we won't have to depend on anyone else, so we won't have to sit around waiting for some petty bourgeois to come and teach us how to fight and liberate ourselves. When the petty bourgeoisie becomes proletarianized, Merry Christmas. But then he's not a petty bourgeois because he's now one of us, a proletarian. But as long as he's still a petty bourgeois, his struggle at our side will be the struggle of a good person, of an honorable man, of a friend, with a heart or with balls. And good people change, honorable men can become corrupt, friends trick you or betray you, heart and balls dry up with time. The only thing that lasts is the suffering of the exploited. And in the petty bourgeois who is proletarianized, that suffering is called discipline. Until exploitation is ended. The exploited man doesn't take part in

481

the revolution for pleasure or from morality, but rather from material necessity. That's why it's better that we workers be the ones who drink directly from the waters of Marxist theory, although it costs us double the effort and time. Without scorning contributions from the outside, since comrade Lenin himself praised them so much.

And this is where I end up my speech, before I start looking like some doctor or priest. The only thing left is to apologize for the awkwardness of my sentences and for how rustic my expressions are. These are illnesses I just can't be cured of, they're chronic, and I think that even if I die of other pains, I'm going to take them along to my grave too – lock, stock and barrel. Also, to end this precisely, I'd like to state a few things. I'd like to state, for example, that in this whole long life of mine that I've portrayed, my best memories are of the moments that followed the imminent danger of death, those moments when you realize you've been reborn. And after that, the trips, the trip to the USSR in 1930 for example. And I'd also like to state that among all the things I've done in my life, the one that makes me the proudest, the one I consider to be a privilege, the greatest of my life, was to have fought shoulder to shoulder with comrades like Agustín Farabundo Martí, the man who is the symbol of communism in El Salvador. On my deathbed, which won't necessarily be a sickbed, my best thoughts will be of Martí and of so many other comrades who fell on the road to liberation. But I don't only want to declare my pride and my revolutionary affections. I don't think it's impolite, or bad manners, that at this closing moment I also talk about my hatreds. My great hatred in life goes to Yankee imperialism and to those who represent it in El Salvador, the Creole oligarchs who have massacred and exploited us. And just as the type of virtue I esteem most is the solidarity of men in the face of adversity, the type of individual men I most detest are the opportunists within our ranks. I hate them more than declared traitors, because with traitors at least you know what you're up against, and side by side, maybe I hate them more than the class enemy, since the latter exist through the law of society. I don't have personal enemies, only political enemies. Of course, everyone has their aversions, people that rub you the wrong way, and it's also true of me that, like the Mexican song goes, "I'm not as good as gold/ for getting everyone to like me," but these are the little unimportant things in life that are forgotten in daily activity. What really is true is that the great love of my life was my children. Of my sweet little kids, the only ones who survive are Hilda Alicia (who they call Angelita, as her grand-mother wished) and my recent crop of boys: Miguelito, two years and seven months old, and the other one whose name I still don't know, because he was born today while I'm out of the country, attending the XXIII Congress of the CPSU. I was able to bury María Elena myself, but not Oscar or Francisquito, who died while I was on the run, underground. Antonita died too, when she was five, and I was also away. And Berta Lilliam, who died in '54 and left me a grandson. I was in Guatemala and couldn't say goodbye to her. I don't like talking about these things, because I get all tearful and a crying old man isn't a pretty sight. I accept that getting older is hard for me to take, because within the very difficult circumstances of my life I tried to take good care of myself, so my health and energy could go to the Revolution. Now that's good advice for young people. The life of a revolutionary is a life of constant struggle that doesn't agree with an undisciplined life: the life of a true revolutionary is a life of moderation in every sense. I always tried to keep it that way: I kept out of bars and tried not to go crazy over women. It's necessary to take care of the body and state of mind in this way, because the political struggle requires tough, sharpened nerves, year after year. I was able to keep my vigor, and even now that I'm old I'm still a man in every sense of the word, though, of course, since I turned fifty I've been taking Testiton pills to fortify myself, pills that are a pure mixture of cock and bull and costs fifty cents. The fatigue I've talked about earlier is of another kind, it's sort of like feeling all your past life suddenly come down on you like a landslide, on your head, shoulders and heart. But this fatigue doesn't make me lose sight of my revolutionary responsibilities, or slack off in the struggle to see realized my most fervent desire: socialist revolution in El Salvador. This is a desire I know will be met sooner or later in all the countries of the world. But what I want is to see socialism among us. Seeing it function for just a week would be enough for me. And on Sunday night, let's say, then I could die happy.

Prague, Summer of 1966.

---

[1] The *Cadejo* is a monster, a hideous creature, that roams the streets as night.

APPENDIX

Letters of Miguel Mármol

LETTER DECLARING A HUNGER STRIKE SENT TO THE GENERAL DIRECTOR OF THE NATIONAL POLICE, COLONEL JUAN FRANCISCO MERINO ROSALES.

General Director of the National Police,
Colonel don Juan Francisco Merino Rosales.

Mr. Director:

In view of the fact that I have not received notification in almost one year of being shut up in seclusion;

Considering that it is arbitrary, according to the tenets of our Political Constitution, not to allow me to be seen at the Honorable Supreme Court of Justice nor to speak with the Minister of Government, General Tomás Calderón;

Considering any possible participation of mine in the bourgeois-democratic revolution of 1932 to have been cancelled upon having executed me on the night of January 26 of that same year in the jurisdiction of Villa de Soyapango, if it is to that matter that my detention is attributable; in view of my continuance, from the first day in shackles, strictly incommunicado, with food insufficient in both quantity and quality, and lacking indispensible and necessary hygiene (characteristics of a semifeudal prison only appropriate for our hardened underclass!); of not having improved my rations even though I have requested it numerous times of the General Inspector of Police, Major Francisco Marroquín, rations which four times have almost killed me with stomach pains, something I can corroborate with the personnel of this same section of the

485

police; in view of what has been stated, Mr. Director, from today–November 12–I declare myself to be on a hunger strike to demand freedom for myself and other comrades arrested since August 20 and at the end of 1934, a strike I will not give up until I and the other comrades are freed. I hope, Mr. Director, that calm and conscientious reflection will not let happen another stain on our blackened political history.

I remain yours most truly,

Miguel Mármol

Official Quarters, Section for Special Investigations, National Police, San Salvador, November 12, 1935.

FAREWELL LETTER OF MIGUEL MARMOL TO THE AUTHOR AFTER ENDING THE SERIES OF INTERVIEWS AND WORK SESSIONS WHICH SERVED AS THE BASIS FOR THE AUTOBIOGRAPHICAL ACCOUNT.

Prague, June 10, 1966.

Roque:

I return home satisfied that you've taken many notes on passages in my life, and sure that those passages won't be lost.

I think we left clear what kind of work you will carry out; that it has to do exclusively with my memoirs. But clearly, since I'm a part of the people, of the working class and of my Party, like it or not, my declarations will have to go further and concern my Party itself.

The object is–as we agreed–to emphasize from my life and actions all the positive things that we can contribute and instruct. And, where it's appropriate, the role we workers play as a class, not as artisans. To reveal the virtues of my Party instead of undermining it with unjust and biting criticism. To enlarge the revolutionary periods lived in the country since 1914, that is, from the First World War until now, for which my people and my Party have fought great battles.

To point out–at the same time–as much the errors and weaknesses of the people, as of the working class and my Party, not to disdain or belittle them, but rather to educate through lived experiences, and with all this, to leave a trail for future researchers.

In all the narration there is no self-criticism of mine, not because I'm infallible or because I don't intend to, but because until now I haven't been able to unravel head nor tail of my weaknesses and errors, but I'll leave the verdict up to the critics and researchers who change around and order everything.

The abundance of details that are an abridgment of lived experiences, I don't think are to be inserted into a document that is supposed to be rather serious and precise. They should only serve–in my opinion–for extensive and minute research, analysis and criticism, since they all relate facts from one whole process and aid in making judgments and deductions.

The fact that on some occasions my name may resonate through this, I think is a funny thing since physically I'm of short height and a whole lot shorter intellectually. This sometime arrogance, without being educated, without being an academic, shouldn't be wrongly interpreted. To my disadvantage, I didn't have an education, no cultural discipline at all. Coming out of poverty and tied up with the battles of an absorbing and unlucky struggle from an early age, I had no time to better myself in any of the classrooms of learning. My privilege has been to have common sense, developed much more with the difficulties of the struggle.

For the formation of the comrades who come to the struggle only with pure desire, only with a burning heart and a soul on fire, but lacking education and culture, perhaps it would be useful to point out my social background and my native soil, with its customs and its ways: to talk about my education at home, my inclinations as a child, my character, emotions and determination. What were my youthful concerns, my preoccupation with economic, social and political problems before I even began to shave. My perseverance; challenging of death, indifference to life and happiness; when it's necessary to be firm, when you mustn't vacillate. To organize the fight even in the midst of defeat. Not to lose perspective, even when the adversary dominates the situation nor even when terror reigns.

This is all I can think of saying right now.

Roque: I will make every effort to send you everything I think useful and necessary. And to you I express my hopes that this will turn into a good work, and it won't take too long to come out.

So, get well soon; much success and happiness.

Miguel Mármol.

LETTER FROM MIGUEL MARMOL TO THE AUTHOR FROM MEXICO.

México, D.F., July 20, 1966.

Dear Roque·

I've written to you from the three places I've stopped in; but according to Toño, those three letters hadn't arrived by the time he left home. I wrote to you in a hurry precisely so that my experieces could be known.

I write again to inform you that very soon I'll be leaving here. So many delays and red tape, because of the carelessness of N . . .

I want to tell you and your wife that I've had another boy. I don't know what his name is, I've only heard about it second-hand since they haven't written to me. I'm anxious to see him.

I have some other notes that will get into your hands when someone comes through here. They are details that I didn't give you entirely about my ancestors and other close relatives, which I think would be good to deliver somehow, because, in addition, I make some slight interpretation of their characters.

Dear Roque, something that always bothers me is the ME that I've been criticized for at other times. I believe that the ME is most relative in most of the cases; not totally absolute. The ME lends itself to various interpretations and various uses; arbitrary use and reasonable use, for example. When it's arbitrary, just mere ego, the ME in some cases is rigidly individualistic; that's why there are selfish, self-adoring men. Because of that, there's the "I command." "I order." "It's my business," etc. But there's the ME which is the expression of the subjective and objective things that make collective action imperative; to act unified. My anxieties, eager desires, tenacity and resignation in being able to combat social wrongs for the collective good is the virtue of thousands and millions of souls who engage themselves in the same action without considering their personal self, without thinking that it is strictly their work, but rather that they participate in something that is the work of many others. The relative, reasonable ME is directed and stimulated by what others have done and continue to do; by what others have

489

written and continue to write. There is, then, the ME conditioned to collective action. Because of this, the true revolutionary is fragile and consistent, sensitive and strong, hard and intransigent under icy conditions. The revolutionary makes the Revolution his, and the Revolution is his, but in the part which his self contributes. This reasoning of mine perhaps may contribute to the focus of my account, since in the struggle I was just one more example whose ME has been vehement, passionate.

I hope you'll write me. You can do it through my friend, so she can pass on to me any correspondence. I don't know if M. gave you my last letter in which I left a series of opinions for your consideration.

I continue to think that with your committed, earnest effort, a good document has to result. I will try, like I said, to give names and dates so the account will be more legitimate. Although if this becomes difficult, I really think that what I have said will be valid, it will be a source of research in any case. Regards to my friends, and I hope you, your wife and kids are happy. Greetings too for JM and the others.

I say goodbye once again with all my affection, yours very fondly,

Miguel Mármol

INTERVIEW

WITH MIGUEL MARMOL, OCTOBER 1986

What follows is an excerpt from an interview with Miguel Mármol, conducted in Spanish by the translators in October, 1986, and faithfully transcribed by Marcia Lifshitz.

To the following people, whose material support helped make our visit with Mármol possible, we owe a deep debt of gratitude: Denise Abercrombie, Fred Arcoles, John Carey, William Chafe, Judy Doyle, Margaret Gibson, Roberta Lichtman, David McKain, New Left Review, Mel Rosenthal, Jeff Schlanger, Alexander Taylor, Faith Wilding, Pamela Vossenas.

How did the idea for the book come about? What was your meeting with Roque like in Prague?

We hit it off right from the start – talking and talking and talking. He proposed an interview with me. He told me he'd like to hear about the events of '32 so he could write some poetry. Gladly, I said.

But concerning the matter of talking: I don't stop when I start talking. Roque was also a hyper type of man, a person who wrote things down very, very quickly. He told me that it would be better to write a book: "Let's write a book, let's talk longer." But in order to do this it would be necessary for me to spend more time in Prague. Therefore, he said, let's propose this idea to the Party. The Party agreed that I stay the necessary time to write

491

the book. Therefore, we had the luxury of talking for a long time, with him writing everything down.

He was a congenial type of person. When I speak of him, people don't understand, foreigners less. He was a happy man, not depressed. He was the kind of man who likes to read everything. Like an inquisitive little child, who, when he gets a doll, wants to know how it was made.

Therefore, we talked. Things were very friendly, congenial. That's how things were in Prague – very happy, dancing, those kinds of things. We were always with a beer, a delicious beer. We spent a long time talking in the cafés. He was enchanting. We argued about certain things, but not everything. So we spent two weeks like that. Two weeks was short, but we worked long hours. We talked for many hours, we spent whole nights talking. To facilitate those talks, Roque took me on long walks to the beautiful places in Prague. Afterwards, we'd return and lock ourselves in and write.

He was a representative for the international magazine of my Party, published in Prague. Therefore, he introduced me to many comrades from Latin America and the Soviet Union. We were very focused in our work, because the idea was that I wouldn't leave Prague until we had gone over everything, until the book could be written.

I believe it has made one of the most important contributions to understanding the events of the '32 revolution. The book received a lot of interest. It continues to get a lot of interest. In Cuba it has appeared in 22 editions. It is published in the Soviet Union, in Costa Rica, in Mexico. I think it's a publication that has been useful in illuminating El Salvador's past.

About Roque: he was a very anxious man. A man who argued a lot. He had his conceptions of the past and I had mine. Roque was an intellectual of petty bourgeois origin. An intellectual comrade is always more radical and extreme than a worker. Because of his theoretical understanding of things, his knowledge, he is always more radical than a worker. I am less radical, because of my experience, because of getting my hands burned. More than anything I am a Leninist. I believe you can't make a revolution without convincing the masses, without mass struggle. We had this in '32. The masses have to be politically conscious, they have to participate in the struggle, to overcome or die. 1932 was a mass movement. I am a Leninist. You have to go to the masses, raise their consciousness, orient them for the struggle, so that they take up their own flag. The Indians of El Salvador fought under the flag of Anastasio Aquino, and later under the flag of Farabundo Martí. The first thing you have to do, I've always thought, is raise political consciousness. This is the most important thing.

Why do you think it is important that the book be translated into English, that it come out in the U.S. and England?

For me it's very important, it's very valuable. So that they know about us, so that they understand about what is going on today, about the struggles of the Salvadoran revolution. And above all, for the working class which is suffering under international capitalism, for the cause of proletarian internationalism.

This revolution is going to triumph. There will be justice in our society. Above all, we don't want the imperialists and we are going to get rid of them. We lost in '32 because we had to lose. This is what history is like. Everything has been exploited – the cotton, coffee, sugar, fishing. We don't have more. Here, the only solution is a radical change, a revolutionary change.

What are the new sectors that read your book for the first time going to learn?

The importance of the message of '32 for people of different languages is to understand the causes of the situation in our country, and to create a reason and the will to struggle – I think the book will contribute to that.

Imperialism will never understand the will of the Salvadoran people. Never. Because the Salvadoran people are politically conscious. They know a lot. The Central American people are

493

political firstly because of their economic condition, and secondly because they work and live together in small communities. We, in El Salvador, have broken with provincialism. There is a class consciousness in El Salvador that is tremendous. This they can never dominate. Never. Unless they throw atomic bombs and end everything. But then they would lose all their interests. They would lose.

In El Salvador the people know who are the 14 richest families in the country. They know who are the biggest thieves. They know the outstanding ones. They know who the progressive democrats are, and who are the authentic revolutionaries. The people know everything; because of these conditions the people are more political, they understand better.

In El Salvador the children are political. General Romero, who was cruel, followed the dictates of the North Americans. Therefore, when this man appeared on the TV screen, the children smashed the TV sets. They demonstrated in large numbers. 10- and 11-year-old children are fighting today. The child knows that the rich live nearby, and that the rich child gets expensive presents for Christmas, and the child sees what his parents have. The child goes to his father and tells him these things.

The most important thing about the book is it shows something of the Salvadoran spirit – is that it?

The Catholic mother prays because her husband loses his job. The child sees these things. The child comes into the world and sees the difficulties of getting food, of life. Because of this, in El Salvador or Latin America, the 12-year-old boy or girl is already a man or woman of responsibility. The oldest girl in a peasant household is very responsible: she makes dinner and takes care of the house while her mother is out getting things that the family needs and the father is working. A child of 12 has a sense of responsiblity.

494

Miguel Mármol too was once 12 years old. At 11, I was a fisherman. At 12, I was a man with a machete, not afraid of anyone. This is characteristic of children in Latin America and in my country. The children think like adults, and when they look at their mothers and fathers – in El Salvador, there are many 12-year-old children who are orphaned – they say, how am I going to stand by and watch as they kill my parents, and they take up arms and go into the struggle. It isn't hard to understand why youngsters are fighting. It is a tremendous question – the spirit of the people.

What about the role of women in the struggle? Did women play a different role in '32 than they do today?

Yes, the role of women was very different. From the '30s up to now, there has been a high level of social, political and economic development. The riches of the country are now greater. Technology and science have prospered in El Salvador. There has been much material development. Highways, for example, have been built. Above all, agriculture, which dominates the Salvadoran economy, has changed. Industry and commerce have also developed, as well as international relations. Therefore, the revolution today has a more highly developed infrastructure than it had in '32.

However, the revolution today doesn't have the preparation it had in '32. In '32 all the masses were organized. The masses had an ideological, social and political scholarship that doesn't exist today. Today, they are doing it without the level of union organization that existed in '32. The proletariat is also larger today. The social exigencies are greater now than in '32.

The current Salvadoran revolution was initiated by several forces. Each group had its own strategy and its own political analysis. The Communist Party was involved in electoral politics. They tried to use this avenue to raise the consciousness of the masses, of the people. Since the revolution was imminent and the people wanted it, the Party summed up its work and changed its strategy. The revolutionary situation is dialectical.

Five groups joined together and, in a non-sectarian way, formed the FMLN.

But unity isn't easy. For there to be unity we must separate out the different ideological questions and deal with these differences. If we don't, things become very grave. Unfortunately, this history is perhaps one in which ideological resistance has not been overcome. They can't overcome all the ideological differences at once. To attempt to do so wouldn't get us anywhere. We are in a war situation. But along the way the differences kept cropping up. Each group maintained its military and political scheme or thesis, each one continued fighting. There wasn't unity in the mass organizations in the '70s. On the one hand, for example, there was the BPR, and on the other, the FAPU. There wasn't unity between the large mass groups. This fact prevented a unified push by the masses. The armed forces banded together in the struggle without the unified backing of the masses.

Today, the masses are coming forward more united. The workers are uniting. The peasants and workers from all the branches – the telephone workers, the bus drivers – all of them are struggling. All the forces are uniting into an organization called the National Salvadoran Workers Union. They are going to Duarte, taking to the streets, organizing demonstrations demanding a solution to the conflict. What is happening is valuable. But with one push this unity could fall apart, because the basic ideological differences have not been overcome. The unity is tenuous. But this unity is, in fact, popularly based. It's a beautiful thing that is coming.

There is hunger, there is misery and imperialism, but socialism is going to win out over these forces. We are preparing for this. We have to prepare and create the new man, the new person. Hunger and economic difficulties are coming. We must prepare for them. We have to survive and be strong. These problems existed in Nicaragua, in Cuba. We cannot despair, we must face these problems.

And the role of women?

496

Ah, yes, of course. Everywhere I go I am asked two questions. How have Catholics participated in the revolution? And how have women participated?

About 90% of the Salvadoran population is Catholic. Of this 90%, the strongest are the women – on the farms, in the factories, in businesses. The women participate with the same fiery spirit as the men. Many women are even braver in the struggle than the men. There are young women who have distinguished themselves. And they will not back down for anything, they would rather die. This is a religious phenomenon, since there are so many people who are religious and the strongest are the women.

Because the masses are exploited and poor, the truth is that women are seen as inferior, they suffer more injuries, and therefore they are politically conscious. They're involved in the revolutionary forces, in the unions, in everything. The religious guerrilla is perceived as one who is beautiful, with a faith in God, and with the anger of her class. Women are conscious, they are conscious.

But in the struggle of '32, did women participate as much?

Of course, of course they did! In the economic struggle, in the unions, in the coffee unions, in the sugar cane unions. They were unionized and brave in their participation. It is a fact that women participated heavily and were strong. How? By taking care of their children, giving them affection. The men didn't have to worry, because women were taking care of the home. The second way was that the women knew where the men were, and they prepared and left food for the men who were fighting or fleeing repression. It was a brave role. Today, there are many campañeras, leaders in military and political roles. It is fantastic. The struggle is contagious.

And did the women in '32 carry arms?

497

In those days, there were few outstanding women in the revolution who carried arms. Among them, I remember, there was compañera Julia Mujica. Julia was a seamstress. She was rather ladina, rather fair. Her family was poor, they were workers. All of her family entered the struggle united with the Indians. The woman was a leader. At the time of the insurrection, some of her brothers were taken prisoner. Julia's house was machine-gunned, her father shot in his house. Manuel, her brother, was taken out of jail and shot by the army in front of his house, in front of his family, and Julia fought back. Julia calling out to her compañeros to fight! At the time, we called Julia the Joan of Arc of El Salvador. We called her that because she was brave, faithful. She was always persecuted, she was a prisoner for a long time. She was a great woman. There was an Indian woman like her, but I don't remember her name. She was combative and had political consciousness. And there were many others who prepared for the battle and participated with the masses, but they didn't fight with arms.

The collaboration of women in '32 was not with arms in hand. It was by supporting the men, by helping out, collaborating in other ways. And then, taking care of their children, taking care of their homes.

You end your testimony in the book with your political activity in Guatemala in 1954, before the fall of Arbenz. Can you now briefly go into your political activities for the last 30 years?

In the '60s I was general secretary of the National Peasant Commission. I had all the rural organizations under my jurisdiction. I dedicated myself with passion to this responsibility.

I dedicated myself to the peasant question. In the '50s I was semi-clandestine, after I returned from Guatemala. The repression was tremendous, but you have to keep working. Therefore, I did a lot of peasant organizing, I did a lot of work.

In the '60s things were very heated, very agitated, and therefore we went to the masses to orient them and prepare them in the event of a sudden social outburst. In this work I did several things: I edited two publications, one of which was called "El Grito Campesino." In "El Grito Campesino," corn was our symbol – on the cover of each issue was a beautiful ear of corn. The people in the countryside loved it. One page was an editorial page where the cruelties and exploitation of the people were denounced. On another page, pure politics – with a picture of a machete. The machete is the most popular weapon in El Salvador and in Cuba. The people loved to see that picture of the machete. What I am talking about was not easy to do. It was very difficult to publish and circulate these magazines.

There was also a school, a clandestine school. We had 14 conferences dealing with the struggle, what was going on, etc. Each person was responsible for one topic, for leading one meeting with the peasants. I was responsible for leading one dealing with morality and fear.

In this school we made a survey – we polled the people about their lives, their work. The result of the survey was that more than 50% of the peasants were paid laborers and did not cultivate their own plots of land. The forms of work were incredibly exploitative, crude. The cotton producers, coffee producers, etc. were all exploitative. Therefore, the issue was to raise the consciousness of the people. Most of us were in the Communist Party. In order to raise the peoples' consciousness you have to be friends with them, the people have to trust you. So we kept the school going, formed delegations, went to the peasants, etc. I knew the countryside better at this time than ever before.

On the 12th of October, 1963, I was captured. We were 4 all together – 3 young men and myself. The truth is I was responsible. They got me with all my documentation, with everything in my hands. It was very costly. The National Guard were murderers. The day they arrested me they hung me up by my thumbs from 2 in the afternoon until 6. It is a terrible thing to be hung, and they beat me silly. I had such horrible pain in my stomach. The second day they hung me up again. They asked me who were the other comrades and I answered them, "You captured me, not the others." It really didn't matter what I told them, they were going to do with me what they wanted. They hung me up by my thumbs 8 times, and beat me senseless 5 times. They did the same thing with my comrades, but not as severely.

So the people and the press protested. The government of Rivera had turned democratic, and so they let me go. But they took all my money, kept all my things. They took everything. Well, the people responded. When I was let go I was cut up – I couldn't drive, I couldn't move, my feet were burned raw.

We went to Mexico. The Guatemalan police tried to terrorize us as well. In November we were in Mexico. By December I was back in the country working clandestinely – continuing the work in the struggle. Finally, I looked for a way to legalize my stay in the country. I set up a business and started working. That was when the head of the National Guard realized where I was and ordered me killed. But, thank God, nothing happened. I continued working in the business, which was a way of legalizing myself. So, they didn't kill me.

How did you get around and travel in, for example, 1966?

Around the time of 1966, I was legitimate because of my business. But I was also doing political work. Because the Party had a lot of work at this time, it was good that I had a certain amount of freedom. But I didn't do all my traveling legally. In '68 I was detained as a suspect. This time the torture was psychological. They tried to get me to tell them things they could use against people. I was there for 17 hours, no more. They took me out and dropped me off at my business, my bread business. So I continued working.

I changed location and began working with young people. I did good work with the youth, and it was during this time that I was asked to give talks at the University. In 1970, I went underground again. In 1972 the army occupied the University and luckily I escaped.

500

In 1974 I left for the Soviet Union, in order to recover from an ulcer and write my memoirs. I was there for 2 years, from '74 to '76.

In 1976 everybody knew me, but the police didn't look for me. When I realized that they weren't looking for me, I went back to work at the University. I worked there until it was occupied in 1980. I was there when they killed Romero, and I participated in the large demonstration of January, 1980. There is a movie where I appear talking. Many people know me. After the persecution that followed Romero's death, I didn't go back to the University. I had to give that up. Every day the death squads went out, the people were scared.

During this time I also worked on the strikes. In this sense I was politically active, but mostly I did cultural work. In the University they couldn't agitate, no revolutionary ideas – only cultural things. If a cop were to ask if you were doing anything political, you would say, "No, just cultural." Things students needed for their studies, history.

Did you give classes? How were things politically in the University at this time?

No, I gave talks. No classes, talks. For example, a professor would tell a student concerning a particular question, to go to the library and read such and such a book . . "And Miguel Mármol is here, he can help you." I was in the Law School. I talked about morality, about what is bourgeois morality, etc. I would ask the students: "Why did you come to the University? Why are you studying?" And so on. There were many strong political currents, many tendencies.

What did we talk about? History, we talked a lot about history, about the founding of the Salvadoran army, the role of the people and of the workers from an historical perspective, the importance of the development of artisan trades in El Salvador. I gave a series of talks on these subjects, about politics, sociology, economics, etc. I didn't talk about communism, only subjects having to do with culture, so that the

501

Guard wouldn't get me. One time, I went to give a talk and a cop, a criminal, came and tried to kill me. But he escaped. That's how things were during this period.

Were you in the Soviet Union when the students were killed in July of 1975?

I was there from '74 until '76. When I returned, things were already serious, awful. The police were killing people in the buses, in the buses! People left their houses and didn't know if they were going to come back. That's how things were.

I want to say something: I don't hate anybody. I don't hate the priests, or the military, or the rich. Why should I hate anyone? We are all people. What I want is a change in the social system. This is what I gave the people, and they said I was kind. I have a lot of friends because I don't insult anyone. There is no reason to insult, there is no reason to threaten, no reason at all. People are very good.

When I was taken prisoner, I didn't give in, I didn't scream, "That's enough!" In the churches the people burned candles and prayed for my release. I wasn't demoralized because of the people, because of the people.

Between 1970 and 1980, I didn't give up my political work. I wasn't outside of the struggle. I was in it. What do I do today outside of El Salvador? The archives that I have are tremendous. I've written many poems here in Cuba. I go to school dedications. I've gone to Europe and the Soviet Union, I've gone to Managua several times to work. I do solidarity work, I work to provide an historical understanding of what is happening. I listen to the Latin Americans who are in refuge in Nicaragua and in Cuba. I also continue writing my memoirs. Tomorrow I am going to give a talk at an event expressing Cuba's solidarity with Nicaragua. I go to many conferences. I'm as busy as ever.

I have tried to maintain my revolutionary stance, not to change for anything. I've tried to lead, to be an example. I remember some movies that I've seen from time to time where the criminal, facing torture, named the bandits. This will never happen to me. I've struggled very hard. I went to Guatemala to do political work, and at the same time I had to support myself as a shoemaker. The comrades in Guatemala at the time didn't have the consciousness to pay me, they didn't realize how important the political work was. One time I even fainted in the street from hunger. So I'm telling you nobody can sweeten me up with money. This is why I am an example.

The people say I'm a relic of the revolution. But they say it with affection, because they know my life, my past. I want to show you a decoration given to me by the Soviet youth – they call me a symbol of the Revolution's continuance. It is for me the most important medal I have. I'm very proud and honored to have received it from the Soviet youth. I have always been considered a loyal, firm, faithful person.

There are people who never wavered: Lincoln, Bolívar, others . . Lenin, Marx. They will never perish, nor will I. There are many things that carry my name – there are songs, books, etc. There was a commission of propaganda that had my name. There were times when I could have run from the struggle, but I never did. Never.

–Kathleen Ross and Richard Schaaf